Resisting Rights

Law and Society Series

W. Wesley Pue, General Editor

The Law and Society Series explores law as a socially embedded phenomenon. It is premised on the understanding that the conventional division of law from society creates false dichotomies in thinking, scholarship, educational practice, and social life. Books in the series treat law and society as mutually constitutive and seek to bridge scholarship emerging from interdisciplinary engagement of law with disciplines such as politics, social theory, history, political economy, and gender studies.

Recent books in the series:

Christopher P. Manfredi and Antonia Maioni, *Health Care and the Charter: Legal Mobilization and Policy Change in Canada* (2018)

Julie Macfarlane, *The New Lawyer: How Clients Are Transforming the Practice of Law*, 2nd ed. (2017)

Annie Bunting and Joel Quirk, eds., *Contemporary Slavery: Popular Rhetoric and Political Practice* (2017)

Larry Savage and Charles W. Smith, *Unions in Court: Organized Labour and the Charter of Rights and Freedoms* (2017)

Allyson M. Lunny, *Debating Hate Crime: Language, Legislatures, and the Law in Canada* (2017)

George Pavlich and Matthew P. Unger, eds., *Accusation: Creating Criminals* (2016)

Michael Weinrath, *Behind the Walls: Inmates and Correctional Officers on the State of Canadian Prisons* (2016)

Dimitrios Panagos, *Uncertain Accommodation: Aboriginal Identity and Group Rights in the Supreme Court of Canada* (2016)

W. Wesley Pue, *Lawyers' Empire: Legal Professionals and Cultural Authority, 1780–1950* (2016)

Sarah Turnbull, *Parole in Canada: Gender and Diversity in the Federal System* (2016)

For a complete list of the titles in the series, see the UBC Press website, www.ubcpress.ca.

Resisting Rights

Canada and the International Bill of Rights, 1947–76

JENNIFER TUNNICLIFFE

UBCPress · Vancouver · Toronto

27 26 25 24 23 22 21 20 19   5 4 3 2 1

Printed in Canada on FSC-certified ancient-forest-free paper (100% post-consumer recycled) that is processed chlorine- and acid-free.

Library and Archives Canada Cataloguing in Publication

Tunnicliffe, Jennifer, author

Resisting rights : Canada and the International Bill of Rights, 1947-76 / Jennifer Tunnicliffe.

(Law & society)

Includes bibliographical references and index.

Issued in print and electronic formats.

ISBN 978-0-7748-3818-4 (hardcover). – ISBN 978-0-7748-3819-1 (pbk.). – ISBN 978-0-7748-3820-7 (PDF). – ISBN 978-0-7748-3821-4 (EPUB). – ISBN 978-0-7748-3822-1 (Kindle)

1. International and municipal law – Canada. 2. Human rights – Canada – History – 20th century. 3. Civil rights – Canada – History – 20th century. 4. International Bill of Human Rights. 5. International law – Canada – History. 6. Canada – Politics and government – 20th century. I. Title. II. Series: Law and society series (Vancouver, B.C.)

JC599.C3T86 2019   341.4′8   C2018-903995-7
C2018-903996-5

Canadä

UBC Press gratefully acknowledges the financial support for our publishing program of the Government of Canada (through the Canada Book Fund), the Canada Council for the Arts, and the British Columbia Arts Council.

This book has been published with the help of a grant from the Canadian Federation for the Humanities and Social Sciences, through the Awards to Scholarly Publications Program, using funds provided by the Social Sciences and Humanities Research Council of Canada.

Printed and bound in Canada by Friesens
Set in Zurich, Univers, and Minion by Apex CoVantage, LLC
Copy editor: Francis Chow
Proofreader: Alison Strobel
Indexer: Heather Ebbs
Cover designer: Martyn Schmoll

UBC Press
The University of British Columbia
2029 West Mall
Vancouver, BC V6T 1Z2
www.ubcpress.ca

Contents

Acknowledgments

I completed this book with the help of many people. Much credit goes to Dr. James Walker at the University of Waterloo. He not only mentored me throughout my MA work on Ontario's human rights history but also suggested that I pursue the topic of Canada's relationship with international human rights and helped me draft my first Social Sciences and Humanities Research Council grant application. He has since become an important colleague and friend. At McMaster University, I was fortunate to have a terrific thesis supervisor, Dr. Ruth Frager. She was a constant source of encouragement and provided insight into my research and writing that greatly improved the quality of this book. I am grateful for her continued friendship. I also benefited from the advice of my thesis committee, Dr. Stephen Heathorn, Dr. Bonny Ibhawoh, and Dr. John Weaver. Their areas of expertise are diverse, and they each provided a unique perspective on my research that helped me create a much richer final project. Dr. Viv Nelles and Dr. David Webster also offered invaluable critiques of earlier drafts of this work. Thank you as well to the faculty and staff in the Department of History at McMaster, who welcomed and supported me as a student and a colleague.

I certainly would not have been able to complete this project without the financial support of McMaster University, the L.R. Wilson Institute for Canadian History, the Social Sciences and Humanities Research Council, and the Ontario Graduate Scholarship program. I am indebted to the staff at Library and Archives Canada, the Archives of Ontario, the Provincial Archives of New Brunswick, the Saskatchewan Archives, the Trent

University Archives, and the Archives of the United Nations. My appreciation also goes out to the many individuals who heard parts of this book at various conferences and provided constructive feedback, especially those involved with the Taking Liberties conference on human rights held at McMaster in 2012. In the process of turning my dissertation into a book, I received excellent support from the people at UBC Press. Thank you to all, but in particular to Randy Schmidt and Ann Macklem for your guidance.

My deepest thanks, of course, go to my friends and family. In different ways you have all provided the advice, inspiration, and assistance I needed to complete this project. To my parents, Marlene and Frank Kivell, thank you for telling me that I could do anything that I put my mind to. You taught me to be a generous, kind, and accepting person, and this has influenced my desire to study and write about issues of social justice and human rights. This book is dedicated to you both. Finally, and above all, my love and thanks to Bruce, Adam, and Emily. You offer the perfect combination of encouragement and distraction. I am not overstating it when I say I could not have done this without you.

Resisting Rights

Introduction: Resisting Rights

A survey commissioned by the Trudeau Foundation in 2010 found that, for many Canadians, support for human rights is an important element of national identity.[1] This extends beyond the domestic realm to include pride in what is perceived to be Canada's strong history of promoting human rights in global affairs and playing an active role in developing human rights norms at the United Nations. The adoption by the UN of the *Universal Declaration of Human Rights* (UDHR) in 1948, and Canada's part in it, is commemorated by Canadians annually on Human Rights Day, and memorialized throughout the year in school curricula, on honorary stamps, on currency, and in various public awareness campaigns, including a Heritage Minute video clip. Accordingly, when the UN's Human Rights Council openly criticized Canada in 2013 for refusing to ratify a number of international human rights instruments, domestic rights activists claimed that then–prime minister Stephen Harper's Conservative government was eroding Canada's "traditional reputation as a human rights leader."[2]

Under Harper, the federal government had opposed the UN *Declaration on the Rights of Indigenous Peoples* (UNDRIP), rejected a General Assembly resolution on the Human Right to Water and Sanitation, and refused to co-sponsor UN General Assembly resolutions calling for a global moratorium on executions.[3] The Conservative government made no secret of its disdain for the UN human rights system, and responded to the Human Rights Council's criticisms by rejecting more than half of the sixty-eight recommendations made, arguing that within Canada's federal structure these issues fell under multiple jurisdictions, making it difficult to institute national programs. Several human rights groups then accused Ottawa of using this federal argument to avoid meeting its international obligations. Taking aim at the Harper government, Amnesty International wrote:

> Partially because of the complexities of federalism, partially because of a lack of political will, and partially because of a failure of leadership, concern about the growing gap between Canada's commitment to international norms on the one hand, and action to implement and live up to those norms on the other hand, has mounted considerably over the past decade.[4]

Since Justin Trudeau's Liberals took power in 2015, Ottawa has gone to great lengths to promote its re-engagement with the UN, and with human rights more broadly. Speaking to the UN General Assembly in 2017, Trudeau acknowledged Canada's poor record of support for the UNDRIP, and the Canadian government's own history of denying and undermining the rights of Indigenous peoples.[5] Trudeau pledged that, moving forward, Canada would work to better meet its international obligations. At home, the Liberal government formally apologized to, and offered compensation to, members of Canada's LGBTQ community for the "tragic act of discrimination" that saw hundreds of civil servants becoming the target of a decades-long "witch hunt" because of their sexual orientation; survivors of the "Sixties Scoop," in which thousands of Indigenous children were forcibly taken from their homes and placed in non-Indigenous care; and former students of residential schools in Newfoundland and Labrador for the "discrimination, mistreatment, abuse, and neglect" they experienced.[6]

These public acknowledgments of historical injustices in Canada have done little to call into question Canada's record regarding international human rights. There remains a sense that the Harper government's unwillingness to engage with the UN's human rights system from 2006 to 2015 was a departure from Canada's longer history of support and leadership in this area. On its website, the federal government continues to promote Canada as "a consistently strong voice" for the protection of human rights at the UN, beginning with a "central role" in the development of the UDHR in 1948.[7] This idea has been reinforced in what Canadians are taught at school, and in reports by media and non-governmental organizations. By invoking Canada's "strong record of accepting international obligations" in its 2013 criticism of Harper, Amnesty International relied on the deeply ingrained belief in Canada's historical leadership in the field of international human rights to try to shame Ottawa into changing its policy.[8] What this rhetoric ignores, however, is the extent to which Canadian policy makers have historically opposed efforts at the UN to introduce and implement international treaties relating to human rights, often relying on arguments of federal jurisdiction to justify their position. Situating recent policies in their proper historical context reveals that Canada's reluctance to be bound by international human rights law is not a recent trend. In fact, Canada resisted the development and implementation of the UN's first human rights initiative, the International Bill of Rights.[9]

At the conclusion of the Second World War, governments around the globe created the United Nations to help foster peace and prevent future global conflict. The UN Charter included a commitment to protect individual rights, calling on member states to promote and encourage "respect for human rights and for fundamental freedoms for all without distinction as to race, sex, language or religion."[10] To fulfill this obligation, the UN established a Commission on Human Rights. A major objective of this commission was to create an international bill of rights, a set of documents that would outline the rights and freedoms to be enjoyed by all humans. In 1947, the commission released the first component of this bill, and over the next two decades, member states debated the bill's form and content, adopting the *Universal Declaration of Human Rights* in 1948 and the two International Covenants on Human Rights and an optional protocol in 1966.

This book is a history of Canada's policy approach towards the development and implementation of these instruments. As such, it has two main objectives. The first is to challenge the image of Canada as a historical champion of international human rights. While scholars such as William Schabas and Michael Behiels have examined Canada's opposition to specific UN documents, this book is the first major historical study of the forces that influenced Ottawa's policy towards the International Bill of Rights from the prewar period through to Canada's ratification of the international covenants in 1976.[11] It argues that, rather than acting as a leader in the push for international standards for the protection of rights and freedoms, Ottawa was very reluctant to support human rights developments at the UN in the postwar period. Canadian policy makers struggled with the expansive definition of universal human rights articulated in UN documents and viewed human rights instruments as a threat to national policy. Unwilling to openly oppose these instruments lest Canada be accused of opposing human rights principles more broadly, Canadian policy makers worked to remain on the periphery of UN efforts to develop an international bill of rights until the mid-1960s. This policy approach runs contrary to the conventional narratives of Canada's contributions to the postwar international order.

Traditional studies of Canadian diplomacy in the postwar period present Canada as a "bold internationalist," a humanitarian state that promoted cooperation and understanding between nations through multilateral organizations like the UN. Within this narrative, the decades after the Second World War are considered a high point in Canada's international engagement. This period has been dubbed the "golden age" of Canadian diplomacy, a time in which Canada was able to "punch above its weight" and play the role of a middle power in global affairs.[12] More recent scholarship disputes this interpretation, with historians such as Greg Donaghy characterizing Canada's postwar diplomacy as "cautious, modest, and pragmatic, echoing long-standing domestic imperatives."[13] These histories emphasize how Ottawa was "mindful of its place" within the Western alliance in the Cold War, more often acting out of national interest or the interests of its allies rather than working to foster constructive solutions or promoting justice in the international community.[14] A number of scholars have begun to challenge Canada's history as a humanitarian state, arguing instead that powerful factors such as economic development, national security, connection to empire, and racialized worldviews continued to inform Canadian foreign policy through the second half of the twentieth century.[15] This book supports this re-evaluation of Canada's postwar diplomacy by detailing Ottawa's reluctance to play a role in the UN Commission on Human Rights, its unwillingness to work with the international community to develop a common set of standards for the protection of human rights, and its resistance to submitting Canada to these standards. It uses Canada's opposition to the development of international human rights in the first decades after the Second World War to question the "self-congratulatory" tone of the historiography on Canada's postwar diplomacy, and to dispel the myth that Canada was leader in the push to include human rights principles as a component of the postwar order.[16]

The second objective of this book is to analyze *why* Canada transformed from a nation initially resistant to the notion of international human rights to one that eventually began to advocate for them. On one level, it will highlight the way in which global developments, and in particular the dynamics of the Cold War and the process of decolonization, impacted the way in which individual states engaged with human rights instruments at the UN. As Roger Normand and Sarah Zaidi point out in their study of the political history of human rights at the UN, discussions over rights were politically and ideologically divisive in the decades after the Second World War.[17] The federal government's efforts to position Canada in a newly aligned world shaped its participation in discussions over an international bill of rights. Early on, Canada's allies pressured Ottawa to support the quick adoption of human rights instruments that would reflect a Western vision of rights; later, the growing power of newly independent states within the General Assembly led to criticism of Canada for its failure to support strong human rights standards. Both forces affected the decisions of federal policy makers.

In addition to examining how external factors transformed Canadian foreign policy, this book places Canada's approach to human rights developments at the UN in the context of its domestic postwar rights culture. It is based on the premise that Canada experienced a fundamental shift in the twentieth century in how its citizens understood issues of rights and freedoms, in their expectations for governments regarding protection of human rights, and in the growth of laws and enforcement apparatus, which eventually formed what Dominique Clément has termed the "human rights state."[18] While government has had a significant role to play in the development and provision of human rights in Canada, primarily through the enactment of protective legislation, the state has not been the primary driver of this "revolution." Scholars such as Clément, James Walker, Ruth Frager and Carmela Patrias, and Ross Lambertson demonstrate that the on-the-ground campaigning of activists, rights organizations, ethnic and racial minorities, church groups, women's associations, and other voluntary organizations has been key to the profound changes in Canada's rights tradition.[19] This book examines the linkages between these activists, customary understandings of civil liberties, and Canada's policies towards the UN's human rights instruments. It therefore provides a unique contribution to a literature on Canadian human rights history that has largely focused inward, on the campaigns to expand rights protections in Canadian federal and provincial laws.

While the work of scholars such as Christopher MacLennan and Stephanie Bangarth has illustrated the ways in which the international discourse of universal human rights influenced rights activism and policy in mid-twentieth-century Canada, this book is most intimately concerned with how domestic discourses of rights, and the growth of Canada's human rights movement, influenced foreign policy and diplomacy.[20] Most studies of Canadian foreign policy largely ignore human rights. A handful of recent historical studies analyze the role of human rights principles in Canada's relations with specific nations, or under certain governments, but there is a need for more comprehensive study.[21] Even in studies of Canada's policy towards the UN's human rights activities, too often scholars have neglected the role of cultural attitudes, rights advocacy, or non-state actors more generally in shaping Canadian diplomacy. Andrew Thompson's recent book *On the Side of the Angels,* a study of Canada's participation in the UN Commission on Human Rights, examines more than sixty years of Canadian diplomacy, effectively situating Canada in the broader study of the development of global human rights.[22] In highlighting Canada's mixed record in its engagement with the commission, Thompson offers a critique not only of Canadian policy but of the UN human rights system itself. Yet it is a fairly conventional diplomatic history, privileging the role of state actors and national interests in shaping Canadian policy. The same could be said for Andrew Lui's *Why Canada Cares,* which seeks to explain why Canada has "underperformed" in the area of international human rights since 1945.[23] Lui, a political scientist, provides a theoretically grounded analysis of the role of human rights in international relations to show that Canada has rarely been willing to sacrifice economic benefit to promote international human rights. He explains changes in Canada's foreign policy by arguing that human rights became a tool that successive federal governments could use to enhance internal national unity and assert federal authority by "externally projecting a particular self-image of Canada as a just-society that was undivided despite its diversity."[24] Although he studies domestic pressures on Canadian foreign policy, Lui continues to give agency to the state. This is a common trend in Canadian foreign policy studies, a field that is preoccupied with Canada's relative status in the world community, particularly after 1945, and the state actors and national interests that have historically guided foreign relations.[25] Yet efforts to define rights were not limited to debates among politicians or diplomats at the UN. More often, they were fought at the level of civil society, involving non-state actors struggling against their personal experiences with inequity and discrimination. There has been a push in recent years for scholars to "rethink" traditional political and diplomatic histories, to broaden definitions of the political and include a wider range of actors, and to explore how cultural practices and understandings affected Canada's worldview.[26] To respond to this challenge, a central objective of this book is to examine how cultural attitudes and civil society actors historically shaped Canadian diplomacy at the UN, in this case Ottawa's participation in debates over the International Bill of Rights.

Universal Human Rights and the United Nations' Rights Regime

Before proceeding, it is useful to discuss some of the conceptual issues within the book. The meaning of the terms "universal human rights" and "fundamental freedoms" was constantly shifting in the period under study. Not everyone conceives of rights in the same way. Conflict over how to define rights and how principles of equality and justice should be enshrined in the provisions of the International Bill of Rights generated intense discussions at the UN, and at home in Canada, in the postwar era. For this reason, I have used the terms as the participants did themselves. Any attempt to define separate categories of rights is a difficult task, yet diplomats, policy makers, and activists frequently relied on classifications to debate which types of rights should be included in the UN's human rights instruments. For example, the desirability of separating civil and political rights from economic, social, and cultural rights became an important topic for discussion in 1949, after the introduction of the first draft covenant on human rights. Traditionally, civil and political rights are understood to relate to individual liberties, such as property rights, basic legal rights, the right to vote and take part in political life, the right to peaceful assembly and association, and the freedoms of worship, movement, thought, and expression.[27] Social and economic rights, on the other hand, are those that enable people to meet basic human subsistence and socio-economic needs, including the right to an adequate standard of health, the right to work and earn an adequate wage in favourable working conditions, support for families, and the right to education.[28] Member states of the UN disagreed over the extent to which economic and social rights could, or should, be implemented in the same manner as civil and political rights. States also came into conflict over the importance of enshrining individual versus collective rights in UN human rights instruments.

These same debates influenced the evolution of a domestic rights discourse in Canada. Throughout the first half of the twentieth century, most Canadians used the term "civil liberties" to refer to a narrow set of individual civil and political rights that were attached to citizenship. When diplomats and politicians communicated about the UN instruments, however, they spoke of "human rights." The UN defined "human rights" as universal, inalienable rights to which everyone was entitled, without distinction of "race, colour, sex, language, religion, political or other opinion, national or social origin, property, birth or other status."[29] The disconnect between these two terms caused significant difficulties as federal policy makers worked to understand how a declaration or covenant on "human rights" might affect Canadian law. By the 1960s, there was a push for a more egalitarian definition of rights in Canada, including the right to live free from discrimination on a series of prohibited grounds. Minority and group rights also became an important component of debates over rights in the late 1960s and early 1970s, as issues such as language rights and Indigenous rights became more prominent. The first chapter of this book outlines the historical roots of Canadian understandings of rights and freedoms leading to the end of the Second World War, to provide context for Canada's resistance to the *Universal Declaration of Human Rights*. Further chapters explore how the language and understanding of rights changed and how these changes influenced Canada's policy towards the International Covenants on Human Rights. A significant argument of this book is that, while there were clear differences in the language and understanding of rights in Canada as compared with the UN in the 1940s, by the 1970s these two discourses of rights had become more aligned.

Within the historiography of international human rights, much debate has focused on this question of timing: When did the concept of human rights take hold and emerge as a global movement? The conventional wisdom has focused on the post–Second World War period and the drafting of the UDHR as the key moment in which a set of universal human rights were first articulated in international law. Other scholars have explored the roots of human rights further back in history, such as in ancient philosophical and religious traditions, in the Age of Enlightenment, or during the anti-slavery movement, culminating in the universalism of the postwar era.[30] Historian Samuel Moyn challenges this long history of human rights, identifying a much more recent origin.[31] Moyn asserts that although the concept of rights stretches back centuries, and the term "human rights" came into usage after the Second World War, the UN's human rights system failed to develop into a broad-based movement in the 1940s because it was rooted in the primacy of nation-states rather than being truly universal. Only in the 1970s, after the collapse of other universalist schemes, did human rights emerge as the "last utopia" for people around the world.[32] This book argues that the support for human rights principles that emerged in the 1970s was the result of a much longer history of grassroots activism at the domestic level. Using Canada as an example, it illustrates the role that domestic movements and civil society actors have played in the development of international human rights.

The terminology surrounding the different United Nations instruments must also be clarified. The International Bill of Rights consisted of a declaration of human rights, two covenants on human rights, and an optional protocol. According to the UN, the term "declaration" is often purposefully selected to indicate that the parties involved want to declare certain principles or aspirations, rather than set binding obligations on states.[33] When the UN Commission on Human Rights drafted the UDHR in 1948, it was presented to member states as a statement of principle or a moral guide. Over time, the UDHR has gained considerable authority and has become more powerful than states originally expected, with international human rights lawyers long maintaining that it is now part of international customary law.[34] In the period under consideration, however, UN members states envisaged the UDHR as having a less direct influence than a covenant.

The terms "covenant" and "convention" are used interchangeably by the UN to refer to specific forms of treaties, either bilateral or multilateral, which are first adopted by the General Assembly and then opened for signature and ratification by member states.[35] A covenant includes provisions that, once the instrument is ratified, are binding on a state. An "optional protocol" to a treaty or covenant is an instrument that provides for additional rights or obligations to which not all states agree. A member state could ratify the covenant but not the optional protocol, meaning that state would be bound only by the provisions in the covenant. The extent to which a covenant is truly binding depends upon the measures of implementation provided in the document. For example, the *International Covenant on Civil and Political Rights* (ICCPR) provides for both a system of reporting designed to exert moral suasion on member states and the establishment of a committee of experts responsible for accepting, considering, and responding to petitions from states and individuals regarding rights violations. At the time of its adoption in 1966, the *International Covenant on Economic, Social and Cultural Rights* (ICESCR) provided only for a system of reporting.[36]

The measures of implementation were the last articles of the covenants to be debated, and so member states were unsure until the mid-1960s as to how these instruments would be enforced. This was significant as governments based their approach on how they believed the covenants would impact both their own domestic policies and those of other member states. In his text on human rights in international relations, David Forsythe defines human rights as "soft law," meaning they are "legal rules that are not the subject of court decisions, but which nevertheless influence extra-judicial policy making."[37] One of the goals of many international human rights advocates is to transform soft law into hard law, creating specific rules that would have concrete protections that could be regularly tested in national and international courts.[38] Particularly in the 1940s and 1950s, Canadian policy makers worried that the binding nature of a covenant would have a significant impact on Canadian policy, but understandings of the legal force of a covenant evolved over the period of study. This evolution is an important component of the story of Canada's approach to the International Bill of Rights.

Methodology and Organization

The study of Canadian foreign policy is multidisciplinary, consisting of works that construct theories and explanatory frameworks to help determine the underlying factors that shaped specific policy outcomes, as well as archival studies that detail the experiences of, and influences on, policy makers in a specific setting. This book falls into the latter category; it is a case study based on extensive archival research that examines Canada's changing foreign policy towards the UN's International Bill of Rights by taking an empirically based approach to the questions of how, why, through what mechanisms, and to what extent Canadian policy changed from the 1940s to the 1970s.

The Canadian federal government had the sole authority to negotiate treaties at the UN. Although the implementation of human rights instruments fell within the power of provincial governments and concerns over jurisdiction influenced policy decisions, officials in Ottawa set Canada's policy towards the International Bill of Rights. The Department of External Affairs took the lead. Robert Bothwell, Greg Donaghy, and Jack Granatstein have written extensively on the unusual political latitude of the department's ministers and public servants in setting Canada's foreign policy in the postwar era.[39] This was certainly the case in relation to Canada's approach to the International Bill of Rights throughout the 1940s and 1950s. While the views of department officials were not homogeneous in this period, a close examination of DEA communications reveals a collective lack of enthusiasm for international human rights. In his study of how ideas of "race" influenced the Department of External Affairs' policy approach to Africa in the same period, Kevin Spooner argues that while there were differences in opinion over policy, all department members were influenced by the common racialized norms and values of the time.[40] Similarly, this book outlines the cultural forces and legal traditions that shaped how federal policy makers understood rights and freedoms in 1940s Canada, and the impact this had on how they collectively approached the UN's first human rights instruments.

By the 1970s, rights activism, growing public awareness of rights issues, the extension of human rights into other government departments, provincial developments, and changing directions in foreign policy resulted in increased oversight of Canada's policy towards human rights at the United Nations. Canada became more engaged with the UN's human rights program at this time not because federal policy makers had come to embrace international human rights but in response to what they perceived as a growing support for human rights principles among the Canadian public. The purpose of this book is therefore to challenge the conventional wisdom that the Canadian government has historically been a driving force in promoting international human rights in order to provide much-needed context for contemporary debates. To do so, it historicizes the decisions of Canadian federal policy makers, taking into consideration both international *and* domestic developments, in order to emphasize the way in which shifting understandings of rights in Canada influenced Canadian policy, and to underline the key role of Canadian rights activists in the process.

Chapter 1 situates the new international concepts of human rights and fundamental freedoms that were coming out of the UN in 1945 in the context of Canadian domestic understandings of civil liberties. By exploring the relationship between rights and the law in early Canada, this chapter demonstrates that Ottawa's opposition to the UDHR was connected to both a narrow view of civil liberties and a strong desire to keep the international community from interfering in its domestic affairs. The chapter argues that the Canadian public and Canadian rights activists were largely disengaged from the international discourse of rights embodied in the UN's human rights instruments, and so the federal government was free to resist their adoption without fear of backlash at home. Only in the face of international pressure did Canada change its vote to support the UDHR in 1948.

Chapter 2 examines Canadian participation in the debates at the UN over the first draft covenant on human rights in the late 1940s and early 1950s in light of the growth of rights activism in Canada. It argues that it is with this covenant, and not the UDHR, that we begin to see a real divergence between the emerging rights movement in Canada and federal policy. At the UN, Canada refused to accept an expansive definition of human rights, and federal officials resisted the idea of submitting Canadian policy to international human rights standards. Although human rights had begun to seep into Canadian popular discourse, domestic rights activism was not powerful enough to influence Canada's policy towards the first draft covenant on human rights. The chapter traces the growing fissure between activists and policy makers to show how it set the stage for the shift in policy that would come in the 1960s.

Chapter 3 examines Canada's participation in the article-by-article debates on the *International Covenant on Civil and Political Rights* and the *International Covenant on Economic, Social and Cultural Rights* from 1954 to 1966. By the early 1960s, a changing balance of power at the UN effectively ensured that the covenants would be adopted in some form. This chapter explores how Canadian policy makers responded to this new reality, especially in light of growing public support for human rights at home. While federal policy makers continued to oppose the expansive definition of universal human rights articulated in the covenants and fear their impact on Canadian policy, the government was persuaded, by what it understood to be international and Canadian public opinion, that it was in Canada's best interest to support the documents in 1966.

Chapter 4 examines the process by which Canada acceded to the International Covenants on Human Rights, arguing that it took a surge in human rights activism in the late 1960s to cause the federal government to push for ratification. An examination of Canada's celebrations of the International Year for Human Rights (IYHR) in 1968 reveals the extent to which cultural attitudes towards rights had changed in Canada, forging a new relationship between domestic and international human rights. The chapter outlines how these changes led to new pressures on the Canadian government to ratify the covenants, and the process through which Ottawa negotiated with the provinces to achieve ratification. Finally, this book concludes by considering why it has been important for the federal government to rewrite the history of Canada's relationship to the UN's early human rights initiatives, and what this means for our understanding of rights and the law in contemporary Canada.

While this book is structured as a chronological narrative of Canada's changing foreign policy towards human rights instruments at the UN, it does not assume that human rights history has evolved in a linear or inherently progressive manner. As international human rights scholar Micheline R. Ishay has effectively argued, all human rights projects generate contradictions and inconsistencies in how rights are understood and applied.[41] Achievements in one direction are often accompanied by counter-balancing pressures, and Canada is no exception to this. Nor does this book suggest that the government's ultimate support for the *Universal Declaration of Human Rights* or the International Covenants on Human Rights was the inevitable conclusion of the story of Canada's response to the UN's attempts to develop an international standard for the protection of human rights. Instead, its purpose is to reveal that Canada's resistance to the International Bill of Rights was the consequence of competing visions over what "human rights" were intended to protect, the proper role of governments in this protection, and the relationship between domestic and international law.

1

The Roots of Resistance: Canada and the *Universal Declaration of Human Rights*

In 1947, the United Nations introduced to its member states the first component of a proposed international bill of rights, the draft *Universal Declaration of Human Rights*. The following year, Canada's foreign minister, Louis St. Laurent, wrote a memo to his UN delegation in Paris on the topic of Canada's position towards the draft document: "I feel sure that you will agree the adoption of the Declaration in its present form at this session of the Assembly might prove to be a source of embarrassment to the Government, particularly if the Canadian delegation were to take an active part in its adoption."[1] St. Laurent's statement reflected the widespread opinion of Canadian diplomats and policy makers at the time that Canada should not support the adoption of the UN's declaration of human rights, and that Canadian delegates should avoid any active involvement in its development. Canada had not been an active participant in attempts to include human rights principles as a key component of the UN when it was first established, and Ottawa had little enthusiasm for international human rights. Consequently, throughout 1947 and 1948, Canada worked against the UN's efforts to draft and adopt its first human rights instrument.

The definitive work to date explaining Canada's resistance to the *Universal Declaration of Human Rights* was written twenty years ago by legal scholar William Schabas. Schabas argues that the lack of a "human rights culture" within the Department of External Affairs and Cabinet caused federal officials to be indifferent, and sometimes outright hostile, to the idea of international human rights.[2] To avoid committing Canada to an instrument they did not support, but unwilling to be open about their opposition, these officials "misled both domestic and international public opinion" by using the pretext of federal jurisdictional issues to justify Canada's position.[3] While Schabas' work brought to light Ottawa's history of opposition to the UDHR and the measures taken to distance Canada from the instrument, it does not provide the cultural context necessary to fully understand *why* federal officials were so hostile towards international human rights as articulated by the UN. Schabas' focus on state actors also obscures the fact that *most* Canadians had a very narrow understanding of rights and freedoms in the 1940s, meaning that the Canadian government's position towards the UDHR was not out of step with broader societal attitudes.

Building on Schabas' work, this chapter explores both the domestic and international context within which the government was working, making three arguments about how they influenced Canadian diplomats at the UN. First, Canada's postwar rights culture conflicted with the broad conceptualization of "universal human rights" emerging at the UN after the Second World War. With a socio-legal tradition that did little to protect citizens from discrimination or promote the rights and freedoms of vulnerable groups, most Canadians struggled with the idea of human rights. Ottawa did not need to "mislead" domestic opinion because the majority of Canadians were either unaware of, or uninterested in, a UN instrument protecting rights and freedoms, and there was little pressure domestically for Ottawa to support the UDHR. Second, federal officials worried that the expansive definition of human rights articulated in the proposed declaration would negatively impact Canadian policy. Fully aware that discriminatory laws in Canada could be considered in violation of the UN's proposals, and concerned with keeping the international community from interfering in Canadian domestic affairs, the federal government was opposed to the UDHR. Finally, Canada's last-minute decision to vote to support the UDHR illustrates the influence the international community had on Canadian diplomacy. There was widespread support for a declaration of human rights among UN member states, particularly Canada's closest allies. Once the Canadian government recognized that withholding its support put it in an uncomfortable minority, consisting primarily of the Soviet bloc, it changed its position, yet it did so with officially stated reservations. Thus, Canada's final decision with regard to the UDHR was more consistent with what historian Hector Mackenzie has described as a "cautious ally" rather than a nation committed to multilateralism, or to taking a leadership role in the development of international law.[4]

Rights and the Law in Early Canada

The Canadian legal system has its foundation in the English common law system. As such, the relationship between rights and the law in early Canada was heavily influenced by ideas of classic liberalism and English constitutionalism. European colonists in British North America brought with them ideas of liberty and the natural rights of man. These ideas had evolved over centuries, tracing as far back as the Magna Carta of 1215 and taking shape in the Enlightenment.[5] By the time of Confederation, a form of rights talk had permeated mainstream political discourse in Canada, and a common language had emerged.[6] Canadians used the terms "civil liberties" or "civil rights" interchangeably in this period to describe a set of customary rights and freedoms inherited from the British political tradition, including property rights, equal treatment before the law, and the protection of an individual's right to formulate or express an opinion and to act freely upon this opinion in the private sphere. Lawmakers and politicians adopted a "negative" vision of these liberties, in the tradition of John Locke, whereby rights were to be protected, not granted, by government; they were a safeguard against undue government interference, as individuals enjoyed liberty in all areas not explicitly limited by law.[7] While rights were often described as *natural,* they were far from universal, often connected to one's status as a British subject and understood as a privilege of long-standing tradition.[8] The concept of equality referred only to the equal protection of the law, and did not include a sense that all people should be treated as equals or have the same political, economic, social, and civil privileges.[9] This narrow conception of civil liberties shaped Canadian law well into the twentieth century.

Perhaps the most notable influence was the lack of codified rights. In 1867, the *British North America Act* created the federal dominion of Canada and endowed it with "a Constitution similar in Principle to that of the United Kingdom."[10] While the *BNA Act* set the framework for how the Canadian government would work and outlined the division of powers between federal and provincial authorities, it was clearly rooted in constitutional conventions arising from centuries of British practice. The act contained only two provisions safeguarding rights: one concerning rights for religious schooling, and the other to protect the French and English languages in federal and Quebec courts and legislatures.[11] It did not contain a specific bill of rights, and placed few limitations on the federal or provincial governments' ability to restrict the civil liberties of their subjects.[12] The main reference to rights can be found in Section 92, which gives authority over "property and civil rights" to the provinces, with no explicit definition of what these rights entailed. Walter Tarnopolsky, a Canadian human rights advocate and legal scholar, has argued that, had the fathers of Confederation been asked to outline a set of rights or fundamental freedoms, they most likely would have pointed to "speech, press, religion, assembly, association," and such legal rights as "*habeas corpus* and to a fair and public trial."[13] None of these were specifically articulated in the *BNA Act*. Instead, property and civil rights, as outlined in Section 92, referred more specifically to the right to enter freely into contract, to own or lease property, and to sue in case of a breach of contract. While the delegates who helped draft the act were committed to the principle of personal liberty, they did not believe in codifying rights in a constitutional document. In part, this was because the Fathers of Confederation privileged the "communal good" over individual interests.[14] More importantly, they believed that the British tradition of relying upon the principles of parliamentary supremacy and the rule of law would be more effective in promoting individual liberty than codifying rights into law.

In 1885, Albert V. Dicey wrote *Introduction to the Study of Law and the Constitution*, strengthening the influence of British liberal understandings of rights on Canadian law.[15] Dicey was a constitutional lawyer and a legal scholar, and his analysis of the British constitution had an enormous impact on the thinking of lawyers, judges, and policy makers in Canada.[16] His work, published at the height of British political and cultural influence, functioned to illustrate the alleged superiority of British constitutional principles.[17] In the United Kingdom, Parliament had absolute sovereignty over the ability to create, change, or repeal legislation for the state. This legislative authority was not limited by a written constitution or the courts, but by the will of the people as expressed through democratic elections.[18]

Dicey argued that, as a central principle in British political institutions, parliamentary supremacy allowed for more effective and democratic governance; it promoted popular sovereignty and it was flexible enough to allow government to act quickly when necessary and adapt the constitution alongside legal and political developments.[19] The role of the courts was to interpret the law and ensure that all citizens were both subject to and enjoyed equal protection under this law. Dicey believed that the rule of law inherently provided for civil liberties, to be upheld by Parliament, making codified rights unnecessary. The British constitution was composed of judicial decisions and legal precedents, all of which dealt with the rights of private individuals. For this reason, Dicey claimed that "individual rights are the basis not the result of the law of the constitution," and as such are protected by the "ordinary law of the land."[20] Dicey considered this method of protecting rights as more effective and natural than an "artificial" constitution or bill of rights, and his ideas remained largely unchallenged in Britain and in Canada leading into the Second World War.[21]

Dicey's conception of civil liberties continued to influence Canadian politicians in the 1940s. Many of them were openly critical of codified rights and argued that Canada's traditional methods provided a surer protection of rights and freedoms. In a 1947 debate over whether Canada needed a national bill of rights, Liberal MP Ian Mackenzie quoted Albert Dicey directly to the House of Commons, arguing that, while the British constitution defined no specific rights, it was "worth a hundred articles guaranteeing constitutional liberty."[22] Federal cabinet minister Paul Martin claimed that all possible rights and freedoms that could be explicitly laid out in a bill of rights were already basic principles within the Canadian tradition. Martin insisted that the remedy for any violation of civil liberties was not a bill of rights but British common law, which, he argued, "proved to be the most lasting and effective guarantee of human liberty the world has ever known."[23] Dicey's views held less meaning for politicians and lawmakers in Quebec, which was the only province in Canada in which civil matters were regulated by a civil code in the French tradition.[24] By the early twentieth century, however, the Catholic Church had increasing power in Quebec, controlling education and dominating social and political life. The Quebec Church was ultramontane, advocating papal and Church authority over the state, and exerting a strongly conservative influence on society. Ultramontane beliefs emphasized duties, to the Church, the family, and the community, over liberal ideas of individualism and rights.[25] For this reason, Quebecers also did not develop a tradition of codifying rights into law in the late nineteenth and early twentieth centuries. Therefore, the codification of rights that characterized efforts at the United Nations in the 1940s was a significant departure from Canada's customary methods for protecting rights and freedoms.

Despite this lack of tradition, when speaking abroad in the 1940s, federal politicians portrayed Canada as a place where rights were upheld. Speaking at a meeting of the Montreal branch of the UN Association of Canada in February 1947, Louis St. Laurent claimed that there was no better example than Canada of the use of British institutions to protect rights and freedoms.[26] St. Laurent pointed specifically to the preservation of linguistic and religious rights for French Canadians within Canada as his example. The following year, Canadian delegate Ralph Maybank told the UN General Assembly that, while Canada had no national declaration of human rights, these rights had instead "developed over many years as the result of the daily concept of free men living together and sharing common basic objectives of individual liberty."[27] In practice, however, the Canadian system did not promote equal protection of the law, and many individuals experienced prejudice and discrimination as a daily part of their lives.

Canadian society privileged white, British, middle-class, Protestant, heterosexual males, and in the period after Confederation the federal and provincial parliaments used their legislative powers to adopt legislation that protected this group of subjects above others. In doing so, governments put laws in place regulating areas such as property ownership, employment, education, voting, and immigration that disadvantaged women, lower classes, and religious and racialized minorities. For example, at the time Albert Dicey was arguing that the principle of parliamentary supremacy allowed for more democratic government, only propertied males in Britain and Canada had the right to vote and several provinces had adopted legislation expressly disqualifying people from the franchise on the grounds of gender and race.[28] Canada's *Indian Act* further discriminated against Indigenous peoples in Canada by restricting their travel and property rights, outlawing traditional ceremonies and rituals, banning the use of

Native languages, and allowing for the establishment of residential schools.[29] Other historical examples of legal discrimination in this period include explicitly racist immigration policies; laws banning visible minorities from holding public office or serving on a jury; restrictive covenants against the presence of certain ethnic, racial, or religious groups within neighbourhoods; discriminatory enlistment policies during the First World War; segregated schooling; and restricted access to services based on gender, race, or religion.

Victims of prejudice fought against these laws. In some cases, individuals or groups who felt their rights had been violated tried to turn to the courts and the safeguards of Parliament. Unfortunately, the Canadian system offered very little in the way of legal remedy for discrimination. The courts offered two options. A person who felt his or her rights had been infringed upon by another individual or a private organization could sue for damages. This civil remedy was available only for cases involving private interactions, however, not those involving perceived violations of rights and freedoms by the government. Since rights were not explicitly protected in Canadian law, the only legal argument open to an individual against government abuse was that the government was working outside of its scope of power or jurisdiction. Individuals could challenge the authority of a government to enact or enforce specific laws, and the courts could determine the constitutional division of powers and judge whether or not these laws fell within the jurisdiction of the legislature that created them, but laws could not be challenged solely on the fact that they violated civil liberties.[30]

James Walker and Constance Backhouse have both used legal case studies from the first half of the twentieth century to demonstrate how racialized minorities used the courts to challenge discriminatory laws in Canada. Victims of racial discrimination expected the courts to uphold their rights on the basis of the British principle of the rule of law, but in many cases individuals were denied rights by a judicial system that maintained a historical systemic racism in Canadian society.[31] Judicial decisions were influenced by "common sense" attitudes that reflected ideas of a racial hierarchy, whereby certain races were considered unfit to participate equally in Canadian society or to qualify for all of the rights and privileges inherent to Canadians of European ancestry.[32] Laws were interpreted in ways that worked to uphold the power of "whites" in Canada, and the courts played a central role in the construction and definition of "race," perpetuating ideas of racial differences.[33] In doing so, many judges and lawyers justified their actions using notions of the fairness and superiority of the British judicial system.[34]

In cases where individuals sued for damages as a result of discrimination, Canadian judges debated the limits of equal treatment before the law, particularly when it came to private interactions. In 1899, a Quebec court awarded damages in a case where management denied admission to certain parts of a theatre to individuals simply because of their colour.[35] Despite this initial decision, federal and provincial courts throughout the first half of the twentieth century upheld the right of taverns, restaurants, and theatres to serve, or refuse to serve, whomever they wanted.[36] In 1940, the Supreme Court considered the case of Fred Christie, who was refused service in Montreal's York Tavern because it was the establishment's policy not to serve "Negroes." In its decision, the court stated: "Any merchant is free to deal as he may choose with any individual member of the public. It is not a question of motives or reasons for deciding to deal or not to deal; he is free to do either."[37]

In cases where individuals challenged discriminatory laws, the Judicial Committee of the Privy Council (JCPC) in London, which served as Canada's highest court until 1949, decided early on that discrimination on racial grounds was not a basis for invalidating legislation.[38] In 1899, the JCPC did determine that a provision in the BC *Coal Mines Regulation Act* stating that no "Chinamen" could be employed in any mine was illegal, but not because of racial discrimination. The judges held that the act was outside the jurisdiction of the provincial legislature.[39] Four years later, the JCPC found that the BC *Elections Act,* which explicitly denied the vote to any "Chinamen, Japanese or Indian," was not illegal because voting legislation related to political rights that were in the jurisdiction of the provinces.[40] The same argument was used in a 1914 case involving Quong Wing, a naturalized Canadian born in China who was convicted of employing white female servants contrary to a Saskatchewan law prohibiting "Chinamen" from hiring or managing white females.[41] The JCPC found that the law dealt with "property and civil rights," which were under the authority of the provincial governments, and so was legal. In the written decision, Justice J. Davies explained that the role of the JCPC was to determine whether or not the law infringed on Dominion jurisdiction, not to consider the "justice or the motives which prompted its passage."[42] These three cases highlight the view of judges in the early twentieth century that, because of parliamentary supremacy, they had no power to stop violations of civil liberties unless the law that caused the violation breached the federal division of powers. Legal scholar Ian Greene has argued that, from the late 1800s to the 1960s, parliamentary supremacy was thought to have "sacrosanct properties," hindering any judicial enforcement of civil liberties.[43]

Beginning in the 1930s, courts began to consider a new legal question: could Canadian laws that violated rights and freedoms considered to be fundamental to the principles of British constitutionalism be subject to judicial review? Judges looked to the *BNA Act* and its explicit reference to the constitution of the United Kingdom, and questioned the extent to which the civil liberty principles that existed prior to 1867 as a part of Britain's unwritten constitution were an essential component of Canada's Constitution.[44] The Supreme Court of Canada faced this question in 1938 in a landmark reference known as the Alberta Press Case. In this case, the court examined several laws enacted by Alberta's Social Credit government, including one limiting the ability of the press to criticize the government.[45] In a six-to-three decision, the court struck down the laws as outside the authority of the provincial government.[46] One justice wrote that press regulation should be considered part of the federal government's power over criminal law. Two other justices, Chief Justice Duff and Justice Cannon, argued that freedom of the press was too fundamental a right to be left entirely to the provinces; only the federal government had the right to limit such fundamental rights. In his decision, Chief Justice Duff wrote that the federal government had sole authority to legislate in the area of public discussion, including freedom of the press. Justice Cannon took this decision further to state that Canadians "enjoy freedom of expression as an incident or privilege of their citizenship status."[47] The decision in the Alberta Press Case supported the argument that, although the provinces did have some authority over rights, the federal government had primacy in the area of fundamental freedoms. However, while this case had an impact on questions of jurisdiction, it did little to help individuals in their fight against discrimination. Simply put, in 1940s Canada, the courts were of limited use in the day-to-day struggle for greater equality. Not only were there barriers to access for vulnerable groups but the courts also perpetuated systemic forms of discrimination. The federal officials who argued that Canadians were adequately protected, denying the existence of prejudice in Canadian society, ignored this reality.

The Growth of Rights Activism in Canada

There were individuals and groups that recognized the inequities in Canadian society and supported marginalized peoples by opposing government action and pushing for enhanced rights protection. A limited form of rights activism developed in Canada in the 1930s, leading to the establishment of the first civil liberties associations. Members of ethnic, religious, libertarian, and other organizations began calling for expanded rights protection, focusing on the ways in which governments in Canada violated the rights of their subjects.[48] Early civil liberties groups were particularly vocal in their opposition to two laws: Section 98 of Canada's *Criminal Code,* and the province of Quebec's "Padlock Law."[49] Section 98 allowed the federal government to abandon the presumption of innocence in cases involving any person belonging to an organization that encouraged the violent overthrow of the government. This section was widely understood to target communist organizations, and civil liberties activists argued that it violated both free speech and freedom of association.[50] Newly formed organizations such as the Canadian Civil Liberties Union (CCLU) made similar arguments against Quebec's Padlock Law, which authorized the Quebec government to shut down any building used for the creation or dissemination of communist materials, without regard for due process.[51] The law also targeted Jehovah's Witnesses, whose religious beliefs caused them to criticize the Roman Catholic Church. The Padlock Law was applied fifty times in Quebec between November 1937 and January 1938, and in response, the CCLU called for a constitutional amendment to the *BNA Act* and the entrenchment of a national bill of rights to protect citizens.[52]

Few Canadians supported the fight for minority rights in this period. This was in part because the minority groups most affected by Section 98 and the Padlock Law, communists and Jehovah's Witnesses, were unpopular and often portrayed as enemies of the state.[53] More importantly, the majority of Canadians, particularly privileged white, English-speaking Canadians, accepted and even supported discrimination. For example, several historical studies illustrate how, well into the 1940s, widespread anti-Asian sentiment in Western Canada led to pressure on government to adopt laws restricting such areas as employment and access to services for Chinese and Japanese Canadians.[54] David Goutor's study of the Canadian labour movement and immigration reveals how organized labour worked to present non-British immigrants as a "menace" to Canada, significantly influencing how Asian, southern and eastern European, and other "foreign" immigrants were viewed in Canada.[55] Such perceptions limited the ability of early civil liberties organizations to gain momentum. In addition to little public support, these organizations suffered internally from a lack of cohesion or coordination, causing them to be fragmented along both geographic and ideological lines.[56] Despite some solidarity, there were significant differences between those fighting for greater rights for women, communists, Jehovah's Witnesses, and labour interests, or for the rights of marginalized ethnic groups. As a result, there was no national civil liberties movement, and activism remained on the margins of Canadian society.[57]

This began to change during and immediately after the Second World War, as broader coalitions of activists used several high-profile cases of government violations of civil liberties to generate public pressure for expanded domestic protection of rights. The first issue involved a series of emergency wartime powers put in place by Prime Minister William Lyon Mackenzie King's Liberal government during the war. These powers, listed in the Defence of Canada Regulations (DOCR), limited traditional civil liberties to enable the government to run the war effort more effectively. This affronted rights activists, who argued that the DOCR violated free speech, *habeas corpus*, freedom of the press, and rights to due process.[58] While many Canadians were willing to accept the suspension of civil liberties in certain cases as a necessary part of the war, continued pressure by activists who argued that the government was going too far caught the attention of the press and led to the creation of a House of Commons Special Committee on the DOCR in 1940. Based on the recommendations of this committee, the Canadian government revised its regulations. While this in itself may not have affected the majority of Canadians, the process of challenging the DOCR generated a public dialogue regarding rights and freedoms in Canada, and their reasonable limits, that went beyond what was perceived to be the special interest of minority groups.

The federal government's attempts to deport Canadians of Japanese ancestry at the end of the Second World War further stirred rights activism in Canada.[59] The initial decision in 1942 to relocate and intern Japanese Canadians along the West Coast met with little opposition from the broader Canadian public.[60] When the war ended, however, the Canadian government not only kept the restrictions on Japanese Canadians in place but also took steps to proceed with deportation. This led to significant criticism from the public, and recognition of the injustice of discrimination based solely on race or ethnicity. The proposed deportation motivated individuals and minority group activists to work with Japanese Canadian organizations to attack racial discrimination.[61] Public protest eventually brought about the repeal of the deportation legislation and resulted in a Royal Commission to consider the government's actions. Stephanie Bangarth argues that this set of events marked "Canada's earliest significant involvement with the discourse on human rights."[62] Rather than relying on traditional British liberties and the safeguards of Parliament, activists opposing the deportation of Japanese Canadians used the new discourse of human rights emerging from the United Nations to articulate their claims and to pressure the Canadian government.

In 1946, a third major civil liberties issue became public as Canadians learned that Igor Gouzenko, a Soviet cipher clerk working in Ottawa, had defected and provided the federal government with details of a Soviet "spy ring" operating in Canada.[63] Prime Minister King kept the details of the affair secret, using the *War Measures Act* to suspend the normal rules of legal procedure to hold a series of secret trials. When the news of the Gouzenko Affair broke, King announced a Royal Commission on Espionage to officially hear testimony in relation to Gouzenko's charges. The public learned that the government had denied detainees and many witnesses the right to consult counsel or to speak to family during the earlier trials, and that suspects had not been made aware of their proper legal rights. Activists objected to such flagrant violations of civil liberties, and their protests built upon the mobilized dissent that surrounded the DOCR regulations and the treatment of Japanese Canadians.

A central aspect of the activism surrounding each of these examples of government violation of rights was the heightening of public awareness and generation of public support that could be used to pressure government. One tactic was increased media coverage, in academic and popular journals and in the daily news. Historically, published debate over civil liberties in Canada was limited to law review journals where legal scholars commented on and discussed important court decisions and debated issues of constitutional law. Beginning in the 1930s, these legal scholars began to offer their views on the high-profile civil liberties issues of the day. Eugene Forsey, a lecturer at McGill University, wrote a series of articles criticizing Quebec's Padlock Law for the *Canadian Forum*, a left-leaning political and cultural magazine.[64] In 1942, Harold Laski of the London School of Economics wrote "Civil Liberties in Canada and Great Britain during War," asking whether or not the Canadian executive was working within the scope of its authority when it curtailed civil liberties in order to further war efforts. Laski argued that, in Canada more than in Britain, the government used its wartime emergency powers to eliminate forces within society that were critical of government or politically unpopular, but that did not interfere with the war effort.[65] Other legal scholars, such as Andrew Brewin and H. Clokie, also published articles examining the Canadian government's violation of civil liberties during the war.[66] Brewin, a lawyer who was retained by the Co-operative Committee on Japanese Canadians to contest the federal government's deportation orders, actively worked to increase public awareness of that issue.[67] The most prolific writer on the topic of civil liberties was Frank R. Scott.[68] Scott began his career of defending the rights of minorities in the 1930s. In 1932, he defended the rights of communists in an article in the *Queen's Quarterly*.[69] Over the next decade, he spoke out in opposition to government infringements on the freedoms of speech and association.[70] In his writings, Scott called for the development of active civil liberties associations across Canada, arguing that although existing local civil liberties groups were taking up specific causes, "the principles at stake concern[ed] every Canadian."[71]

Issues of civil liberties had also become a more frequent topic in the daily and weekly press by the 1940s. Media sources commented heavily on the internment and scheduled deportation of Canadians of Japanese ancestry.[72] Newspapers and magazines such as *Canadian Forum*, the

Toronto Daily Star, the Toronto *Globe and Mail*, the *Winnipeg Free Press*, the *Ottawa Citizen*, and *Saturday Night* regularly printed articles opposing the government's policies, connecting arguments surrounding human rights to concerns over the treatment of Japanese Canadians.[73] Throughout the spring and summer of 1946, newspapers across the country also reported heavily on the espionage trials, as did magazines such as *Maclean's*, *Saturday Night*, and *Canadian Forum*, and professional journals such as the *Dalhousie Law Review*, the *Canadian Bar Review*, and the *Fortnightly Law Journal*.[74] These reports did not simply outline the details of the Royal Commission on Espionage or the Gouzenko Affair; they also debated the limits of civil liberties and of government power within Canadian society, bringing this debate into public conversation.[75]

Increasingly, activists pointed to the need for a domestic bill of rights to rectify the lack of legal protection for civil liberties in Canadian society, and in a few cases members of government also took up the cause. Historian Arthur Lower, a member of the Civil Liberties Association of Winnipeg, wrote prolifically in the *Winnipeg Free Press* on the topic.[76] Members of the newly formed Co-operative Commonwealth Federation (CCF), including leader J.S. Woodsworth, called on Ottawa to entrench a bill of rights into the constitution, but there was insufficient support from either the public or within government. The cause took on new meaning after the events of the war, in the wake of the relocation and internment of Japanese Canadians and the espionage trials. In 1945, Alistair Stewart of the CCF introduced a resolution in the House of Commons to create a Canadian bill of rights.[77] This resolution was defeated, as the majority of MPs remained opposed to the idea that Canada needed codified rights. The following year, Progressive Conservative MP John Diefenbaker attempted to have a bill of rights added to the Liberal government's *Citizenship Act*.[78] Diefenbaker was one of the most vocal supporters within the federal government of the protection of individual rights from government interference. Historians have characterized him as a Prairie populist whose commitment to the idea of a bill of rights was a reflection of his upbringing in Saskatchewan, particularly his own experiences of discrimination based on his German ancestry.[79] However, Diefenbaker was also a strong proponent of the principle of parliamentary supremacy and therefore supported statutory protection of rights and freedoms rather than an entrenched bill of rights. He had been a vocal critic throughout the war of the King government's use of executive power to curtail the rights of citizens, and saw a bill of rights as a way to preserve traditional British liberties and reaffirm the role of Parliament, not the courts, in protecting civil and political rights.[80] In 1946, Diefenbaker suggested the creation of a parliamentary committee to determine the status of rights in Canada and the question of a national bill of rights in particular. His motion led to extensive debate in the House of Commons over the idea.[81]

Objections to a national bill of rights focused on three main arguments: (1) that it would break from the British tradition of parliamentary supremacy; (2) that it would infringe on provincial rights in the area of "property and civil rights"; and (3) that it was unnecessary as the existing judicial system in Canada already guaranteed the protection of civil liberties. This opposition reflected the degree to which Albert Dicey's views on civil liberties continued to inform the way in which Canadian politicians understood rights in the 1940s. Diefenbaker's motion failed, and these same objections would become key elements in the opposition to an international bill of rights the following year. Therefore, while civil liberties organizations and a handful of federal politicians supported the idea of enshrining a set of fundamental rights and freedoms in Canadian law, the majority of parliamentarians did not agree, and it was not until 1960 that Diefenbaker, as prime minister, successfully introduced and passed his *Canadian Bill of Rights*.

Regardless of this lack of support for a national bill of rights, public discourse surrounding civil liberties in Canada in the 1940s did reflect an emerging concern that traditional social and political safeguards were insufficient to protect individual rights from government interference, and that certain fundamental freedoms needed to be protected in law. According to an editorial in the *Winnipeg Free Press*, "all these disquieting developments have compelled Parliament to ask itself whether the citizen's civil rights, assumed under the BNA Act are, in fact, safe."[82] Some governments in Canada had responded to pressure from activists, albeit in a very limited manner. In 1932, the Ontario government amended its *Insurance Act* to make it an offence to discriminate based on race or religion.[83] Member of Provincial Parliament E. Frederick Singer introduced the amendment. His own insurance policy had been cancelled after he had begun inquiring into the company's policy of charging higher premiums or refusing policies for Jewish Canadians, and Singer persuaded fellow MPPs to denounce this type of discrimination.[84] Two years later, in response to rising anti-Semitism in Manitoba, Independent Labour Party member Marcus Hyman introduced an amendment to the province's *Libel Act*, outlawing libel against a race or creed that would likely expose a person of that race or creed to hatred, contempt, or ridicule.[85] The amendment would permit members of a racial or religious group to sue for an injunction against a defaming publisher or author, and it gained full support in the Manitoba legislature.[86] Such amendments were rare, however, and it was not until the mid-1940s that two provinces adopted laws whose sole purpose was prohibiting discrimination. The first was Ontario's 1944 *Racial Discrimination Act*, which prohibited the publication or public display of any signs or advertisements that discriminated on the basis of race or creed.[87] Ontario MPPs had refused to support similar legislation a decade earlier, arguing it gave government too much power to interfere with individual freedom. Examining the evolution of human rights policy in Ontario, Brian Howe credits the adoption of the 1944 act to a growing sensitivity towards discrimination in Ontario after the war.[88] Yet the law was very limited in scope. It was restricted to public acts, leaving discrimination that occurred within the private interactions of individuals or businesses acceptable.[89] In 1947, Saskatchewan became the first province to adopt a general law prohibiting discrimination when it passed the *Saskatchewan Bill of Rights*. The legislation protected basic civil and political rights, and prohibited discrimination on the grounds of "race, creed, religion, colour or ethnic or national origin."[90] Despite having a broader scope, its application was inconsistent and weak, and few cases were ever formally tried under the bill.[91]

According to Walter Tarnopolsky, part of the difficulty in implementing and enforcing these new laws was that the judiciary remained reluctant to convict for discrimination, based on the belief that discrimination was not really illegal.[92] Both the *Racial Discrimination Act* and the *Saskatchewan Bill of Rights* were to be administered through the courts, and convictions were difficult to achieve because early legal interpretations of discrimination never strayed far from the original idea that an act of discrimination must include an element of intent. Discrimination was associated with "ill-willed behaviour caused by bigotry, prejudice and intolerance" rather than any larger societal issues, and as a result enforcement of early anti-discrimination laws used a quasi-criminal approach that required proof beyond a reasonable doubt.[93] Individual cases were therefore difficult to prove, and the legislation failed to address policies or actions that were neutrally motivated yet resulted in discrimination. Despite shortcomings in scope and application, both the Ontario and Saskatchewan laws were important landmarks in the development of human rights legislation in Canada. They marked the first significant codification of rights, and the perceived limitations of these laws would help shape the development of fair practices legislation in the 1950s, and aid the push for a federal bill of rights.[94] Nonetheless, at the time the UN was debating its first human rights instrument in 1948, legislative protection for rights and freedoms in Canada was very weak, and federal and provincial laws continued to discriminate against citizens in a variety of ways. This socio-legal tradition helps to explain why Ottawa took the negative approach it did towards an international bill of rights. The lack of a "human rights culture" described by William Schabas in his work on Canada's resistance to the UDHR extended far beyond the Department of External Affairs and Cabinet, to Canadian society more generally.

Even activists within the limited rights movement that had emerged in Canada prior to the Second World War viewed rights very narrowly. In their study of Ontario's early human rights campaigns, Carmela Patrias and Ruth Frager describe Canada's early civil liberties organizations as being composed largely of "civic-minded English-Canadian scholars, educators, clerics, journalists, and labour activists."[95] Many of these individuals gained their inspiration to fight for greater rights protection from liberal, socialist, pacifist, or social gospel ideals rather than out of personal experiences with discrimination, and this shaped their understanding of rights and freedoms.[96] Members of civil liberties associations often defined rights in the British tradition, taking what Dominique Clément has termed a "minimalist approach to human rights" that equated human rights with civil, political, and legal rights, which could be extended with little government interference.[97] Many early rights activists, influenced by an interpretation of liberalism that placed individualism before equal rights, emphasized a libertarian rather than an egalitarian approach to rights and freedoms.[98] They therefore hesitated to support anti-discrimination laws on the basis that they would give the government power to regulate social relations, and instead focused on government violations of the rights of citizens. As an example, B.K. Sandwell, the influential editor of *Saturday Night* and an outspoken advocate of a national bill of rights, was an avowed disciple of laissez-faire liberalism in the 1940s and could not initially support anti-discrimination laws that gave governments authority to regulate employment, accommodation, or the provision of services.[99]

While members of minority groups and activists did push for greater equality, how they defined equality affected to whom the rights protections they sought would apply, and in what situations. The language of rights coming from the UN in the 1940s reflected a universal understanding of equality, applying to all humans by virtue of their humanity. Although the term "human rights" came into more common usage in Canada after the war, many Canadians, including rights activists, continued to believe that there were essential differences between people based on characteristics such as race or sex, and that discrimination was acceptable in certain circumstances, particularly in private interactions. Common prejudices, such as those against Indigenous populations, communists, French Canadians, homosexuals, or the disabled, permeated these associations in the same way that they permeated Canadian society generally. Rather than campaigning for a broad application of equality in the 1940s, civil liberties associations tended to focus their efforts either on specific cases of discrimination, such as the forced deportation of Japanese Canadians, or on specific categories of discrimination, such as race or creed. Alice Kessler-Harris argues that, while race-based inequality became harder to justify in light of the atrocities of the Second World War, discrimination against women continued to be justified, even by many activists pushing for expanded rights.[100] For this reason, clauses to prohibit discrimination based on sex were largely absent from Canada's early human rights laws. However, as Patrias and Frager point out, these types of biases also affected women's groups: "Men and women who fought against racist injustice were frequently unaware of gender injustice. Conversely, some of the most outspoken advocates of women's rights were unconscious of – or chose to ignore – racism."[101] Recognizing the limits of the ways in which activists themselves understood rights and freedoms in this period sheds light on why these activists were not pushing federal and provincial governments for a more expansive definition of human rights, and helps to explain in part the limitations of Canada's early human rights laws.

A second characteristic of Canadian rights activism in this period was its domestic focus. While civil liberties organizations and minority groups did connect with groups outside Canada to further their cause, and at times used the language of rights coming from UN discussions, they did not engage with any larger international human rights movement. Nor did they see the development of an international bill of rights as relevant or important to Canada. Other than Frank Scott, there is little evidence that activists or scholars were writing about Canada's participation, or lack thereof, in the development of international human rights instruments at the UN. French Canadian humanist Richard Arès did write several articles in the Jesuit journal *Relations,* exploring Catholic teachings on human rights and supporting the development of an international bill of rights, but the earliest of these was published in December 1948.[102] The media were similarly unaware of, or uninterested in, human rights developments at the UN. There were very few press reports on the UN's human rights initiatives, or reports that referenced the draft Declaration of Human Rights, unless it was to use the discourse of universal human rights emerging from the UN to help defend rights in Canada. This is not to say that individuals and groups in Canada that were pushing for expanded rights protection did not support the UN's efforts in principle – if they were aware of them – but they never focused their efforts on lobbying the federal government to support international human rights, or connected the need for greater protections in Canada to a broader international movement.

The major exception to this was John Humphrey, a Canadian legal scholar and human rights advocate who began working for the UN Secretariat as director of its Human Rights Division in 1946. A strong supporter of international human rights, Humphrey was the most active advocate for the *Universal Declaration of Human Rights* in Canada, using his position at the UN to try to generate enthusiasm for the instrument at home. He had some success within the CCF party and from individuals such as R.G. Nik Cavell, chair of the Canadian Institute for International Affairs.[103] More often, however, he met either opposition or indifference to the declaration. The opposition came primarily from the Canadian Bar

Association, which felt that the UDHR was too "socialist," or conservative business circles, which worried about the implications of economic rights.[104] Most Canadians, including rights activists, were either unaware of developments at the UN or did not consider them a priority for Canada. In a letter to Cavell, Humphrey expressed his frustration at being unable to stimulate more interest in the UDHR: "One thing that has appalled me since coming down here is the realization that, in our own country Canada, there is relatively less interest in this question than in certain other countries which we sometimes think are less democratic than our own."[105] Humphrey's comments reveal an important characteristic of rights activism in Canada at the time of the adoption of the UDHR. There were two parallel discourses on rights. The first was a domestic discourse, developed through the hard work of individuals and groups across the country, gaining momentum and beginning to exert pressure on Canadian governments to enhance domestic rights protections. The second was the international discourse, embodied in the UN's human rights instruments, with a much broader definition of rights, and from which the Canadian public and Canadian rights activists were largely disengaged. As a result of this disconnect, there was no pressure on the federal government to support the proposed *Universal Declaration of Human Rights*, and this allowed federal politicians to pursue the policies they wished.

The Push for an International Bill of Rights at the UN

The United Nations organization was an important component of the peace plan designed by the Allied nations in the early 1940s. Intended to promote security and stability for the world, the UN would replace the defunct League of Nations, which had been created at the end of the First World War. Human rights provisions had not been a part of the League, although its covenant did contain a series of clauses to recognize the collective rights of ethnic minorities in certain states in Eastern and Central Europe.[106] For these new territories, entry into the League was conditioned upon their willingness to guarantee the life and liberty of their citizens, without distinction of nationality, and to ensure certain linguistic and religious rights for minorities.[107] The League's minority clauses were an early attempt to use international law, enforced through an international body, to limit how a sovereign state could treat its citizens.[108] The failure of this rights regime was a reflection of both weaknesses within the League itself and the marginal interest among nations in creating strong international protection for rights in the interwar period.[109]

Canadian foreign policy was isolationist prior to the outbreak of the Second World War, a position the public widely supported.[110] The government took a cautious and somewhat unenthusiastic attitude towards the League of Nations under the leadership of Mackenzie King. The prime minister's primary goals within the League were the promotion of Canada as an independent nation at the international level, a minimal commitment for Canada to collective security, and assurance that the League would not interfere in domestic affairs such as immigration or taxation.[111] Although Canada wanted to see the League take a role in resolving and mediating international disputes, the King government displayed little interest in taking part in or developing this role.[112] The invasion of Poland in 1939 convinced both King and the Canadian Parliament to take an active role in the war against Germany. While Canada provided considerable military and industrial support to Britain, the federal government seemed content to allow the British, later in conjunction with the Americans, to determine the high policy of the war.[113] By 1945, the experience of two world wars had caused many Canadians to believe that in order to preserve future domestic security, Canada would need to play a more active role in promoting security abroad, yet King remained cautious in his approach.[114] Aware that the public was in favour of Canadian participation in the United Nations, the federal government worked to strike a balance between internationalism and isolationism.[115] Within the Department of External Affairs, there were two conflicting views on the proper future for Canadian foreign policy. Diplomats such as Lester Pearson and Escott Reid wanted to see Canada play an enhanced role in world affairs. Under-Secretary of State for External Affairs Norman Robertson and long-time diplomat Hume Wrong often worked to rein in these ideas, arguing that Canada should continue to act with restraint.[116] As this latter position was in line with King's own approach, in the immediate postwar period Canadian foreign policy was more careful and far less committed to that of a middle power than the public was aware.[117] In characterizing King's form of internationalism after the war, Robert Bothwell has noted that "King might rhetorically embrace the service of humanity, but he knew that it was his task to represent only the Canadian section thereof."[118]

The end of the Second World War saw new demands for the development of a system of international human rights law, rooted this time in individual rights. Wartime atrocities, the experience of the Nazi regime with its disregard for the rights of the individual, and the dismal failure of the League of Nations to protect minority rights all contributed to a desire to include the protection of individual rights as a central aspect of the newly formed United Nations.[119] At the founding conference in San Francisco, non-governmental organizations, largely from the United States, called for the inclusion of human rights provisions in the UN Charter. These organizations had the support of member states from Latin America, as representatives from Chile, Cuba, and Panama submitted proposals to include a legally binding bill of rights in the Charter.[120] The United States, Britain, and the Soviet Union were less enthusiastic; these states were concerned that, because human rights could fall within domestic jurisdiction, their inclusion could threaten national sovereignty. Yet it was difficult to ignore the pressure from the NGOs, particularly when Allied forces had championed human rights during the war. The introduction of a clause to protect domestic jurisdiction finally convinced the major powers to include human rights provisions, although not a complete bill of rights, in the UN Charter.[121]

Canada played virtually no part in these debates, but King, Norman Robertson, and Hume Wrong all shared the concern that human rights provisions in an international treaty could infringe on domestic jurisdiction. They instructed Canadian delegates to be cautious in their comments, speaking only in broad support of the principles and objectives of human rights rather than committing Canada to any specific position.[122] This was consistent with Canada's approach to other UN initiatives. Hector Mackenzie argues that Canada exhibited only lukewarm enthusiasm for the organization during its first few years, with King and St. Laurent being hesitant about Canada's role on the Security Council in 1948–49.[123] Historian Adam Chapnick also stresses that it was not unusual for Canada to refrain from commenting on issues at the UN, and that the Department of External Affairs was cautious in its early relations with the international body.[124]

In the field of international human rights, the desire to limit Canada's commitment to foreign affairs and outside influence on domestic policy caused the King government to distance itself from any meaningful role. This was, in part, because many External Affairs officials did not view human rights provisions as the most appropriate tool with which to achieve peace and stability after the war. Lester Pearson was a Canadian representative at the Dumbarton Oaks Conference, where the great powers first negotiated the structure of the UN, and a delegate to the founding conference in San Francisco in 1945. He criticized framing any peace settlement in terms of rights, supporting instead a focus on the welfare, not the rights, of individuals and states. In a 1944 article in *Canadian Affairs,* he stated: "We may get further in this 'welfare' approach to international organization than we ever did along the road of glittering political abstractions."[125] Having participated in the founding of both the Food and Agriculture Organization of the United Nations (FAO) and the United Nations Relief and Rehabilitation Administration (UNRRA), Pearson applauded the more "workmanlike approach to practical problems" of these organizations and argued that "a pint of milk a day for everyone may in the long run prove a greater help to international cooperation and provide a surer basis for international organization than thunderous declarations about the rights of man."[126] Mackenzie King also connected peace and social welfare. As early as 1942, in an address to the American Federation of Labor convention in Toronto, he stated that "the era of freedom will be achieved only as social security and human welfare become the main concern of men and nations."[127] This focus on welfare, and the sense that the rhetoric surrounding human rights was too abstract to have real effect in promoting justice, peace, or stability in the world, was widely accepted within External Affairs.

One exception to this was Escott Reid. Reid had joined External Affairs in 1938 and served as a delegate to the San Francisco conference alongside Pearson. In January 1945, he prepared a draft UN Charter, which he hoped to distribute to Canadian diplomats prior to the conference to help guide Canada's participation. This document contained an entire chapter on the importance of human rights to the UN, but the department refused to allow Reid's charter to be included in its official documents.[128] Privately, in letters to his family, Reid complained about the constraints placed on the Canadian delegation by the prime minister's cautious approach to the UN.[129] Ultimately, however, he found no support within External Affairs for his position on rights, and Canada remained non-committal.

Despite Canada's reluctance, there was sufficient support among the founding states of the UN to include a provision in its charter calling upon members to promote "universal respect for, and observance of, human rights and fundamental freedoms."[130] In 1946, the UN's Economic and Social Council (ECOSOC) established a Commission on Human Rights (UNCHR) consisting of representatives from eighteen member states and chaired by the American delegate, Eleanor Roosevelt.[131] Canada was not a member. Within a year, the commission had completed a draft bill of rights that included three parts: a declaration that would act as a broad statement of principle, a covenant that would be binding on all signatory states, and a document to outline measures for implementation. This tripartite structure was a compromise, as member states could not agree on what type of instrument to use to outline an international standard for the promotion of human rights. Questions over how to define and implement rights had become increasingly political; collaboration between the wartime allies collapsed almost as soon as the UN was established, and the organization became a battleground in the Cold War. Both the United States and the Soviet Union spoke out against adopting a binding treaty or any measures of implementation, arguing that a declaration was more appropriate. The majority of other states on the commission supported the adoption of a binding covenant. Concerned that disagreement over the format of the instrument would stall the process entirely, and anxious to adopt some form of human rights instrument quickly, the commission chose to focus on a declaration first and work towards a covenant later. Throughout 1948, the draft *Universal Declaration of Human Rights* was revised by the UNCHR and debated at ECOSOC and then within the General Assembly, before it was put to a final vote and adopted on 10 December.

Canada's Reluctant Participation

Public servants working in the Department of External Affairs were the primary architects of Canadian policy regarding an international bill of rights from the late 1940s through to the 1960s. Officials in the department's UN Division were responsible for coordinating Canadian policy on the draft UDHR in 1948, while the Legal Division commented on the details of the instrument. These two divisions worked together to respond to any queries the department received relating to international human rights, and prepared the instructions for the Canadian UN delegation. While these instructions were subject to the approval of the minister, the prime minister, and Cabinet, their substance was shaped largely by the work of public servants who were very entrenched in Canadian cultural and legal understandings of rights and freedoms. When Louis St. Laurent became prime minister after Mackenzie King's retirement, Lester Pearson replaced him as minister of external affairs in time for the final deliberations and votes on the UDHR. Supported by St. Laurent and sustained by a "disciplined Liberal majority in Parliament," Pearson and his foreign policy advisors had unusual political latitude towards the instrument, and there was broad agreement that Canada should once again proceed cautiously, and an underlying resistance to the idea of international human rights instruments.[132] By 1948, even Escott Reid, whose views on the importance of human rights in foreign affairs had conflicted with those of King and senior officials in 1945, shared the department's concerns over the UDHR and its possible negative consequences for Canada. While the mandarins of Canada's so-called golden age may have viewed the UN as an agency to promote peace and stability in the world, they were not prepared to accept its interference in the domestic affairs of sovereign states. The role of international law was understood as governing state-to-state relations, not regulating how states governed their own citizens, and so the officials responsible for setting Canada's policy on the draft declaration saw it as an unnecessary document that could infringe Canadian sovereignty.

To support the work of the foreign ministry, the federal government established a Joint Committee of both Houses of Parliament on Human Rights and Fundamental Freedoms. This committee was established after the UN first declared its intention to draft an international bill of rights in 1947, to consider how the human rights obligations set out in the UN Charter could best be implemented in Canada, and the legal and constitutional implications of these obligations.[133] Jointly chaired by Minister of Justice J.L. Isley and Senator L.M. Gouin, the committee met eighteen times from June 1947 to June 1948, and heard evidence from officers of the departments of External Affairs and Justice, as well as from John Humphrey, who by then was working at the United Nations.

In the 1930s, Humphrey developed an interest in international law and foreign affairs. While teaching at McGill University, he became active in the UN Society of Canada and the Canadian Institute of International Affairs, supporting an enhanced role for Canada in the postwar world.[134] During the war, Humphrey became friends with Henri Laugier, a French academic who taught at McGill while on exile from German-occupied France. When Laugier became the assistant secretary-general for social affairs at the UN at the conclusion of the war, he invited Humphrey to take a position in the UN Secretariat as director of its Human Rights Division. In this capacity, John Humphrey worked closely with the UNCHR, actually writing the preliminary draft of the international bill of rights that would eventually be introduced to UN member states. Throughout 1947 and 1948, he appeared before the parliamentary committee to outline the purpose of the proposed declaration and to encourage Canadian support. Humphrey did not, however, represent the Canadian government in his work at the UN. As a member of the Secretariat, he played no role in setting, nor was he privy to, Canadian policy on human rights initiatives at the UN. Despite this fact, the Canadian government continues to use Humphrey's accomplishments as evidence of Canada's historical commitment to the UN's human rights program. In particular, his role in drafting the UDHR forms the basis of the claim that Canada played a "central role" in the development of the document. There is little recognition that, during this period, Humphrey's support for the UDHR, and international human rights law more generally, stood in opposition to the Canadian government's position.

Members of the parliamentary committee spent most of their first meetings working to understand the language of an international bill of rights. The terms "human rights" and "fundamental freedoms" were not well understood, and all UN member states struggled to comprehend how "human rights" aligned with or diverged from their own customary understandings of rights. Part of the difficulty for Canadians was a lack of definition of the terms in Canadian law. Senator Gouin noted that human rights may be "so evident that it was not necessary to define them," but as a result they came out as "rather vague."[135] Senator Thomas Crerar tried to define the term in the following way:

> My own judgment is that human rights really get down to a few principles such as the right of the individual to free expression; free criticism of his

> government; to worship as he desires to worship; to read what he wants to read and to have the privilege of exercising free thought without influences to prevent him doing so; to be secure in his person and property so long as he does not violate the law of the land.[136]

In attempting to better define human rights, the parliamentary committee examined a series of historical and contemporary examples of codified rights, including the Magna Carta, extracts from a number of state constitutions, and the brand-new *Saskatchewan Bill of Rights*. Given the ambiguity in how the *BNA Act* referred to rights, several committee members wondered whether the types of rights listed in the documents studied would fall under provincial or federal jurisdiction. The committee also spent considerable time discussing the difference in force between an international declaration and a covenant, in order to understand the implications of these instruments for domestic policy. These questions consumed discussions in 1947, with little resolution.

In the spring of 1948, the Department of External Affairs asked the Joint Parliamentary Committee to comment specifically on the draft declaration provided by the UN's Commission on Human Rights. When it reported its findings to Cabinet, the committee treated an international declaration as a moral guide for nations that, although not legally binding, would "influence the course of legislation."[137] With this in mind, in its report the committee suggested that the UN draft would be more effective if it was shorter and limited to general statements of principle rather than specific articles that defined the duties of the state.[138] Committee members had debated the importance of reflecting Christian values in human rights agreements, both domestic and international. As a result of a successful motion by Liberal MP Eugène Marquis, the committee also suggested to Cabinet that Canada propose an amendment to the UN's draft declaration to add an explicit reference to God within the document.[139] According to historian George Egerton in his study of the religious dimension of human rights questions in the postwar period, an unwavering belief that rights policies must maintain the supremacy of Christian values, even in light of pluralist societies, limited Canada's approach to rights domestically and internationally.[140] Egerton further argues that, as the human rights discourse became increasingly pluralistic, with the potential to move to a

form of secular pluralism, it provided a challenge to both Anglo-Canadians' concepts of a British Protestant nation and French Canadian Catholic culture, and should therefore be resisted by government.[141] In contrast to the report of the Joint Parliamentary Committee, there is little evidence within the internal communications of the Department of External Affairs to support the idea that its officials were concerned about the lack of Christian values in international human rights instruments. For its part, the Canadian government made little effort at the UN to lobby for a reference to God in the UDHR.

In addition to the parliamentary committee, Ottawa also set up an Interdepartmental Committee on Human Rights, consisting of civil servants from the departments of External Affairs and Justice, to brief federal policy makers on the extent to which the articles found in the draft declaration were already covered by Canadian law.[142] This committee was less concerned about the spirit of the draft declaration and more focused on the implications of specific articles on existing Canadian legislation and government policy. Committee members asserted that, for the most part, the broad principles outlined in the UN's instrument were not only acceptable but already law in Canada. Yet they also pointed to statutes that discriminated on the basis of race, ethnicity, religion, or political purpose, thereby contravening articles in the draft declaration.[143] Specifically, they cited federal and provincial election acts prohibiting Indigenous peoples, Doukhobors, Hutterites, or Mennonites from voting; Quebec's Padlock Law, which limited the activities of communists; laws in British Columbia limiting the employment of Japanese Canadians in the lumber and fishing industries; and the federal Orders-in-Council that controlled the mobility of Canadians of Japanese ancestry during and after the war, including deportation orders.[144] Committee members also questioned how the draft's article guaranteeing the right to life would influence laws on capital punishment, or how the right to asylum might limit Canada's ability to set its own immigration policies. It is clear that the Interdepartmental Committee on Human Rights understood that there were many laws in Canada that violated human rights as defined in the draft declaration, yet rather than debating whether or not these laws ought to be changed, members were most concerned with whether or not an adopted UN declaration on human rights would necessitate policy change in Canada, revealing the limits of how rights were understood and accepted by Canadian politicians.

Neither the parliamentary nor the interdepartmental committee supported the inclusion of economic and social rights in a declaration, and both acknowledged possible constitutional constraints for the federal government. It was clear, however, that by the end of their deliberations each committee understood that a declaration would be a quasi-legal document, and that its authority in Canada would take the form of a recommendation or moral guide. For this reason, and not wanting to appear to oppose the protection of human rights, both committees supported the idea of a declaration in principle, and urged the federal government to do so as well. The Interdepartmental Committee went so far as to argue that Canada must "take a firm stand for the adoption of a Declaration of Rights," stating that a lack of support may be understood within the international community as an admission that "our house not being in order, we refuse to clean it up."[145]

Debates over the Draft Declaration in Parliament

The introduction of a draft declaration on human rights at the UN led to some debate in the Canadian House of Commons, although domestic interests continued to override any interest in Canada's position towards the instrument. When the UN Commission on Human Rights was first established in 1946, Progressive Conservative MP Gordon Graydon asked Prime Minister King what Canada's position was on the proposed international bill of rights. King replied simply that, as Canada had yet to see a draft copy, the government had formed no opinion.[146] The matter did not come up again until 1947, when Ian Mackenzie, the Liberal minister of veterans affairs, moved that a joint committee be struck to consider Canada's human rights obligations as a member of the United Nations. This led to a debate over rights protection in Canada, with some MPs arguing that these rights were not adequately protected.[147] The debate tended to focus on domestic rights protections, as John Diefenbaker and CCF members Alistair Stewart and Stanley Knowles took the opportunity to call for a Canadian bill of rights. Social Credit Party members J.H. Blackmore, Ernest G. Hansell, and Norman Jacques spoke out against a bill of rights, either for Canada or at the United Nations, arguing that such legislation was an unnecessary limitation on government, providing rights to undeserving groups such as communists or Jehovah's Witnesses.[148] Several MPs from Quebec, including Liberals Eugène Marquis and Roch Pinard, also opposed a Canadian bill of rights, reflecting the Duplessis government's position that the Catholic faith provided the surest protection for human rights.[149]

A year later, there was a more heated exchange between Diefenbaker and the Liberal government. Diefenbaker asked Mackenzie King directly in February 1948 if the government had made any recommendations to the UN regarding the International Bill of Rights, and he was told that it was "under consideration."[150] In April, after the UN deadline for comments from member states had passed, the Liberals told MPs that the government had written the Secretary-General of the United Nations informing him of Canada's "inability" to provide the necessary comments because it had not had adequate time to allow its legislature to consider the draft.[151] Diefenbaker chastised the Liberals for their meagre support for the idea of an international bill of rights. He questioned why, if the government had received a copy of the draft declaration in January, it waited until 9 April, six days after the deadline for feedback to the United Nations, to present the draft to the House of Commons. He pointed to the fact that two months earlier he had asked outright whether Ottawa had received a copy of the draft. Diefenbaker stated that he was amazed that the government had shown so little interest in the International Bill of Rights; in the two years since it the draft was first published, Canada provided no recommendations to the UN and made no attempt to send a representative to the Commission on Human Rights. The Liberal government also did not make the draft available to MPs, NGOs, or the public after receiving it in January. In contrast, Diefenbaker pointed to the fact that the American government had sent more than 350 copies of the draft declaration to NGOs throughout the country for feedback.[152] Diefenbaker also questioned the lack of consultation between the federal government and provincial governments on the issue of Canada's participation in the development of the International Bill of Rights. He warned that if Canada did not sort out its jurisdictional issues quickly, it would "be in the position of being not in the vanguard but in the rearguard of the march on the part of the nations of the world to these better things conducive of international peace."[153]

Despite these pointed criticisms by Diefenbaker, there was no sustained interest in Canada's position towards international human rights, and opposition parties did not pressure the King government to take action regarding the UDHR. Even Diefenbaker himself was much more interested in a national bill of rights than in international human rights, and he did not follow up on his comments, which allowed the Liberals to avoid having to justify their actions. The House of Commons adjourned in mid-1948, and was not in session when the UDHR was being debated at the United Nations. As a result, the federal government was able to take the position towards the UDHR that it wanted without fear of being questioned in Parliament.

Resistance: Canada's Policy Approach to the UDHR

Some of the recommendations from the parliamentary and interdepartmental committees on human rights made their way into the instructions External Affairs sent the Canadian UN delegation in the fall of 1948. Delegates presented suggestions to make the declaration more concise, and argued for the removal of articles relating to economic and social rights. External Affairs also instructed delegates that Canada should "at least place on the record the view that the name of God should be embodied in the first article of the Declaration."[154] When the Brazilian delegation submitted an amendment suggesting this very thing, Canada was therefore prepared to offer its support despite opposition from the United States.[155] The amendment was withdrawn, however, and the Canadian delegation did not pursue the question. An explicit reference to God never made its way into the UDHR, and debates over the importance of reflecting Christian values in the instrument did not reappear in correspondence between External Affairs officials, politicians such as Lester Pearson, and the UN delegation.

Rather than taking a firm stand to support the draft declaration, as proposed by the two committees, the Canadian government followed the advice of policy makers in External Affairs and proceeded cautiously. The department instructed delegates at the UN to push to delay consideration of the document by the General Assembly until the following year. This decision was influenced by the advice of the Canadian Bar Association (CBA) and its president, John Hackett. In September, the CBA adopted a resolution calling for any draft declaration on human rights to be examined "with the utmost care in all its juridical aspects before further action is taken."[156] Hackett, a Progressive Conservative MP who opposed the idea of an international bill of rights, met with Louis St. Laurent in October to discuss the topic, and also corresponded with Pearson. In a letter to Hackett dated 28 October, Pearson indicated that Canada would focus on proposing that the existing draft be sent to the International Law Commission for review before being passed on to the General Assembly.[157] This proposal was repeated throughout October and November 1948 but found little support among other member states. By October, External Affairs had also begun to focus increasingly on the question of jurisdiction. Picking up on some of the concerns brought forward by the Joint Parliamentary Committee relating to possible constitutional constraints on Canada, the foreign ministry began to highlight potential issues arising from provincial jurisdiction over rights to property ownership, marriage, employment, and education.[158] In a speech to the UN General Assembly, Canadian delegate Ralph Maybank declared that the extent to which Canada could take international action in the field of human rights was "circumscribed" by its constitutional arrangements and that the federal government was not prepared to "invade" on provincial jurisdiction.[159] Canadian delegates avoided taking a prominent role in any discussions of the specifics of the draft declaration while the government decided on a new course of action. Three options were under review: to support a simplified declaration with an officially stated reservation concerning constitutional issues; to abstain from voting on the basis of a lack of federal jurisdiction; or to vote against the declaration. External Affairs originally suggested that Canada abstain. Cabinet fully supported this decision but, as the debates at the UN continued, diplomatic considerations came into play.

International Pressures: Canada Supports the UDHR

As support for international human rights grew at the United Nations throughout 1948, the Canadian government worked to convince member states that, despite its reservations regarding the draft declaration, Canada supported the principles of human rights. The challenge for politicians and the Canadian delegates was to balance their public support for the UN's broad goals in the area of human rights with a policy of avoiding any real commitment to the protection of these rights.[160] Louis St. Laurent publicly assured Eleanor Roosevelt, chair of the Commission on Human Rights, of Canada's "sympathetic interest" in the work of the commission.[161] Canadian delegate Ralph Maybank told the Third Committee of the General Assembly that Canada had established a "sensitive and deep-rooted devotion to the further development of rights."[162] This rhetoric meant little, however, when the Canadian delegation was not actively participating in the debates over the draft declaration.

One of the difficulties for Canada was the fact that its two greatest allies, the United Kingdom and the United States, both wanted to see a declaration of human rights adopted in 1948. Pressure for an international system of human rights had come, in part, out of US president Franklin D. Roosevelt's Four Freedoms Speech in 1941. After Roosevelt's death and with the intensification of the Cold War, the State Department's enthusiasm for the International Bill of Rights diminished, but the American government saw the propaganda value in a non-binding human rights instrument that would include no measures for implementation but reflect a Western interpretation of individual rights. The State Department instructed the head of its delegation to the UN, Eleanor Roosevelt, to push the declaration through quickly, with little debate.[163] British historian Mark Mazower argues that the urgency with which US and British policy makers pushed for the adoption of the UDHR reflects their desire for a non-binding human rights document focused on individual rights rather than the alternate tradition of minority rights that had been articulated in the League of Nations.[164] British officials, although skeptical as to the enforceability of an international human rights instrument, saw the UDHR as both a means of raising human rights standards around the world and a weapon of political warfare. In 1947, the British government submitted a proposed bill of rights it hoped would form the basis for any instrument that would come out of the UN Commission on Human Rights. This draft contained a preamble and eighteen articles, all of which existed in British law. The draft contained no economic and social rights, and was designed to have as little impact on Britain as possible.[165] Historian A.W. Brian Simpson argues that the British Foreign Office considered human rights to be a matter of foreign relations, and not a domestic issue. Believing Britons to be the inventors of liberty, it took for granted that Britain would play a positive role in the development of international human rights.[166] It was not until after the adoption of the UDHR, with the rising influence of anti-colonial arguments in the UN Economic and Social Council that Britain's Colonial Office convinced other officials of the implications of international human rights instruments on Britain itself.[167]

Strong support for a UN declaration by both the United States and Britain put Canada in a difficult position. In September, Commonwealth representatives to the UN met to discuss Britain's view on the draft instrument. They included representatives from Australia, New Zealand, South Africa, Pakistan, India, and Ceylon. The British representative made it clear that, on the whole, the United Kingdom was in favour of having the declaration adopted, with minor changes relating to the right to asylum, the right of equal pay, and the right to work.[168] Britain wanted to keep the textual changes to a minimum, however, in order to speed up adoption. Later that same month, Canadian delegates in Paris met with Eleanor Roosevelt and the American delegation. Roosevelt also expressed her desire to see the declaration adopted in 1948. The Canadian delegates reported to External Affairs that, while there were certain aspects of the declaration the United States did not like, it was willing to support the document without any major changes to avoid prolonged discussions. For Roosevelt, the opportunity to adopt a human rights document that would act as a "moral authority" for the world outweighed any concerns over specific elements of the declaration.[169] The Canadian delegation was also well aware that its constitutional concerns were not shared by other federal states. The United States and Australia, both federal states, supported quick adoption of the declaration and seemed unconcerned about jurisdictional issues. By October, the Canadian delegation was reporting to External Affairs that, in addition to Britain and the United States, the declaration had the support of India, New Zealand, the Western European countries, and Latin America.[170] Pearson responded that the government was feeling pressure from the "Western powers and in particular the delegation of the United States" for Canadian support for the UDHR.[171] Even with these pressures, Canadian representatives remained committed to abstaining in the final vote, stating that "we must avoid embarrassing the government on the provincial rights issue, at the same time recognizing that any hesitation might be construed as opposition to human rights by those who are active in their support."[172] All public addresses given at the United Nations in November and early December 1948 were drafted and redrafted in an attempt to convey the message that Canada supported the protection of human rights but was limited by its Constitution.[173] Canada's continued resistance to the draft declaration was a testament to the depth of opposition within External Affairs and the fear of the declaration's effect on national policy.

Despite the warnings, many UN delegates were surprised by Canada's abstention in the Third Committee on 6 December 1948. Immediately after the vote, representatives from the United States and Britain approached the Canadian delegation, urging support for the final vote on 10 December. Canadian delegates reported to External Affairs that their allies stated that they regarded Canada's abstention as "a serious weakening of the propaganda position which they were hoping to achieve."[174] In their weekly progress report, they wrote: "There was considerable surprise at this association of Canada with the Slavs. It certainly is regrettable that it had to occur, but in view of the message from Ottawa, we felt we had no alternative."[175] John Humphrey, the Canadian diplomat who had helped to draft the declaration and urged Canada to support it, wrote in his diary that he was shocked by Canada's decision.[176] Other members of the UN Commission on Human Rights, including drafting committee members Eleanor Roosevelt, P.C. Chang, and Charles Malik, told the Canadian delegation they were at a loss as to why Canada had taken such a stand.[177]

By this point, it was obvious to External Affairs, and the Canadian government more generally, that Canada was in a minority in its continued opposition to the UDHR. Out of a total of fifty-nine UN member states in 1949, none had opposed the draft declaration in the Third Committee, and only eight others had abstained: Saudi Arabia, South Africa, the Soviet Union, Byelorussia, the Ukraine, Poland, Czechoslovakia, and Yugoslavia.[178] In considering the impact of an abstention in the final vote, Pearson wrote to his department that "we might find ourselves in a rather undesirable minority – including principally the Soviet bloc and South Africa."[179] While Pearson and other External Affairs officials opposed the adoption of the declaration, they were mindful of the broader global context. Only a few months earlier, the Reunited National Party had won the national election in South Africa with its platform of apartheid, a system of institutionalized racial segregation and discrimination. Within a few years, South Africa would become an international pariah. This was also the early days of the Cold War, and despite a rhetoric of international cooperation, Canadian diplomats were well aware of the importance of working with their two historical allies and of avoiding finding itself aligned too closely with the Soviet Union. Ottawa was therefore willing to change its final vote, disregarding its substantive opposition to the document and alleged constitutional constraints, to avoid international stigma. Policy makers were aware that the UDHR might exert moral pressure but would not be legally binding, require ratification, or necessitate legislative change in Canada. This allowed the government to change its position quickly without having to consider the legal ramifications on Canadian policy, and Canada voted in favour of adoption of the *Universal Declaration of Human Rights* on 10 December 1948. Thus, despite Canada's reluctance to support the initial draft, its delegation's attempts to delay the vote, and an eleventh-hour change in position, Ottawa could proclaim that it had supported the *Universal Declaration of Human Rights.*

The Reasons behind Ottawa's Resistance

In the debates leading to the final vote on 10 December, Ottawa's primary justification for its resistance to the UDHR centred on the ways in which the instrument would pose jurisdictional challenges for Canada. The Canadian delegation presented these challenges as the major obstacle to Canada's support for the UDHR, frequently stressing that an abstention should in no way be interpreted as opposition to the principles set forth in the document. While there is evidence that the question of jurisdiction was on the minds of politicians and government officials working to set Canada's policy on a proposed UN declaration on human rights, the extent to which this provided an obstacle to Canadian support for the document is less clear. As early as 1945, External Affairs had conducted a study of the jurisdictional implications of international human rights. Diplomat Hume Wrong looked at the effect of the human rights provisions in the Dumbarton Oaks proposal and concluded that there was nothing that would constitute an invasion of the authority of the provinces.[180] The question of jurisdiction came up again at the first meeting of the Joint Parliamentary Committee in 1947, when committee members compared the proposed International Bill of Rights to labour legislation negotiated at the International Labor Organization (ILO) in the 1930s. In the case of the ILO, federal states were obliged to refer all treaties to their subgovernments for legislative implementation. In 1935, when the Parliament of Canada enacted three laws to implement ILO conventions relating to working hours and wages, the provinces challenged this legislation on the basis that it was outside the authority of the federal government. The Judicial Committee of the Privy Council supported this challenge two years later, stating in its decision that the federal government could not use its treaty-making powers to expand its authority to implement treaties without provincial support.[181] Members of the Joint Parliamentary Committee on Human Rights and Fundamental Freedoms therefore asked in 1947 whether these same principles would apply to Canada's attempts to negotiate human rights treaties. Several witnesses were brought before the committee to outline the different legal obligations of a declaration versus a convention on human rights. E.R. Hopkins, a legal advisor for External Affairs, described a declaration as a "quasi-juridical force, a moral force having the character of a strong recommendation," whereas a convention would require ratification, after which it would be binding on all signatory states.[182] In its final report to the House of Commons in 1948, the parliamentary committee pointed specifically to the limited authority of a declaration when urging the government to support the instrument drafted by the UN Commission on Human Rights.[183] In the House of Commons, committee chair J.L. Isley explained to MPs that the UN's draft declaration would *not* be legally binding on the state.[184] The differences between a declaration and a covenant were also made clear to Canada's UN delegates in instructions sent by External Affairs in September 1948.[185] Civil servants and elected officials alike were therefore aware that the *Universal Declaration of Human Rights* would not obligate the Canadian government to take any action that would interfere with provincial authority.

Despite this, the correspondence between External Affairs and diplomats at the UN illustrates that provincial jurisdiction continued to be a point of discussion. In a memo dated 4 October 1948, delegates Lionel Chevrier and Ralph Maybank expressed concern that proponents of provincial rights might "misinterpret the government's position in supporting the Declaration."[186] The government had no direct evidence that the provinces would object to the federal government's support of the UDHR, however; nor did policy makers make any attempt to test provincial support for the instrument. There was no consultation between the federal government and the provinces regarding actions taken by the UN relating to human rights. When Senator P.F. Bouffard suggested at the Joint Parliamentary Committee that it would be useful to have provincial representatives appear before the committee to consider jurisdictional issues, co-chair Senator Gouin told him that representatives of the federal Department of Justice would appear instead to answer these questions.[187] The Joint Parliamentary Committee did send a letter to all provincial attorneys general and the heads of Canadian law schools in 1947, but this letter focused on the issue of a Canadian bill of rights rather than the UN instruments.[188] When the question of international human rights came before the House of Commons in April 1948, John Diefenbaker proposed that the question be dealt with by a referral to the Supreme Court: "Let us ascertain for once and for all whether or not we have the power to discharge, first, our responsibility as a nation in the United Nations, and, second, if a [national] bill of rights is necessary for Canada."[189] Diefenbaker argued a referral was essential so "no longer will anyone be able to hide behind the concept that under our confederation Canada cannot maintain the fundamental freedoms of Canadians within Canada."[190] The Liberal government refused to refer the question to the Supreme Court on the basis that the Joint Parliamentary Committee on Human Rights and Fundamental Freedoms had been struck for the very purpose of ascertaining the legal and constitutional situation in Canada with respect to human rights, and that a referral would therefore be redundant.[191] Although the parliamentary committee concluded that the draft declaration would not impose legal obligations upon the Canadian government, federal officials never explained to provincial authorities or the public the difference between a declaration and a covenant to convince advocates of provincial rights that Canadian support for the instrument would not infringe provincial jurisdiction. One of the options open to the federal government from the outset had been to support the UDHR with official reservations that would outline the jurisdictional concerns, yet for months External Affairs and Cabinet both supported the more severe approach of abstention. Then, when it became clear that abstention would have an unfavourable diplomatic effect, policy makers quickly reversed their position to support the UDHR with reservations even though nothing had changed in their understanding of the possible constitutional constraints. The question is, then, why did the federal government resist the adoption of the *Universal Declaration of Human Rights* if policy makers understood the quasi-legal nature of a declaration and knew that Ottawa could support the instrument with reservations designed to address possible provincial concerns?

Clues can be found in a speech given by Pearson to the United Nations just before the final vote on 10 December 1948. He assured the UN that Canada supported the general principles of the declaration, referring to it as "inspired by the highest ideals."[192] In outlining Canada's reservations to the document, he cited constitutional constraints but included references to other areas of concern, including the language of the declaration, problems with the definition of rights expressed in the document, and differences between the declaration and Canada's traditional methods of protecting rights.[193] Further exploration of these areas reveals that the government had three significant substantive objections to the instrument. First, officials argued that the codification of rights that characterized the UDHR challenged the principles of British parliamentary democracy. As discussed earlier in this chapter, the majority of Canadian lawmakers and politicians in 1940s Canada supported the British tradition of protecting rights through parliamentary supremacy and the rule of law, not through codified rights. Many External Affairs officials were uncomfortable with the idea of an international bill of rights, feeling not only that it undermined British traditions but that Canadian support for codified international human rights might provide an argument to domestic activists pushing for a national bill of rights. Second, policy makers were concerned with how the declaration defined and articulated "universal human rights." Given the narrow conception of rights in Canada, the idea of universal human rights, and the inclusion of economic and social rights, seemed too expansive for Canadian politicians.

Finally, Canadian politicians and policy makers saw the UDHR as an unnecessary legal instrument that would interfere with Canadian sovereignty and make Canada vulnerable to potentially embarrassing propaganda attacks. Diplomats continued to argue that Canada did not have a problem with its minorities, and that the rights laid out in the UDHR were already protected in Canada. Furthermore, despite the Domestic Jurisdiction Clause laid out in Article 2 of the UN Charter, and the quasi-legal nature of the declaration, policy makers worried about how the UDHR would influence the ability of the government to set its own policies in relation to rights and freedoms. For example, Louis St. Laurent and Minister of Justice Stuart Garson questioned how the adoption of the declaration would limit Canada's ability to pursue less formal policies, such as preventing the spread of communism.[194] In its study of the draft declaration, the Interdepartmental Committee had identified a number of provincial and federal statutes that would have to be altered or repealed to meet all of the standards of the UDHR, the most common example of which was election acts. The government was well aware, however, of other laws, such as Quebec's Padlock Law, the Order-in-Council restricting Japanese Canadians after the Second World War, immigration policies, and regulations surrounding the treatment of Indigenous peoples, that could be considered in violation of the principles of the draft declaration. Unwilling to debate the validity of these laws in an international forum, federal policy makers worried about how the UDHR could be used as a tool to embarrass Canada. For these reasons, there was little enthusiasm for the instrument.

This is not to say that there was no support in Ottawa, or from individuals and NGOs in Canada, for universal human rights or the codification of rights more generally. To the contrary, there was such support, but it remained marginal until the 1960s. With virtually no pressure from opposition parties, the public, or domestic rights activists, there was no reason for the federal government to take a positive policy approach towards an instrument it opposed. It was not until Canadian diplomats realized the international implications of failure to support the UDHR that Canada changed its position.

The lack of awareness or any sense of relevance within Canada regarding international human rights is further illustrated by the absence of any public reaction to either the government's decision to abstain in the Third Committee or its subsequent decision to support the UDHR in the final vote. With the House of Commons adjourned at the time, there was no comment in Parliament. The major newspapers were silent on the issue of Canada's abstention. In fact, the only press clipping sent to External Affairs was from the 7 December edition of the *New York Times,* which mentioned Canada's abstention.[195] Even the adoption of the UDHR on 10 December was not big news. Papers such as the *Winnipeg Free Press,* the *Montreal Gazette,* the *Globe and Mail,* and the *Ottawa Citizen* ran only small front-page stories on the United Nations' "historic document on rights."[196] Although these papers explained that, after voting in support of the UDHR, Lester Pearson gave a speech to the General Assembly indicating that the Canadian government had no intention of infringing on provincial rights, no reference was made to the abstentions. Ironically, the papers did make a point of emphasizing the "bitter Russian opposition" to the declaration.[197] Other Canadian newspapers, such as *Le Droit,* the *Toronto Star,* and the *Ottawa Evening Journal,* barely mentioned the UDHR, focusing instead on the closing of the UN session.[198]

By the end of the 1940s, the Canadian government could say it had supported the adoption of the first component of the United Nations' International Bill of Rights. In no way, however, did Canada play a central role in its development. John Humphrey's accomplishments as a member of the UN Secretariat and his advocacy of the UDHR ought to be celebrated, but cannot be appropriated by the Canadian government as representative of Canada's role. Not only was Ottawa not a leader in the international community's first steps towards setting human rights norms but Canadian policy makers worked against the UN's efforts, belying the popular image of Canada as a key player in crafting the institutions and structures that shaped the postwar world. Canadian politicians and policy makers struggled with the broad conceptualization of human rights laid out in UDHR, and despite understanding that it held no legal weight in Canada, they worried about its implications on domestic policy. What is important to understand is that the "rights culture" of these federal officials was not incongruous with that of most Canadians. In spite of a growth in rights activism, the majority of the population would have had a hard time reconciling the UDHR with Canada's rights tradition in the 1940s.

The work of the United Nations Commission on Human Rights was not finished in 1948. The UDHR represented only one part of the proposed International Bill of Rights. Only months after its adoption, the Commission on Human Rights distributed a draft covenant on human rights to act as a clearer articulation of the principles outlined in the UDHR. A covenant on human rights would be legally binding on all signatory states, and provided a much greater challenge to Canadian policy makers than the declaration. Throughout the 1950s, then, the Canadian government would once again find itself in opposition to international human rights law.

2

Canada's Opposition to a Covenant on Human Rights

Less than a year after the adoption of the *Universal Declaration of Human Rights,* the United Nations released the second component of its International Bill of Rights, a draft covenant on human rights. This document generated intense debate as member states disagreed on how to best define human rights, and on the appropriate role for national and international law in promoting these rights. Whereas the UDHR could accommodate competing visions because it was understood to be a moral guide only, a covenant was a form of multilateral agreement that included obligations that would be binding on signatory states. Nations were therefore much less willing to commit to an instrument that did not reflect their own legal and political traditions. Mounting Cold War tensions and the pressures of decolonization further complicated discussions at the United Nations over rights, and as a result progress on the development of a covenant stalled in 1950. The most contentious issue was the question of whether or not to include articles providing for economic and social rights. Fierce debate among member states caused the General Assembly to adopt a resolution in 1951 instructing the Commission on Human Rights to rework its first draft into two distinct covenants, separating economic and social rights from the more traditional civil and political rights. This process took three years, and in 1954 the UN presented its draft *International Covenant on Civil and Political Rights* and its draft *International Covenant on Economic, Social and Cultural Rights* to its member states.

Having voted for the adoption of the UDHR to satisfy international pressure rather than out of genuine support for the document, the Canadian government had little enthusiasm for another international human rights agreement. Diplomat John Halstead voiced the doubts of many of his colleagues in External Affairs when he accused the UN's Human Rights Commission of holding on to "the misbegotten idea that a convention, such as the Covenant on Human Rights, actually 'gives' human rights in some obscure way."[1] Working with, although not always supporting, the position of the United States and Britain, Canadian policy makers pushed for the inclusion of federal state and colonial clauses, and vocally opposed the inclusion of economic and social rights.[2] Unsure as to whether or not these demands would be met, the Canadian government instructed its delegates to the United Nations to remain on the periphery of debates and to avoid making any comments that could be interpreted as support for the draft. The period between 1949 and 1954 therefore represents the Canadian government's strongest opposition to an international covenant on human rights. Meanwhile, rights activism in Canada was growing. The language of human rights began to seep into popular discourse following the adoption of the UDHR, and activists rallied around calls for enhanced legislative protections against discrimination, often referencing developments at the UN to promote their cause.

This chapter analyzes Ottawa's position towards the International Covenants on Human Rights in light of three competing forces: (1) the expansion of Canada's domestic rights movement, and its connections to international discourses of human rights; (2) the substantive opposition to the content of the documents from the departments of Justice and External Affairs; and (3) international pressures relating to the onset of the Cold War and the impact of decolonization on UN membership. It suggests that it is with the covenants, not the *Universal Declaration of Human Rights,* that we begin to see a real divergence between the emerging human rights movement in Canada and federal policy in Ottawa. Yet, calls from activists for provincial and federal laws to promote equality and prohibit discrimination had no immediate impact on Canadian diplomacy with regard to the UN's human rights instruments. The federal and colonial clauses, debates over the inclusion of economic and social rights, Cold War divisions, and the process of decolonization all provided convenient grounds for the federal government to maintain that Canada did not need greater statutory protections at the international level.

Canada's Nascent Human Rights Movement

During debates over the adoption of the UDHR, there had been virtually no pressure from civil liberties activists, voluntary organizations, or the broader public for the Canadian government to support the instrument. This was due in part to a lack of awareness of the UN's human rights initiatives, something Canadians shared with people around the world. Recognizing the need for public education, in 1949 the UN began pushing to increase awareness in member states of existing international human rights protections, and to foster the idea that domestic and international human rights were interrelated. A General Assembly resolution encouraged member states to educate citizens about the UDHR and its meaning, and required them to report back to the Secretary-General on any domestic progress in the field of human rights.[3] UNESCO, the education division of the UN, worked with domestic organizations, providing materials to be used in publicity campaigns. Copies of the UDHR, available in multiple languages, were distributed to member states. In Canada, the Canadian Citizenship Council and the national branch of the United Nations Association worked with the federal government to supply interested organizations, individuals, and educational institutions with these leaflets. French copies were disseminated through the Société canadienne d'enseignement postscolaire and the Société d'éducation des adultes.[4] Several government departments included a copy of the text of the declaration in departmental bulletins, often providing some commentary on the relevance of international human rights to Canadians.[5] UNESCO also prepared educational resources specifically for teachers, including a teaching guide, a series of booklets on the rights outlined in the UDHR, radio programs, films, and booklets for debating clubs. Schools were also able to obtain a UN human rights filmstrip, *The Declaration of Human Rights*, which came with a set of posters, including the text of the UDHR and a discussion guide.[6] These UN outreach campaigns helped bring the language of human rights to Canadians.

Much of the public education took place around the anniversary of the adoption of the UDHR, as the United Nations encouraged its member states to commemorate the occasion. This became official in 1950, when the General Assembly adopted a resolution declaring 10 December "Human Rights Day."[7] The Canadian government initially had reservations about this resolution, preferring to combine a day to celebrate human rights with United Nations Day, observed on 24 October, but as the majority of member states supported the idea, Canadian delegates decided to vote in favour of the resolution. In preparation for the yearly celebrations, UNESCO created a pamphlet suggesting possible initiatives to be taken by either governmental or non-governmental organizations. Examples included in-school curricula such as projects, essay contests, exhibits, or readings; public ceremonies such as addresses, concerts, and proclamations; media attention, including reprinting the UDHR, writings articles and editorials, and drawing cartoons; radio programming, including concerts, readings of the UDHR, and speeches by national authorities; and film and visual displays.[8] Canadian programming for the first few anniversaries of the UDHR was minimal, and coordinated largely through programming of the Canadian Broadcasting Corporation (CBC). In 1949, the CBC aired a special recording of the New York Junior Symphony Orchestra and a reading of the UDHR. This was repeated the following year, along with an interview with Canadian John King Gordon, the human rights and information officer for the United Nations Secretariat.[9] By the third anniversary of the adoption of the UDHR, Canada's commemoration programs had expanded to include both national and regional programs.[10] The federal government sent letters to all provincial governments asking for details on provincial activities organized for UN Day. Quebec, Ontario, New Brunswick, and Saskatchewan all replied, outlining programs that were being run, primarily through their ministries of education, in primary and secondary schools.[11]

On the fifth anniversary, then–Secretary of State for External Affairs Lester Pearson addressed the public. Despite his own role in resisting the UDHR in 1948 and Ottawa's continued opposition to international covenants, Pearson spoke of Canada's tradition and experience with supporting the principles of international human rights. He told Canadians that not all nations around the world were as fortunate as Canada, as many people continued to live without rights. Pearson outlined the difficulties encountered at the UN in reaching a consensus on human rights, but urged people to resolve to "press forward on the long and difficult road" leading to enhanced human rights.[12] The way in which this commemoration was performed, including the positive rhetoric Pearson used in speaking about the UDHR, encouraged those Canadians listening to believe that their government supported the document. The UN's outreach programs did not bring sudden awareness of international human rights to Canadians; knowledge of the specific initiatives was often limited to government officials, rights activists, and elite intellectuals. Yet the UN-sponsored commemorations and the public awareness campaigns involving media, voluntary organizations, and the public school system helped to diffuse knowledge of, and support for, the idea of universal human rights throughout the Canadian public more generally. The celebrations of the UDHR's adoption also provided a focal point around which voluntary groups, educators, and activists could talk about rights and push to expand the narrow conception of rights held by many Canadians.

At the time the UN was debating the UDHR, Canada's rights movement was just establishing itself, and its attention was fixed on domestic issues. Little had changed by the time the UN released its first draft covenant. It was not until the early 1950s that domestic rights activism began to connect with efforts for an international bill of rights, but this did not mean that understandings of rights had remained static. On the contrary, the continued expansion of Canada's rights movement to include greater representation from groups such as ethnic minorities, organized labour, and women's organizations led to calls for a more egalitarian society based on the principle that all people deserve equal rights. A series of successful campaigns to enact anti-discrimination laws helped raise public awareness of the reality of prejudice in Canadian society, and garnered further support for government action to protect rights and freedoms. Activists increasingly used the discourse of international human rights and developments at the UN to press for expanded protections in Canada. This, combined with the efforts of the UN's educational division, raised the profile of the UDHR and the idea of an international bill of rights among rights activists and the broader public.

Canada's early civil liberties associations had focused on state violations of rights and freedoms, challenging discrimination in the courts, distributing petitions calling for the repeal of unfair laws, and supporting labour activism to push for expanded citizens' rights. These efforts had limited success.[13] Discrimination in private interactions, such as in employment, housing, or the provision of services, remained largely unchallenged into the 1940s. The public was wary of laws granting governments the power to limit individual freedom in private matters, as most Canadians still took a very "negative" vision of rights that opposed government interference. A *Globe and Mail* editorial from 1948 gave voice to these concerns in its assessment of an Ontario Superior Court decision to uphold the validity of a restrictive covenant forbidding the use of a summer resort property to anyone of "Jewish ... or coloured race or blood."[14] The author expressed doubts as to the wisdom of "denying the right of choice of association in private relationships," arguing that "regardless of emotional prejudices for or against the matter under consideration, there can be no acceptance of the limitation of contractual rights which is not founded solidly on statutory law."[15] While the events surrounding the Second World War had heightened sensitivity to the idea of racial discrimination, most Canadians continued to see incidents of prejudice at home as isolated and intentional acts rather than common or systemic behaviours. Such perceptions undermined the ability of Canada's early rights movement to gain widespread support, and so activists began to employ new strategies to more successfully lobby government.

The first of these was to form coalitions to broaden the scope of the movement and bolster the argument that rights activism was not driven by the desire of specific groups to gain privilege. Groups such as the Jewish Labour Committee of Canada (JLC), the Joint Public Relations Committee of the Canadian Jewish Congress (JPRC), and the Association for Civil Liberties (ACL) played a vital role in mobilizing grassroots activism, pulling together individuals and groups who agreed that racial and religious discrimination should be limited by law, and encouraging all citizens to take action to promote greater rights.[16] According to historian Christopher MacLennan in his work on campaigns for a Canadian bill of rights, as new groups began adding their voices to demands for expanded rights protections, understandings of rights moved beyond the arguments made by the early civil liberties groups that had pushed for a bill of rights; the discourse was expanded to include alternate forms of equality protection, especially in the form of anti-discrimination laws.[17] Organized labour became a powerful force in Canada's growing human rights movement.[18] Union membership was on the rise, and organizations such as the Canadian Congress of Labour (CCL) and the Trades and Labor Congress (TLC) began to connect the basic needs of the trade union movement in the area of human rights to the needs of other marginalized groups in Canadian society.[19] The JLC, based in Montreal, encouraged other labour organizations to establish human rights committees, and these committees circulated bulletins and reports to their membership that spoke out against racial discrimination, arguing that it divided the working class and so hurt all workers.[20] While labour organizations were inconsistent in their opposition to racial prejudice, labour leaders were intimately involved in campaigns to pressure government for expanded rights protection.

Public education became an important tool in expanding the movement. Minority groups such as African Canadians, Japanese Canadians, and Jewish Canadians played a particularly vital role in increasing public awareness of the reality of prejudice and discrimination in Canadian society, challenging the idea that racist acts were aberrations.[21] These groups developed radio programs, distributed pamphlets and bulletins, and used the media to highlight examples of how racism affected their communities on a daily basis. In late 1949, the town of Dresden, Ontario, captured public attention after its residents participated in a municipal referendum, voting five to one against a by-law preventing local restaurants from refusing service based on "race, color or creed."[22] Activists within the African Canadian community had protested the racial discrimination and segregation in Dresden for years, but the referendum acted as a catalyst to publicize the explicitly racist policies of the town. Newspapers in Ontario and across the country reported on the "shocking" results, and civil libertarians and human rights activists used Dresden as an example of how racial discrimination was more prevalent in Canada than previously understood.[23]

The campaigns of the late 1940s and early 1950s were carefully coordinated, and included a range of voluntary organizations, women's groups, ethnic minorities, churches, citizens' groups, veterans' associations, members of political parties such as the Co-operative Commonwealth Federation, and the Communist Party, and social, political, and intellectual elites. Language became a tool in the fight to disassociate the growing movement from earlier campaigns for reform, which had often been labelled as special interest rather than for the benefit of all Canadians. The traditional notion of civil liberties began to be articulated in ways that reflected more universal ideas of rights as something to be shared among all people and that lay outside the power of national government.[24] For example, at the 1947 convention of the Canadian Congress of Labour, the national director of the Jewish Labour Committee urged the CCL to take "vigorous action" in the "fight for full equality of all peoples, regardless of race, colour, creed or national origin."[25] Legal scholar Frank Scott began writing about a revival in the "concept of natural law in Canada," and urged more positive state action in the form of human rights law and the establishment of a national human rights commission.[26] As early as 1949, Scott began to differentiate between civil liberties and human rights, defining the latter as "a new concept of the claims of an individual upon society," and a term that "embraces all the various kinds of rights together – political, religious, economic and social."[27] Activists began to more commonly use the phrase "human rights" in place of "civil liberties" or "civil rights," and other UN terminology used to describe rights, such as "inalienable," "natural," or "universal," also began to seep into the domestic discourse. Increasingly, rights advocates relied on this language of the UN and the universality of human rights in their call for enhanced rights protections in Canada, rather than the language of British civil liberties. It is important to note, however, that while activists increasingly used the language of universal human rights in this period, and spoke of the "equality of all peoples," their definition of universal and of equal remained limited. Many activists conceptualized equality in ways that prioritized certain forms of discrimination, such as racial and religious discrimination against non-Indigenous peoples, above others. Prejudice against women, Indigenous populations, sexual minorities, and the physically or mentally disabled continued to be of marginal concern, both for the public and for many activists. The voices of these groups were often silenced in the calls for enhanced rights protection.[28]

In the late 1940s, rights activists lobbied government to adopt two different but related types of legislation: (1) provincial and federal fair employment and fair accommodation practices laws, and (2) a national bill of rights. The fair practices laws were modelled on legislation first introduced in New York state in 1945 and then adopted by numerous other American states throughout the 1950s.[29] Activists in Canada pushed to make it unlawful for employers to discriminate against a person in hiring, promotion, or termination, for trade unions to exclude membership, or for landlords and business owners to deny accommodation, services, or facilities based on race, religion, colour, or nationality. Pay equity laws were also included under the broader umbrella of fair practices legislation. Ontario took the lead. In 1951, a coalition of individuals and organizations led by the Canadian Jewish Congress and the Association for Civil Liberties successfully pressured Progressive Conservative premier Leslie Frost to adopt Canada's first *Fair Employment Practices Act* and the first *Female Employees' Fair Remuneration Act*. Frost had resisted calls to enact these laws when he was first elected in 1949, but the publicity generated by the campaigns, growing support from the public for anti-discrimination legislation, and the American example of fair practices laws combined to gain his support.[30] Similar campaigns were launched throughout Canada, and within three years fair employment practices legislation or equal pay acts were adopted in Saskatchewan, Manitoba, and British Columbia, and by the federal government, and Ontario passed the first fair accommodation practices act in 1954. These laws were an important step in the evolution of human rights law in Canada because they called on the government to play a new role in discouraging discrimination by intervening in private interactions, and articulated broader acceptance of the idea that it was illegal to discriminate in certain areas based on a set of prohibited grounds. They also reflected the growing opinion that human rights were more than a tool to right past wrongs, but could also be used to create a more equitable society.

In addition to pressure for fair practices laws, there was a resurgence in demand for a national bill of rights. In November 1949, Senator Arthur Roebuck tabled a draft bill of rights in the Senate, challenging Louis St. Laurent's Liberal government to discuss the matter at the upcoming Dominion-Provincial conference. Roebuck had been a member of the Ontario legislature in the 1930s, and also served as Ontario's attorney general. In 1945, Prime Minister Mackenzie King appointed him to the Senate, and throughout the postwar period he was an important advocate for the civil liberties movement.[31] The federal government was reluctant to place human rights on the agenda of the Dominion-Provincial conference, however, because the primary goal at this meeting was to draft an amending formula for the Constitution, and there was a sense that a discussion of human rights could disrupt the proceedings.[32] To avoid this, the government suggested a special Senate committee to study human rights and fundamental freedoms and invited Roebuck to act as chair. He agreed and withdrew his bill.[33] The Senate committee held eight public sessions and heard from thirty-six witnesses from April to May 1950, and released a report the following year. The report concluded that many Canadians supported greater statutory protection of human rights, and recommended that Ottawa entrench a bill of rights in the Constitution.[34] More than three hundred activists met with Prime Minister St. Laurent, Minister of Justice Stuart Garson, and Secretary of State for External Affairs Lester Pearson to call on the government to follow through on the committee's recommendations. Despite this, Ottawa took no action. Under St. Laurent, the Liberal Party maintained the view that traditional methods of protecting rights and freedoms made a bill of rights unnecessary, and simply ignored the recommendations of the Senate committee. The fact that they were able to do so reflects the limits to the power of the human rights movement in Canada in the early 1950s, and according to historian Christopher MacLennan, much of the spirit of the bill of rights movement dissipated. Many long-time civil libertarians felt that as long as a Liberal government was in power in Ottawa, there would be no national bill of rights.[35]

One of the strategies activists began to employ to strengthen their demands and to persuade governments to change their position against codified rights was to connect to rights activism and legislative developments outside of Canada. For decades, civil liberties organizations and minority groups had established formal links with their counterparts in the United States, sharing strategies and resources to further their causes.[36] Rosanne Waters' historical study of transnationalism in the US civil rights movement illustrates the strong connections between Canadian anti-discrimination activists and American civil rights organizers.[37] She demonstrates how Canadians adapted ideas and resources from American organizations, brought prominent civil rights activists to Canada to speak, and leveraged the American example in their own campaigns.[38] Beginning in the late 1940s, rights activists in Canada also began utilizing international developments as a tool in their campaigns, invoking UN human rights instruments to pressure the Canadian government to adopt similar laws at home. For example, in 1952 the CCL's National Committee on Racial Discrimination used the UDHR to lobby the federal minister of labour to support national fair employment practices legislation. In its memo to the ministry, the CCL argued that, since the government had supported the declaration, and the basic principles of fair practices legislation were recognized by the declaration, the government had no legal basis to oppose fair practices laws.[39] At the hearings of the Senate committee on a national bill of rights, several witnesses testified to the importance of the UN's interests and activities in the field of human rights.[40] B.K. Sandwell of the Civil Liberties Association, an organization that had submitted a draft bill of rights to the committee for consideration, argued that all of the rights listed in its draft were consistent with those listed in the UDHR. Sandwell reminded the committee that the UDHR had been considered and discussed for over two years before being approved by Canada and fifty-seven other nations. He stated:

> In subscribing to the United Nations Universal Declaration of Human Rights, Canada undertook to promote by progressive measures, universal and effective recognition and observance of human rights and fundamental freedoms in its territory. We feel that Canada would be setting an example for the rest of the world if it now proceeded to implement this undertaking.[41]

Organizations such as the National Japanese Canadian Citizens Association and individuals such as F.R. Scott also used Canada's support for the UN Charter and the UDHR to claim that Ottawa ought to move forward with a national bill of rights.[42] These claims found a receptive audience in the Senate committee, whose final report not only recommended an entrenched bill of rights but also suggested that, as an interim measure, Parliament enact a declaration of rights modelled on the UDHR.[43]

The distinction between international and domestic rights remained, however. Sandwell articulated the attitude of many rights activists when he insisted that a national bill of rights would be more relevant to Canadians than an international covenant on human rights.[44] Activists were more interested in how they could use international instruments to press for domestic developments, rather than in pressuring for further developments at the UN. In some cases, however, individuals and organizations were interested in Ottawa's policy position on human rights initiatives at the UN. One example was the Canadian Jewish Congress (CJC), which lobbied the federal government to be more active in promoting the UN's human rights activities more generally.[45] The UN's Sub-Committee on the Status of Women and the UDHR drew the attention of women's organizations such as the Canadian Federation of University Women, which pressured Ottawa to take a more prominent role on the subcommittee. In 1951, the Tenth Annual Convention of the Saskatchewan Women's Co-operative Guild passed a resolution calling on federal and provincial governments to "consider ways and means, possibly through Dominion-Provincial Conferences, to have a commission set up to divide the provisions of the U.N. Universal Declaration of Human Rights, and take steps to have legislation passed on subject."[46] Members of women's groups also wrote letters to the Department of External Affairs and the Privy Council Office on the matter of Canada's participation on UN bodies such as the Sub-Committee on the Status of Women.[47] These activists saw a connection between the development of international human rights and the enjoyment of rights and freedoms at home, but they remained in the minority in this period.

Some politicians recognized this connection as well. The Ontario legislature explicitly linked its fair practices laws to international developments. Both the *Fair Employment Practices Act* of 1951 and the *Fair Accommodation Practices Act* of 1954 included a preamble stating that the principle of non-discrimination expressed in the laws was "in accord with the Universal Declaration of Human Rights as proclaimed by the United Nations."[48] No other governments in Canada expressly connected domestic rights protections to the UN's human rights instruments, but beginning in 1949, several MPs questioned the Liberal government on its plans for the UDHR. CCF MPs asked Prime Minister St. Laurent whether Canada intended to bring all Canadian legislation in line with the human rights outlined in the new document.[49] St. Laurent told the House he believed that Canadian law already incorporated all of the principles of the declaration. When several MPs stood and asked whether the government was therefore prepared to end sex discrimination, get rid of the closed shop, and promote equal pay for equal work, it seemed that the worries of federal policy makers about the influence of the UDHR on Canadian policy had come to pass.[50] St. Laurent dismissed their comments, however, and nothing more was said on the topic. In 1952 and then again in 1953, MPs submitted private member's resolutions to have the government reflect Canada's acceptance of the UDHR in Canadian law, but these resolutions were quickly dismissed as the government explained the quasi-legal nature of the declaration.[51] While it is clear that parliamentarians were aware of the adoption of the UDHR, there was not yet enough support for international human rights to force the government to take any action, and there is no evidence that the draft covenant was ever the focus of debate in the House of Commons in this period.

By the early 1950s, then, Canadian understandings of rights and freedoms had begun to expand beyond the traditional definition of civil liberties. Canada's nascent human rights movement intersected with the UN's outreach programs, which were specifically designed to increase awareness about international human rights instruments. This facilitated the convergence of the two parallel movements, and the linkages between Canadian activists and the universalist rhetoric of the UN provided tools that could be used to pressure for domestic changes in Canada. Interestingly, this is what federal policy makers feared at the time of the debates over the UDHR – namely, that the broad conceptualization of human rights emerging from the UN would force changes in Canadian policy.

Politicians responded to the increased public debate over rights by talking more about rights themselves. In his study of Canadian national party platforms from the nineteenth century through to the late 1960s, Owen Carrigan reveals a significant increase in references to either individual or collective rights from the late 1940s to the late 1950s.[52] Federal political parties understood that Canadians were becoming more responsive to human rights, as rights-related issues had become a topic for conversation. This affected political discourse, at least at a rhetorical level. While none of these legislative or cultural developments led to direct pressure on the government to support the covenants on human rights, and rights activists continued to focus on domestic issues, it was becoming increasingly obvious to federal policy makers that Canadians would likely support the basic principles of the covenants. Furthermore, the growth in Canada's human rights movement led to a greater demand among some sectors of the population for enhanced statutory protections for rights and freedoms, and to a challenge to governments that refused to see legislation as the proper tool to promote equality. At the UN, however, the federal government was able to continue using jurisdictional issues, opposition to economic and social rights, and the pressures of the Cold War and decolonization as convenient grounds for Canada not to support a covenant on human rights.

The Draft Covenant on Human Rights

The UN Commission on Human Rights drafted a covenant as a part of its international bill of rights in 1947, but member states had no time to consider this instrument until after the adoption of the UDHR. The purpose of a covenant was to more clearly articulate both the specific rights outlined in the declaration and their limitations. A covenant would be more than a moral guide; it would create a binding multilateral agreement for the promotion and protection of human rights, and set specific measures for implementation. Throughout its fifth session in 1949, the commission revised its original draft covenant. Determined to achieve a speedy adoption, it excluded the articles that had generated the most controversy in debates over the UDHR: Articles 22 through 27, protecting the right to work, the right to just working conditions, social security, education, and adequate health, and the right to participate in cultural life. Instead, the new draft contained eighteen articles safeguarding civil and political rights – such as the right to life and liberty; freedom of movement, thought, conscience, religion, association, and peaceful assembly; legal rights allowing for equal protection under the law – and prohibiting slavery and torture. The commission styled this as a "First Covenant of Human Rights" with the intention that economic and social rights would be included in a later document.[53] The UN released the draft First Covenant to its member states in 1950 with a request for comments.

In Ottawa, Louis St. Laurent's Liberal Party remained in power, having won a strong majority government in June 1949.[54] The Department of External Affairs, under the leadership of Lester Pearson, resumed responsibility for reporting to the UN on the topic of human rights and preparing instructions for the Canadian delegates, subject to the approval of Cabinet and the prime minister. Recognizing the different legal implications of a covenant, External Affairs sought the advice of both its own Legal Division and the Department of Justice. The minister of justice at the time was Stuart Garson. Garson had practised law in Manitoba before being elected to the province's legislative assembly in 1927. As a Liberal-Progressive, he became premier in 1943 and maintained close ties with Mackenzie King's federal Liberal government. Mark Vajcner has described Garson as a moderate liberal who viewed liberalism as the most effective tool to balance the reactionary forces of conservatism and socialism in Canada.[55] At the request of St. Laurent, Garson moved to federal politics in 1948 and became minister of justice. He kept this position until the Liberals' defeat in 1957, assuming an important role in St. Laurent's government. After the release of the UN's draft covenant, Garson provided specific comments on the instrument, and External Affairs relied heavily upon these comments in setting its policy. The government also resurrected its Interdepartmental Committee on Human Rights to provide support; the committee included representatives from External Affairs, Justice, and the Privy Council.[56] Other federal departments expressed only limited interest, and the government did not solicit any broader political or public opinion on Canada's policy towards human rights instruments at the UN.[57] Instead, it was a select group of federal civil servants and politicians, largely from External Affairs and Justice, many of whom had resisted the adoption of the UDHR, who determined Canadian policy towards the UN's first attempt at a covenant on human rights. Unsurprisingly, these officials were unenthusiastic about the instrument.

External Affairs attributed its lack of interest in a covenant to "skepticism as to the value of the international instruments to protect rights."[58] Garson declared in 1950 that Canadian law already provided most of the provisions included in the draft, and argued it could only have been designed to improve conditions in other countries.[59] Having already supported a declaration on human rights, officials in these departments were unsure about the need for another instrument, particularly one that would bind signatory states. Canada would not be able to take the same position towards a covenant as it had with the UDHR, supporting it with officially stated reservations.[60] David Mundell, a Justice representative on the Interdepartmental Committee, suggested that the United Nations should go no further than the UDHR in its attempts to legislate international human rights. He argued that it was "hopeless" to expect that a covenant could ever be implemented because those states in need of such a convention would never follow it, while states for which it was unnecessary, like Canada, would only be opening themselves up to propaganda attacks through the use of the new machinery of the international human rights regime.[61] Mundell's ideas were not at odds with those of other representatives on the Interdepartmental Committee on Human Rights, and they reveal the hostility many federal officials felt towards the draft covenant.

The belief that a covenant on human rights would be a tool to be used against Canada rather than a tool to promote equality and justice around the world illustrates the extent to which many Canadian policy makers failed to understand the potential of international human rights, or the connection between human rights and peace. Within the larger context of Canadian foreign policy in the early 1950s, the UN's instruments were considered marginal. The government continued to be involved in postwar reconstruction efforts, Cold War tensions had reached new heights and erupted into conflict in Korea, and External Affairs was focused on establishing Canada's position in a newly aligned world, particularly given the decline of the British Empire and the rise in power of the United States. Given these other concerns, Canadian officials questioned both the need for an international treaty on human rights and its usefulness to Canada.

To help determine what approach Ottawa should take, External Affairs, Justice, and the Interdepartmental Committee all prepared reports summarizing their views on both the content of the draft First Covenant and its potential impact on Canadian policy.[62] These reports eventually became the basis for Canada's criticisms of the instrument. None of the reports suggested that Canada should push for a quick adoption of the draft, or viewed a covenant as beneficial to Canadian domestic or foreign policy, although there were differences in how officials advised the federal government to proceed at the UN. Stuart Garson, civil servants in the Ministry of Justice, and officials in the Legal Division of External Affairs focused on the negative impact of the draft covenant on specific legislation in Canada and were therefore strongly opposed to its adoption. David Mundell argued that a covenant on human rights might set a precedent for international agreements that set limits on Canada's freedom of action, and for that reason advised that Canada withhold its support.[63] Garson agreed that if the government had a free choice in the matter, Canada should oppose the draft.[64] Members of the Interdepartmental Committee felt, however, that Canada may already have been bound to support a covenant because of obligations incurred in signing the Charter of the UN, and Canada's support for the UDHR. The committee went so far as to report to Cabinet that "the protection of human rights is now a matter of international concern and has ceased to be one of exclusive domestic jurisdiction of States."[65] This was a remarkable comment, considering that Canada's opposition to the UDHR had in part been premised on concerns that the declaration would allow the UN to interfere with domestic sovereignty, a principle that was revered by federal politicians at the time. While this committee did not support the draft covenant in its current form, and had many of the same reservations as Garson, rather than advising the government to oppose the document outright, it suggested that Canadian delegates state that the present text of the draft covenant was unsatisfactory and required substantial revision before Canada would be in a position to support it.[66] External Affairs remained undecided throughout 1950 and 1951 on which approach to take, and therefore sent no comments to the UN Commission on Human Rights outlining Canada's position. Officials felt it was "inadvisable to make even preliminary comments which might be interpreted as committing the Canadian government to a particular position before the whole document was subjected to detailed scrutiny."[67] As it had in 1948 with the UDHR, the department instructed delegates to hold off on participating in debates at the UN over specific articles of the document. It encouraged delegates instead to reiterate Canada's support for human rights principles, and to speak only generally about the government's concerns.[68]

Of these concerns, delegates almost exclusively pointed to constitutional issues when justifying Canada's hesitation at the UN. Under-Secretary of State for External Affairs Arnold Heeney told the Canadian delegation to emphasize that the draft First Covenant could cause difficult domestic problems for Canada as a result of possible conflicts of jurisdiction between the federal and provincial governments.[69] Federal-provincial relations were a significant issue for Canadian politicians. In the late 1930s, Mackenzie King had established the Rowell-Sirois Commission to study the distribution of powers between the federal and provincial governments. Aided in part by the recommendations of this commission, King obtained agreement from the provinces to centralize power to aid efforts in the Second World War and help guide postwar reconstruction. By the late 1940s, however, provinces such as Nova Scotia, Quebec, Ontario, and Alberta were challenging this centralized federal authority.[70] None of these provinces posed a specific concern for policy makers relating to the draft covenant, however. Even Quebec, which in the 1970s would demand its own authority in the field of international relations, exhibited no interest in human rights initiatives at the UN during this period. Regardless, federal officials advising the government on how to proceed with a covenant on human rights questioned whether or not Ottawa would have the authority to enforce provisions that fell within provincial jurisdiction, particularly in the provinces that were already resisting centralization. It was therefore in the best interest of the federal government to show respect for Canadian federalism when working at the United Nations. Within the Ministry of Justice, there was a sense that Canadian support for the covenant could be "a political weapon of considerable force" for proponents of provincial rights.[71] Officials warned that it would be unwise to agree to support the instrument without consultation with provincial governments.

Historian Michael Behiels argues that, because a covenant was a similar instrument to the International Labor Organization conventions that had proven so problematic for Canada's federal government in the 1930s, it was natural that Canadian policy towards the draft covenant would be driven primarily by constitutional constraints.[72] External Affairs officials were therefore only being honest with the international community when they stated that the implementation and enforcement of the draft covenant's articles would be difficult given Canada's federal system. To take this further, it could be argued that the Canadian government should be commended for its honesty and realism when other states, such as the United States or the Soviet Union, both of whom supported the adoption of a covenant in the late 1940s, had no genuine intention to implement its provisions. Canada was also in a much different position from its Commonwealth allies: Britain and New Zealand were unitary states, and although Australia had a federal system, its states were very weak. From this perspective, Canada's approach to the draft covenant is understandable. The problem, however, is that too close a focus on Canada's constitutional issues obscures the extent to which Canadian federal policy makers also opposed the *substance* of the draft covenant and had little desire to see its provisions implemented or enforced. Jurisdictional issues aside, these policy makers were reluctant to support the instrument because the concept of universal human rights it articulated conflicted with their own limited vision of rights.

Substantive Opposition to the Draft First Covenant

Beyond the question of jurisdiction, several key concerns were repeatedly mentioned in the internal communications of federal officials involved in evaluating the draft First Covenant: the language of the document, its definition of rights, the question of economic and social rights in particular, and possible restrictions on the Canadian government's ability to set its own policies and to decide to whom those policies applied. These concerns, many of which had been apparent in debates over the UDHR, became more pronounced when Canadian policy makers considered the impact of a binding international human rights instrument. Federal officials simply could not, and would not, accept the need for an international covenant that included such an expansive interpretation of human rights.

A.J. Pick, a legal advisor in External Affairs, complained that because human rights in Canada were largely a matter of common law, it was difficult to comment critically on the draft First Covenant because Canada had no basis for comparison.[73] Officials agreed that, as a legal document, a covenant needed proper statutory language and should be as precise as possible, but questioned whether it should include general rules only or list specific limitations and exceptions to each article. If limitations and exceptions were included, how could the document possibly accommodate the range of different legal and social systems represented in the United Nations? From the standpoint of Canada's political alignment, did officials really want a covenant that accommodated all of these systems?[74] Canadian delegate G. Davidson complained to members of the UN Economic and Social Council (ECOSOC) that, in attempting to find common ground among member states, the Commission on Human Rights had drafted articles that were often inconsistent, sometimes with "burdensome detail," at other times too vague.[75] The problem, as Minister of Justice Stuart Garson saw it, was that the draft covenant was neither clear nor comprehensive, acting as "some sort of hybrid between a general statement and an

American style Bill of Rights."[76] The uneven language and structure of the document alarmed Canadian policy makers, especially those in the Ministry of Justice.

All the Canadian civil servants involved in the internal discussions over Canada's policy approach to the draft covenant had difficulty coming to terms with the way in which rights were defined in the document. As they had with the UDHR, officials argued for a more simplistic definition of rights that focused on individual rights, and civil and political rights in particular. Accordingly, Canada opposed any articles in the First Covenant that it believed articulated collective rights. It did so on the basis that these were neither rights nor principles under international law. Canada used these arguments to justify its opposition to the inclusion of articles on self-determination. While the delegation assured other member states that it was sympathetic to the "problem" of self-determination, Canada could not support its inclusion in a covenant because it saw the issue as "more of a goal than a right" and "a collective matter rather than an individual human right."[77] This was in line with the position of most Western powers at the UN at the time, and Canada met privately with other delegations that were opposed to the inclusion of an article on self-determination to discuss how best to proceed, including the United Kingdom, France, Belgium, the Netherlands, Norway, Denmark, Sweden, Turkey, Australia, New Zealand, and Brazil.[78] Ottawa also opposed suggestions from Yugoslavia to include articles to protect the language and other rights of minorities, again on the basis that they were an expression of a collective right. External Affairs instructed its delegates that "as a country of immigration and a country where all residents are substantially treated equally, we would be reluctant to support such legal provisions for the perpetuation of minority characteristics."[79] Not only did this comment ignore the inequities that many Canadians experienced daily but it reflected assimilationist ideas of the time and a reluctance to promote egalitarian rights for minority groups.

Economic and social rights posed an even greater challenge for Canadian officials. While the revised draft covenant excluded many of the economic and social rights outlined in the UDHR, there remained significant pressure within the UN for these articles to be reinserted into the document. The Canadian delegation was told to support any attempt to exclude these rights from the covenant and, if the majority of states supported inclusion, to avoid participating in the debate and to abstain on all votes.[80] Canada's position was that civil and political rights were fundamentally different from economic and social rights. The former were "safeguards against the abuse of power by Parliaments and Governments," whereas the latter were "essentially matters of detailed social legislation and economic and financial policy on both the national and international scale."[81] According to this argument, economic and social rights, such as the right to work or to education, could not be achieved by simply declaring them in a covenant. They required the application of legislation, and for this reason were not considered legitimate rights by Canadian policy makers.[82] At the United Nations, the Canadian delegation argued that economic and social rights could not be protected in the same manner as civil and political ones, largely because there was no way to create "practical and enforceable legal remedies in the case of their violation."[83] In 1953, the deputy attorney general of Canada commented on economic, social, and cultural rights by stating, "I am somewhat dubious about the effect of numerous articles which 'recognize the right' to certain things, but I presume that these have a certain value as an enunciation of idealistic objectives."[84] Other delegates were far less supportive, such as L.A.D. Stephens, who claimed that the Latin American and Asian countries that advocated for economic and social rights were looking to create a "welfare world."[85]

Opposition to the inclusion of economic and social rights in the draft covenant was not limited to civil servants in External Affairs and Justice. It reflected a dominant understanding of rights within both the Liberal and Progressive Conservative parties in this period. Many party members were suspicious of economic and social rights, believing them to be a threat to the traditional values of individual freedom, the rule of law, and freedom in the marketplace.[86] Throughout the 1940s, the Liberal government had opposed calls for a domestic bill of rights in part due to concerns over the inclusion of economic and social rights.[87] In 1948, Social Credit MP Ernest Hansell stood in the House of Commons and accused members of the Civil Rights Union, a civil liberties group advocating a national bill of rights that included economic rights, of being communists and "traitors" to the Canadian way of life.[88] While this was an extreme view, advocacy for these types of rights was believed to be the domain of the CCF, not the Liberals or Conservatives.[89] In the communications between Justice and External Affairs officials, the concerns over economic and social rights were articulated in a way that did not reflect Cold War ideologies so much as a limited vision of what constituted rights and freedoms.

Closely linked to this was a narrow understanding of the role of governments in implementing human rights policies. Officials argued that the concept of rights embodied in the UDHR and the draft First Covenant required state involvement not only in the protection of political and civil rights but also in the promotion of the economic, social, and cultural well-being of all. Justice and External Affairs officials noted that the First Covenant contained articles that called for greater government interference than was the tradition in Canada. Under-Secretary of State for External Affairs Jules Léger claimed that this degree of interference was incompatible with Canada's form of parliamentary democracy.[90] The Interdepartmental Committee had expressed this same concern during the process leading to the adoption of the UDHR, stating that some of the articles were "based on the premise that the State should be paternalistic" and that this may not be acceptable to the Canadian government, whose thinking was "laissez-faire."[91] The quasi-legal nature of the UDHR had soothed these concerns somewhat, but the draft First Covenant caused them to resurface.

The Canadian government also had difficulty reconciling the obligations inherent in a covenant with its desire to maintain national sovereignty. In its initial response to the draft, External Affairs indicated that it felt that the way in which rights and freedoms were promoted and protected in individual states was a matter of decision for that state, in accordance with its own constitution and traditions.[92] By drafting international treaties that explicitly guaranteed a set of rights and freedoms for individuals around the world, the United Nations was implying that the way in which a state treated its citizens was no longer simply a matter for domestic law.[93] Stuart Garson worried that a covenant on human rights might place Canadian legislation under subordinate statutory authority to international law, and asked why the government would want to "barter away" control over its own affairs.[94]

Contrary to claims made by delegates at the UN that Canadian law already included all of the principles outlined in the draft covenant, federal civil servants discussed in private their concerns over how the document could be used to challenge existing legislation in Canada. The Interdepartmental Committee once again listed provincial and federal statutes that would have to be altered or repealed to meet UN standards, such as election acts. The committee pointed to specific examples, such as Alberta's *Communal Property Act,* which prevented Hutterites from purchasing land within forty kilometres of other Hutterite communities and limited the size of their land holdings, to show how provincial laws conflicted with the principles of the International Bill of Rights. Quebec's infamous Padlock Law was another example, along with laws in Quebec that limited women and Jehovah's Witnesses.[95] Deputy Minister of Citizenship and Immigration Laval Fortier wrote a letter to External Affairs in defence of Canada's selective immigration policy, stating his unwillingness to enter into an international debate over the appropriateness of that policy.[96] Fortier also worried that the draft covenant could limit Canada's policy of deportation and its restrictions on the issuance of passports and visas.[97] Robert Gordon Robertson of Northern Affairs and Natural Resources wrote a similar letter to Jules Léger regarding Canada's policies towards "Eskimos" and other Indigenous groups, claiming that a covenant "might well leave us vulnerable to outside criticism from those who do not, or who will not, understand the peculiar conditions of the north at this stage of human history."[98] The letters from Léger and Robertson illustrate a common understanding among federal officials at this time that Canadian laws that discriminated did so in a manner that was acceptable within the particulars of Canadian society, but that this would not be well understood by outsiders. This fear was exacerbated by the fact that Canadian officials were unsure as to exactly how a covenant on human rights would be implemented and enforced, as the measures for implementation remained incomplete. They questioned the type of UN committee that would be created to enforce the covenant, what would inform the judgments of this committee, and what relationship would exist between this committee and Canadian authorities.[99]

Canadian Participation in Debates over the Draft

The federal government's dissatisfaction with the proposed human rights covenant put Canadian delegates in a difficult position at the UN. Canada's closest allies all continued to support the quick adoption of international human rights instruments. Whereas Ottawa viewed human rights as a domestic issue, matters of rights and freedoms were more visible in the foreign policy of states such as Britain and the United States. The British cabinet considered the protection of rights and freedoms to be a major component of its foreign policy in Europe in the late 1940s, and the Foreign Office viewed human rights as a resource to be used in dealing with other states, particularly the Soviet Union.[100] While international human rights may not have been a priority for the United States, the American government recognized the propaganda value of a covenant on human rights, particularly one that reflected Western understandings of rights. In 1950, the American delegation pushed to have the draft First Covenant sent quickly to the General Assembly for a vote. The Australian government supported a covenant for more ideological reasons. Under the leadership of Labor prime minister Ben Chifley and Minister of External Affairs H.V. Evatt, Australia advocated the inclusion of economic and social rights in the UN's human rights instruments, viewing a covenant as a tool to promote higher levels of governmental responsibility over economic and social programs among member states of the UN.[101] Australia was therefore actively involved in the UN Commission on Human Rights and in debates over the draft First Covenant. In contrast, Canada's approach wavered between a desire for the idea of a covenant to be abandoned altogether, hope that if it was completed its content would be such that Canada could easily oppose it, and fear that if it emerged in a form Canada felt obliged to sign, it would contain articles that would be problematic.[102] Canadian delegates to the UN met regularly with their Commonwealth and American counterparts to discuss their respective positions, demonstrating that Ottawa was cognizant of the importance of working with its allies even if it was reluctant to change its own policy.

In light of the support for a covenant on human rights among Canada's allies, the federal government did not want to make its opposition to the substance of the draft public. This influenced Canadian participation in the debates over the document at the UN. Focusing primarily on concerns over jurisdiction benefited policy makers, who, while they also opposed the content of the instrument, were afraid to stress substantive concerns lest Canada be accused of opposing human rights more generally. It was not in the interest of External Affairs to attempt to resolve or bring clarity to questions over jurisdiction, and the department did not discuss the draft First Covenant with the provinces or test provincial attitudes.[103] Federal officials did nothing to persuade provincial authorities, or Canadians more generally, of the urgency of adopting international agreements protecting universal human rights because they did not want to take any positive action towards international instruments that they saw as both unnecessary and potentially embarrassing for Canada. Instead, External Affairs instructed delegates to make clear to other member states that the addition of a federal state clause was required in order for Canada to support any covenant on human rights. Such a clause would allow federal states to become party to the covenant without being bound by international law to carry out obligations that would be under the jurisdiction of provincial governments, and the push to include such a clause came to define Canada's participation in debates over international human rights throughout the 1950s. Canadian delegates spoke of it so frequently that representatives from other UN member states accused Canada of linking its support of the covenants to the federal clause in order to provide a future justification for failing to support or ratify the instruments, which was not far from the truth.[104]

Beyond repeated calls for a federal clause, Canada participated very little in discussions over the draft covenant. Ottawa worried that any active participation would be interpreted as a sign that Canada was committed to the instrument. Officials urged Canadian delegates to refrain from participating in discussions over articles the government opposed, and to abstain from voting on many proposals and amendments. Uncertain of the status of a federal clause, the Canadian delegation was also instructed not to participate in discussions in areas deemed to be outside federal jurisdiction. Even relating to articles it supported, the delegation was told to avoid specific statements of support or enthusiasm because the most modest expressions of support could potentially be awkward. In 1951, members of External Affairs became upset when a Canadian delegate referred to the covenant as an "admirable project" and a "positive achievement."[105] Deputy Under-Secretary of State for External Affairs Escott Reid worried how this wording would misrepresent a government that, in his own words, "considers that the project is far from admirable and sincerely hopes that it will be stillborn."[106] Reid and Arnold Heeney contacted the head of the Canadian delegation in Paris and requested that, from that point forward, Stuart Garson do all the speaking.[107] Canada also refused an invitation to sit as a representative on the UN Commission on Human Rights out of fear that such active participation would be interpreted as support for the covenant. When Canada was approached to join this commission in 1953, Acting Under-Secretary of State for External Affairs S. Morley Scott argued that, as its attitude towards the covenants had been so lukewarm, the government would gain little from a seat.[108] This strategy to avoid any clear policy towards the covenant on human rights, and to avoid participation on the UNCHR, is strikingly similar to Canada's early policy towards the UN Security Council. Hector Mackenzie outlines how, during Canada's first term on the council from 1948 to 1949, delegates were instructed by External Affairs not to "take unauthorised initiatives," to abstain in votes whenever unsure, and to generally keep a low profile.[109] He goes on to argue that, contrary to studies that emphasize Canada's postwar success as a middle power, there is little evidence of attempts to establish a strong role for Canada in international affairs through the Security Council. The same could be said for Canada's role in the area of human rights, which was characterized more by caution and a desire to protect Canada's traditions than by attempts to influence international policy or promote universal human rights.

Any contributions Canada did make to negotiations over the covenant were largely critical. Policy makers took a very legalistic approach to the document because a covenant was a binding agreement. This led to two seemingly contradictory criticisms. First, officials, particularly in the Department of Justice, claimed that the language used in the draft was too imprecise to be effective, pointing to the use of vague terms such as "democracy," "peoples," and "nations," and ambiguous statements such as "within a reasonable time."[110] Yet these same officials also resisted attempts to make the covenant more specific through the inclusion of lists of restrictions and limitations. Garson warned that such lists could have the effect of overriding the basic rights outlined in the covenant.[111] At times these two criticisms appeared in the same documents. The challenge was in drafting a covenant that was consistent, precise, and definite *without* listing limitations and exceptions within each article. The Canadian government seemed disinclined to help work towards this goal, however, and Canada offered few amendments to improve the details of the draft. Instead, delegates were instructed to support only the text for articles that included a clear statement of principle with no details about how the article would be implemented, or any comprehensive definition of the right. In all other cases, the delegates were to refrain from participating in the discussions and to abstain in all votes.[112] This excluded Canada from the majority of discussions, preventing delegates from constructively contributing to the development of the covenant.

Global Obstacles: The Draft Covenant Stalls

By the early 1950s, progress on the draft covenant had slowed considerably. Differences in opinion among member states as to the appropriate format and content of the document stalled the process. States that had previously supported the quick adoption of a covenant, such as the United States, realized this was no longer possible, and in some cases re-evaluated their position. Under the leadership of Democratic president Harry Truman, the US State Department had reluctantly supported US involvement in the development of an international bill of rights. Shortly after Republican Dwight Eisenhower's election in 1952, however, newly appointed Secretary of State John Foster Dulles announced that, due to an unfavourable climate at home, the United States no longer planned to ratify the covenant.[113] Human rights issues had become progressively political, and US politicians were less convinced that the final form of a covenant on human rights would be compatible with US interests.[114] Consequently, the US government instructed its delegates to withdraw from active participation in the debates. By mid-decade, Canada's Department of External Affairs was reporting that other "friendly" states, such as Britain, Australia, and, to a lesser extent, New Zealand, were all becoming increasingly unsympathetic towards a covenant on human rights.[115] These shifts in policy were the result of changing domestic and international environments, as the process of adopting an international treaty on human rights was hampered by the mounting political and ideological divisions of the 1950s.

In their broad history on the human rights movement at the United Nations, Roger Normand and Sarah Zaidi argue that the divisions over human rights among member states in this period illustrate the "reemergence of competing national interests" after a brief period of consensus at the end of the Second World War.[116] Conflicts over how to incorporate the concept of universal human rights in a legally binding covenant were shaped by many international factors. The emergence of the Cold War heightened political and ideological tensions between the Soviet Union and the United States, and the process of decolonization brought anti-imperial discourses into discussions over rights. These pressures were made more complex when added to the desire of world powers to protect their own national sovereignty by resisting strong measures of implementation.

By the early 1950s, the tensions of the Cold War were out in the open and causing evident conflict within the UN. Events such as the 1948 communist coup in Czechoslovakia and the 1948–49 Berlin Blockade had a tremendous impact on relations between the Soviet Union and Western states. This carried over into debates at the UN, as human rights became a propaganda tool in the ideological war between the Soviets and the Americans and their allies.[117] Cold War events further exacerbated the already difficult atmosphere at the UN. The Eleventh Session of ECOSOC, during which member states debated the content of the draft First Covenant, began only days after the outbreak of the Korean War. A final decision on the inclusion of economic and social rights in the covenant was delayed until 1951, due in part to the Soviet boycott of UN functions over the issue of Chinese representation.[118] Debates over the draft covenant became bogged down in Cold War rhetoric. Most vocal within the Soviet bloc were delegates from the Soviet Union and Poland, who attacked Western states for perpetuating racially discriminatory laws, and condemned the United States for, "its warmongering policies and its economic exploitation of underdeveloped countries."[119] The United States, and to a lesser extent Britain and France, responded by accusing the Soviet Union of totalitarian rule and by attacking communist states for their lack of political freedom and legal rights.[120] The Canadian delegation reported that these five states consumed most of the time dedicated to discussing the draft covenant as debates over individual articles were constantly being interrupted with bickering, insults, and points of order that involved lengthy, repetitive, and tiresome discourses.[121] Canada remained on the margins of these discussions.

Particularly in debates over the inclusion of economic and social rights, the Cold War created an ideological divide between the Soviet bloc, which backed a socialist vision of human rights coordinated through centralized state planning, and Western Europe, North America, Australia, and New Zealand, which supported individualism and a free market. This divide influenced the attitude of individual states towards the instruments on human rights, and caused two of Canada's closest allies, the United States and Australia, to withdraw their initial support for the draft First Covenant. Anti-communism was the driving force behind US domestic and foreign policy by the 1950s, and US officials worried about Soviet influence over the content of the UDHR and the covenant. In 1949, the inclusion of articles on economic and social rights in the UDHR caused Frank E. Holman, president of the American Bar Association, to refer to the document as a manifesto on "pink paper" that would "promote state socialism, if not communism, throughout the world."[122] The US government responded by demanding that any covenant on human rights include only civil and political rights. When it became obvious that this would not be the case, the United States withdrew its support. A rise in anti-communist and anti-socialist sentiments in Australia by the 1950s also caused the Australian government to take a more negative approach to the draft. The Liberal government of Robert Menzies reversed the earlier Australian policy of advocating the inclusion of economic and social rights, and Australian policy makers began to view the draft covenant as a document that needed to be contained.[123] Canadian officials shared the desire of both the United States and Australia to limit the influence of a covenant on human rights, but Cold War rhetoric did not permeate the debates among federal policy makers over Canada's position towards the draft covenant. Political scientist Denis Stairs explains this by arguing that Canada's foreign policy throughout the Cold War period was shaped by calculations over power and national interest, not ideology.[124] The archival records of the communications between Justice and External Affairs regarding international human rights support this, as the focal point of the criticisms of the covenant related to how it defined rights from a legal perspective, and the ways in which it infringed domestic sovereignty, as opposed to more ideological or political discussions. In their reports to External Affairs, Canadian delegates did comment on the unrelenting use of propaganda by the Soviets in debates over rights, but this was more of a general observation than a comment intending to inform policy. If anything, Canadian policy makers saw the divisions caused by the Cold War as useful, hoping they would induce members of the UN to abandon the project of a covenant on human rights. In 1952, Under-Secretary of State for External Affairs Arnold Heeney told the Canadian delegation that Cabinet and the ministers of external affairs and justice hoped that project of a covenant on human rights would be "delayed for a long, perhaps indefinite, time."[125] Heeney went on to say, however, that this "real view" of the ministers could never be expressed in public.[126]

In addition to Cold War tensions, the process of decolonization influenced discussions over the First Covenant in ECOSOC and at the General Assembly. In *Decolonization and the Evolution of International Human Rights,* Roland Burke asserts that it was this process above all others that "transformed the UN and the shape of human rights discourse," producing global human rights as we understand them today.[127] There was tremendous pressure on European colonial powers to grant independence to their colonies after the Second World War, but the slow pace of decolonization led to a great deal of criticism at the UN.[128] The most vocal anti-colonial states were those that had only just won their own independence, such as India, Pakistan, and the Philippines.[129] These states supported the inclusion of economic and social rights and an article on self-determination in the draft covenant, and they openly criticized the position of what they characterized as the "Western colonial states." The Canadian government was well aware of the influence of decolonization on attempts to develop a covenant on human rights, with External Affairs reporting that the UN sessions were increasingly reduced to "acrimonious debate" between anti-colonial and so-called colonial countries.[130] Latin American nations such as Chile, Mexico, and Peru supported the anti-colonial arguments, and there was a growing and visible gap between "developed" and "underdeveloped" member states. Soviet delegates attempted to take advantage of this gap, often attacking the West for its history of colonialism, racial discrimination, and overseas exploitation, fashioning the USSR as the champion of colonial peoples.[131] This was initially effective, but Western states learned to take the offensive by pointing out the poor conditions behind the Iron Curtain, the absorption of the Baltic states, and the suppression of political and religious freedom in Soviet territory.[132] Human rights were a powerful political weapon, but one that cut in many ways.

By the early 1950s, Canadian delegates were reporting to External Affairs that there were three main alliances in the debates over the draft covenant on human rights: the Western bloc, led by the United States and Britain; the Soviet bloc; and the non-aligned states.[133] As the non-aligned states became increasingly vocal in debates over issues of economic and social development, they realized that, because of their numbers, they could control the debate and the fate of the resolutions presented in the General Assembly.[134] This is what happened, to a large extent, in debates over economic and social rights.

The Debate over Economic and Social Rights

Within months of the introduction of the draft First Covenant, the desirability of including economic and social rights in the same covenant as civil and political rights had become a clear issue for debate.[135] When the Commission on Human Rights submitted the draft to ECOSOC for consideration, it included only articles covering civil and political rights, along with articles of implementation. ECOSOC took a full week to debate the merits of the draft, and economic and social rights figured largely in this debate. Some states, such as Canada, were satisfied with the focus on civil and political rights and opposed any inclusion of economic and social rights. They argued that economic and social rights differed from civil and political rights because they were not immediately realizable and justiciable; they claimed that, because economic and social rights were not easily adjudicated and enforced by traditional court systems and the legal process, they should not be included in a covenant.[136] The United States argued that economic and social rights were too different from civil and political rights, and that their inclusion in the First Covenant would slow down the process of adoption.[137] Canada and Britain both agreed with this sentiment, proposing that economic and social rights be added at a later date. Despite all the internal communications to the contrary, Canadian delegates publicly told other UN members states that Canada did *not* oppose the inclusion of economic and social rights, but felt that their inclusion in 1950 was "over-ambitious and premature" and could "jeopardize, if not make impossible" the adoption of the covenant.[138]

Other states insisted that a covenant that did not include economic and social rights was not in the true spirit of the Universal Declaration of

Human Rights.[139] Chile, Mexico, Brazil, and Peru, among others, argued that without economic and social rights, a covenant on human rights was incomplete.[140] Not all states that supported inclusion were from Asia or Latin America. Prior to the defeat of Ben Chifley's Labor government in 1949, Australia was a leading advocate for the addition of fundamental economic and social rights in the First Covenant, insisting that if the number of this type of article was limited, the covenant could be adopted within a year.[141] The "red scare" in Australia in the late 1940s undermined the Labor Party's policies, however, and led to the election of the openly anti-communist Liberal Party of Robert Menzies, who reversed Australia's position towards economic and social rights.[142] The Soviet Union and its satellite states also supported the inclusion of economic and social rights in the First Covenant, but opposed any serious implementation measures.

At the end of the ECOSOC session, the American delegation pressed strongly to have the First Covenant sent directly to the General Assembly, hoping it could be taken to a final vote quickly to avoid further debate on economic and social rights. Before the General Assembly could take a serious look at the content of the instrument, a lobby group of states convinced a majority of the General Assembly that the document was inadequate. The most vocal delegates in this lobby represented Latin American states and the Soviet bloc.[143] Based on their arguments, the covenant was returned to the Commission on Human Rights with instructions to include a clearer expression of economic, social, and cultural rights. Seriously concerned at this point, the Canadian government instructed its delegates to avoid any participation in the debates.[144] Canadian delegates met privately with representatives from other states that opposed the inclusion of economic and social rights, hoping to find middle ground through which compromise could be achieved; states involved in the consultation were Canada, Britain, the United States, France, India, Belgium, Sweden, and Uruguay.[145] They discussed the possibility of putting forth a resolution to have the Commission on Human Rights prepare two separate covenants to be introduced and debated simultaneously, one including civil and political rights and the other including economic and social rights. This was first proposed by American delegates who opposed the inclusion of economic and social rights but recognized that they were in the minority in the General Assembly, and suggested this alternative as a way of keeping the two types of rights apart. Canadian officials were initially skeptical of the American proposal. Policy makers in Ottawa argued that support for a two-covenant solution would presuppose the need for economic and social rights, and questioned which of the two covenants would take priority.[146]

When the idea of two covenants was proposed at ECOSOC, member states debated this question of a hierarchy of rights. The majority of states supported the inclusion of economic and social rights, but were at this point divided into two camps: those that supported a unitary covenant, and those advocating for two covenants to be presented simultaneously.[147] In its instructions to the Canadian delegation in 1951, External Affairs expressed its desire to prevent the creation of two covenants, but admitted that this would be difficult to do without making Canada look like it opposed human rights. In a memo, the department argued that the inclusion of economic and social rights was "unworkable and inadvisable" and that, as these were already covered by the UDHR, it would "tend to weaken the position of the Universal Declaration."[148] The Canadian government therefore found itself in a dilemma; it opposed a single covenant that included both civil and political and economic and social rights, yet it also objected to the creation of two covenants, because one would be dedicated to economic and social rights, which the government opposed. One covenant with only civil and political rights was no longer an option, and so federal policy makers had to make a difficult decision. In January 1952, the Canadian delegation voted against a Chilean resolution to include economic and social rights in the same covenant as civil and political rights, and in favour of two covenants. Preferring to abstain in the vote on two covenants to show its displeasure, the Canadian delegation had to vote in support instead, because the vote was so close that the government feared that by abstaining Canada would help those in favour of a unitary covenant to carry the vote.[149] The close results illustrate just how contentious this issue was for member states of the UN. In the final count, thirty states voted in favour of drafting two separate covenants, while twenty-four opposed the division of the First Covenant and seven states abstained; because abstentions did not count as a negative vote, the motion passed.[150] Beginning in 1952, therefore, the Commission on Human Rights worked to prepare revised drafts for the two covenants. Canada played no role in this process, as only member states sitting on the commission were involved. Two years later, the *International Covenant on Civil and Political Rights* and the *International Covenant on Economic, Social and Cultural Rights* received first reading.

The Federal State and Colonial Clauses

In addition to losing the debate over economic and social rights, Canadian policy makers were unhappy with the lack of progress towards inclusion of a federal state clause in the draft covenant to alleviate jurisdictional concerns. In 1950, External Affairs proposed the following text for such a clause:

> In the case of a Federal State, the following provisions shall apply:
>
> (a) With respect to those articles of this Convention that come within the legislative jurisdiction of the federal legislative authority, the obligations of the federal government shall, to this extent, be the same as those parties which are not federal states;
> (b) With respect to those articles of this Convention that come within the legislative jurisdiction of the legislative authority of the constituent states, provinces or cantons, the federal government shall bring such articles, with favourable recommendation, to the notice of the appropriate authorities of the states, provinces or cantons at the earliest possible moment.[151]

Canadian delegates were instructed to resist sending the First Covenant to the General Assembly for a vote until this clause, or a similar version, was included. The United States, another federal state anxious to limit the covenant's authority over domestic policy, was Canada's greatest ally in this. States such as Britain and India supported Canada in principle, but argued that a federal clause put a greater legal obligation on unitary states.[152] The vast majority of states, however, opposed a federal clause, arguing that all states should have an equal responsibility to uphold the obligations of the covenant. Pakistan went so far as to accuse the Canadian government of fabricating the constitutional concerns.[153] With such meagre support, the Canadian delegation was unsuccessful in its push for a federal clause, although Canada continued to restate its constitutional concerns at every opportunity.

The call for addition of a colonial clause limiting the application of the covenant in the dependent territories of a colonial state also provoked heated debate. This clause would let colonial powers choose whether or not to extend the application of the instrument to all or any of such territories. Colonial states such as Britain, France, Belgium, and Denmark had the mild support of smaller powers such as Canada and Australia in their push for the inclusion of such a clause. In a memo to Cabinet in 1950, the Interdepartmental Committee on Human Rights recommended that Canada vote in favour of a colonial clause because it was important to Britain, and because this could help secure British support for a federal state clause.[154] Again, any limitation on the application of the covenant was strongly opposed by the majority of states. Latin American and Asian states argued that this clause would provide an excuse for Britain, France, and Belgium to circumvent the obligations of the covenant, perpetuating the already inequitable treatment of colonial peoples.[155] These opposing states considered both the federal and colonial clauses as loopholes designed to suit the interests of colonial powers and their allies, and Canadian delegates reported that Asian and Latin American states were becoming "loud and frank about their discontent, despite the way in which this might influence American versus Soviet alignment."[156]

~

By 1954, conflicting national positions at the United Nations had forced a compromise transformation of the draft First Covenant on Human Rights into two instruments: the *International Covenant on Civil and Political Rights* and the *International Covenant on Economic, Social and Cultural Rights*. From the introduction of the first draft in 1949, the Canadian government participated as little as possible in the development of, and refrained from committing itself in any way to, a covenant on human rights. As a result, the Canadian delegation was often isolated and the subject of criticism by other member states. Although policy makers used jurisdictional problems and the need for a federal clause as the primary justification for their position, in reality officials also had significant substantive concerns with the draft. Especially with regard to economic and social rights, the government was reluctant to accept the expansive definition of human rights that other member states wanted to see embodied in the instrument. Ottawa had become increasingly dissatisfied with the status of international human rights. Canadian officials had been unenthusiastic over the draft First Covenant released to member states in 1949, but by 1954 the situation seemed much more complicated. The evolution of debates over the best form for a covenant on human rights, the decision to draft two separate instruments in order to incorporate economic and social rights, and the continued exclusion of a federal clause alarmed policy makers. With support for the covenants declining among Canada's closest allies, most federal civil servants working on Canadian policy towards the International Bill of Rights in External Affairs and Justice could not envision a situation in which it would be in Canada's best interest to support an international covenant on human rights.

In her study of the federal government's policy towards the 1951 UN *Convention Relating to the Status of Refugees*, Laura Madokoro argues that Ottawa's reluctance to support the refugee convention has been "disguised by accounts of the postwar period as a time of linear liberal progress along with an insistence by officials and citizens alike that the character of the Canadian nation was, and remains, a humanitarian one."[157] The hostility Canadian policy makers felt towards a covenant on human rights has been similarly downplayed. In the first decade after the end of the Second World War, Canadian politicians and bureaucrats did not view international human rights policies as a means to promote peace and improve the conditions of marginalized peoples around the world. Instead, they were suspicious of the benefits of human rights treaties, believing that they threatened Canadian sovereignty and fearing that they could be used as a propaganda tool against Canada. Ottawa's resulting approach to attempts to adopt an international covenant on human rights was therefore rooted not in humanitarianism but in a form of protectionism.

Cold War tensions and the pressures of decolonization stalled the progress of the First Covenant, as did the serious concerns over enforcement. Despite this, the divisions within ECOSOC and the General Assembly demonstrated to the Canadian government that Canada was in a minority position in its opposition to the covenants. At home, a small but growing rights movement was working to challenge historical understandings of civil liberties. The UN's discourse of human rights was making its way into public and political discourse, and Canadians were becoming aware of, and more supportive of, human rights principles. Although this had yet to influence Canadian policy towards a UN covenant on human rights, it did represent the beginning of a real divergence between the attitudes of Canadian policy makers and Canadian rights activists in relation to international human rights. This was important because it would set the stage for Canadian policy makers to gradually shift from opposing the International Covenants on Human Rights to working to improve the text of these covenants so that Canada could ultimately vote in favour of their adoption by 1966.

3

A Reversal in Policy: The Decision to Support the Covenants

The UN Commission on Human Rights submitted copies of its draft *International Covenant on Civil and Political Rights* (ICCPR), and *International Covenant on Economic, Social and Cultural Rights* (ICESCR) to the General Assembly in 1954 for article-by-article debate. It would take more than a decade for member states to revise and adopt these instruments, and the debates over their form and content reflected the deepening political and ideological divisions of the Cold War period. While questions over how to best articulate and implement international human rights were influenced by international relations and the expanding membership of the United Nations, domestic developments in the 1950s and 1960s shaped the foreign policy approach of individual members. As a result, some states that had been enthusiastic about a covenant on human rights, such as the United States, withdrew their support. Canada worked in reverse, as officials initially resisted the idea of a binding human rights instrument but reluctantly came to support both covenants.

Ottawa's policy approach did not change significantly through the first years of the article-by-article debates. Publicly, Canadian officials invoked jurisdictional issues as their primary reason for failing to support the covenants, but policy makers continued to oppose the expansive definition of universal human rights articulated in the documents and feared their impact on domestic policy. The Department of External Affairs instructed its UN delegation to resist active participation in the debates, hoping the covenants would prove too contentious for adoption. By the mid-1960s, however, Canada was playing a more active role on the Commission on

Human Rights, constructively contributing to debates over the ICCPR and the ICESCR, and positioning itself to vote in favour of the adoption of both instruments. This change in approach was shaped by two realities of the early 1960s. First, Canadian policy makers recognized that, with support for both covenants increasing, the instruments *would* be adopted in some form in the near future, with or without Canadian support. This forced Ottawa to make a decision. Second, growing public support for human rights at home and an active human rights movement caused federal officials to consider for the first time how Canadians would react if their government refused to support the adoption of human rights treaties at the UN. This public support for human rights significantly affected the government's policy approach to the two covenants, as federal politicians realized that they would have to at least pay lip service to the importance of signing the documents. By the 1960s, External Affairs was instructing its delegation to contribute more constructively to the article-by-article debates. Minister of Justice Stuart Garson, whose report on the draft First Covenant had been so critical, encouraged the delegates to "make the best of a bad job" and contribute to the UN's efforts to produce documents that would be amenable to all states.[1] It was therefore Canadian civil society, and the changing international environment, that inspired changes to Canadian policy. Ultimately, the government was persuaded, by what it understood to be international and Canadian public opinion, that it was in Canada's best interest to support the International Covenants on Human Rights.

The Article-by-Article Debates

Originating from the same document, the two draft covenants shared a common preamble as well as an identical first article outlining the right of self-determination. The *International Covenant on Civil and Political Rights* was a longer document, consisting of twenty substantive articles protecting the right to life, liberty, dignity and security of the person; legal rights allowing for due process and equality before the law; freedom of movement, expression, religion, thought, opinion, assembly, association, and marriage; and the right of all humans to be recognized as persons. An additional sixteen articles outlined measures for implementation, including rules requiring member states to provide periodic reports to the UN Human Rights Commission on their progress as well as provisions to establish a human rights committee to administer the covenant and review complaints of violations. The *International Covenant on Economic, Social and Cultural Rights* contained eleven substantive articles, defending the right to education; the right to work in just conditions and to join unions and access social security; the right to an adequate standard of living, including sufficient food, clothing, and housing; and the right to the highest attainable standard of health. Due to previous debates over the difficulty of enforcing economic and social rights, and the appropriateness of including these rights in a covenant, this instrument required periodic reporting to the UN Human Rights Commission but did not establish a committee to oversee implementation or review complaints.

In addition to the two covenants, the UN also produced an optional protocol linked to the ICCPR. The protocol expanded on enforcement measures, outlining the procedures whereby individuals could petition the UN regarding their rights under the covenant. It did not address any new substantive areas, only influencing the way the treaty operated and could be enforced. The decision to allow individual petitions was contentious, and the optional protocol allowed states that disagreed with its provisions to still support and ratify the ICCPR.

The Third Committee of the General Assembly was responsible for dealing with issues regarding humanitarian affairs and social development, and therefore hosted the article-by-article debates. In its ninth session in 1954, the committee undertook a first reading of the drafts, allowing only for a general discussion of their contents and the debate procedures. Canadian delegates participated very little, but restated the constitutional problems facing Canada given that neither draft contained a clause accommodating the division of powers in a federal state.[2] The general discussion at the ninth session highlighted issues over which states were most divided: the article on self-determination, the inclusion of economic and social rights, the federal state and territorial application clauses, the possibility of allowing reservations to the covenants, and questions over who would be allowed to petition any committee established by the ICCPR. The Canadian delegation reported that "the general debate had a sobering effect on the self-appointed champions of human rights in the Third Committee" because it underlined the "fundamental differences still separating various groups of states in spite of the painstaking efforts of the Human Rights Commission to produce drafts which would provide a common denominator."[3]

A lengthy debate over the order in which the draft articles would be discussed suggested that the process of adopting the two covenants would be difficult and take longer than originally expected. The Soviet bloc and states from Latin America, Asia, and Africa called for an immediate discussion of Article 1 on self-determination, arguing that this article was a precondition of the enjoyment of all other rights.[4] Canada joined other Western delegates in proposing to hold off this debate. Britain argued that an article-by-article debate did not require the articles to be discussed in order and suggested that the committee start with "less controversial items."[5] In private communications with its High Commissioners in Canada, Australia, New Zealand, and South Africa, the Commonwealth Relations Office expressed concern that "rabid anti-colonials" would pressure the Third Committee to begin its debates with the article on self-determination, thereby "plunging the Committee into acrimonious debate at the very onset."[6] Britain's predictions were correct, as most member states did vote to start debate in 1955 with the preamble and common first article, to be followed by the substantive articles of the ICESCR and then those of the ICCPR, ending with the articles on implementation. This decision forced member states to deal with the most divisive articles of the covenants first.

Earnest debate and voting on specific articles commenced in 1955. The Canadian delegation reported that the debates were "exhausting," and the committee was able to get through only four to six articles per session on average.[7] Intense deliberation, lengthy speeches, and frequent proposals for revising each article were common to all of the sessions. For example, the Third Committee dedicated thirty-eight meetings in 1956 to examining Articles 6 through 13 of the ICESCR, and member states participated in more than one hundred votes over amendments and subamendments.[8] It took until 1963 for the Third Committee to discuss and vote on all of the substantive articles for each covenant. It then turned its attention to the implementation provisions, and member states debated the extent to which either covenant would be subject to an international supervisory system.

The article-by-article debates concluded three years later, and on 16 December 1966, the General Assembly voted to adopt both International Covenants on Human Rights.

The Reluctant Critic: Canada's Early Participation in the Debates

After its general discussion of the covenants in 1954, the Third Committee invited member states and the UN's specialized agencies to comment on the drafts.[9] Yet again, the Canadian government did not offer a submission, deliberately avoiding a definite stand with respect to the covenants. Policy makers continued to question the need for an international treaty on human rights for Canada. In an internal memo, External Affairs officials noted that, while the draft ICCPR seemed to be satisfactory and provide for rights and freedoms already enjoyed by Canadians, the articles in the draft ICESCR were still too vague; officials remained skeptical of the appropriateness of including these rights in a binding treaty.[10] The department also pointed to ongoing concerns over the article on self-determination, and the absence of meaningful federal state and colonial clauses. For these reasons, External Affairs described its position as "very guarded, unenthusiastic and non-committal."[11]

In part, Canada's indecision was shaped by the changing positions of its closest allies. Whereas in the late 1940s Canada had been under intense pressure from the United States and Britain to support the UN's human rights initiatives, by the 1950s these states seemed to have lost interest in a covenant. Even the United States' strongest advocate for international human rights, Eleanor Roosevelt, realized the difficulty of designing a binding instrument that would be acceptable to the American government in the Cold War era.[12] From 1951 to 1953, Senator John Bricker, a Republican from Ohio, campaigned against American support for the covenants, describing them as "utter nonsense," "a blueprint for tyranny," and the "greatest threat to American sovereignty."[13] Bricker's campaign was influential, and in 1953 the new Eisenhower administration replaced Roosevelt with Mary Lord on the UN Commission on Human Rights. Lord had experience as a civic worker in several charitable organizations, including the US Committee for UNICEF, and had been heavily involved in President Eisenhower's electoral fundraising. She had no diplomatic experience and very little knowledge of the American position towards human rights at the United Nations.[14] Unlike Roosevelt, she appeared uninterested in a covenant on human rights.[15] Secretary of State John Foster Dulles announced later that year that the United States would no longer participate in the commission's work of drafting a binding human rights instrument, and did not intend to ratify the covenants. The official justification for this change was that the covenants would not be effective because of the widespread lack of respect for human rights, and were unlikely to be widely ratified.[16] Among Canadian policy makers, the first part of 1954 was therefore taken up with discussions over what Canada would do now that it had lost its greatest ally in the fight for a federal state clause.

Britain, although publicly supportive of the principles of the covenants, had also stopped taking a lead role in human rights work at the UN. British delegates were pessimistic that an effective covenant could be adopted, and discouraged by the way in which their attempts to shape the documents were received by other member states. In a report on the progress of the Commission on Human Rights, Samuel Hoare of the British Home Office claimed that British proposals were repeatedly viewed with suspicion by other delegates, who argued that Britain was either protecting its colonial power, working to design an instrument that reflected only British law, or attempting to "hamstring" any article it did not approve of.[17] Frustrated, Britain continued to participate in debates over the draft covenants, but focused its support on the new *European Convention for the Protection of Human Rights,* a regional document that was more in line with its own traditions.[18] Even Australia, which had enthusiastically advocated the inclusion of economic and social rights and supported the draft First Covenant in 1949, changed its position. The Cold War led to a rise in anti-communism in Australia, and the Labor Party was replaced with a Liberal government that worked to limit both the content and the power of the covenants throughout the 1950s.[19]

Despite the concerns expressed by states such as Britain and Australia, only the United States took a definitive stance against ratifying the covenants. Fearful of criticism, the Canadian government was unwilling to state such a strong opinion. External Affairs officials gave their "true opinion" on the drafts minimal publicity, focusing instead on jurisdictional problems.[20] Participation in the article-by-article debates was to be marginal, lest delegates appeared either too critical or too supportive of the documents, thereby committing Canada to a course of action. Stuart Garson claimed it was too early to decide whether or not Canada would support the covenants.[21] External Affairs provided few specific instructions to its UN delegates, preferring that they speak in generalities and abstain in votes where possible.[22] Even two years into the article-by-article debates, External Affairs legal advisor Marcel Cadieux noted that little progress had been made in determining Canada's position. Rather than playing an active role in shaping the International Covenants on Human Rights, Canada was excessively cautious and therefore often peripheral to their development. In an internal departmental memo, Cadieux observed that "the fundamental question which does not appear to have been answered definitely is whether the Canadian government is really interested in the covenants being drafted in a form which will facilitate signature and ratification by Canada."[23] Unfortunately for the Canadian government, which preferred to speak as little as possible in committee discussions, the Third Committee decided to begin by voting on the articles on self-determination and social and economic rights. As Canada opposed the inclusion of all these articles, the early contributions of its delegates to the debate were largely negative.[24] This caused other member states to openly question Canada's claim to support the principles of the covenants.

The article-by-article debates began with a discussion of the only right to appear in both covenants, that of self-determination. When the UN Charter was written in 1945, it listed the development of "friendly relations among nations based on respect for the principle of equal rights and self-determination of peoples" as a key purpose of the organization.[25] Recognized at this point as a principle rather than a right, self-determination did not appear in the UDHR. The concept evolved throughout the postwar period, however, heavily shaped by both the socialist doctrine of self-determination, traced back to Marx and Lenin, and a growing anti-colonial movement.[26] By the 1950s, members from Latin America, the Soviet bloc, and a number of newly independent states were calling on the UN to move beyond the "principle" of self-determination to recognize instead the "right" for peoples to organize as a state. By 1952, this had gained sufficient support for the General Assembly to direct the Commission on Human Rights to include a common article on self-determination as the first article of each of the international covenants.[27] It became one of the most divisive human rights issues in the debates, as statehood brought with it political, economic, and military power.[28] At issue was the question of *which* national groups would be eligible. The proposed text of Article 1 of each covenant was: "All peoples and all nations shall have the right of self-determination, namely the right freely to determine their political, economic, social and cultural status."[29] This right would also include "permanent sovereignty over their natural wealth and resources."[30] The meaning of these terms remained unclear. Canadian delegate Paul Martin argued that the notion of self-determination was "susceptible to multiple interpretations" and that the question of who would be entitled to such a right remained "too loose, too vague to be defined with the desirable accuracy" in a covenant on human rights, and should therefore be left out.[31] John Humphrey, still working for the UN Secretariat, also opposed the inclusion of an article on self-determination, but for more practical reasons. He worried the issue could hinder progress on the covenants, causing the colonial powers to withdraw their support entirely.[32]

Humphrey had a point. In the literature on international human rights, there is much debate over the significance of the addition of an article on self-determination to the covenants. A.W. Brian Simpson has argued that the campaign to persuade the UN that the principle of self-determination amounted to a human right was politically motivated, used by anti-colonial powers to mobilize support at the UN for decolonization, and used by the Soviet Union to weaken the position of the Western powers.[33] In this way, although self-determination came to be articulated in the language of rights, it was not essentially a rights movement and so delegitimized the UN's human rights program. Roland Burke disputes this, arguing that the campaign was initially premised on the value of individual rights, but that it evolved throughout the 1950s and 1960s to focus more on the rights of states, mirroring a broader trend away from the focus on individual rights in the human rights movement.[34] Samuel Moyn agrees that the decision to include an article on self-determination led to the reconceptualization of human rights as more collective, but argues that this marginalized human rights as it became apparent that the UN had become more of a forum for the promotion of sovereign states than for individual rights.[35] Although UN states were not discussing self-determination in this way, they were conscious of the significance such a right would have for the covenants, and for the global community more broadly. Western states such as the United States, Britain, and France were staunchly opposed to the right of self-determination, fearful that it would legitimize nationalist movements around the world, destabilizing the international system.[36] Canada's specific position was that self-determination was a collective right, and therefore did not belong in covenants that expressed the rights of individuals. Canada's opposition was also linked to its continued support for British imperialism, particularly as the Canadian government worked closely with its Commonwealth allies in setting policies towards the covenants on human rights in this period.

Canada joined Belgium, the Netherlands, Australia, New Zealand, Britain, and Turkey in arguing that discussions over self-determination were premature and should take place in another forum.[37] The Canadian delegation tried to assure member states that Canada did take the issue of self-determination seriously; delegates argued that they were only being cautious, and questioned whether or not self-determination could be achieved overnight, simply through the creation of an article in a covenant.[38] Despite these assurances, Canada was criticized for its position. Most member states in the Third Committee argued that self-determination was an essential component of any draft covenant, and that opponents of this article were supporting colonialism.[39] The debate over Article 1 lasted for twenty-six meetings, consuming most of the time allowed by the Third Committee in 1955 to discuss the draft covenants. Eventually, the article was adopted, with thirty-three states voting in support, twelve, including Canada, voting against, and thirteen abstaining.[40] For the Canadian government, it was not the ideal way to establish Canada's policy towards the covenants.

Canada drew further criticism for its position on the substantive articles of the *International Covenant on Economic, Social and Cultural Rights*. Reluctant to oppose these rights but also unwilling to support many of them, Canada abstained in eight of the eleven votes. Delegates pointed to the Canadian federal government's lack of authority to negotiate international treaties that infringed on provincial jurisdiction. For example, they abstained on the articles guaranteeing the right to work, to just working conditions, and to free compulsory education, arguing that these articles would impose obligations in areas under the jurisdiction of Canada's provincial governments. In the case of Article 8, on the right to join trade unions, delegates abstained, insisting that the inclusion of the right to perform specific functions, such as the right to strike, also infringed on provincial jurisdiction.[41] Canadian delegates criticized the vague language used in the articles on economic and social rights. They also argued that articles on the right to social security, to an adequate standard of living, and to protection of the family were too imprecise to be included in an international treaty. Even in the case of articles the delegation supported, such as those on the right to adequate health and to participate in cultural life, Canada was clear that its support depended on the inclusion of a federal state clause.[42] During the first two years of the article-by-article debates, therefore, a pattern of Canadian participation emerged. The delegation began each session with a reminder that Canada's division of power made it impossible for the government to commit to a covenant that did not include a suitable federal clause; delegates spoke infrequently but critically about the text of the articles; and Canada abstained on all articles that could even potentially fall under provincial jurisdiction, including articles on the right to work and to enjoy adequate conditions at work, to join unions, to social security, to the protection of family, to adequate food and clothing, to an adequate standing of living, and to compulsory education.[43] This pattern does not fit into Thomas Keating's description of Canadian foreign policy in the postwar period as demonstrating a persistent commitment to multilateralism and to international cooperation.[44] Rather it supports interpretations of Canadian foreign policy in this period as cautious, pragmatic, and protective of Canadian interests.

Pressures from Home: The Influence of Canada's Growing Human Rights Movement

At first, federal officials seemed unconcerned about any negative repercussions at home of their policy approach towards the draft covenants. Canadians continued to be unaware of the documents' existence, and there was very little pressure on Ottawa to support them. There was, however, mounting public support for human rights more broadly. Campaigns to expand anti-discrimination laws and greater social movement activity at both the provincial and federal levels triggered an important cultural shift in how Canadians understood the concept of human rights and the role of governments in promoting equality. As a result, External Affairs policy makers grew increasingly sensitive to how their policy decisions would be interpreted by Canadians.

By the end of the 1950s, most jurisdictions in Canada had passed fair practices legislation in the areas of employment and accommodation, and several had also enacted equal pay laws.[45] Unlike earlier anti-discrimination laws, which took a quasi-criminal approach, the fair practices acts were based on the methods and procedures used in labour relations, emphasizing conciliation and the settlement of complaints over criminal prosecution. Rather than using the courts, victims would bring complaints to administrative officials, who would investigate and then try to negotiate a settlement. This avoided the high burden of proof involved in criminal cases and offered a wider range of remedies to victims. Although this was an improvement on earlier laws, enforcement of the fair practices acts was problematic.[46] There were no administrative bodies to deal with human rights complaints, so civil servants, often within departments of labour, took on the responsibility. Budgetary and time constraints prevented human rights cases from becoming a priority for government workers. A lack of public awareness of the available laws and procedures also meant that many victims of discrimination failed to file complaints because they were unaware of their rights or the proper procedures for launching a complaint.[47] Finally, by requiring citizens to initiate a case, the legislation was designed to minimize government interference in the private interactions of individuals; this reflected the persistent attitude that discrimination was the result of individual infractions rather than larger societal problems, and limited the scope of the legislation.[48] Despite these limitations, the adoption of fair practices laws across the country demonstrated a new awareness of discrimination as a problem in Canadian society, and a greater acceptance of codified rights as an important tool for solving this problem. Citizens had begun to expect their government to play a role in protecting human rights.

This expectation must be seen in the broader context of Canada's postwar social policy, as anti-discrimination laws were a part of a larger legislative shift towards the creation of a welfare state. Throughout the first half of the twentieth century, the dominant political philosophy was that responsibility for well-being rested with the individual or the family, with support coming from local charities when needed.[49] Municipal or provincial governments set social policy, not Ottawa. However, the experience of the Depression and two world wars led to the adoption of interventionist policies by the federal government, and Canadians began to increasingly accept an expanded role for Ottawa in social and economic life. In 1940, the Rowell-Sirois Commission on federal-provincial relations recommended that the federal government implement a national unemployment insurance plan and expand social security programs. Penny Bryden's work on the Liberal Party's postwar social policy reveals that, despite the commission's recommendations and growing public support, the King and St. Laurent governments were reluctant to include social security measures as a key component of their domestic policy.[50] By the late 1950s, although Ottawa had introduced a family allowance program, an agreement on old age pensions, and a national hospital insurance plan, there was no comprehensive social welfare policy at the federal level. Provincial governments also adopted a number of social security measures, many of which dealt with rights outlined in the UN's draft covenants, including workers' compensation, mothers' allowance, mandatory education, and living accommodations for the aged.[51] These policies were increasingly popular, and according to Bryden, public opinion supported greater national responsibility for the social and economic well-being of Canadians.[52] This support added impetus to the push for greater government involvement in protecting rights and freedoms.

The adoption of fair practices laws and accompanying pressures to combat discrimination in Canadian society also influenced other provincial and federal policies. Most notably, by 1960, racial and religious discrimination was no longer a factor in voter qualification, and no major group was explicitly deprived of the franchise in Canada. This began in the years after the Second World War, in the context of the campaigns against the deportation of Japanese Canadians and for the repeal of the *Chinese Immigration Act*. By 1949, the federal and all provincial governments had removed voting exclusions for Chinese, Japanese, and South Asian Canadians. The enfranchisement of religious minorities such as Mennonites, Hutterites, and Doukhobors followed, and all these groups were allowed to vote by the mid-1950s. Non-Status Indians began receiving full voting rights at the provincial level in 1949, most Inuit had the franchise in 1950, and the federal franchise was extended fully to Non-Status and Status Indians in

1960.[53] Changes also occurred in other policies. Property laws were amended to prohibit discrimination in the sale or leasing of property. In 1950, a legal team headed by law professor Bora Laskin and supported by the Canadian Jewish Congress successfully challenged the legality of restrictive covenants that limited land ownership to "persons of the white or Caucasian race."[54] Six years later, the Supreme Court of British Columbia considered a case in which a woman was barred from inheriting her father's estate as long as she was "married to a Jew." In this case, the court set aside the clause on the grounds that it constituted racial discrimination and was contrary to public policy and the public interest.[55] This was a significant departure from the legal tradition of the first half of the twentieth century. Canadian judges did not, however, choose to advance the earlier suggestion, arising out of the Alberta Press Case (see Chapter 1), that government laws could be subject to judicial review for violating fundamental rights and freedoms.[56] Instead, courts continued to limit themselves to the question of whether the law was within the authority of a government based on the constitutional division of powers. In some cases, this worked in the favour of rights activists. In 1957, the Supreme Court of Canada struck down Quebec's infamous Padlock Law, ruling that the creation of "the crime of promoting communism" was *ultra vires* the provincial government.[57] Two years later, the same court ruled that Maurice Duplessis had committed a civil wrong when he revoked the liquor licence of Frank Roncarelli on the grounds that Roncarelli frequently provided bail for Jehovah's Witnesses charged with distributing pamphlets attacking Roman Catholicism.[58] This decision set a legal precedent for the rule of law in Canada, as Duplessis was the premier of Quebec at the time. However, because a protection for rights was not explicitly entrenched in Canada's Constitution, most judges continued to believe that Parliament was a more appropriate forum for resolving civil liberties or human rights questions.[59]

The Department of External Affairs was well aware of Canada's legislative developments in the area of human rights protection because states were obligated to provide periodic reports on their progress to the Secretary-General of the United Nations. The UN's annual *Yearbook on Human Rights* contained extracted texts and summaries of significant constitutional provisions, legislative acts, executive orders, and judicial decisions for each member state, documenting how each either promoted or limited the observance of human rights within that state.[60] In 1956, the UN Economic and Social Council (ECOSOC) adopted a resolution requiring states to also produce triennial reports summarizing progress made and difficulties encountered in safeguarding human rights.[61] In Canada, the departments of Labour, Justice, External Affairs, Citizenship and Immigration, and National Health and Welfare were responsible for generating these documents, and officials could be working on several at one time. In 1957, for example, public servants were working on material for the *Yearbook,* a triennial report, and specialized reports on arbitrary arrest, discrimination with regard to religious practice, discrimination in employment and occupation, and discrimination in the field of political rights.[62] It was therefore impossible for External Affairs to ignore the changes taking place within Canada, especially as Ottawa worked hard to demonstrate in its reports that Canada continued to make progress in the field of human rights.

One of the most significant changes, at least in terms of codification of rights, was the development of a Canadian bill of rights in the late 1950s. Impetus for such a bill re-emerged when John Diefenbaker and his Progressive Conservatives won the 1957 federal election, ending twenty-two years of Liberal Party rule and signalling a break in Liberal tradition. During the campaign, opposition parties argued that the Liberals had become arrogant and out of touch with the needs of Canadians during their long tenure. The Progressive Conservatives won by offering a new vision of Canada at a time when Canadians were questioning their nation's role in the Empire and the larger world, the meaning of citizenship, and the place of marginalized peoples in society.[63] Diefenbaker attempted to answer these questions with his New National Policy and his concept of "one unhyphenated Canada," a single Canadian nation where people of all ethnic backgrounds could live under a government that would respect their fundamental rights and freedoms.[64] An important part of this was the concept of a national bill of rights. Diefenbaker had been outspoken in the 1940s about the need for a national bill of rights to protect Canadians from what he perceived as civil liberties abuses on the part of the Liberal government. Under pressure from rights activists to follow through on his words, he introduced Bill C-60, *An Act for the Recognition and Preservation of Human Rights and Fundamental Freedoms,* in 1958. The bill included a preamble that recognized the supremacy of God and primacy of the rule of law in promoting freedom, as well as three articles enumerating a set of fundamental rights and freedoms.[65] Bill C-60 recognized the right to life, liberty, personal security, the enjoyment of property, and equal protection under the law; it also recognized freedom of religion, speech, assembly, association, and the press. To the great disappointment of advocates in the bill of rights movement, Diefenbaker introduced his bill of rights as a federal statute rather than an amendment to the Constitution. For this reason, it would apply only to federal matters, but it did prohibit discrimination based on race, national origin, colour, religion, and sex.[66]

For eighteen months, the public debated the merits of Diefenbaker's *Canadian Bill of Rights* before it was adopted in 1960. Critics questioned his commitment to and understanding of human rights, and attacked the decision to introduce a statute.[67] Arthur Roebuck, who had chaired the 1950 Senate committee that recommended an entrenched bill of rights, argued that a statue "did very little for the people of Canada."[68] Bora Laskin, law professor and founding member of the Canadian Civil Liberties Association, condemned Diefenbaker for being too "timid" with the bill.[69] Examining the legislation and Diefenbaker's motivations in retrospect, historians Christopher MacLennan and Ross Lambertson explain Diefenbaker's choice of a statute over a constitutional amendment by arguing that his support for a bill of rights had never been grounded in a liberal concern for the rights of individuals, but rather in a fear of executive despotism and a desire to reaffirm British tradition and the role of Parliament in upholding individual liberty.[70] Diefenbaker himself was a strong defender of the British parliamentary tradition, and his bill of rights focused on civil and political rights such as speech, religion, peaceable assembly, and legal rights, rather than economic and social rights. For these reasons, it did not reflect the more expansive concept of universal human rights coming out of the United Nations by the 1960s.[71]

Regardless of the effectiveness of the *Canadian Bill of Rights* in promoting equality in the country, it had a tremendous impact on public awareness of both rights issues and Canada's foreign policy towards human rights initiatives at the UN. The bill was heavily influenced by the *Universal Declaration of Human Rights,* to the extent that some of the articles in the Canadian law used phrasing found in the declaration.[72] Section 1(a) of the

Canadian Bill of Rights protects "life, liberty and security of person," which is identical to the phrasing found in Article 3 of the UDHR. The original wording of Section 2(b), prohibiting "cruel, inhuman or degrading treatment or punishment," is identical to Article 5 of the declaration. In August 1960, as MPs debated Bill C-60 in the House of Commons, there was a long discussion comparing its substance with that of the UDHR.[73] Both Diefenbaker and Pearson, who was then leader of the opposition, discussed the history of the UDHR, their experiences with its adoption, and its relationship to the bill being debated. The two laws had a somewhat circular relationship in that the UN's discourse of rights and the UDHR influenced the development of Canada's own bill of rights, and the codification of a set of rights and freedoms in Canadian law made the UDHR a more familiar instrument to Canadians.

The process of enacting Bill C-60 brought the question of how to codify rights and freedoms into public discussion. Popular journals such as *Saturday Night, Canadian Forum, Maclean's,* and *Relations* printed articles on the topic, and daily news sources regularly reported on the proposed legislation.[74] Parliament established a special committee on human rights and fundamental freedoms to discuss the issue, and a coalition of voluntary organizations, including churches, trade unions, women's organizations, and ethnic groups presented briefs, attempting to shapes the bill's form and content.[75] According to Ross Lambertson, what is most important about the people who appeared before this parliamentary committee is that they were not radicals but "moderate" and "respectable" individuals and groups, signalling an acceptance, at least in English Canada, of the need for greater legislative protection for human rights.[76] Few francophones took part in the campaign for a national bill of rights, and the Quebec government under Duplessis remained opposed to the idea.[77]

Diefenbaker's election also heralded a new, more positive approach to the United Nations. A 1957 External Affairs report quoted him as stating that, "so far as Canada is concerned, support of the United Nations is the cornerstone of its foreign policy."[78] External Affairs' tone towards the UN became more optimistic, with historian Adam Chapnick describing the 1960s as the height of the department's confidence in the international body.[79] The Canadian public also held the UN in high esteem. Lester Pearson's 1957 Nobel Peace Prize for his role in resolving the Suez Crisis made Canadians proud of their country's achievements at the UN. By the 1960s, Canadians believed they had a special leadership role to play at the world body, that of promoting peace and security throughout the world.[80] This leadership role carried with it an obligation to act as a model, and rights advocates pushed Ottawa to play a greater role in international human rights initiatives.

In 1956, External Affairs reported that "pressure from women's organizations for a more active participation by Canada in the activities of the United Nations in the field of human rights has been building up steadily at least for the past 9 years."[81] Activists sent letters and briefs to the government, admonishing federal officials for their lack of commitment to the status and situation of women around the world, and for failing to support UN resolutions and instruments.[82] These letters focused on issues such as Canada's lack of representation on the UN Human Rights Commission or the Commission on the Status of Women, and called on the federal government to ratify the *Convention on the Political Rights of Women,* which was adopted by the General Assembly in 1953.[83] External Affairs noted that the most vocal organizations, including the Federated Women's Institutes of Canada, the Canadian Federation of Business and Professional Women, the National Council of Women of Canada, the National Board of the YWCA, and the Canadian Federation of University Women, had branches throughout Canada, including French-speaking branches in Quebec. Their pressure on the federal government represented early attempts to hold the Canadian government accountable to international human rights law.

The UDHR also continued to garner attention. Private member's resolutions throughout the 1950s called on the federal government to officially affirm Canada's support of the declaration.[84] This was in part an attempt to pressure the government to introduce a national bill of rights, but it also demonstrated an interest in Canada's approach to international human rights instruments. Prime Minister St. Laurent had previously informed Parliament that, since the declaration was not a legal instrument, the government was not required to endorse its approval.[85] Upon request, the permanent delegation to the UN reported to members of the House of Commons that the UDHR had not been endorsed in the legislature of any other member state.[86] Nonetheless, pressure continued from voluntary organizations and individuals who wanted the government to make a formal statement of commitment to the principles embodied in the UDHR. One example is a 1957 brief from the Canadian Jewish Congress, which called on the government to either create a national bill of rights or write the declaration into Canadian domestic law.[87] After the adoption of the *Canadian Bill of Rights,* this pressure faded.

Rights activism did not fade, however. Most of the literature on Canadian human rights history has focused on important moments: the development of civil liberties groups in the 1930s, the growth of rights activism around the Second World War, campaigns for fair practices laws in the 1950s, the adoption of a national bill of rights in 1960, and the resurgence of social movement activity in the late 1960s and early 1970s. Little attention had been paid to the continued growth of activism, with periods such as the early 1960s often skipped over in accounts of Canada's "rights revolution." In the existing scholarship, more attention has been given to formal campaigns and the most active rights organizations than to the subtler ways in which human rights principles began to seep into Canadian society. Although there was no central or nationally organized movement, and many of the rights associations from the 1930s had become dormant, there were significant developments in the field of human rights in the early 1960s, and an explosion of human rights–related activity across the country. External Affairs was well aware of this. In 1961, it asked Citizenship and Immigration to conduct a study on the nature of human rights advocacy in Canada. The author of the subsequent report, George Davidson, noted the lack of national rights-based organizations.[88] He also stated that while there were some national outlets for public opinion and information relating to human rights, such as the National Council of Women or communications organizations such as the National Film Board and the CBC, "the geographic pattern of voluntary involvement in human rights is by no means clear-cut."[89] Davidson argued, however, that to properly understand rights activism in Canada, one had to look beyond self-described civil liberties or human rights organizations. He explained that groups that might not, by name alone, be identified as "human rights" organizations, including labour, citizenship, or community groups, were nonetheless responsible for channelling a great deal of literature to local communities to increase public awareness of rights, prejudice, and discrimination.[90] There was tremendous activism on the ground in the early 1960s, a period that witnessed the diffusion of human rights ideas and principles from elite intellectuals, human rights organizations, and minority groups activists to Canadian society more broadly, primarily through public education and the growth of human rights–related committees in other voluntary organizations. It was a patchwork of grassroots organizations across the country that brought these issues to public attention in the 1950s and early 1960s, helping to initiate what Ruth Frager and Carmela Patrias have characterized as "a fundamental reconsideration of the concepts of democracy and equality that guided postwar reconstruction."[91]

Celebrations of the tenth anniversary of the adoption of the UDHR provided an opportunity for rights activists in Canada to take stock of domestic developments in the field of human rights and generate momentum for further activism. The impetus for the celebration came from the United Nations, with a Commission on Human Rights resolution in 1956 calling on member states to facilitate "the widest possible celebration" of the anniversary and recommending that governments encourage "leading civil or social organizations" to arrange for national conferences and meetings on human rights in 1958.[92] This focus on non-governmental organizations suited External Affairs officials, who feared that government participation would either lead to questions about Canada's position towards the covenants or signal too great a commitment to international human rights.[93] The Canadian government turned down the opportunity to sit as a member of the UN's organizing committee for the celebrations, stating that "unless we are firmly convinced that a refusal would be badly regarded and considered as an open manifestation of disinterest we would prefer that Canada should not repeat not [sic] be nominated."[94]

Federal officials were nervous about the impact of wide-scale celebrations in Canada. Aware of the growing interest in human rights issues, they worried that the event could be a catalyst for criticism of government policy. Laval Fortier of the Citizenship and Immigration wrote:

> I must confess that I do not view the 1958 celebrations without some apprehension. It is doubtful that in a country like Canada, the proposed seminar will be used to "celebrate" any advance in the field of human rights; it will more likely turn into a critical analysis of certain situations

> where these rights are not yet fully enjoyed. Furthermore, it is the experience of this Department that whenever such study is undertaken by community leaders, governments are likely to be apportioned more than their fair share of the blame. It is therefore my view that the whole project should not be given too much encouragement.[95]

A.H. Brown of the Department of Labour also opposed the organization of a national conference on human rights, arguing that government coverage and observance would be enough.[96] Gordon Robertson, deputy minister of northern affairs and national resources, formerly of External Affairs, cautioned the other ministers that "while it is true, as you mention, that Canada voted in favour of the Declaration in 1948, my impression is that we did so without any real enthusiasm and generally because of a feeling that it would be extremely hard to do otherwise."[97] Robertson was critical of the effect of the UN's human rights instruments: "I think a good many Canadians would feel that the first problem was to demonstrate that the adoption of the resolution [the UDHR] has signified anything whatsoever."[98] Despite this negative feedback from other departments, and under pressure from the UN, N. Currie of External Affairs sent a letter to NGOs interested in a national conference, stating that it would be inappropriate for the government to be too involved and asking for their help in organization.[99]

Despite government's lack of enthusiasm, voluntary organizations were eager to move forward, illustrating the willingness of civil society to take the lead in the push for greater awareness of human rights. John P. Kidd of the Canadian Citizenship Council and Max Swerdlow of the Canadian Labour Congress established the Human Rights Anniversary Committee for Canada, announcing that the committee would organize a national conference to be held in Ottawa on 10 December 1958.[100] By the end of 1957, more than forty organizations had volunteered to help plan the celebrations, including many national organizations such as the Canadian Welfare Council, the Canadian Jewish Congress, the National Council of Women in Canada, the Canadian Association for Adult Education, the Canadian Citizenship Council, the UN Association of Canada, and the Canadian Institute of Public Affairs. In outlining proposed themes, the planning committee focused on domestic rights issues, such as the need for enhanced legislative protections in the form of a national bill of rights, and the possibility of writing the UDHR into domestic law.[101] Gordon Hockin of the Canadian Labour Congress stated the purpose of the conference should be to help make the Canadian public more aware of the real human rights problems many Canadians faced on a daily basis, and to provide reports and a source of information to be used by the federal government in instructing its representatives at international conferences regarding Canadian attitudes towards human rights.[102]

The connection between domestic and international rights, and more specifically the idea that human rights in Canada ought to be shaped by the principles of the UDHR, was explicit in the organization of the celebrations. In September 1958, a press release announced that nineteen Canadian organizations, representing national groups in the areas of "church, education, welfare, labour and women's groups," were holding a national conference to explore "Canadian life in relation to the principles set forth in the three main areas of the Universal Declaration – civil liberties, social rights and economic rights."[103] The national conference was held in Ottawa from 8 to 10 December. The organizing committee also encouraged community organizations to devote time to discussing human rights at five regional conferences, in Vancouver, Winnipeg, Ottawa, Montreal, and Halifax.[104] The national conference included a keynote address on "The Universal Declaration of Human Rights – Its Influence in Canadian and International Scenes," as well as panels on the nature of civil liberties and economic and social rights within Canada.[105] The regional conferences included similar panels, as well as more specific workshops on a variety of topics, including "Human Rights and Racial Problems," "Canadian Immigration Laws," "Legal Rights," "Labour Relations," "The Indian," "The Eskimo," and "Threats to Human Rights."[106] All of the conferences were well attended, and they were significant because, although participants continued to focus on the issues of discrimination and prejudice particular to Canada, they framed their discussions through the lens of international human rights, considering how the principles of the UDHR might influence Canadian law and society.

The activities of the tenth-anniversary celebration extended far beyond the national and regional conferences, reflecting a growing interest in human rights on the part of a diverse group of voluntary organizations.

There were public education campaigns similar to those for previous Human Rights Day celebrations: distribution of resources examining national and international developments, a focus in primary and secondary schools on the UDHR and human rights laws in Canada, and a variety of local activities promoting human rights. While these campaigns reached a broader range of Canadians, the celebrations also reveal the groups and issues that remained outside of the mainstream human rights movement in Canada. Whereas discrimination on the basis of race, religion, colour, and nationality had become central to discussions of human rights, and therefore an important part of the activities for the tenth anniversary, discrimination on other grounds, such as sex, physical and mental disability, and sexual orientation were missing from the conversation. Despite decades of activism, women's rights continued to be considered separate from human rights. Other groups had yet to formally mobilize. In the late 1950s, disability activists were still working towards deinstitutionalization, and it was not until the 1970s that people with disabilities began forming their own groups to advocate for greater rights.[107] Homosexual acts were a criminal offence in Canada until 1967, with prevailing societal attitudes towards homosexuality overwhelmingly negative, and it was not until the late 1960s that gays and lesbians began organizing.[108] With the exception of women, international human rights law had almost nothing to say about these vulnerable groups either.

Although the UDHR was widely discussed during the tenth-anniversary celebrations, the international covenants and Canada's policy towards them were not. Yet again, the exception was John Humphrey, who continued working for the UN while spending time in Canada promoting the world body's work in the field of human rights. During the preparations for the national conference, Humphrey spoke very negatively about the drawn-out process of the article-by-article debates, complaining that the text of the covenants had become "progressively worse."[109] Government observers reported that other than Humphrey, none of the other representatives at the meetings showed any interest in the possible ratification of the covenants or seemed unduly perturbed by Ottawa's use of constitutional issues to justify a lack of support for the instruments.

At the conclusion of the year, some members of the planning committee questioned the true impact of the celebrations. Muriel Jacobson of the

Canadian Association for Adult Education wrote that, while "almost everyone is for human rights," feelings ranged from "skepticism about the existence of sufficient public interest" to an "opaquely complacent view that human rights in Canada were not burning issues" except to those most directly affected.[110] Close examination of the internal communications in External Affairs reveal, however, that government officials did note the growing support for human rights not only among activists and those directly affected by discrimination but also in the Canadian public more broadly. This perception of public opinion weighed heavily on the federal departments responsible for setting Canada's policies towards human rights initiatives at the UN; policy makers were aware that the rights culture in Canada was changing, and this made them sensitive to how their decisions could be interpreted at home.

Ottawa's Changing Approach to Human Rights at the UN

Policy makers were also sensitive to the increasingly vocal criticism of Canada's policy towards the covenants by other UN member states. These criticisms focused on two aspects of Canada's early participation in the article-by-article debates: the inconsistent and overly negative contributions of Canadian delegates to the process, and Canada's insistence on a federal state clause. As early as 1956, Canadian delegates were reporting to External Affairs that Canada's position was under attack.[111] The few articles in either covenant that Canada did support were "of such a weak and declamatory nature" that most member states were disinclined to pay much attention or to see such support as constructive participation.[112] In addition, the department's instructions were often inconsistent or contradictory. In early versions of the draft covenants, delegates had been instructed to work to replace technical terms and detailed provisions with general terms in order to find common ground between the legal systems of member states. Three years later, the government was arguing that responsibilities and obligations must be closely defined and that the excessive generality of the draft covenants was a problem.[113] These inconsistencies eroded the delegation's credibility with the Third Committee, and delegates expressed their frustration, insisting that, while they understood that the provinces might misinterpret a vote in favour of articles that could fall within provincial legislative jurisdiction, they needed some flexibility. Unless they were free to participate in the debates, working under the assumption that a federal clause would be included, "our approach to the majority, if not all, of the articles of substance will necessarily be so negative that the value of our participation in the discussion should be questioned."[114] They worried that the government's instructions would force them to put forward extremely unpopular proposals to "water down" each article, and that when Canada inevitably abstained, it would have "incurred the displeasure of the other members of the Committee for taking up its time unnecessarily and to no avail."[115]

Canada's insistence on a federal state clause was intensely scrutinized by other states, who understood that such a clause would enable Canada to become a party to a covenant while only committing itself to those articles that fell under federal jurisdiction. The question of how a binding human rights instrument would impact federal-provincial jurisdiction had persisted since the International Bill of Rights was first introduced in 1947. Canada had informed other states that, without provincial agreement, the Government of Canada could not ensure the enforcement of articles relating to areas under provincial jurisdiction, and that by agreeing to the covenants, it would therefore be signing on in bad faith. Nonetheless, by the 1950s there was some question, even within the federal government, as to how serious the jurisdictional arguments really were. Legal scholars such as Frank Scott and George Szablowski claimed that the federal government *did* have the authority to enforce international treaties and agreements.[116] Szablowski argued that, unless a treaty dealt with matters expressly assigned to the provinces, if it was deemed of national importance, Parliament had the power to implement it treaty through the "Peace, Order and good Government" clause of the *British North America Act*.[117] To test this, the Ministry of Justice conducted a thorough study of the articles of the draft covenants on human rights. Deputy Attorney General F.P. Varcoe reported to External Affairs that, although some articles dealt with matters that were primarily under provincial jurisdiction, all articles involved some form of federal jurisdiction and none dealt with issues wholly under the authority of the provinces.[118] Having never consulted the provincial governments, federal officials had no specific information on how they would respond to the instruments. If, as Varcoe suggested, it was within the power of the federal government to enforce the covenants, federal officials worried that Canada could be criticized for misrepresentation by focusing too closely on the question of jurisdiction.

At the same time, External Affairs officials recognized the opportunity that Canada's federal system offered, enabling them to abdicate responsibility in an area where they were not strongly favourable to UN action. They suggested to Stuart Garson that it was time to consider whether or not the government truly wanted to support the covenants, and if not, whether it should instruct its delegates to simply cease to work for the inclusion of a satisfactory federal state clause so that Canada could use the lack of the clause as justification for abstaining altogether.[119] Garson was reluctant to take such action. At the United Nations, advocates for a federal state clause were already being openly accused of using their constitutional systems as an excuse to avoid committing to international human rights. Even Canada's allies questioned the government's intentions. At a meeting of Commonwealth states in 1956, the British delegation noted that Canadian officials seemed pleased to be able to use the lack of a federal state clause to absolve themselves of responsibility over the covenants.[120] Rather than providing a reasonable justification for Canada's resistance to the drafts, the federal state clause was causing other states to question Canada's sincerity. This did not sit well with officials such as Secretary of State for External Affairs Lester Pearson, who was unhappy to have his department "hiding behind its federal constitution in treaty matters."[121] Policy makers also worried about what would happen if a suitable federal state clause *did* make its way into the covenants. By repeatedly tying its inability to support the drafts to issues of jurisdiction, Canada might be placing itself in a position where, if a federal state clause was inserted, it could hardly refrain from supporting the covenants without coming off badly.[122]

By the end of 1956, then, External Affairs officials were sensitive to two competing pressures: continued indecision over whether to support the development of binding international covenants on human rights, and unease over how Canada's participation in UN debates, or lack thereof, was being perceived both internationally and domestically. According to Marcel Cadieux, Canada had been "dithering" for several years between "hope that the covenants would emerge in such a form that we wouldn't be able to sign them and a fear that, if we did in the end feel obliged to sign them, they might contain articles which would be embarrassing to us."[123] Cadieux went on to say that policy makers had been "reluctant to take an active part in framing the covenants for fear we would give the impression that we were interested," and argued that it was time for Canada to "get off this particular fence."[124] Even Garson encouraged Ottawa to give UN delegates more latitude.[125] Nevertheless, throughout the late 1950s, Ottawa was in no hurry to change its approach. Policy makers in both Justice and External Affairs were content with the slow progress. When Greece, Morocco, and Tunisia presented a resolution in 1958 calling on the General Assembly to expedite the drafting of the covenants, External Affairs advised its delegates that, while Canada would not want to appear to wish to put off the covenants forever, it had no desire to accelerate their consideration. The delegates duly informed other states that "another ten or fifteen years in their drafting would not unduly delay the advent of the era of Human Rights when viewed in the long prospect of world history."[126]

The first real step External Affairs took to change its policy was to collect feedback from other branches of the federal government.[127] External Affairs sent each department a copy of the draft covenants in late 1956, along with a summary of the progress of the debates in the Third Committee, asking for comments on specific articles. Responses were prompt, in most cases mirroring External Affairs' own views: a general support for the principles of the instruments but concern over the way in which specific articles conflicted with existing policy and could therefore embarrass Canada. Deputy Minister of Citizenship and Immigration Laval Fortier pointed to articles in the *Covenant on Civil and Political Rights* that he felt would affect Canada's practice of deportation, restrictions on issuing passports and visas, and the political and electoral organization of Canada's "Indian Bands."[128] He also indicated that his department was not prepared to enter into an international debate over the detailed provisions of Canada's immigration laws and regulations.[129] The Department of Labour worried about the impact of the *Covenant on Economic, Social and Cultural Rights*, particularly the article on the right to work, arguing that the instrument dealt with matters that were more appropriately handled by the International Labor Organization.[130] Gordon Robertson of the Department of Northern Affairs and Natural Resources worried that the instruments would cause Canada's policies towards "Eskimos" to be the subject of criticism,[131] arguing: "While we are in agreement with the broad principles covered by the draft Covenants, I feel there is a great amount of detail in the Articles which could be made embarrassing to Canada, or any other country, if referred to out of context and without relation to the special circumstances that may exist."[132] These comments expose how protective federal bureaucrats were of Canada's existing laws, their acceptance that some circumstances warranted discrimination, and their anxiety that an international covenant on human rights might infringe on Canada's ability to do what it considered necessary to best serve Canadians. In response, External Affairs instructed its delegates at the UN to continue opposing or abstaining in votes relating to the issues mentioned by other departments. In other areas, they were given more flexibility and were encouraged to work with other states to bring the texts more in line with the Canadian position.

Based on this subtle change in policy, it is easy to assume that the election of John Diefenbaker and his Progressive Conservative Party in 1957 heralded a new era in Canada's approach to human rights at the UN. As previously discussed, Diefenbaker had openly criticized the Liberal government's policy towards the UDHR in 1948, and then introduced a national bill of rights as prime minister in 1960. Diefenbaker's record with international human rights is mixed, however. On one hand, as a result of a greater enthusiasm for the UN by the late 1950s, Ottawa did take positive action on several other UN declarations and conventions relating to human rights. In 1959, Canada ratified both the *Convention on the Political Rights of Women* and the *Convention on the Nationality of Married Women*, and supported the adoption of the *Declaration of the Rights of the Child*. In the early 1960s, Canadian delegates also helped develop the *International Convention on the Elimination of All Forms of Racial Discrimination*.[133] It was easier for Canada to support the instruments relating to women's rights that came out of the Commission on the Status of Women because they dealt entirely with civil and political rights. In addition, women's organizations in Canada had specifically lobbied the federal government to increase its involvement with these instruments. Canada's support for children's rights can be traced back to the League of Nations. In her work on the topic, historian Dominique Marshall argues that children held a pre-eminent place in early efforts to protect a set of universal human rights, largely because the protection of children was widely popular, both in Canada and around the world.[134] The conventions and declarations on women's and children's rights of the 1950s avoided the most contentious aspects of the covenants on human rights, such as self-determination, broad economic and social rights, and the concept of universalism. However, they all dealt with topics at least partially under provincial authority, providing examples of UN treaties that Ottawa was willing to support, sign, and in some cases ratify, jurisdictional issues aside.

Despite these examples of support for other UN documents, Diefenbaker's election did little to change Ottawa's policy approach to the draft covenants. The Progressive Conservatives shared many of the Liberals' concerns over a binding covenant on human rights, and the internal reports and summaries produced while Diefenbaker was in office often simply recycled the points, and in some cases entire paragraphs, found in older reports.[135] External Affairs' internal communications contained the same views on the vagueness of the instruments' language, the need for a federal state clause, and the persistence of articles that should not be included in a covenant. The Diefenbaker government did continue the softer approach that the Liberals had begun to take, but their specific policies did not differ significantly.[136] This can be explained in part by the fact that Diefenbaker himself did not take a personal interest in the adoption of the International Covenants on Human Rights. His advocacy of a Canadian role in the adoption of the UDHR in 1948 had been more closely linked to his desire to pressure government for a national bill of rights than to genuine interest in the development of international human standards, and so the covenants were not a priority. Even the adoption of the *Canadian Bill of Rights* did not have an immediate impact on the instructions from the federal government to its UN delegates. A second factor was the influence of career civil servants in External Affairs. One of Diefenbaker's most trusted foreign policy advisors was Basil Robinson, who had worked in foreign affairs under the Liberals for twelve years. Several senior civil servants in the department also kept their positions under the new government, providing much consistency in policy. For example, Norman Robertson joined the foreign service under Mackenzie King and served a second term as under-secretary of state from 1958 to 1964. John Holmes joined External Affairs in 1943 and became Permanent Delegate to the United Nations from 1950 to 1953 and then assistant under-secretary of state from 1953 until his retirement in 1960. Allan Gotlieb worked in the External Affairs Legal Division in the 1950s and was assistant under-secretary of state until the end of the 1960s. All played a significant role in helping to set, articulate, or implement the Liberal Party's policies towards the UN's human rights activities, and continued in the same vein under Diefenbaker, making the transition between parties more seamless in this area than might be expected. The fact that neither party was enthusiastic about international human rights meant that Ottawa was unlikely to significantly change its approach without external pressure.

An Environment for Policy Change

The real impetus for policy change on the part of the Canadian government was the realization that the instruments *would* eventually be adopted in some form by the General Assembly. After more than a decade of hoping that the covenants would prove too divisive to be adopted, Canadian delegates recognized that a strong enough majority in the General Assembly supported the idea of binding human rights instruments and were determined to see covenants on human rights adopted, even if reaching agreement on the details was extremely time-consuming. The delegation warned External Affairs that Canada needed to decide whether or not to vote in support of the draft covenants.[137] There were several options: (1) continue with the current policy and use the lack of a federal clause to justify Canada's hesitation; (2) actively oppose the covenants on the basis of their content; (3) follow the lead of the United States in supporting the principles of the covenants but announce that Canada would not be ratifying the documents; or (4) play a more active role in shaping the covenants with the intention of voting for their adoption. Ultimately, the government decided to play a more positive role, not only in the debates but also in human rights programs at the UN more generally. It did so for three reasons.

The first was pressure from new UN members who were critical of states that did not support the covenants. Canadian officials continued to worry about Canada's image among these newly established, often non-aligned states. UN membership grew from 51 countries in 1945 to 133 by 1966.[138] Sixty-three joined in the period of the article-by-article debates alone.[139] This new membership included a wider representation from Asia and Africa, causing the proportion of European and American nations to drop.[140] Many new states had only recently gained independence. They denounced the slow pace of decolonization and saw the covenants as tools to further their goals of self-determination and development. Following the 1955 Bandung Conference, 29 new member states formed an Afro-Asian bloc in the General Assembly that grew yearly in size and power. Asa McKercher's work on Canada's relations with this bloc reveals the federal government's competing interests at the UN. Ottawa wanted to gain influence with the newly formed states, both for economic benefit and to limit Soviet control in Africa and Asia. One way to do this was to support initiatives or resolutions put forward by the Afro-Asian bloc. However, Canada remained closely connected to Britain and supported British interests at the United Nations. As former colonies, newly independent states were often in conflict with British interests, which created tensions for Canadian policy makers.[141] Robert Bothwell argues that Canada's growing sensitivity to the non-aligned states was a matter of self-interest; in order for Ottawa to exert any influence in the postwar, postcolonial world, it had to maintain the image of an "honest broker," and this required the support and respect of those states.[142]

In the debates over the human rights instruments, the most outspoken former colonies were Lebanon, Afghanistan, and Saudi Arabia, who condemned member states they believed were opposing or attempting to weaken the draft covenants, arguing that they were supporting colonial rule.[143] For various reasons, these arguments found support from Latin American and Soviet bloc nations,[144] and a large majority of the Third Committee was prepared to vote for adoption of the covenants. Canadian delegates often referred to this group collectively as the "anti-colonial majority."[145] This was an oversimplification, of course, as regional and national differences and Cold War ideology continued to permeate the debates over individual articles. Even as this greatly slowed the process, Canada and other Western states became convinced that the covenants would inevitably be adopted, and that any states that opposed or even abstained from voting for their adoption would be portrayed as opposing the fundamental principles of human rights.

Second, the realization that the covenants would be adopted caused many of Canada's allies to modify their approach to the debates over the instruments. Canadian delegates reported these changes to External

Affairs,[146] writing that "during the past few sessions certain countries have tended to consider these covenants not as legal documents but as ideals and principles to serve as a guide for national legislation."[147] Countries became less anxious about the legal implications of a covenant on human rights, which enabled them to support its principles, as in the case of the UDHR. External Affairs suggested two explanations. First, after fifteen years of experience with the UN system and ten years of debating how to articulate human rights principles in international instruments, member states recognized that consensus was impossible and that there would be some flexibility in the implementation process. Since the covenants would eventually be adopted, some member states were working to improve the text of articles to make the instruments acceptable enough for adoption. Second, countries such as the United States no longer intended to ratify the covenants and so ceased to argue legal points.[148] Canadian representatives routinely met with officials from friendly states such as Australia and New Zealand to discuss the progress of the covenants and to exchange reports to help inform policy decisions. These communications confirmed for Canadian officials that, despite widespread disillusionment with how the debates had unfolded, by the 1960s the "main Western countries" were prepared to see the covenants project to its completion.[149]

Finally, and most significantly, Canadian legislative and cultural developments in the early to mid-1960s created an environment in which federal policy makers felt increasingly uncomfortable in not actively supporting the covenants. A new wave of human rights developments at home, marked by the transition from fair practices laws to the enactment of human rights codes and the development of human rights commissions, represented another shift in understandings of rights in Canada. Ontario led the way. By the 1960s, it was becoming clear that the province needed a more comprehensive and focused approach to human rights; in many ways, the fair practices acts were declarations of principle and were difficult to enforce.[150] In 1962, the *Ontario Human Rights Code* came into effect, consolidating all existing rights policies. The government established the Human Rights Commission and gave it the sole function of administering and enforcing the new code. Thus, one agency became responsible for education, administration, promotion, and enforcement of human rights, which raised the importance of protecting rights within the province. By the end of the decade, seven Canadian provinces had enacted similar acts.[151] This was a significant difference from the environment in which the draft First Covenant had been introduced in 1949, when there had been virtually no domestic legislative protections for rights and freedoms. Between the introduction of the UN's International Bill of Rights in 1947 and the final votes on the ICCPR and the ICESCR in 1966, the legislative foundation for Canada's human rights state was established.

The infrastructure for the human rights state extended beyond legislative developments. By the 1960s, rights and freedoms had become the subject of a growing number of formal and informal educational programs, and all regions saw the development of workshops and seminars for employees in specialized fields such as teaching, health care, police, and government work.[152] Human rights became a field of study for credit in Canadian universities, and an area of wider academic research and publishing. Legal and constitutional scholars such as F.R. Scott, Douglas Schmeiser, Bora Laskin, S.J. Godfrey, and Andrew Brewin wrote extensively on civil liberties and Canadian federalism, civil liberties and the Supreme Court of Canada, the legal impact of federal and provincial rights legislation, race relations, and discrimination in Canadian society.[153] Moreover, the rights literature was not limited to legal experts. There was an increase in reporting on rights in English- and French-language newspaper articles, editorials, trade journals, and popular magazines. Publications such as *Saturday Night, Relations, Maclean's,* and *Canadian Forum* all produced articles on the meaning of human rights, campaigns for further human rights laws, the work of the UN, and the significance of international human rights instruments.[154]

In June 1963, with information provided by provincial education ministries, the Canadian Education Association (CEA) produced a report outlining the extent to which teaching about human rights and the United Nations had made its way into public school curricula.[155] In many provinces, rights-related topics were covered in elementary and secondary school, in social studies, history, civics, or citizenship classes. This included Quebec, where both Protestant and Catholic schools taught about the UN and human rights.[156] The report also noted that resources such as the United Nations Association of Canada's *World Review* publication and UNESCO and CBC publications were well used by provincial school systems.

School-wide activities such as celebrations of UN Day in October and Human Rights Day in December, model UN clubs, annual UNICEF collections, and a number of other activities supported the official curricula. The UN Association of Canada played a key role in promoting public awareness of the world body and its human rights instruments, and provided services for educators and educational institutions. The association published its monthly *World Review* and an annual catalogue of materials on the United Nations, including pamphlets encouraging schools to form UN clubs. It reported that by 1963 there were more than 2,000 students in junior UN clubs in Saskatchewan, Manitoba, and British Columbia alone, and over 350 UN clubs across the country.[157] Most universities in Canada hosted branches of the Student UN Association, and more than twenty model General Assemblies were held nationwide, drawing from high schools. A week-long leadership education seminar on the UN and world affairs was hosted in twelve centres across the country, and the first interprovincial seminar was held in April 1963, involving 32 senior secondary school students who were addressed by UN Secretary-General U Thant himself.

On 10 December 1963, Canadians commemorated the fifteenth anniversary of the adoption of the UDHR. Of the celebrations five years earlier, Norman Robertson wrote that "it must be admitted that on the occasion of the celebration of the tenth anniversary of the Universal Declaration the Canadian government took little initiative other than to have several departments issue special publications or press releases to mark the anniversary."[158] In 1963, however, the government assumed a larger role, both at the United Nations and at home. Canada co-sponsored a UN resolution to plan for the fifteenth anniversary and volunteered to sit on a special organizing committee.[159] External Affairs encouraged other federal departments to take a lead in domestic preparations; in response, Citizenship and Immigration chaired a meeting with representatives from voluntary organizations to establish the Canadian Anniversary Conference of Canada Committee. Those attending the committee's first meeting in August 1963 debated the purpose of a nationwide celebration, deciding that it would both recognize the gains made in the field of human rights and assess what remained to be done to fulfill Canada's international and domestic obligations.[160] Rather than focusing on a handful of regional conferences and a single national conference, as had been the case for the tenth anniversary, the committee concerned itself with stimulating public and community participation at a grassroots level by facilitating the development of materials to be used, working with local organizations and communities to plan events, and providing information about Canadian human rights achievements since 1958.[161]

While voluntary organizations once again took the lead in planning these initiatives, the government helped produce and distribute materials, and representatives from several federal agencies acted as consultants to the anniversary committee, including the English and French networks of the CBC, the Department of Citizenship and Immigration, the Canadian National Commission for UNESCO, the Department of External Affairs, the Department of Labour, and the National Film Board.[162] NGOs that had been heavily involved five years earlier continued to play a role in 1963, but were joined by a broader variety of organizations across the country, such as the Association canadienne des éducateurs de langue française, the Canadian Bar Association, the Canadian Daily Newspapers Association, the Canadian Federation of Mayors and Municipalities, the Canadian Home and School and Parent-Teacher Federation, the Canadian Teachers' Federation, the Confédération de syndicats nationaux, the Institut canadien d'éducation des adultes, and the National Federation of Canadian University Students.[163] Some provincial governments were also more actively involved than they had been five years earlier. The Ontario government was particularly enthusiastic, with Premier John Robarts proclaiming a province-wide celebration culminating with a special ceremony at the Ontario legislature.[164] The Nova Scotia government established an interdepartmental committee on human rights, established a Human Rights Day committee, wrote to service clubs in the province suggesting steps they could take to celebrate the anniversary, and facilitated the distribution of UNESCO resources.[165] When External Affairs asked provincial governments about their level of participation in the anniversary, both New Brunswick and Alberta responded that they had no plans to hold special ceremonies beyond the customary educational programs run through their schools. New Brunswick went so far as to argue that UDHR commemorative programs were "of a federal nature" and therefore would be most appropriately organized from a federal rather than a provincial point of view.[166] Other provinces, including Quebec, British Columbia, and Saskatchewan, did not reply. The observance of the fifteenth anniversary was diverse and widespread, however, involving the media, schools, churches, ethnic groups, and governmental and non-governmental organizations at local, provincial, and national levels. The federal government's interest and involvement in this programming, particularly in light of its lack of participation only five years earlier, reflects the view of policy makers that Canada needed to take action to satisfy interested groups and individuals at home, as well as demonstrate to other UN member states that Canadians did support the principles of human rights.

These human rights developments took place in the context of other developments in early 1960s Canada. In 1963, the "Diefenbaker Interlude" ended with the Liberals' return to power, now under the leadership of Lester Pearson.[167] In attempting to draft their own vision of an independent Canada as a force within the international system, they encountered many of the same challenges that had faced Diefenbaker. Within Canada, the most significant was the rise of nationalist sentiment in Quebec. The death of Premier Maurice Duplessis in 1959 altered the political, economic, and cultural landscape of the province. The election of Liberal Jean Lesage the following year heralded a new era in Quebec politics, and the Quiet Revolution was the culmination of intellectual and cultural change that had begun even before Duplessis' death.[168] This period was characterized by a rejection of traditional French Canadian values, modernization of the state, economic reform, growing secularization, and the development of a welfare state. Campaigns by groups such as the Montreal Jewish Labour Committee and the Quebec Federation of Labour led to the adoption of the province's first anti-discrimination law in 1964, *An Act Respecting Discrimination in Employment in 1964*.[169] The early 1960s also witnessed the establishment of Quebec's first independence groups, including the Action socialiste pour l'indépendence nationale in 1960, and the Comité de libération nationale in 1962. Along with their tremendous impact on the Québécois, these developments also had significant implications for Quebec's relationship with Ottawa. A new generation of politicians challenged earlier notions of the role of francophones in developing Quebec society, and the place of the French language and culture within Canada.[170]

In response, and to promote the image of a government eager to serve both English- and French-speaking citizens, Pearson established a Royal Commission on Bilingualism and Biculturalism shortly after his election. The commission's task was to investigate "the existing state of bilingualism and biculturalism in Canada" and to make recommendations for policies to "develop the Canadian Confederation on the basis of an equal partnership between the two founding races."[171] Its findings, which were released in a preliminary report in 1965 and a final report in 1969, led to changes in French education across the country, the passage of the *Official Languages Act,* and the appointment of a federal Commissioner of Official Languages. In its final report, the Commission on Bilingualism and Biculturalism concluded that, as a result of problems in the relationship between English and French Canadians, Canada was "passing through the greatest crisis in its history."[172] The creation of the Royal Commission, its recommendations, and the debate surrounding the topic of language rights in Canada added a new dimension to discussions of rights in this country, particularly since language rights were understood collectively rather than as individual rights.

Social unrest in this period was not limited to Quebec. The 1960s and early 1970s were a tumultuous time in Canadian history, against the backdrop of a boom economy that generated a sense of optimism about Canada's future. In a recent collection on the "long 1960s," Lara Campbell and Dominique Clément describe this era as "a historical moment that fomented a revolution in education, racial divisions, anxieties about national security, consumerism, Indigenous mobilization, anti-Americanism, the search for national identity, clashes between capital and labour, innovations in public policy, and debates surrounding the family, health and the environment."[173] This extensive activism, which began during the period of the article-by-article debates at the UN, made federal officials wary about how its attitude towards universal human rights might be viewed by Canadians.

Canada's Changing Policy towards the Covenants

External Affairs understood that the legislative and cultural changes taking place in Canada were closely linked to how Canadians understood rights and freedoms, be they language rights, political rights, social rights, or the right to live free from discrimination. In a report to the UN, it identified a number of trends as most relevant to Canada's human rights development: growing attention to bilingualism and biculturalism; a new focus on the "third element" and Canadians of non-French and non-English origin; federal legislative changes, culminating in the *Canadian Bill of Rights;* provincial legislative changes; changes experienced by certain minority groups in the country; and public education and community awareness of human rights.[174] Aware that most UN member states supported the adoption of the covenants, Ottawa worried that if it abstained in a final vote, it would face a backlash from the Canadian public. An internal External Affairs memo from 1962 articulated this concern:

> Given the present inclination of some of the Western countries [to support the covenants], we might find ourselves isolated with a few countries such as South Africa, Portugal and China. Abstention in such circumstances is likely to be misunderstood not only by the non-aligned countries but perhaps even within Canada itself.[175]

The government was loath to appear opposed to universal protection of human rights, and recognized that its objections on constitutional grounds would not be accepted by other UN members or by rights activists at home. Policy makers in External Affairs and the Interdepartmental Committee on Human Rights began discussing whether Canada should continue approaching the covenants from a legal standpoint or give more weight to political considerations, and also considered other steps to increase Canada's engagement with human rights at the UN more generally.[176]

The Interdepartmental Committee suggested that Canada apply for the vacant seat on the Human Rights Commission. It argued that, although Canada had never sat on this committee, growing interest in the field of human rights in Canada had been stimulated by the recent adoption of the *Canadian Bill of Rights,* and that it was therefore time for Canada to play a greater role in developing international human rights.[177] Canada was elected to the commission for a three-year term that officially began on 1 January 1963.[178] This was a significant departure from the government's official position ten years earlier, when it had declined the invitation for Canada to sit on the commission lest it commit Canada to support the human rights instruments.[179]

Canada played an active role during its tenure on the Commission on Human Rights. Representatives were involved with three main tasks: organizing studies of specific rights or groups of rights; collecting triennial reports from member states; and developing advisory services in the field of human rights. These advisory services consisted of a series of international institutes and training courses that would enable member states to exchange views and experiences in human rights matters in the hope of fostering the development of these rights and freedoms in all countries. Canadian officials discussed the possibility of holding a regional seminar in Canada, to be attended by representatives from North and South America and Europe, possibly lasting six to eight weeks.[180] During this period, Canada also sat on the special committee appointed by the Secretary-General to help plan the UDHR fifteenth-anniversary celebration. Canada's greater role in human rights committees at the UN influenced the instructions that federal policy makers sent to delegates, as officials believed that Canada would now be "expected to take a much more active part in the debates on Human Rights in the Third Committee" and "could not afford to abstain as frequently" for fear of sending a mixed message to other members.[181] In 1966, Canada also worked with other countries to submit a draft resolution on the creation of the post of High Commissioner for Human Rights, and in the Preparatory Committee for the International Year for Human Rights (1968), it suggested awarding a prize in the field of human rights during the year.[182]

The Liberals' return to power in 1963 coincided with both the beginning of Canada's term on the Human Rights Commission and the conclusion of the debates on the substantive articles of the draft covenants. At this point, M.H. Wershof, one of the key policy makers in External Affairs, conceded that there was no real prospect of a federal clause being included in the final form of the covenants. He told senior officials within the department that it was time to decide, based on this, whether or not Canada would support adoption of the covenants when they came before the General Assembly in their final form: "Although we know that Canada's record in respecting human rights is very good, it will nevertheless be embarrassing – or worse – for Canada to be unable to accede to the Covenants, and perhaps unable even to vote for their adoption."[183] Wershof suggested assembling a panel of professors and other experts in the field of human rights to "discuss the problem of Canada's constitutional capacity to carry out the Covenants," and possibly even consult the attorney generals of the provinces on this matter.[184]

External Affairs rejected the idea of involving NGOs, and also argued against consulting the provinces lest such consultation be seen as a commitment to obtaining their prior agreement before supporting adoption of the covenants.[185] There was, however, a difference in opinion in the department as to how to proceed. Officials in the Legal Division identified eight articles in the draft *Covenant on Civil and Political Rights,* and four articles in the draft *Covenant on Economic, Social and Cultural Rights* that related to matters falling under provincial jurisdiction and could therefore be problematic for the federal government.[186] Members of the UN Division suggested that, despite the concerns with these articles, Canada vote in favour at the General Assembly, with the understanding that it would not be able to ratify the treaties immediately. The Legal Division of External Affairs and in the Ministry of Justice had previously rejected this course of action on the grounds that supporting adoption would place Canada in a bad position if it was later unable to accede to the covenants, and proponents of provincial power could use this against the government. By 1964, however, analysts in the UN Division felt that it would be more embarrassing for Canada to be one of the only countries not to support adoption of the covenants.[187] They argued that abstention might make the government appear to oppose core values of the international human rights regime: freedom, respect for universal human dignity, equality of peoples, and peace among nations. As an example, officials pointed to a series of restrictive clauses that had recently been added to the draft covenants prohibiting racial discrimination and the spread of war propaganda. They asked how Canada could possibly abstain from supporting these articles when its government had recently taken a stand in a number of international forums against racial and religious discrimination and nuclear testing.[188] In the end, the government decided to consult with its allies and align its policy as closely as possible with Britain, Australia, New Zealand, and the United States, voting with the majority.

The Third Committee did not have an opportunity to consider the final articles of the draft covenants, those on implementation, until its twenty-first session in September 1966. These articles outlined the reporting procedure for both covenants, and the complaints process for the *Covenant on Civil and Political Rights*. Canada had supported these provisions when they were first introduced in 1954. A subcommittee composed of France, the United States, Britain, and India had been largely responsible for drafting the articles of implementation, so these articles enjoyed the support of most Western states. The Canadian delegation reported that some of the newly independent states in Africa and Asia were nervous about the impact the international supervisory system outlined in these articles would have on their national sovereignty. From the beginning, the Soviet Union and its allies had taken the stance that human rights were a matter for national enforcement, and so opposed the articles on implementation. Of greatest consequence to member states were the articles outlining the complaints process for the *Covenant on Civil and Political Rights,* which involved the creation of a new body to be known as the Human Rights Committee. When the UN Commission on Human Rights first decided to include the extra level of supervision for this covenant, there was significant debate over who would have the power to appeal to this committee. When the draft First Covenant was introduced in 1949, the Canadian government argued that the right to petition should be limited initially to signatory states, and not be given to individuals or NGOs.[189] By 1966, however, Canadian officials were discussing the "advantage" of Canada's taking a strong stand for implementation and supporting the right to individual petition. This position gained support for several reasons: other, like-minded Western states supported these measures, strong articles on implementation would place the Soviet Union on the defensive, and such a stand would demonstrate Canada's belief that the covenants should be properly enforced. Canadian officials did have concerns about allowing individuals to petition the Human Rights Committee, but in an internal memo they recognized a growing trend in international law to "recognize the enhanced status of the individual" and believed that before long the individual might be "generally recognized as being a legal unit in international law."[190] For this reason, External Affairs instructed delegates that if most member states supported individual petition, Canada could also support it. In the end, Canada voted in favour of the implementation measures, including the Optional Protocol to the *Covenant on Civil and Political Rights,* which outlined the mechanisms for creating the Human Rights Committee and set the parameters of the complaint process.[191]

The UN held the final vote on the adoption of the *International Covenant on Civil and Political Rights* and the *International Covenant on Economic, Social and Cultural Rights* on 16 December 1966, and Canada voted in support of both instruments.[192] Ottawa's policy had evolved significantly from the time the International Bill of Rights was first introduced in 1947, and it was in Canada's best interest to downplay its earlier resistance to the UDHR and the draft covenants. Instead, politicians and bureaucrats presented an image of Canada as having always supported the principles behind international human rights. A press release to commemorate the fourteenth anniversary of the adoption of the UDHR stated: "In the United Nations, Canada has consistently taken a strong stand in favour of the full application of the principles expressed in the Universal Declaration and has emphasized that the rights and freedoms therein guaranteed are intended to be enjoyed in all corners of the world."[193] Leading up to the adoption of the covenants, politicians often referred publicly to Canada's role on the UN Human Rights Commission and its work to promote the UN's human rights initiatives as proof of their engagement with international human rights. Yet, the Canadian government's decision in favour of these instruments was influenced more by concerns over the political implications of not doing so than by genuine support for the concept of universal human rights or the provisions of the covenants themselves.

In supporting the adoption of international treaties on human rights that did not include any federal state exemptions, the Canadian government decided that the cultivation, at home and abroad, of an image of Canada as an advocate of human rights, fundamental freedoms, and international justice was more important than any potential constitutional conflicts that might arise as a result. Federal officials knew, however, that the covenants would not be binding on Canada unless the government ratified them. Other nations, such as the United States, also supported adoption of the covenants without any intention of ratifying them. This offered Canadian politicians the opportunity to speak publicly throughout the late 1960s and early 1970s about Canada's commitment to the UN's human rights regime and its historical support for both the UDHR and the covenants in the General Assembly, without having to commit Canada to any legislative or policy changes – which suited the federal government.

At the same time, federal officials knew that they could no longer put off a dialogue with provincials governments over Canada's relationship to international human rights law.[194] In September 1966, two months before the covenants were adopted, External Affairs drafted a letter to the deputy attorneys general of each province and to Claude Morin, Quebec's deputy minister of federal-provincial affairs. The letter brought provincial officials up to date on developments relating to the covenants, and indicated that the federal government would be in contact in the near future to discuss the possibility of ratification by Canada.[195] It would take another ten years for the Canadian government to sign and ratify both international covenants, a period witnessed even greater political and cultural change in Canada, at the United Nations, and throughout the world.

4

The Road to Ratification, 1966–76

At the twenty-first session of the United Nations General Assembly in 1966, the Canadian government voted for adoption of the *International Covenant on Economic, Social and Cultural Rights* (ICESCR), the *International Covenant on Civil and Political Rights* (ICCPR), and the Optional Protocol to the ICCPR, lending its support to instruments it had resisted for almost two decades. Such support was made easier by the fact that the vote in the General Assembly did not commit Canada to become a party to the treaties. None of the articles in either covenant would be binding until Canada acceded to the documents. To do so, the government needed approval from Parliament authorizing ratification, which by tradition also required formal agreement from all ten provincial governments that they would adopt any necessary legislation to bring Canada into compliance. Federal officials initiated this process with little sense of urgency.

This chapter considers how Canada's road to ratification of the international covenants was influenced by three competing forces: (1) the continued apathy of the federal government towards international human rights; (2) the social movement activity of the period, which resulted in the first organized campaign to pressure Ottawa to support the UN's human rights instruments; and (3) the power struggle between the federal government and the province of Quebec over who would represent provincial interests at the UN. It suggests that, while federal policy makers were no longer hostile towards international human rights, there was still insufficient support to make them a priority in 1966. This was a period of intense social and political change in Canada and the world, however. The UN proclaimed 1968 as the International Year for Human Rights (IYHR), and the Canadian program to celebrate the IYHR tapped into a resurgence of social movement activity. It stimulated extensive discussion, research, and public education. The celebrations reveal the extent to which cultural attitudes towards rights had changed in Canada and stimulated a closer relationship between domestic and international human rights movements. As different groups in Canadian society called for enhanced rights, using the UN covenants as ammunition, for the first time there was a public campaign demanding that Ottawa take action in the area of international human rights. These developments influenced both Canada's human rights infrastructure and the federal government's mindset with regard to ratifying the covenants on human rights.

The Pearson Government and Ratification

The Liberal government did not immediately initiate the ratification process. A month after the United Nations adopted the covenants, Leader of the Opposition John Diefenbaker stood in the House of Commons and asked Prime Minister Lester Pearson whether the Liberals intended to ask Parliament to ratify the instruments.[1] Pearson admitted that he was "not as familiar as [he] perhaps should be with these particular international covenants," and promised to look into it.[2] Four days later, he gave a short speech to the House in which he reversed his earlier opposition to an international covenant on human rights by describing the instruments as a "significant step forward by the international community," reminding MPs that Canada had voted in support of the covenants at the UN the previous year.[3] Using a rhetoric similar to that of Canadian diplomats at the UN, Pearson applauded Canada's "constructive contributions" to the development of international human rights, downplaying almost two decades of Canadian resistance. He told Diefenbaker that the government would strike an interdepartmental committee to consider the contents of the covenants and, as a number of provisions fell within provincial jurisdiction, consult with the provinces before any steps would be taken towards ratification.

As a matter of law, the federal government had the authority to negotiate and ratify international treaties. Ratification required only that the Governor General exercise Royal Prerogative, which could be obtained through an Order-in-Council from Cabinet. However, the federal government did not have the power to implement by legislation a treaty whose subject matter fell under provincial jurisdiction, or to force provincial governments to execute domestic policies that fell under provincial authority. Since the 1937 *Labour Conventions* case, in which the Supreme Court of Canada declared that only provincial legislatures had the authority to pass labour laws to implement an international convention the federal government had signed, Ottawa had secured formal agreement from all provinces to accept and fulfill any necessary legislative obligations before the federal government acceded to treaties involving matters under provincial authority.[4] With this in mind, in February 1967 the Department of External Affairs forwarded copies of the text of both covenants and the Optional Protocol to the provincial governments. A letter followed from Pearson asking the premiers to study the instruments and indicate their willingness to enact the necessary legislation, and informing the provinces of the government's intention to initiate a federal-provincial dialogue on the covenants in the near future.[5]

External Affairs convened a meeting of the federal Interdepartmental Committee on Human Rights to formulate recommendations for Cabinet concerning the question of ratification. One option was for Canada to begin by signing the instruments, which would be a more formal endorsement of their principles and signal the government's intention to take steps to ratify at a later date. Glen Shortliffe, a career civil servant in the UN Division of External Affairs, suggested that an early signature could be used to counter pressure from non-governmental organizations and opposition politicians such as Diefenbaker. Canada had taken a similar path with the *Convention on the Elimination of All Forms of Racial Discrimination,* which was also adopted by the UN in 1966, signed by Canada the same year, and then ratified in 1970.[6] The Interdepartmental Committee felt that pressure for ratification would grow, citing a brief that Cabinet had received from the Canadian Labour Congress (CLC) barely a month after the adoption of the covenants, calling on the Liberals to ratify them.[7] The committee therefore recommended that Canada sign on to the instruments at the earliest possible date, and that the federal government work quickly to achieve the consensus required for ratification.[8]

This was a major change in approach for civil servants who had, only a decade earlier, worried about the perceived negative impact a covenant on human rights would have on domestic policies. These concerns had diminished by the late 1960s, however, for several key reasons. First, policy makers were no longer worried that the instruments would put Canada in an embarrassing position, as most of the federal and provincial laws that explicitly violated their provisions were no longer in place. The Supreme Court of Canada had declared Quebec's Padlock Law to be unconstitutional in 1957. Legislation in Alberta to prevent the sale of land to "enemy aliens, Hutterites, and Doukhobours" was amended in 1960. The 1960s saw several reforms that virtually eliminated racial discrimination as a major feature of immigration policy; in 1967, the Pearson government established the points system for evaluating prospective immigrants, easing anxiety that Canada's policy would contravene the human rights commitments embodied in the covenants. Federal and provincial voting laws had also changed to allow for universal adult suffrage, as restrictions based on gender, race, ethnicity, and religion were removed.

Second, Canada's domestic rights legislation had developed to the point that the codification of rights in an international bill of rights was no longer considered contrary to Canadian tradition. Most jurisdictions had anti-discrimination laws, and the federal government had enacted the *Canadian Bill of Rights* in 1960. Several provincial governments were expanding their human rights infrastructure. By 1967, Ontario, Nova Scotia, New Brunswick, and Alberta had all adopted human rights acts, with the first three establishing human rights commissions to administer these acts. Alberta and New Brunswick had created the office of "Ombudsman" to help safeguard individuals against discriminatory acts by government. The Diefenbaker and Pearson governments had also expanded the Canadian welfare state. Under the Progressive Conservatives, permanent programs for the funding of hospitalization, higher education, and vocational rehabilitation were introduced or extended. The Liberals built on this, implementing the Canada Pension Plan, the Canada Assistance Plan, and Medicare in 1966. In its annual reports for the UN *Yearbook on Human Rights,* the Canadian government regularly pointed to the extension of the welfare state to demonstrate Canada's progress in the field of rights. For example, the 1967 report highlighted new provincial laws to increase the minimum wage, guarantee equal pay for female employees, provide vacation pay, and extend workers' compensation.[9] These laws made officials in the departments of External Affairs and Justice feel more comfortable that Canada's social and economic policies were in line with the ICESCR. The legislative changes taking place in Canada did not solve the problem of discrimination – several provinces had yet to enact human rights legislation, and even in those that had, many vulnerable groups remained unprotected – but they were sufficient to make the public servants in External Affairs and Justice who were responsible for Canada's UN human rights policy comfortable advising the federal government to proceed with ratification.

Third, policy makers no longer worried about the "binding" nature of the covenants, which eased earlier concerns over sovereignty. After more than two decades of experience at the UN, Canada's diplomats understood its limitations. In the 1950s, the divisions of the Cold War had paralyzed the UN, as had the veto power of the Soviets, the Americans, the British, the French, and the Chinese in the Security Council. Achieving consensus over the content, form, and measures of implementation for a set of binding instruments on human rights had been virtually impossible, yet in 1966 the General Assembly adopted the two covenants unanimously. The Canadian delegation reported that member states were increasingly viewing these instruments as ideals and principles to serve as a guide for legislation, rather than legal documents.[10] The covenant that the Canadian government had opposed most strongly, the *International Covenant on Economic, Social and Cultural Rights,* would be enforced only through annual reporting and moral suasion. Canadian policy makers had a clearer understanding of what a "binding" covenant would mean for Canadian policy, and they were experienced enough to appreciate that Canada would remain in control of its own domestic policies.

Despite the alleviation of these concerns and the Interdepartmental Committee's recommendation of a quick ratification, the process took almost another decade. This was due in part to the fact that the provinces were slow to reply to Pearson's letter. International covenants on human rights were not a priority for these governments either. By the end of 1967, only Alberta's Social Credit government had given formal support to ratification.[11] British Columbia, Nova Scotia, Ontario, and New Brunswick had provided an interim reply, tentatively supporting ratification. External

Affairs had received no reply from the other provinces, but officials were unconcerned. Under Pearson's leadership, the federal Liberal Party's foreign policy was more focused on arms control and peacekeeping initiatives at the United Nations, Canada's role within the North Atlantic Treaty Organization (NATO) and the North American Air Defence (NORAD) system, increasing international trade, and reducing global economic disparity.[12] At home, the government concentrated on economic and industrial expansion, national unity and the relationship between Canada's two founding cultures, the repatriation of the Constitution, and a review of policies dealing with national health care, labour standards, pensions, unemployment insurance, and immigration.[13] While the governing Liberals were not opposed to the idea of ratifying the International Covenants on Human Rights, these were simply not a priority. With no direct pressure to act, nothing came of the Interdepartmental Committee's suggestion that Canada sign on early to the covenants, and the government did not schedule a federal-provincial meeting to discuss international human rights. More than a year after Pearson wrote the premiers, the Canadian delegation told the United Nations that Canada was "awaiting affirmative reply" from the provinces before pressing forward.[14] Having made initial contact with the premiers, the Pearson government was not in a hurry to sign or ratify the covenants. It took a surge in human rights activism in the late 1960s to make the federal government reconsider.

Activism and Social Change: The International Year for Human Rights

The late 1960s witnessed significant social and political change in Canada and abroad. At home, the 1960s were marked by a questioning of Canadian identity, challenges to established authority, and a growth in social movement activism. Central to this was a rethinking of French-English relations. The Quiet Revolution was redefining Quebec society, and with it Canadian politics. The preliminary report of the Pearson's Royal Commission on Bilingualism and Biculturalism had noted that "Canada, without being fully conscious of the fact, is passing through the greatest crisis in its history. The source of the crisis lies in the Province of Quebec."[15] With a growing number of Quebecers calling for the creation of a separate state, and Daniel Johnson's Union Nationale government testing the limits of Canadian federalism, this period saw a challenge to traditional power structures in both provincial and federal politics.[16] The forces of modernization and secularization and the demand for change that characterized the Quiet Revolution were also evident in English Canada. Canadians were becoming more secular, as part of a larger postwar trend in Western nations of declining influence of formal Christian religions and institutions in areas such as politics, the economy, and public education.[17] This reflected a move away from religion as the dominant source of social mores. At the same time, Canada's historical ties to Britain, its political and economic relationship to the United States, and the position of Indigenous and other non-Anglo minorities in Canada had all become the subject of public debate. Canada's celebration of its centennial in 1967 offered both the opportunity for the mass education of Canadian citizens about Canadian history and identity and an occasion for further questioning of that identity.[18] In his study of the "rebellious" 1960s, Brian Palmer argues that forces such as the independence movement in Quebec, the rise of the New Left and youth counterculture, growing Indigenous unrest, militant labour activism, and demands for women's liberation all challenged ideas of what it meant to be Canadian and the idea of Canada as a peaceful nation.[19] By the end of the decade, Canada's self-conception as a British country had begun to dissolve, and the dominant national narrative of belonging, which privileged white Anglo-Canadians, was under attack.[20]

This was the period in which Canada's baby boomers came of age. According to Doug Owram, as this self-consciously unique generation was confronted with the difficulty of reconciling postwar ideas of personal liberty and opportunity with the constraints of the Cold War, it became dissatisfied and restive.[21] "The demographic wave led by the baby boomers," writes Dominique Clément, "and the social, economic, and political contexts of the period, had a profound impact on social movements [of the 1960s and 1970s]."[22] For example, this period witnessed the intensification of the women's movement in Canada. Existing francophone and anglophone women's organizations began to regroup and campaign in support of peace and disarmament, equality in education and employment, birth control, and an end to violence against women. The launch of the Royal Commission on the Status of Women in 1967 significantly increased public awareness of women's issues in Canada, and acted as a rallying point for the movement.[23] The following year, as minister of justice, Pierre Elliott

Trudeau initiated a massive overhaul of the *Criminal Code*, relaxing laws relating to divorce, amending abortion laws, and decriminalizing homosexuality. In asserting that "there's no place for the state in the bedrooms of the nation," Trudeau helped redefine the role of the state in people's lives.[24] When Pearson announced his retirement from politics, Trudeau ran for leadership of the governing Liberal Party, promoting his vision of a "Just Society" in Canada. He won the race and in April 1968 ushered in a new era in Canadian politics and culture. All of these changes had a profound effect on Canadian culture, values, and norms.

This was also an important period in global affairs. Competition between the United States and the Soviet Union for spheres of influence continued, with former colonial states in Africa and Asia increasingly becoming a focus of attention. The European imperial project had come to an end as the vast majority of colonies achieved independence. This transformed the UN General Assembly, and an influx of new, non-aligned states continued to alter the balance of power, bringing greater attention to issues of decolonization, development, and economic inequity.[25] The Non-Aligned Movement (NAM) was formalized in Belgrade in 1961, and by the late 1960s more than fifty states were involved, condemning imperialism, opposing the continued production and stockpiling of weapons of mass destruction, and challenging US and Soviet hegemony.[26] This was a crucial time in the Cold War, as the two superpowers were confronted with the cost – both financial and in terms of image – of their global foreign policy. The year 1968 marked the height of US engagement in the Vietnam War. The number of American troops deployed, the number of casualties, and military spending all peaked in this year.[27] At home and abroad, Washington faced intense criticism for its involvement in the region and condemnation of the way in which the war was being fought. In Europe, 1968 was the year of the Prague Spring, a period of political liberalization and economic reform in Soviet-controlled Czechoslovakia. As citizens called for the greater democratization of government, Soviet armed forces invaded the country, took control of the government, and reversed the reforms.[28] This invasion illustrated the lengths to which Moscow would go to prevent the splintering of the Eastern bloc. Carole Fink, Phillip Gassert, and Detleff Junker refer to 1968 as a "watershed" year in the Cold War, with Washington and Moscow caught between a period of intense confrontation and the beginning of the era of détente; in the context of external pressures, this caused the superpowers "to reexamine the framework of the postwar order, to rethink their own national interests, and to renew efforts to strengthen international stability."[29]

A powerful new force was also at play, as a rise in global activism helped created a climate of social unrest. Much of this unrest was the result of long-simmering anger towards exploitive structures of power, including undemocratic governments, an oppressive capitalist system, and legalized racism. In his study of the connections between great power diplomacy and social protest, Jeremi Suri argues that by the late 1960s activism had turned revolutionary on a global scale, alarming world leaders.[30] In the United States, the civil rights movement was entering a new phase of Black Power, as individuals such as Stokely Carmichael began to promote a form of revolutionary Black nationalism. In April 1968, Martin Luther King Jr., the movement's key proponent of non-violence, was assassinated, resulting in a wave of civil unrest across the nation.[31] Just two months later, Democratic presidential candidate Robert Kennedy was also assassinated, deepening concerns about violence in the United States. This same year, a series of popular rebellions took place around the world, in many cases involving violent clashes between government, police, and protesters. In May, students and workers in France took to the streets to push for social and economic change, paralyzing the state for weeks. In Mexico in October, students protested that country's hosting of the Olympic Games, calling instead for a revolution to bring about democratic reform and social justice. Similar protests took place in countries such as Poland, West Germany, Spain, Brazil, and South Africa.[32]

It was in this context that the UN commemorated the twentieth anniversary of the adoption of the *Universal Declaration of Human Rights*, designating 1968 as International Year for Human Rights (IYHR). The UN first discussed the idea of a human rights year in the early 1960s, hoping to reinvigorate the international human rights movement and facilitate more intensive efforts and undertakings by national governments in the field of human rights.[33] After more than a decade of debate, the International Covenants on Human Rights remained incomplete, and many member states were disillusioned with the process. Ottawa initially had misgivings about the value of a year to celebrate human rights but quickly realized that the idea was popular among other UN members, and so Canadian delegates voted in support of the related resolutions.[34] The UN Human Rights Commission established a committee with representatives from thirty-four states to consider the possibility of holding an international conference to review the progress made in human rights since 1948 and to assess the UN's effectiveness in the field. As a member of the Human Rights Commission at the time, Canada sat on the Committee for International Year for Human Rights, and the Canadian government played an active role in preparations for the year, both at the UN and at home.

The IYHR stimulated tremendous activity around the globe. At the international level, the celebrations revealed three significant trends in the field of human rights: the growing influence of non-Western states on how the UN conceptualized rights; the desire of NGOs to play a more substantive role in the design of international human rights law; and the penetration of human rights principles into other fields of global policy. The major event organized by the UN was an intergovernmental conference in Tehran, Iran. Its major objective was to review the total UN effort to further human rights, and to discuss how the international body ought to move forward.[35] Delegates from over eighty nations attended, with Canada sending six representatives.[36] Mirroring the challenges experienced at the UN, a substantial amount of time at the Tehran conference was spent on political issues. For this reason, the conference agenda was split into two parts: one to consider human rights questions in general, emphasizing the technical problems involved in defining and protecting human rights, the other to discuss more political questions such apartheid, colonialism in Rhodesia, and conflict in the Middle East.[37] Even in the more technical sessions, delegates disagreed over how best to enforce the human rights principles outlined in the various UN declarations and conventions, illustrating that even after two decades of work these instruments remained deeply contentious.[38] The lack of agreement caused most analysts at the time, and historians since, to label the conference a disappointment, or, as Andrew Thompson puts it, "a missed opportunity to move beyond standard-setting toward a regime that was capable of actually protecting the rights of vulnerable populations."[39]

What the Tehran conference did reveal was the extent to which the changing balance of power at the UN was influencing the international human rights project. Many of the states that attended had not even been members of the UN when the UDHR was adopted, with many delegates opposing the UN's traditional focus on civil and political rights. Roland Burke cites Tehran as "the culmination of a shift from the Western-inflected concept of individual human rights exemplified in the 1948 Universal Declaration to a model that emphasized economic development and the collective rights of the nation."[40] He argues that, at Tehran, Western states were willing to cede power to smaller non-aligned states in the realm of human rights in exchange for support in matters of Cold War security.[41] This compromise allowed for the adoption of a number of small but constructive resolutions to improve the protection of women's rights and the rights of detained persons, as well as to eradicate illiteracy and improve education around the globe. More importantly, the conference's final report explicitly affirmed the indivisibility of economic, social, and cultural rights from political and social rights, proclaiming that "the widening gap between the economically developed and developing countries impedes the realization of human rights in the international community."[42] In contrast to the earlier policy of remaining on the margins of debates over human rights, Canada played a more active role in Tehran, introducing a resolution urging all countries to develop a legal aid system, which received widespread support, and co-sponsoring resolutions on rights for refugees and on fuller implementation of the *Declaration of the Rights of the Child*.[43] Ultimately, Canada's contributions were eclipsed by the conference's inability to deal with the fundamental question of how to ensure effective implementation of international human rights policies.

The Tehran conference was restricted to representatives from states and specialized UN agencies. Individuals and NGOs were excluded from this analysis of the UN's international human rights system, symbolizing the desire of states to maintain control over the development of human rights law. Unsurprisingly, there was a tremendous demand from non-state actors to contribute substantively to the UN's initiatives. In response, the Johnson Foundation of Racine, Wisconsin, sponsored a World Assembly on Human Rights to be held in Montreal in advance of the intergovernmental conference. Financial support came largely through American non-profit organizations and private donors. American NGOs had taken the lead on pressuring member states of the UN to include human rights in the agenda in 1948, and the Montreal conference followed in this tradition. The bulk of the money came from the Johnson Foundation, the Eleanor Roosevelt Memorial Foundation, Fund for Tomorrow, Inc., Lakeview Fund, Inc., and private donors such as Jacob Blaustein.[44] The World Assembly provided a venue for non-state actors to discuss the current status of human rights at the UN and produce recommendations to be sent to the organizers in Tehran.[45] Louis B. Sohn, a key architect of the United Nations and the international legal system, helped organize the conference. Sohn wanted delegates at Tehran to adopt an official statement acknowledging the binding force of the UDHR, and hoped to use the World Assembly to promote this idea.[46] Thirty-five human rights experts from various nations met for six days and the proceedings were attended by dozens of observers.[47] Participants discussed the prevalence of racial discrimination around the world, the urgency of putting into effect the International Covenants on Human Rights, new dangers to rights and freedoms as a result of scientific developments, and how to induce national compliance with and public awareness of international human rights.[48] Included in these discussions were many representatives from Canada: Maxwell Cohen, dean of law at McGill; Justice Harry Batshaw of the Superior Court of Montreal; John P. Humphrey, McGill law professor and former director of the UN Human Rights Division; Ronald St. John Macdonald, dean of law at the University of Toronto; and Gerard Rancourt, president of the United Council for Human Rights in Montreal.[49] The assembly's final report contained twenty-nine pages of statements on the status of human rights in the world and called on UN members to reaffirm their support for the human rights provisions outlined in the UN Charter and to bring national legislation in line with the principles of the UDHR.[50] A key focus of the final report was on how important it was for all states to ratify the two International Covenants on Human Rights and the Optional Protocol. While the World Assembly's report did not exert influence in the way proponents like Sohn had hoped, it signified to world leaders and diplomats the broad support that international human rights had within civil society. For Canadian officials in particular, the location of the assembly in Montreal and the significant involvement of Canadian rights activists and legal scholars illustrated the growing connection between the national and international human rights movements.

In addition to the Tehran conference and the Montreal World Assembly, other international conferences were organized in 1968 to stimulate discussion and action relating to human rights. In September, UNESCO hosted the International Non-Governmental Organization (NGO) Conference on Human Rights at its headquarters in Paris. Canada sent two delegates to this conference, which brought together representatives from over three hundred organizations around the world.[51] Many of the annual meetings of international associations used human rights as their organizing theme in 1968, reflecting the extent to which human rights questions had spread into other areas of global policy. For example, in August the International Conference on Social Welfare was held in Helsinki.[52] Seventy-five Canadian delegates attended this event, which focused on "Social Welfare and Human Rights." Canadian representatives also travelled to Dublin to attend the annual meeting of the World Confederation of Organizations of the Teaching Profession, which discussed "Education and Human Rights." Events such as these fostered international discussion of human rights–related topics and increased awareness within a wide range of Canadian professional organizations of the ways in which human rights were protected in international law.

The Canadian Program for the International Year for Human Rights

The International Year for Human Rights was also widely celebrated in Canada. As in the past, individuals and voluntary organizations sponsored initiatives and coordinated public education relating to a wide variety of topics falling under the umbrella of human rights. The IYHR differed in several ways from previous celebrations, however: the federal and provincial governments played a much more active role; Canadians were more connected to the international program, and events in Canada were more closely linked to global human rights; and the breadth of participation and the topics discussed revealed that understandings of rights in Canada had evolved beyond the narrow concept of civil liberties to embrace a more universal vision of human rights.

When planning began in 1965, the Canadian Citizenship Branch of the federal Department of Citizenship and Immigration noted that there was a receptive climate in Canada for the launching of a human rights year.[53] Officials pointed to the development of provincial commissions on human rights, the attention given to the new role of ombudsman, interest in issues of bilingualism and biculturalism, the growth of training in human rights in a variety of sectors, and the proliferation of national conferences on related topics as signs that it was "unquestionably a period in Canadian life when governments, voluntary groups and individuals are vitally concerned with human rights issues."[54] The human rights movement in Canada, which had grown steadily since the 1940s, was strengthened by the rise in social movement activism in the 1960s, including the second-wave women's movement, the student youth movement, the rise of a New Left in Canada, Indigenous activism, and successive waves of protest demanding enhanced rights for marginalized groups. These movements were dedicated to addressing issues of discrimination and inequity, and many were heavily involved in the IYHR celebrations.

From the beginning, the federal government was closely involved in the planning. The Interdepartmental Committee on Human Rights, which had expanded to include representatives from External Affairs, Justice, National Health and Welfare, Labour, and Manpower and Immigration, discussed what form Canada's observance would take, and suggested two main features: a national conference, and a nationwide program of promotion, coordination, and liaison in the area of human rights.[55] Federal officials encouraged the development of a national committee, composed of representatives from Canadian voluntary organizations, to coordinate the conference and program.[56] The resulting Canadian Commission, IYHR met for the first time in 1966.[57] John Humphrey was its president, and human rights activist Kalmen Kaplanksy was chair. The commission's executive invited more than three hundred Canadian organizations to a national consultation in Ottawa in September 1966. The response to this invitation foreshadowed the wide-ranging participation in Canada's program for 1968.[58] Eighty delegates from more than seventy national associations and thirty representatives from federal and provincial governments met in Ottawa to set an agenda and discuss goals for the year. Delegates generated a long list of what was to be achieved by the end of 1968, including development of human rights legislation and a human rights committee in every province; establishment of a national council for human rights; public support for ratification of the International Covenants on Human Rights; a review of existing legislation in Canada and a strengthening of the *Canadian Bill of Rights;* establishment of Royal Commissions on Indigenous peoples and on the status of women; and a culminating national conference to assess achievements and work still to be done.[59]

For the first time, Ottawa viewed a UN-sponsored celebration of international human rights as politically valuable. External Affairs tapped into the widespread support for the IYHR, recognizing that it could help build support for a number of the government's other proposed policies. It informed Cabinet that "the development of favourable public opinion through the activities of voluntary organizations at national and regional levels would add considerable weight to the federal position in negotiations with the provinces in such matters as a Charter of Human Rights, language rights legislation and ratification of international agreements."[60] It is noteworthy that External Affairs spoke of the importance of this year in terms of how it could further policy objectives rather than how it might advance the principles of universal human rights. Still, this was a much more positive approach than that of only five years earlier, when Ottawa distanced itself from the fifteenth-anniversary celebrations because it had yet to commit to supporting the international covenants on human rights. Things were much different in 1967 and so, sensing the benefit of a well-organized human rights year, the Citizenship Branch provided most of the funding for the planning committee, in the form of a $99,500 grant. In April that year, the Canadian Commission, IYHR held a second planning conference in Montreal that lasted three days. At this meeting, government officials worked with private individuals to chair workshops on international human rights as well as wide range of new topics now considered under the umbrella of human rights, including social welfare, immigration, Indian affairs, the protection of minority groups, and the need for voluntary action.[61]

The federal government also encouraged provincial participation. The Citizenship Branch, the Interdepartmental Committee on Human Rights, and the Canadian Commission, IYHR all saw the human rights year as a tool to draw the provinces into a national discussion of human rights.[62] This was another reversal in the federal position, which in 1950 was against consultation with the provinces out of fear that this would "paralyze all action" in the area of human rights.[63] In 1967, Cabinet wrote the premiers urging their participation in planning for the IYHR.[64] Significantly, Cabinet used the fact that parts of the UDHR and the International Covenants on Human

Rights fell within provincial jurisdiction to encourage provincial input, hoping this would ease negotiations over both ratification of the international covenants and discussions over a Charter of Rights and Freedoms. The letter stated that "no Canadian observance of International Year for Human Rights would be really complete without some form of provincial participation."[65] Federal officials recommended that each province or region establish a planning committee. The Canadian Commission kept in contact with these committees, monitoring progress and reporting to Canadians and the UN Secretary-General on what actions Canada was taking to celebrate the year.

There was a range of provincial participation. Ontario, which had participated actively in the fifteenth-anniversary celebrations, ran the most extensive IYHR program. The province was a leader in Canada in the development of human rights law, enacting the first fair practices laws in the 1950s and the *Ontario Human Rights Code* in 1962, and establishing the nation's first provincial human rights commission. Walter Tarnopolsky, a professor at Osgoode Hall Law School and legal expert in human rights, chaired the Ontario Planning Committee for IYHR, which wrote in 1967 to more than seven hundred organizations around the province to encourage their involvement.[66] The committee was so supportive that it also wrote to other provinces to encourage their full participation. It described the IYHR as "a golden opportunity" for advancements in the field of human rights, and suggested that the provinces exchange resources to take full advantage of the opportunity.[67] The biggest project in Ontario was a provincial conference held in March, which included a panel dedicated to the importance of ratifying the International Covenants on Human Rights.[68] Ontario's enthusiasm for IYHR heralded its strong support for Canada's ratification of the covenants.

New Brunswick was also particularly active. In 1966, it established the New Brunswick Human Rights Commission, and its IYHR program was heavily influenced by the enthusiasm of the commission's chair, Noël Kinsella. A variety of groups from across the province, including religious institutions, university clubs and faculty, Indigenous groups, women's organizations, and educational societies, held seminars and sponsored studies on the topic of rights throughout 1968. A provincial conference in Fredericton in March focused on the equal status of the two official languages and the day-to-day experiences of marginalized groups in New

Brunswick.[69] The New Brunswick Human Rights Commission was very active in sponsoring events and in reporting back to the Canadian Commission, IYHR. Quebec also actively organized IYHR events. After the death of Daniel Johnson in early 1968, Jean Lesage became premier. Lesage had been a federal Member of Parliament before moving to provincial politics, and in 1950 he represented Canada as a delegate to the UN, where he worked on the draft covenant on human rights.[70] Although no specific anti-discrimination or human rights laws were adopted in Quebec under Lesage's government, Quebecers had become more accepting of human rights principles throughout the 1960s and widely supported the IYHR. In April 1968, the government launched the Commission du Québec des Droits de l'Homme, which included 135 delegates from all regions of the province, representing approximately seventy different organizations.[71] The commission set two goals for the year: inclusion of all regions in the celebrations, and initiation of a series of studies of human rights problems in the province in relation to the standards of the UDHR.[72] Reporting on its progress, Quebec's organizing committee made special note of its ability to attract participants from ten regions outside Montreal, the city that had previously generated most of the province's human rights activities.[73] Quebec's participation in the IYHR celebrations was greatly enhanced from that of either the tenth- or fifteenth-anniversary celebrations, reflecting the transition away from the Duplessis government's earlier opposition to civil liberties and the growing interest in rights in the province.[74] Other provinces, such as Alberta, Manitoba, Nova Scotia, and British Columbia, set up provisional human rights committees to work with voluntary organizations in coordinating events for the year. Alberta hired a full-time human rights officer to bring provincial human rights laws to the attention of the public, while in Manitoba the government sponsored a number of studies on issues such as discrimination towards the province's Indigenous people, linguistic rights, and rights in housing.[75]

Some provinces played a less active role. The differences in the extent to which each province celebrated the year reveals less about the support of these provinces for international human rights, however, and more about the uneven development of domestic human rights legislation and infrastructure in Canada in the 1960s. Saskatchewan, which strongly supported the protection of rights and freedoms under Tommy Douglas' CCF government, enacting the nation's first bill of rights in 1947, was less committed under the Liberal government in the late 1960s and had yet to enact any comprehensive human rights laws. During the IYHR, Saskatchewan held a provincial conference in December, but focused most of its attention on developing a constitution and a set of bylaws for its new Human Rights Association.[76] Prince Edward Island, which had not adopted any anti-discrimination legislation in the 1950s or 1960s, did not create a formal IYHR committee but did report some activities to the Canadian Commission.[77] Newfoundland had neither rights-related legislation nor a strong structure of voluntary organizations. There were rights-related issues of concern in Newfoundland, such as the right to work and the right to education, but the government did not identify them are human rights questions. Provincial officials also argued that there was "no race problem" in the province.[78] One of the important consequences of IYHR was that it made visible the differences in provincial support and infrastructure in the area of human rights, and for many provinces it stimulated the development of stronger human rights laws.

Another effect of the greater participation of provincial governments in the IYHR was that it helped foster greater federal-provincial discussion in the area of human rights. Before the adoption of the covenants in 1966, Ottawa had initiated virtually no contact with the provinces relating to the UN's human rights activities. The provincial ministries of labour, which administered most of the early anti-discrimination laws, met regularly under the umbrella of the Canadian Association of Administrators of Labour Legislation (CAALL). By the 1960s, this association was setting aside more time to address human rights, but its focus remained more broadly on labour legislation.[79] Other than a 1965 conference of provincial human rights administrators organized by the Ontario Human Rights Commission, there had been little opportunity for government officials from across Canada to discuss human rights problems.[80] However, with the federal government's encouragement of provincial participation in IYHR planning, provincial representatives attended the national consultation in 1966 and the Montreal planning conference in 1967. Both events had workshops dedicated specifically to discussion of provincial human rights legislation, human rights commissions, and provincial ombudsmen. Provincial governments also kept in contact with the Canadian Commission, IYHR throughout the year, reporting on their programs and any legislative developments. This paved the way for greater federal-provincial dialogue over human rights in the future, and in particular set the stage for discussions over Canada's accession to the international covenants on human rights.

The IYHR also gave Canadians an opportunity to engage more actively in global discussions of human rights. Canadian representatives participated in Tehran's intergovernmental conference, in the Montreal World Assembly, and in a number of related annual meetings of international associations. This participation enabled a growing number of Canadians outside government circles to consider human rights from a global perspective, and to bring ideas relating to the international promotion of human rights back to Canada. The president of the national IYHR planning committee, John Humphrey, brought his experience as former director of the UN Human Rights Division to Canada's planning process. As a long-time advocate for international human rights, Humphrey worked to ensure that international developments shaped Canada's program for the celebration. At the national conference held in December 1968, all seminars and topics discussed were explicitly linked to the principles of the UDHR. Each workshop was responsible for creating recommendations based on the following underlying questions: (1) how does Canada measure up to the standards set by the *Universal Declaration of Human Rights*? (2) what was achieved in 1968? and (3) what further action must be taken?[81] For example, the workshop on human rights commissions recommended that all jurisdictions in Canada "review the adequacy of their human rights legislation with respect to the Universal Declaration."[82] The workshops on women's rights and on social welfare and human rights urged the federal government to work with the provinces to implement the outstanding international conventions.[83] For the first time, the need for Canada to fulfill its international obligations by ratifying outstanding UN human rights instruments became a major talking point in Canada. At the Montreal planning conference in 1967, Dr. Manfred Saalheimer of the Canadian Jewish Congress gave a talk on this very topic. David Bartlett, a representative of the Canadian National Commission for UNESCO chaired a workshop on the ratification of the covenants.[84]

The way in which the federal government talked about the importance of Canada's relationship to the UN human rights regime also began to change. At the national consultation to begin the planning for the IYHR in 1966, Secretary of State for External Affairs Judy LaMarsh stated that "we in Canada can – and should – be in the forefront of the world community in our respect for and dedication to the basic rights of our citizens."[85] She urged delegates to see the International Year for Human Rights as an opportunity for Canada to distinguish itself in the world community. Maxwell Cohen, the keynote speaker for the culminating national conference in December 1968, picked up on LaMarsh's comments. He noted that "Canada cannot have an international image of any significance in the human rights field, whether legal, political, economic or social, or even a 'sense of community,' if she is not a good model at home of what is expected from abroad."[86] This was a theme of the IYHR: the idea that Canada must bolster its domestic human rights regime and record in order to gain credibility and authority internationally. After 1968, this idea of Canada as a model in the area of human rights, establishing a key role for Canada within the international human rights system, became more prominent in the rhetoric of diplomats, also trickling into the way in which members of NGOs and the public began to talk about Canada's role in the world.[87]

In an article in the *Canadian Bar Review,* Cohen further considered the interrelationship between domestic and international human rights.[88] He explained that there had been a radical change in awareness of rights since the end of the Second World War, and that the 1950s and 1960s offered a more sensitive environment for new ideas about rights and new standards in Canadian society.[89] He provided four reasons for this greater sensitivity: the lesson of the Holocaust, the influence of the anti-colonial movement, increased interaction between "white" populations and people of colour, and the rise of the welfare state. In the international system and at the UN, Cohen argued, decolonization and changes in the global power structure created a "new majority" and put pressure on privileged whites.[90] He also pointed to the growing use of the term "human rights," and argued that the rights language and the rights-related documents that came out of the United Nations were useful tools in calls for enhanced rights protection at home. He wrote: "No one could have predicted in 1945–46 the power or the semantic consequences of this kind of language, or its absorption into the wider area of political debate in this generation, and the ease with which it has become part of the political dialogue, part of the debating experience of peoples in all parts of the world, even those in affluent societies."[91] As Cohen's comments illustrate, rights activists in Canada had begun to connect global developments and the international human rights movement to their own quest for enhanced rights protections in Canada.

The evolution of understandings of rights in Canada was evident in the IYHR celebrations, implicitly through the diversity of groups involved and the broad range of topics discussed, and explicitly in the resources produced for the year. At the official launch of the year in Canada, a total of 283 representatives from more than 150 different organizations attended the opening ceremony. Scheduled events ranged from highly organized conferences to informal presentations in local churches and essay-writing contests for secondary-school students.[92] The planning committee published a monthly brochure, *Resources,* which tracked "Action Notes" of many of the activities taking place throughout the year. A survey of these notes reveals that the groups involved were diverse in focus and represented local, provincial, and national interests.[93] National organizations such as the Canadian Council of Christians and Jews participated, as did provincial organizations such as the Groupement Latino-Canadien du Québec or the Home and School Federation of New Brunswick. Local groups with a wide range of interests, such as the Peace River Human Rights Committee, Sudbury's Local 6500 of the United Steelworkers, and the Morell Women's Institute, hosted a variety of events. Only a small percentage of the organizations self-identified as a human rights group; the rest were voluntary organizations looking to connect their own interests to the pursuit of greater equality and enhanced rights protections. Public education was key, and the Canadian Commission, IYHR acted as a clearinghouse for information about the year. The demand for resources was so great that only a month into 1968, the commission worried that it could not afford the cost of meeting regular requests from individuals, organizations, and school groups for human rights literature and educational materials.[94]

The culminating event of the year was a three-day national conference held in early December. More than five hundred delegates attended this conference, representing 147 national voluntary organizations, provincial human rights committees, religious institutions, government departments, universities, ethnic groups, women's groups, Indigenous groups, and unaffiliated but interested individuals.[95] At a series of plenary sessions, federal and provincial governments provided a summary and analysis of Canada's domestic human rights policies and programs. These sessions were followed by ten workshops, spread over several days, on such topics as Canada's Constitution and a Charter of Human Rights, Social Welfare, Labour Rights, Human Rights Commissions, Women's Rights, Aboriginal Rights, and Children's Rights.[96] This was a much broader array of topics than at the tenth- and fifteenth-anniversary celebrations, which had focused on broader categories, such as Civil and Political Rights, Economic and Social Rights, or a Bill of Rights. In particular, the new focus on topics such as women's and Aboriginal rights reflected the influence of social movements of the late 1960s on how conference organizers conceptualized human rights in Canada.

One of the significant barriers to federal support for the UDHR and the covenants had been cultural attitudes towards rights; in the late 1940s, federal officials and Canadians more generally defined rights as a narrow set of legal and political rights attached to citizenship. In preparation for the launch of the IYHR, the Canadian Commission produced a pamphlet titled "Canada & Human Rights: 21 Questions and Answers," which defined human rights for the purpose of the year's program.[97] Rather than relying on British tradition and on how the Fathers of Confederation understood rights, as federal officials had done in 1948, the commission looked to the UDHR and described human rights as "the conditions necessary for each individual to live truly as a human being in society."[98] The human rights outlined in this pamphlet were vastly different from the understanding of rights that had guided the policies of External Affairs in the 1940s and 1950s. According to the commission, human rights were universal and should be designed to meet the needs of both individuals and minority groups; in categorizing which rights should be protected, the pamphlet listed political rights, legal rights, egalitarian rights, and linguistic rights. It defined egalitarian rights as guarantees against discriminatory treatment by government or other action by reason of race, national origin, religion, or sex. It also pointed out that significant portions of Canada's population, including "Negroes, Prairie Métis, Northern Eskimos and most of Canadian Indians," had not historically been afforded these rights, and that the remedy for this would be to enshrine the principles of the UDHR in the Canadian Constitution and then to educate all Canadians about these constitutional rights.[99]

At the UN in the 1950s, the Canadian delegation fought to exclude group rights and economic and social rights from the covenants because these were understood to be a matter of social policy rather than a matter of right. By 1968, however, the Canadian Commission, IYHR was arguing that individual rights were insufficient for many members of minority groups, and that these groups also needed the right to preserve their language and other cultural traits. In this case, the commission was referring explicitly to French-speaking populations in Canada. The pamphlet made reference to the importance of the Royal Commission on Bilingualism and Biculturalism in creating an "equal partnership" between French and English Canadians. Economic and social rights had become a significant point of conversation, and were the topic of many talks and workshops throughout 1968. Many social movement organizations of the late 1960s focused on the poor economic and social conditions of Canada's marginalized peoples, including women, children, Indigenous peoples, and new immigrants. Organizations such as Toronto's Just Society Movement organized anti-poverty rallies.[100] The Canadian Human Rights Foundation argued that a study of economic and social rights would not "demote civil and political rights to a status of minor importance," but instead allow for a more complex and self-fulfilling understanding of rights.[101] While federal officials continued to view rights more narrowly than this, it is noteworthy that public discussions of rights in the late 1960s were much broader than they had been two decades earlier.

Throughout the different activities in 1968, activists were quick to point out the ways in which Canadian laws fell short of protecting this broader understanding of human rights. They also challenged not only the government but also the historic lack of support from Canadian citizens. Alan Borovoy, a member of the Jewish Labour Committee, stated that "Canadians are not sufficiently in favour of human rights. We are not 'hate-mongers' we are 'comfort-mongers.' Our problems concern not the ill-intentioned wrong-doer, but the well-intentioned non-doer."[102] For long-time activists such as John Humphrey, one important goal of the IYHR was to highlight the shortcomings in Canada's domestic and international human rights policies in order to press for further developments. Humphrey told delegates: "We have lived with a national smugness for so long, believing we had such an advanced enlightenment toward equality for all people, that we are only beginning to recognize with a shock that we are just people after all."[103] Humphrey described how he had been "embarrassed" by Canada's decision to abstain in the vote on the adoption of the UDHR in 1948, and that he continued to be disappointed with the government's lack of commitment to international human rights.[104]

The International Year for Human Rights had a significant effect on Canada. The year's activities brought human rights to the forefront of public debate, and subsequent pressures led to an expansion of existing human rights structures, both federally and provincially. In setting goals for the IYHR, participants at the national consultation in 1966 had recommended the adoption of a human rights act by all of the provinces. At that time, only Saskatchewan, Ontario, and Nova Scotia had such legislation. By the end of the IYHR, Alberta, New Brunswick, and Prince Edward Island had acts in place, and by the mid-1970s all Canadian provinces had adopted some form of human rights bill.[105] The year was also instrumental in encouraging the creation of human rights associations throughout Canada. The federal government had called on all provinces to establish planning committees to prepare for the observance of the year, and several of these provisional committees evolved into permanent provincial human rights commissions. Nova Scotia, New Brunswick, Newfoundland, British Columbia, and Manitoba all developed commissions either immediately before or shortly after the IYHR celebrations.[106] Even the federal government developed a short-lived Canadian Council for Human Rights from 1969 to 1970. This new council adopted the executive and the structure of the IYHR planning commission, but from its inception it struggled financially and members had difficulty agreeing on its goals.[107] Before any decisions could be made, the council collapsed due to insufficient funds.[108] This period also saw the creation of a number of new NGOs that specifically self-identified as human rights organizations, such as the Canadian Foundation for Human Rights in Montreal.[109] These groups continued to press for expanded rights protections in Canada, and formed a part of the larger global human rights movements that developed in the 1970s.

One of the significant effects of the IYHR was the first organized campaign to pressure the Canadian government to accede to the international covenants. The UN Commission on Human Rights had adopted a resolution in 1966 calling on all member states to ratify these instruments by the end of the human rights year. Almost all international conferences, as well as those held in Canada, included information sessions on the UN's human rights conventions. The fact that a number of these conventions had not yet been signed or ratified by Canada was widely publicized during and after the year.[110] As a result, a range of governmental and non-governmental organizations at the national conference recommended that Canada ratify the International Covenants on Human Rights and the Optional Protocol at the earliest possible date.

In the House of Commons, the UN's human rights instruments became a more common point of reference. Some MPs called for legislative change, arguing that Canadian legislation had to be consistent with the principles of the UDHR. Progressive Conservative MP Robert Thompson called on Prime Minister Trudeau to amend the *Industrial Relations and Disputes Investigation Act,* "in view of the fact that Canada has given such full and complete endorsement of [the] universal declaration."[111] This same argument was used repeatedly in 1969 and 1970 to promote hate propaganda amendments to the *Criminal Code.*[112] Other MPs called on the federal government to ratify the covenants, although confusion between the UDHR and the two international covenants persisted.[113] The most direct pressure on the Trudeau government for action on the covenants, however, was exerted by a nationwide petition campaign led by B'nai Brith Canada's League for Human Rights. B'nai Brith, an international Jewish advocacy group with an active branch in Canada, had been involved in the movement for racial equality in the postwar period.[114] At the Montreal World Assembly, its representatives were particularly interested in the assembly's sense of urgency to have national governments ratify the international covenants and to arouse public awareness and support for their effective implementation.[115] In 1971, B'nai Brith Canada established its League for Human Rights, and appointed Roland de Corneille, a human rights activist, Anglican priest, and member of the Canadian Conference of Christians and Jews, as its national director.[116] One of his first tasks as director was to initiate a petition campaign to push the federal government to ratify the International Covenants on Human Rights.[117] Neither covenant was given priority; the campaign called for the ratification of both.

According to the League for Human Rights, the petition campaign was designed to "urge our Federal and Provincial Governments to exert their greatest efforts to the end that Canada become a party to the most fundamental and far reaching instruments in the field of human rights."[118] The Petition Committee agreed that apathy was a major obstacle in the implementation of human rights in Canada, and made public education a key component of the campaign.[119] The league began by using its system of fraternal lodges to educate its members about human rights and about the UN instruments specifically. Members were encouraged to sign the petition and then were sent to visit as many Canadian organizations and religious and ethnic groups as possible to distribute resources about the campaign and obtain signatures for the petition.[120] The league targeted local, provincial, and federal politicians as well, seeking signatures and involving the media where possible. The mayor of Oshawa, Ontario, proclaimed Human Rights Petition Week when he provided his support for the campaign, and the *Oshawa Times* printed an article, the proclamation, and a photo of the mayor signing the petition.[121] This type of publicity generated momentum. Throughout 1971, B'nai Brith worked with many other organizations to promote ratification and educate the public about the covenants. The UN Association of Canada involved hundreds of UN Clubs in schools across the country.[122] Other supporting organizations included the National Indian Brotherhood, the Anglican Church of Canada, the Indian-Eskimo Association of Canada, the Ontario Human Rights Commission, the Human Rights Committee of the Ontario Federation of Labour, the National Council of Women of Canada, the Union of Ontario Indians, the World Federalists of Canada, and the National Council of Jewish Women.[123] Increasingly, Canada's human rights organizations were taking up the call for the federal government to ratify the covenants.

The official petition campaign ran from October to December 1971. Almost 22,000 Canadians signed the petition, including 91 Members of Parliament representing all of the major political parties.[124] A delegation led by de Corneille met with Prime Minister Trudeau on 10 December 1971 and submitted the petition. Trudeau responded:

> I am very pleased to be receiving today a petition signed by thousands of Canadians calling for Canada to become a party to the International Covenants. This petition, sponsored by the League for Human Rights of B'nai Brith embodies the hopes and desires of large numbers of Canadians

> who seek to advance the cause of human rights both within Canada and internationally ... I welcome this particular initiative and pledge my support for its worthy objective.[125]

With this speech, the federal government publicly supported ratification for the first time. Trudeau did not commit to a specific deadline, however. When Progressive Conservative MP David MacDonald asked him in the House of Commons a few days later whether or not the Liberals had a timeline for ratification, he simply reverted to the government's stock response that consultation with the provincial governments was ongoing.[126]

Although the petition campaign was complete, the League for Human Rights continued to disseminate information about the covenants and human rights. Roland de Corneille travelled throughout Canada, speaking on a range of topics. In 1973, he told a crowd at the Jaycees National Convention in Kingston, Ontario, that there was much to be done in Canada in the area of human rights and that Canada had fallen off track. He said, however: "There is one thing we can do that will get us back on the track – that will give us back leadership in Human Rights. It is clear. It is simple. It is concrete. It is effective. It is to have Canada become a party to the International Human Rights Covenants."[127]

The Slow Road to Ratification

According to the Department of External Affairs, the International Year for Human Rights, "resulted in very widespread public interest and participation in human rights programs across Canada," and the year "developed expectations of continuing federal and provincial support for the realization of human rights goals."[128] Indeed, in terms of domestic developments, the momentum continued into the 1970s, as provincial governments further enhanced human rights protections and the federal government pushed for an entrenched Charter of Human Rights. Trudeau told provincial representatives at the First Ministers' Meeting in 1969 that his government intended to work towards a constitutionally entrenched bill of rights, and this topic became an important aspect of federal-provincial discussions.[129] On the other hand, there was less movement in the area of international human rights. Despite Trudeau's positive response to the B'nai Brith petition campaign, the federal government took no significant steps between 1971 and 1974 to hasten the ratification of the covenants.

This inaction was not the result of any opposition to the covenants or the Optional Protocol. In fact, many of the Liberal government's policies, and indeed Trudeau's own vision for a "Just Society," were premised on individual rights and equality of opportunity, and therefore consistent with the international human rights regime. Trudeau's Just Society was focused on civil and political rights, however. In 1962, he had written an article on "Economic Rights" for the *McGill Law Journal*, arguing that "if this society does not evolve an entirely new set of values ... it is vain to hope that Canada will ever reach freedom from fear and freedom from want. Under such circumstances, any claim by lawyers that they have done their bit by upholding civil liberties will be dismissed as a hollow mockery."[130] Trudeau's position on economic rights had changed by the time he was prime minister, however. When he proposed an entrenched Charter of Rights in 1968, he argued that it would be difficult to secure agreement on the issue of economic rights, and for that reason it was "advisable not to attempt to include economic rights in the constitutional bill of rights at this time."[131] He was more determined to expand language rights. In 1969, based on the recommendations of Lester Pearson's Royal Commission on Bilingualism and Biculturalism, the *Official Languages Act* was passed, recognizing the right of both French- and English-speaking Canadians to access federal services in either language.[132] Also, cognizant of the growing influence of the "Third Element" in Canadian society, the federal Liberals introduced a policy of official multiculturalism in 1971. This policy was designed to promote and protect cultural diversity within Canadian society, and also addressed the rights of Indigenous peoples and supported the use of Canada's two official languages.[133] Most importantly, Trudeau was determined to entrench a bill of rights in the Canadian Constitution. Between 1969 and 1971, the federal Liberals hosted five first ministers' conferences at which Trudeau attempted, unsuccessfully, to enshrine individual rights and language rights in the Constitution.[134] These policies illustrate his commitment to expanding human rights protection, but he concentrated his efforts on domestic policy. This was consistent with the priorities of many Canadian rights activists of the time, who continued to advocate domestic initiatives because of limited resources and the sense that domestic developments were more urgent, and would have a more profound impact on the lives of marginalized Canadians.[135] Trudeau's focus on domestic issues was not limited to human rights. In fact, New Democrat MP Andrew Brewin complained that Trudeau's throne speeches barely mentioned international affairs.[136] Domestic matters, constitutional reform, and the place of Quebec within the federation stood highest on Trudeau's agenda, not international human rights instruments or human rights initiatives at the UN.[137]

Despite Trudeau's personal lack of enthusiasm for the covenants, had all ten provinces provided formal support for ratification, the Canadian government likely would have deposited its instruments of accession much sooner than it did. Members of the Interdepartmental Committee on Human Rights and officials in the Department of External Affairs had been urging Cabinet to push for ratification since 1967. Cabinet's ability to do so was hindered, however, by a lack of support from Quebec. In 1971, four years after Lester Pearson asked the provinces to officially confirm their willingness to enact the necessary legislation to implement the three instruments, Quebec had yet to respond. Secretary of State for External Affairs Mitchell Sharp asked Quebec premier Robert Bourassa for the province's position on ratification. Receiving no formal reply, he wrote a second letter in January 1973 indicating that eight of the ten provinces had indicated their agreement to Canada's accession to the covenants and the Optional Protocol, and asking again for Quebec's position.[138]

Bourassa finally replied in March 1973, six years after Pearson's initial letter. He noted that a number of the articles in both covenants concerned matters falling under provincial authority.[139] He further stated that, although Quebec had no objections to the principles and objectives of the covenants, and in fact supported them, the government had concerns with the modalities of provincial participation in the reporting and accountability system established by the three instruments. More specifically, the Government of Quebec wanted the authority to appear before international bodies to defend Quebec institutions or laws that might become the subject of a complaint at the UN, and provincial officials wanted the right to author and file any reports relating to provincial developments, as was the case in the International Labor Organization (ILO).[140] In light of the rise of nationalist sentiment in Quebec, its provincial policy makers and politicians were continually looking for new opportunities to expand the powers and responsibilities of the provincial government.[141] Quebec wanted the power to represent itself in the international arena, particularly when dealing with matters that fell at least partially under provincial jurisdiction, such as the international covenants. Trudeau, on the other hand, was an ardent federalist who opposed any attempt by the provinces to infringe on the authority of the federal government.[142] In 1973, however, he was not sufficiently interested in the ratification of the covenants to bother with Quebec's demands.

Despite Trudeau's lack of interest, by 1974 the federal government was feeling pressure from all sides to take more decisive action towards ratification. The IYHR and its public education campaign had made individuals and organizations aware of the UN's human rights instruments and of the federal government's failure to accede to them. After three years of virtual inactivity relating to the International Covenants on Human Rights, Canadians began writing or inquiring informally about the government's timeline for ratification. Organizations such as the Canadian Unitarian Council passed resolutions demanding that the federal government take action.[143] Letters arrived from individuals such as Betty Stillwell, a Canadian of Japanese heritage who supported ratification and sent copies of her letter to the Greater Vancouver Japanese Canadian Citizens' Association, the Toronto Japanese Canadian Citizens' Association, and the BC Civil Liberties Association.[144] Letters were sent to provincial governments as well. Saskatchewan premier Allan Blakeney, a vocal supporter of ratification, forwarded letters that his government received to the prime minister and External Affairs for their consideration.[145] Human rights experts such as Roland de Corneille, John Humphrey, and Walter Tarnopolsky continued to write on the subject, speak critically of the government's lack of action, and encourage other individuals to pressure the government. Tarnopolsky grabbed headlines when he told a conference of human rights ministers from across the country in 1974 that racist conflict in Canada was a "time bomb" that would explode without immediate action on both domestic and international fronts.[146]

Support for ratification among federal officials had also grown since the 1960s. External Affairs officials noted that, of fifteen international conventions adopted by the United Nations, Canada had ratified only five.[147] Concerned that this number reflected poorly on Canada's commitment to international human rights, officials in the UN Division, such as

W.H. Barton, called on the government to resolve this problem. Barton and others believed that the momentum arising from the IYHR would make gaining the support of the provinces easier. As time dragged on, however, and there was a possibility that Quebec would withhold its support indefinitely, External Affairs officials began questioning whether or not the federal government was really obligated to obtain consent from the provinces before ratifying the international treaties. A.W. Robertson, the director of the Legal Advisory Division, wrote to other members of the department that "it would be unfortunate if the impression were to be given that this Department thought that the prior consent of provincial authorities was necessary from a legal, as opposed to (sometimes) a practical, point of view."[148] The Federal-Provincial Coordination Division asked other External Affairs officials to take care in responding to letters from the public asking why Canada had not ratified the covenants, so as to not overemphasize the role of provincial governments in case the government decided to move unilaterally at a later date.[149]

Members of the federal Progressive Conservative and New Democratic parties also took up the call for ratification in the mid-1970s. In 1973, when the Liberal minister of justice announced in the House of Commons that the government was proposing the creation of a new federal commission for the protection of egalitarian rights, several MPs criticized the government's failure to fulfill its international obligations in the area of the human rights. Progressive Conservative Gordon Fairweather pointed out that "twenty-five years after the United Nations voted for the Declaration of Human Rights Canada has not yet ratified some of the covenants on human rights adopted as long ago as 1966."[150] New Democrat Andrew Brewin picked up on Fairweather's comment and denounced Canada's "poor record" with respect to ratification of international conventions on human rights.[151] As provincial governments became more active in enforcing human rights protection, provincial officials also became more vocal in their demands on the federal government. Noël Kinsella, chair of the New Brunswick Human Rights Commission, argued that the federal government had a role to play in helping provincial human rights administrators keep abreast of human rights developments at the United Nations and in Canada.[152] He told External Affairs that, within provincial governments, there was a sense that "the clock stopped in 1948" with regard to international human rights.[153] Instruments developed in the 1950s and 1960s were almost unknown to provincial officials. He argued that the work to ratify the international covenants and the Optional Protocol would have been much quicker, and the work of the provincial governments much easier, "if they had been enabled to follow the development of the work of the Commission on Human Rights and the debate in the General Assembly and particularly in the Third Committee."[154] To compensate for this lack of knowledge, Kinsella recommended that the External Affairs sponsor seminars or courses for provincial human rights administrators and appoint a human rights officer to the department's UN desk to foster a federal-provincial dialogue.[155] At his advice, the Canadian Association of Statutory Human Rights Administrators (CASHRA) organized a week-long course for provincial human rights officers in Ottawa in 1973.[156] The course covered topics such as the UN *Convention on the Elimination of All Forms of Racial Discrimination,* women in society, the work of the ILO and UNESCO, and the effect of the UN's work in the field.[157]

The Canadian Government's Strategy for Ratification

By 1974, sufficient pressure had been brought to bear on the federal government for it to finally take the question of ratification seriously. In considering its different options, it faced two questions. First, was the government comfortable enough with the provisions of the two covenants and the Optional Protocol to bind itself to their implementation? Second, if the government was prepared to ratify, what should be done about Quebec? In order to answer the first question, the Department of Justice conducted a final analysis on the content of each covenant with respect to their compatibility with Canadian law. When similar studies had been conducted in the 1950s, federal officials had expressed concern that binding covenants would open Canada to criticism in areas such as immigration and voting laws, and policies relating to Indigenous peoples. According to A.W. Robertson of External Affairs' Legal Advisory Division, the 1974 study revealed no serious impediments to Canada's accession to the covenants. Minor legislative changes might be required upon accession, but the Department of Justice had determined that any such change was already under consideration by policy makers.[158] External Affairs argued that, as the language of the covenants explicitly allowed for "progressive implementation," any legislative changes that did need to be made could take place over a period of time.[159] More specifically, officials pointed to Article 2(1) of the ICESCR, which stated:

> Each State Party to the present Covenant undertakes to take steps, individually and through international assistance and cooperation, especially economic and technical, to the maximum of its available resources, with a view to achieve progressively the full realization of the rights recognized in the present Covenant, by all appropriate means, including particularly the adoption of legislative measures.[160]

They argued that, with nine of the ten provinces already supporting accession and this type of flexibility built into the covenant, Canada was in a good position to initiate the process of ratification immediately.

The Justice Department did have a concern over Canada's accession to the Optional Protocol, which set in place the complaint mechanism for the ICCPR. Officials were concerned over the protocol's implication for Canada, because of its provision that individuals who alleged that they were the victim of a violation by a state party to the covenant could bring forward a complaint to the new Human Rights Committee once it was formed. External Affairs was not concerned about the implications of this new UN body, but Justice did not like the fact that the committee would be able to render a judgment that would supersede the decisions of Canada's highest courts.[161] It therefore took the position that Canada should not accede to the Optional Protocol until the federal government was convinced it would not slip out of compliance with the covenants.[162] Justice continued to raise this issue in interdepartmental discussions, but by this point, External Affairs was determined to have the covenants and the Optional Protocol ratified. Officials reminded their minister that Trudeau had publicly supported ratification of the covenants in 1971, and maintained that the Canadian public would not understand why the government would later withdraw its support from one of the three human rights instruments.[163]

The second major concern of the federal government was how to approach Quebec. By 1974, all the other provinces had given their approval for ratification. The Quebec government had not indicated it would challenge Canada on the matter of accession, but continued to state its concerns over the protocols surrounding implementation. Federal politicians realized that the government would have to take action to resolve the stalemate, so External Affairs, the Privy Council Office, and Britain's Foreign and Commonwealth Office (FCO) created a two-pronged strategy: Trudeau would take a personal approach with Bourassa, writing the premier and assuring him that Canada understood Quebec's concerns and was willing to work with the province on the technicalities of implementation; at the same time, federal-provincial meetings were set up for October and December 1975 to facilitate the negotiations. Trudeau did send a letter to Bourassa. Bourassa did not reply personally, but the Quebec government expressed its intent to attend the federal-provincial meetings.[164]

In October 1975, the federal government hosted a meeting to provide the provinces with necessary information on the technicalities of the ratification process. The formal Federal-Provincial Conference on Human Rights would not be held until December, but the federal government hoped that these preliminary discussions would alleviate some of Quebec's concerns over implementation and allow for an easy agreement. At the October meeting, federal representatives encouraged provincial support for Canada's accession to the covenants and the Optional Protocol, once again emphasizing that the language of the covenants allowed for a "progressive implementation" of its provisions.[165] Ontario representative Thomas Symons chaired an informal working group to discuss specific questions or problems, and it was at this group's meetings that the provinces worked on a proposal to allay Quebec's concerns.[166] Representatives from Ontario, Quebec, Saskatchewan, and Nova Scotia worked through the night to reach a tentative agreement that included several key points: the ability of provincial governments to renounce in the future their willingness to subscribe to any part of the instruments that fell under provincial jurisdiction; an agreement that the federal government would consult with the provinces when forming a Canadian delegation to the UN Human Rights Committee; an agreement to allow any province under attack in the field of human rights to provide a representative to defend itself at the UN as part of the Canadian delegation; the ability of provincial governments to write the portions of any reports to the UN that dealt with provincial developments; and a proposal for annual federal-provincial meetings for continued consultation.[167] This represented a major concession to provincial rights. By the conclusion of the October meeting, all the provinces had indicated their satisfaction with the agreement reached by the working committee and resolved to return in December to make an official decision regarding ratification.[168] In advance of this second meeting, the federal Cabinet met and agreed that Canada would accede to both covenants and the Optional Protocol if all ten provinces gave their official support. Cabinet also indicated that, if the provinces did not unanimously agree, then External Affairs and the Secretary of State should report to Cabinet on both the pros and cons of acceding without unanimous consent.[169]

At the Federal-Provincial Conference on Human Rights in December, delegates further discussed the ratification of the covenants. The federal delegation was composed of representatives from the departments of Justice, External Affairs, Labour, and the Secretary of State. In most cases, the ministers responsible for human rights represented their provinces, although Quebec was represented by the minister of intergovernmental affairs, François Cloutier. Cloutier outlined Quebec's position to the other delegates, highlighting the province's accomplishments in the field of human rights and making a particular note of its newly adopted *Charter of Human Rights*.[170] He indicated that Quebec subscribed, "without any reservations," to the objectives of the International Covenants on Human Rights. He explained that the premier of Quebec had exchanged letters with the federal government for three years, and stressed the importance of "adequate participation of his government in enforcing international agreements."[171] The federal government stated that it agreed in principle to the points set out in the preliminary agreement written in October, but proposed several changes. First, while Ottawa accepted that provincial governments would write reports to the UN concerning provincial developments, it reserved the right to request edits to these documents as it was ultimately responsible and accountable for all reports submitted to the UN. Furthermore, while the federal government would accept provincial representation on the Canadian delegation to the UN Human Rights Committee in cases where provinces were facing a complaint, federal officials stressed that these representatives would work with, and not independently of, the federal representatives.[172] With these changes in place, the federal government accepted the agreement. At the conclusion of the conference, all ten provinces agreed in principle to Canada's accession to the covenants and on the modalities of their implementation, with a proviso from Quebec's representative that he needed authority from his cabinet to formalize his agreement.[173] The Canadian government issued a press release outlining the agreement reached by all provinces and the federal government to "act in concert in the implementation of the Instruments."[174]

The Final Push for Ratification

Despite the agreement reached at the federal-provincial conference in December, the Canadian government was in the same position it had been in at the beginning of 1974: Quebec had yet to formally provide its support. The government's initial plan was to wait to hear from Quebec, but Canadian policy towards international human rights was influenced once again by international developments. On 23 December 1975, Czechoslovakia became the thirty-fifth state to ratify the *International Covenant on Civil and Political Rights,* which meant that the covenant would officially enter into force three months later. Once it was in force, the Optional Protocol would also come into force, and the United Nations Human Rights Committee would come into existence within six months. To be eligible to have a representative sit on this committee, member states would have to ratify the covenant by 19 May 1976.[175]

None of Canada's allies had ratified either covenant. The United States maintained that it did not plan to ratify the covenants, and while the United Kingdom, Australia, and New Zealand planned to ratify, none of these states was far enough in the process to be able to file the instruments of accession. Britain's Foreign and Commonwealth Office (FCO) contacted the Canadian government in early 1976. Noting that all of the Warsaw Pact states except Poland had become party to the covenants, the FCO was concerned that there would be a "lack of Western influence" on the Human Rights Committee.[176] Britain would be unable to accede before the deadline, and the British government hoped that Canada could push through accession so that it could nominate a candidate for the committee. In response, External Affairs wrote Cabinet to explain that Canada must decide in favour of accession by 19 May 1976. If it decided not to accede, it would not be able to nominate Canadian candidates to the Human Rights Committee, which "otherwise will be subject to very little Western influence and will in effect be controlled by representatives of various totalitarian regimes."[177] Only Quebec had yet to provide formal consent for ratification, but François Cloutier had provided tentative support.[178] External Affairs had learned, through unofficial channels in Quebec, that Cloutier had obtained the necessary approval from his government, but despite his knowledge of the important deadline, he had yet to reply to the federal government.[179] External Affairs was concerned that the Quebec government might be using its formal agreement as a bargaining chip to obtain concessions from the federal government in other areas.[180]

J.S. Stanford of the Legal Advisory Division of External Affairs advised the minister that, in light of Quebec's refusal to provide its formal agreement, and the tight deadline to be eligible for the Human Rights Committee, the minister ought prepare a letter from the prime minister to Premier Bourassa to put pressure on Quebec.[181] At the same time, the department discussed the possibility of ratifying the covenants without unanimous support. Officials provided two previous examples of similar circumstances, in which the federal government was forced to wait for one or two provinces to provide formal consent to Canada's signature on an international treaty.[182] In each of these cases, the federal government waited instead of moving forward without unanimous support; thus, Stanford was concerned about the precedent that would be set if the Canadian government ratified the international covenants without Quebec's agreement.[183] He expected that, if Ottawa chose to proceed, Quebec would attack the government for acting unilaterally and overstepping federal jurisdiction. Despite these concerns, there was support in External Affairs for moving forward since it had been publicly established that, on the question of substance, Quebec agreed to Canada's accession, and that the problems of modalities had been settled at the December conference. The question was whether it was more important to meet the 19 May deadline or to wait for Quebec's formal agreement.

In the end, it did not matter. On 11 May, the minister cabled François Cloutier, drawing attention to the urgency of Canada's accession to the covenants. While awaiting Cloutier's reply, he sent a memo to the Governor General stating that "policy approval, in principle, for Canada to become party, by accession, to the two Human Rights Covenants and the Optional Protocol, was granted on December 4, 1975."[184] Only days before the deadline, Quebec's formal agreement did come through, and on 18 May, Secretary of State for External Affairs Allan MacEachern announced to the House of Commons that the consultation with the provinces was complete and that Canada's instruments of accession were to be filed with the Secretary-General of the United Nations the following day.[185] Canada had finally ratified the International Covenants on Human Rights, completing a process that had begun almost three decades earlier.

In 1966, although the Canadian government was less resistant to the idea of binding international human rights instruments, it remained unenthusiastic about their ratification. After taking initial steps to inform the provinces of the government's intent to begin the ratification process, federal officials were content to allow the process to take ten more years. To say, however, that the government's attitudes towards the covenants had not changed would be to confuse apathy with resistance. The Trudeau government's priorities were decidedly domestic, but the principles behind many of his initiatives were consistent with the principles of the International Bill of Rights. Despite the slow road to ratification, there was considerable support for the covenants within the federal and provincial governments. More importantly, the awareness of and support for human rights generally that had been building since the late 1950s exploded during the International Year for Human Rights in 1968 and led to direct pressure on the government to accede to the covenants. While this did not have an immediate effect, by 1975 the federal government recognized that it could no longer put off ratification. The process encountered an obstacle in the form of Quebec. Whereas the other nine provinces had given their official support for accession by 1974, the politics of handling Quebec were more difficult. Enmity between the Trudeau and Bourassa Liberals had developed after unsuccessful attempts to amend the Constitution in 1971, and had deepened by the mid-1970s. The root of the conflict was a struggle over power, and the question of whether federal or provincial governments had primacy within Canada's federal system.[186] In terms of the human rights covenants, this played out in negotiations over who would represent provincial interests in human rights matters at the United Nations. Ultimately, however, neither Ottawa nor Quebec wanted to appear to oppose the promotion of universal human rights. Pressures from the other provincial governments, the Canadian public, and Canada's allies at the UN accelerated the negotiations and led to the ratification of the international covenants in 1976.

Conclusion: The Making of the Myth

The momentum that had built surrounding Canada's policy towards international human rights was not limited to the International Covenants on Human Rights. The International Bill of Rights, now complete, was only one aspect of the United Nations' human rights regime. By 1975, the Canadian government had decided to re-engage with international human rights more generally. Canada supported a resolution at the General Assembly to designate 1975 as the launch for International Decade for Action to Combat Racism and Racial Discrimination, and played an active role in the 1975 World Conference on International Women's Year, held in Mexico City. The same year, Canada successfully applied for a second term on the UN Commission on Human Rights. Andrew Thompson describes this as the beginning of a period of robust engagement with the commission, which was focused on apartheid in South Africa, the colonial actions of Portugal, and human rights violations in Southeast Asia, the Middle East, and South America.[1] Canadian efforts to play an active role in human rights developments at the UN intensified after the ratification of the covenants. In 1979, Ottawa agreed to a second term on the UNCHR, and Canadian diplomat Yvon Beaulne served as chair until 1984. Beaulne gained a reputation for "energetic, concerned, and effective delegation leadership."[2] He took his position seriously, working, often unsuccessfully, to broker compromise over issues such as the drafting of a convention against torture, reform of the commission, and ongoing human rights violations around the globe.[3] During this time, Canada was also represented on the Commission on the Status of Women and the Committee on the

Elimination of All Forms of Racial Discrimination. The government successfully put forth a candidate, Walter Tarnopolsky, for the new Human Rights Committee established to monitor implementation of the *International Covenant on Civil and Political Rights,* and another one, Ronald St. John Macdonald, for the position of director of the UN Division on Human Rights. Whereas External Affairs had previously devoted very little in the way of resources and personnel to the issue of human rights, by the end of the 1970s it had created a division specifically dedicated to human rights issues, with a director and a small staff.[4] This active involvement was a profound departure from Canada's determined lack of participation in developing human rights instruments from the 1940s through the 1960s.

Canadian politicians and bureaucrats had begun to recognize the benefits of playing a more central role in the UN's human rights regime. At home, decades of campaigning by rights activists had resulted in a new understanding of rights as "human rights" and a growing expectation that government would promote and protect these rights. Many Canadians saw a connection between issues of discrimination and racism at home and Canada's commitment to international human rights law, and there was greater interest in Canada's participation in human rights developments at the UN. For example, after the declaration of 1971 as the International Year for Action to Combat Racism and Racial Discrimination, the UN Association of Canada noted that "our office has been deluged with requests for information on the Universal Declaration of Human Rights and on Canada's record of ratification of the covenants."[5] In this climate, active participation at the UN in the field of human rights was politically valuable. It also fit into the Trudeau government's broader vision of Canada as a "Just Society," which itself built upon the social protest and rights activism of the postwar period. Active support for the UN's human rights initiatives also raised Canada's status in the world community, as it promoted itself as a human rights protector.[6]

These examples of Canada's newfound enthusiasm for the global human rights regime tell only part of the story, however. In looking at Canada's involvement with the UNCHR, Thompson argues that even at the height of Canada's commitment, its record of support for human rights was mixed.[7] There were many cases throughout the 1970s and 1980s in which Canada refused to submit to international human rights standards or support UN human rights instruments. The most glaring was Ottawa's approach to the UN's Working Group on the Rights of Indigenous Populations (WGRIP), which was established in 1982. One of the goals of this group was to develop UN instruments that would translate Indigenous understandings of rights into international law. Canadian politicians and policy makers opposed this, worried that a declaration or covenant would include an article on the right to self-determination, giving legitimacy to nationalist movements and posing a threat the territorial integrity of Canada.[8] Ottawa approached a possible UN instrument on Indigenous rights the same way it had approached the *Universal Declaration of Human Rights* or the international covenants in their early years: fearful of openly opposing such a document, it remained non-committal and spoke of jurisdictional concerns. Canada was the subject of intense criticism from Indigenous representatives who condemned its past and present policies before the Working Group, from other nation states, and in the Working Group's final report. In response, Canadian officials did everything in their power to sideline the issue of Indigenous rights in the UN's human rights agenda.[9] When the UN did adopt the *Declaration on the Rights of Indigenous Peoples* in 2007, Canada was one of only four states that voted against the declaration.[10] Under intense pressure from the international community, Indigenous activists, and the Canadian public, the Harper government reversed its position on UNDRIP in November 2010. Canada's support was qualified, however, by a statement that it remained concerned with the meaning and interpretation of certain provisions of the declaration, and endorsed it as an aspirational document rather than a document of customary international law.[11] This approach to the UNDRIP was reminiscent of Canada's earlier policy towards the UDHR and Lester Pearson's own speech to the UN in 1948 qualifying Canada's support of that instrument.

Recent historical studies of Canadian foreign policy in the 1970s also demonstrate the limits of the government's willingness to allow human rights principles to influence its relations with other states. With significant pressure on the Canadian federal government from human rights organizations, women's groups, ethnic, labour, and church organizations, left-wing political groups, and opposition Members of Parliament, all of whom wanted to see Canada play a stronger role in global affairs in promoting social justice and protecting human rights, Canadian diplomats had begun to acknowledge their obligation to promote rights abroad.[12] One area where this played out was foreign aid, which Ottawa viewed as a means to demonstrate Canada's new trend of "humane internationalism."[13] Under the leadership of Maurice Strong and Paul Gérin-Lajoie, Canadian development assistance experienced unprecedented vitality in the 1970s, with programs expanding into all parts of the developing world.[14] Yet a significant portion of this aid went to states with poor human rights records, and even when Canada suspended aid to countries such as Vietnam, Uganda, Afghanistan, Chile, El Salvador, and Guatemala, no clear messages were sent to indicate that this was tied to their human rights records, and government cuts were not accompanied by any limitations on a state's access to public sector economic links.[15] While there was in some cases genuine support for human rights principles, and an interest in promoting them outside Canada, human rights were constantly in competition with other, more powerful factors, such as economic development or national security.[16] According to David Webster, who examines Canada's historical bilateral human rights dialogues (HRDs) with China, Cuba, and Indonesia, federal officials were reluctant to implement human rights principles in foreign policy decisions. He argues Canada has used its HRDs as a "tactic" to promote human rights without having to sacrifice a focus on trade, and that successive governments have "segregated rights from the mainstream of Canadian foreign policy, treating it as an optional extra."[17]

The same criticisms can be applied to the implementation of the UN's human rights conventions. While Canada had a much better record after 1976 of ratifying these conventions, Amnesty International's 2014 concern about a "growing gap" between the federal government's commitment to, and implementation of, international human rights norms reflects Ottawa's continued inconsistencies.[18] One reason for Canada's apparent unwillingness to take the necessary measures to ensure the consistent enforcement of UN human rights instruments relates to the fact that in many cases, such as with the International Bill of Rights, the government supported these instruments as a result of pressure from the public, from domestic rights activists, and from the international community rather than out of genuine commitment to their underlying principles. The Canadian public needs to understand Canada's long history of resisting international human rights, and focus more attention on holding Ottawa accountable for its international obligations rather than allowing politicians and policy makers to rely on the myth of Canada as a historic and vocal advocate for the protection of rights and freedoms around the world.

Making the Myth

What is perhaps most interesting in the story of Canada's policy towards the development of human rights at the UN is how quickly the federal government remade the story. Even as Ottawa was resisting the adoption of the UDHR in 1948, and then the draft First Covenant in the early 1950s, its delegates insisted that Canada did support the underlying principles of human rights. By the 1960s, as Canada's policies towards the two covenants shifted, federal politicians and diplomats began to embellish Canada's role in the development of early UN human rights initiatives. In a news release launching the Federal-Provincial Conference on Human Rights in December 1965, the Canadian government stated: "The United Nations General Assembly adopted the Universal Declaration of Human Rights on December 10, 1948. Since that time, Canada has played an active role in the preparation of international instruments designed to incorporate the objectives of the Declaration into law."[19] The following year, on the eve of the adoption of the international covenants at the United Nations, federal officials claimed that "Canada has always expressed strong support for international agreements which are designed to promote international behavior and respect for the rights of the individual."[20] Even Lester Pearson's comment in the House of Commons in 1967, that the international covenants on human rights instruments were a "significant step forward by the international community," obscured twenty years of opposition;[21] this was the same Pearson who had criticized the abstract notions outlined in the UN's human rights provisions as ill-suited to improving social, economic, or political conditions.

Canadian public awareness of human rights issues around the globe was on the rise and the federal government experienced a surge in the 1970s in the number of letters and informal inquiries into Canada's policy towards human rights abuses in other states. J.D. Livermore of External Affairs' UN Division wrote: "The past few years have seen an increasing awareness and concern in Canada regarding human rights in the international context."[22] Livermore went on to say: "Given that public interest on human rights issues is likely to remain high, it has been thought worthwhile to re-examine the basis for our present policy, which has in the past been interpreted by some as a lack of real concern on the part of the government."[23] His comments caused External Affairs to intensify their efforts to change this vision of Canada's historical policy towards international human rights. Phrases such as "strong support" and "active role" were increasingly used by Canadian politicians to describe Canada's past policy approach to the development of the UN's human rights instruments. Three years after Canada's ratification of the ICCPR and the ICESCR, the Department of External Affairs went so far as to claim that "Canada has been at the forefront of multilateral human rights initiatives designed to promote human rights."[24] This attempt to recover a new image for Canada as a global human rights defender not only was a response to a surge in public support for human rights principles but also complemented several important goals of Pierre Elliott Trudeau's Liberal government. At home, Ottawa had announced its policy of multiculturalism, which was designed to preserve cultural freedom for all individuals and help recognize the cultural contributions of diverse ethnic groups to Canadian society, and Trudeau was pushing the provinces to support the inclusion of a bill of rights in a repatriated constitution. In its relations with other states, the Department of External Affairs was working to forge positive relations with states in newly decolonized Africa and Asia, often using its image as a "humanitarian" state to distinguish itself from the United States and Britain. Canada's true history of prejudice and discrimination, and its early opposition to the development of human rights laws at the international level, contradicted the idea of a state that recognized the value and dignity of Canadians of all races and ethnic groups, all languages and all religions. Certainly, government officials did not want Canada to be remembered as a state that resisted human rights.

Andrew Lui argues that a crisis in internal national unity caused the changes in Canadian policy towards international human rights in the 1970s and that human rights became a tool that successive federal governments could use to project an image of Canada as a just society that was united despite its diversity.[25] While this book argues that the actual changes to government policy towards the International Bill of Rights were more of a response to pressure from a growing human rights movement and a shift in how most Canadians understood rights, it does support the argument that anxieties over national identity and unity contributed significantly to the federal government's desire to rewrite its history in relation to international human rights. The image of Canadians as historical rights advocates at home and as key players in the design of the UN's human rights regime was a tool that politicians used to promote a particular understanding of what it meant to be Canadian in a multicultural society. A statement inscribed on copies of the *Canadian Charter of Rights and Freedoms* widely distributed by the federal government following its formal adoption in 1982 reflected this understanding when it described the rights and freedoms in the new law as "the basic principles, the basic values and beliefs which hold us together as Canadians so that beyond our regional loyalties there is a way of life and a system of values which make us proud of the country that has given us such freedom and such immeasurable joy."[26]

As Canada's identity crisis intensified into the 1990s, fuelled by sovereignty movements in Quebec, concerns over American influence, and increased diversity as a result of changing immigration patterns, governmental and non-governmental institutions worked to counter ideas of difference in Canadian society by emphasizing, and in many cases exaggerating, those qualities that unified. In 1997, Canadian historian Desmond Morton noted these efforts: "As Canada once again threatens to disintegrate, a host of history and heritage organizations have emerged or revived with nation-saving concerns."[27] Perhaps the most well-known effort in this regard were the Heritage Minutes, a series of video clips depicting what were considered significant individuals, events, or stories in Canada's history, produced by the Historica Foundation beginning in 1991. Historica had been established by Charles R. Bronfman and the CRB Foundation to "enhance Canadianism" and, according to Erin Peters, the dramatized scenes featured in the Heritage Minutes were designed to encourage the Canadians watching them to assume these episodes as a part of their own personal heritage.[28] In 1997, Historica dedicated one of its Heritage Minutes to John Humphrey.[29]

The clip begins by depicting Humphrey defending the universalism of a proposed declaration of human rights to members of the UN Commission on Human Rights in 1947, and then fast-forwards to a scene from the European Court of Human Rights in 1986 in which lawyers are using the UDHR to challenge national employment laws that discriminate based on physical disability. In the background sits Humphrey, with a member of the audience leaning over and whispering: "Isn't that the Canadian that actually wrote the Universal Declaration of Human Rights?" That Humphrey is identified as "the Canadian" obscures not only the fact that he was not representing the Canadian government when he worked on the UDHR, but also that the Canadian government openly resisted the document. Emily West's work on collective memory, national identity, and popular culture illustrates how governments and institutions used popular culture, such as the Heritage Minutes clips, to "fill gaps in the Canadian collective memory."[30] John Humphrey, and in particular his role in helping to draft the UDHR, had become a symbol of the Canadian government's "central" role in developing international human rights instruments, despite the history to the contrary. This idea was furthered in 1998 when the government of Canada designed a commemorative stamp, recognizing the fiftieth anniversary of the signing of the UDHR, with Humphrey's portrait on it along with text from the declaration in the background.[31] Again, implicit in this celebration of Humphrey's role was the message that Canada was key in the drafting and development of the UN's International Bill of Rights. This is the message that the federal government wants us to hear.

Final Thoughts

What can be learned from a study of Canada's changing policy towards the International Bill of Rights? First, it illustrates the agency of non-state actors in the development of foreign policy. In their recent collection on Canada's relations with the Third World, editors Karen Dubinsky, Sean Mills, and Scott Rutherford argue that cultural attitudes and non-state actors have been central to the forging of relationships between Canada and the developing world.[32] Canadian diplomacy at the UN in the field of human rights reveals a similar pattern. Federal policy makers opposed the UN's efforts, but as a result of decades of hard work on the behalf of voluntary organizations, minority groups, rights associations, and individuals across the country, Canada's rights culture transformed from the 1940s to the 1970s, altering the environment in which the federal government set its policy. As members of civil society adopted the language of human rights and pushed for greater public awareness of rights issues, federal policy makers felt increased pressure to support the UN's human rights instruments. This supports the work of Canadian human rights historians who argue that governments have not been the drivers of Canada's rights revolution, and also suggests that we ought to rethink the role of non-state actors and cultural attitudes in our study of Canada's foreign policy approach to human rights.

Second, the debates over how to define human rights, and which rights ought to be included in law, demonstrate clearly that not all parties conceived of rights in the same way. Negotiating human rights laws required prioritizing rights in ways that generate inconsistencies and contradictions, and that excluded entire groups from the debate. In Canada, many vulnerable groups such as women, Indigenous peoples, gays and lesbians, and the disabled did not participate equally in the rights revolution in the period under study. Their silence teaches us as much about human rights as do the debates detailed throughout these pages. Even Canadian rights activists themselves prioritized rights, both when they negotiated to whom rights should apply and when they argued that domestic rights protections were more important to Canadians than the development of a set of international human rights. This book therefore reveals some of the limits to Canada's so-called Rights Revolution. The universalist discourse of human rights that came out of the United Nations in the 1940s challenged the more limited discourse of civil liberties that existed in Canada, and as a result policy makers resisted the adoption of the UDHR. Although understandings of rights in Canada evolved, even in the 1970s many Canadian activists struggled with the expansive definition of human rights articulated in the UN's human rights instruments.

Third, and in relation to the ongoing debate over the periodization of human rights history, a study of Canadian attitudes towards the International Bill of Rights demonstrates that the concept of universal human rights that emerged in the postwar period did influence the way in which Canadians talked about and ultimately understood rights. As early as the 1940s, government officials, non-governmental groups, and individuals throughout Canada were talking about "human rights," not simply "civil liberties" or "British liberties." Long before Ottawa formally supported the adoption of the International Covenants on Human Rights, politicians, scholars, rights activists, and marginalized Canadians adopted the UN's language of human rights to reformulate customary understandings of rights and freedoms in Canada. It was not until the late 1960s, however, that Canada's domestic human rights movement intersected with the global human rights movement and drove the federal government to take international human rights seriously. In addressing the question of exactly *when* this transformation took place, James Walker suggests that we have it wrong in looking for one moment in which a truly universal idea of human rights prevailed. He suggests rights are the product of a struggle; there have been many moments, and distinct movements, in Canada's human rights history, each of which brought about dramatically different ways of understanding the problems of inequality, prejudice, and exclusion in Canadian society.[33] In support of this idea, a goal of this book has been to demonstrate that the changes in Ottawa's policy towards the International Bill of Rights came slowly, heavily influenced by decades of work by individuals and groups outside of government who fought for a more inclusive and equal society. In the early years of the movement, many activists did not conceive of rights as universal, nor did they look to the UN or its human rights instruments as a solution to discrimination in Canada, but they did use the language and the example of the UN's human rights project as tools to push for enhanced rights protections at home. It has been through the struggle of these activists, and of marginalized groups across the country, that understandings of rights and freedoms in Canada changed. As Walker argues, it is the cumulative impact of these movements for greater equality that has shaped how Canadians interact with one another, their expectations of the state, and their understanding of the relationship between domestic and international human rights.[34]

Similarly, the adoption of the UDHR in 1948 represented yet one moment in the history of human rights, one in which a universal concept of inalienable rights was articulated into law. Yet in the decades that followed, the nature of these rights and to whom they applied remained contentious, both between and within states. This is made obvious by the nearly two decades it took to develop international conventions to more clearly define the principles laid out in the UDHR, and by the continued gap between the rhetoric of human rights and the reality of continued discrimination and prejudice around the globe. While states were certainly influenced by global factors, including the Cold War and decolonization, more attention needs to be paid to on-the-ground developments. By attributing the widespread acceptance of human rights principles by the

1970s to the collapse of other universalist schemes, Samuel Moyn ignores a much longer history of grassroots activism, and the growth and influence of domestic rights movements and civil society actors on international human rights. Any talk of the "triumph" of international human rights also ignores the reality that the fight for greater equality and the realization of human rights for all is an ongoing process. As we approach the seventy-fifth anniversary of the adoption of the UDHR, international human rights remain fragile, and many marginalized peoples have yet to feel the full benefit of the UN's human rights instruments.

Finally, by historicizing Canada's participation in the development of early human rights instruments at the United Nations, this book helps situate current debates and criticisms over Canada's adherence to contemporary instruments. Canada has historically viewed international human rights law with skepticism, resisted the development of international human rights standards, and used Canada's federal structure as justification for this resistance. Many of the same arguments that existed at the time of the adoption of the UDHR and the covenants continue to be used by federal policy makers today. Canada's ultimate support for the International Bill of Rights did not signify the triumph of international human rights in Canadian society, despite the rhetoric of government. The Canadian government never fully embraced the idea of submitting Canada to international human rights standards. When the federal government posts on its website that Canada has been "a consistently strong voice for the protection of human rights" since 1947, and NGOs criticize current governments for eroding Canada's "traditional reputation as a human rights leader," neither statement accurately represents Canada's historical relationship with international human rights law.

Appendix 1

Universal Declaration of Human Rights

Preamble

Whereas recognition of the inherent dignity and of the equal and inalienable rights of all members of the human family is the foundation of freedom, justice and peace in the world,

Whereas disregard and contempt for human rights have resulted in barbarous acts which have outraged the conscience of mankind, and the advent of a world in which human beings shall enjoy freedom of speech and belief and freedom from fear and want has been proclaimed as the highest aspiration of the common people,

Whereas it is essential, if man is not to be compelled to have recourse, as a last resort, to rebellion against tyranny and oppression, that human rights should be protected by the rule of law,

Whereas it is essential to promote the development of friendly relations between nations,

Whereas the peoples of the United Nations have in the Charter reaffirmed their faith in fundamental human rights, in the dignity and worth of the human person and in the equal rights of men and women and have determined to promote social progress and better standards of life in larger freedom,

Whereas Member States have pledged themselves to achieve, in cooperation with the United Nations, the promotion of universal respect for and observance of human rights and fundamental freedoms,

Whereas a common understanding of these rights and freedoms is of the greatest importance for the full realization of this pledge,

Now, therefore,

The General Assembly,

Proclaims this Universal Declaration of Human Rights as a common standard of achievement for all peoples and all nations, to the end that every individual and every organ of society, keeping this Declaration constantly in mind, shall strive by teaching and education to promote respect for these rights and freedoms and by progressive measures, national and international, to secure their universal and effective recognition and observance, both among the peoples of Member States themselves and among the peoples of territories under their jurisdiction.

Article 1

All human beings are born free and equal in dignity and rights. They are endowed with reason and conscience and should act towards one another in a spirit of brotherhood.

Article 2

Everyone is entitled to all the rights and freedoms set forth in this Declaration, without distinction of any kind, such as race, colour, sex, language, religion, political or other opinion, national or social origin, property, birth or other status. Furthermore, no distinction shall be made on the basis of the political, jurisdictional or international status of the country or territory to which a person belongs, whether it be independent, trust, non-self-governing or under any other limitation of sovereignty.

Article 3

Everyone has the right to life, liberty and security of person.

Article 4

No one shall be held in slavery or servitude; slavery and the slave trade shall be prohibited in all their forms.

Article 5

No one shall be subjected to torture or to cruel, inhuman or degrading treatment or punishment.

Article 6

Everyone has the right to recognition everywhere as a person before the law.

Article 7

All are equal before the law and are entitled without any discrimination to equal protection of the law. All are entitled to equal protection against any discrimination in violation of this Declaration and against any incitement to such discrimination.

Article 8

Everyone has the right to an effective remedy by the competent national tribunals for acts violating the fundamental rights granted him by the constitution or by law.

Article 9

No one shall be subjected to arbitrary arrest, detention or exile.

Article 10

Everyone is entitled in full equality to a fair and public hearing by an independent and impartial tribunal, in the determination of his rights and obligations and of any criminal charge against him.

Article 11

1. Everyone charged with a penal offence has the right to be presumed innocent until proved guilty according to law in a public trial at which he has had all the guarantees necessary for his defence.
2. No one shall be held guilty of any penal offence on account of any act or omission which did not constitute a penal offence, under national or international law, at the time when it was committed. Nor shall a heavier penalty be imposed than the one that was applicable at the time the penal offence was committed.

Article 12

No one shall be subjected to arbitrary interference with his privacy, family, home or correspondence, nor to attacks upon his honour and reputation.

Everyone has the right to the protection of the law against such interference or attacks.

Article 13

1. Everyone has the right to freedom of movement and residence within the borders of each State.
2. Everyone has the right to leave any country, including his own, and to return to his country.

Article 14

1. Everyone has the right to seek and to enjoy in other countries asylum from persecution.
2. This right may not be invoked in the case of prosecutions genuinely arising from non-political crimes or from acts contrary to the purposes and principles of the United Nations.

Article 15

1. Everyone has the right to a nationality.
2. No one shall be arbitrarily deprived of his nationality nor denied the right to change his nationality.

Article 16

1. Men and women of full age, without any limitation due to race, nationality or religion, have the right to marry and to found a family. They are entitled to equal rights as to marriage, during marriage and at its dissolution.
2. Marriage shall be entered into only with the free and full consent of the intending spouses.
3. The family is the natural and fundamental group unit of society and is entitled to protection by society and the State.

Article 17

1. Everyone has the right to own property alone as well as in association with others.
2. No one shall be arbitrarily deprived of his property.

Article 18

Everyone has the right to freedom of thought, conscience and religion; this right includes freedom to change his religion or belief, and freedom, either alone or in community with others and in public or private, to manifest his religion or belief in teaching, practice, worship and observance.

Article 19

Everyone has the right to freedom of opinion and expression; this right includes freedom to hold opinions without interference and to seek, receive and impart information and ideas through any media and regardless of frontiers.

Article 20

1. Everyone has the right to freedom of peaceful assembly and association.
2. No one may be compelled to belong to an association.

Article 21

1. Everyone has the right to take part in the government of his country, directly or through freely chosen representatives.
2. Everyone has the right to equal access to public service in his country.
3. The will of the people shall be the basis of the authority of government; this will shall be expressed in periodic and genuine elections which shall be by universal and equal suffrage and shall be held by secret vote or by equivalent free voting procedures.

Article 22

Everyone, as a member of society, has the right to social security and is entitled to realization, through national effort and international co-operation and in accordance with the organization and resources of each State, of the economic, social and cultural rights indispensable for his dignity and the free development of his personality.

Article 23

1. Everyone has the right to work, to free choice of employment, to just and favourable conditions of work and to protection against unemployment.

2. Everyone, without any discrimination, has the right to equal pay for equal work.
3. Everyone who works has the right to just and favourable remuneration ensuring for himself and his family an existence worthy of human dignity, and supplemented, if necessary, by other means of social protection.
4. Everyone has the right to form and to join trade unions for the protection of his interests.

Article 24

Everyone has the right to rest and leisure, including reasonable limitation of working hours and periodic holidays with pay.

Article 25

1. Everyone has the right to a standard of living adequate for the health and well-being of himself and of his family, including food, clothing, housing and medical care and necessary social services, and the right to security in the event of unemployment, sickness, disability, widowhood, old age or other lack of livelihood in circumstances beyond his control.
2. Motherhood and childhood are entitled to special care and assistance. All children, whether born in or out of wedlock, shall enjoy the same social protection.

Article 26

1. Everyone has the right to education. Education shall be free, at least in the elementary and fundamental stages. Elementary education shall be compulsory. Technical and professional education shall be made generally available and higher education shall be equally accessible to all on the basis of merit.
2. Education shall be directed to the full development of the human personality and to the strengthening of respect for human rights and fundamental freedoms. It shall promote understanding, tolerance and friendship among all nations, racial or religious groups, and shall further the activities of the United Nations for the maintenance of peace.

3. Parents have a prior right to choose the kind of education that shall be given to their children.

Article 27

1. Everyone has the right freely to participate in the cultural life of the community, to enjoy the arts and to share in scientific advancement and its benefits.
2. Everyone has the right to the protection of the moral and material interests resulting from any scientific, literary or artistic production of which he is the author.

Article 28

Everyone is entitled to a social and international order in which the rights and freedoms set forth in this Declaration can be fully realized.

Article 29

1. Everyone has duties to the community in which alone the free and full development of his personality is possible.
2. In the exercise of his rights and freedoms, everyone shall be subject only to such limitations as are determined by law solely for the purpose of securing due recognition and respect for the rights and freedoms of others and of meeting the just requirements of morality, public order and the general welfare in a democratic society.
3. These rights and freedoms may in no case be exercised contrary to the purposes and principles of the United Nations.

Article 30

Nothing in this Declaration may be interpreted as implying for any State, group or person any right to engage in any activity or to perform any act aimed at the destruction of any of the rights and freedoms set forth herein.

Appendix 2

International Covenant on Civil and Political Rights

Adopted and opened for signature, ratification and accession by General Assembly resolution 2200A (XXI) of 16 December 1966, entry into force 23 March 1976, in accordance with Article 49

Preamble

The States Parties to the present Covenant,

Considering that, in accordance with the principles proclaimed in the Charter of the United Nations, recognition of the inherent dignity and of the equal and inalienable rights of all members of the human family is the foundation of freedom, justice and peace in the world,

Recognizing that these rights derive from the inherent dignity of the human person,

Recognizing that, in accordance with the Universal Declaration of Human Rights, the ideal of free human beings enjoying civil and political freedom and freedom from fear and want can only be achieved if conditions are created whereby everyone may enjoy his civil and political rights, as well as his economic, social and cultural rights,

Considering the obligation of States under the Charter of the United Nations to promote universal respect for, and observance of, human rights and freedoms,

Realizing that the individual, having duties to other individuals and to the community to which he belongs, is under a responsibility to strive for the promotion and observance of the rights recognized in the present Covenant,

Agree upon the following articles:

PART I

Article 1

1. All peoples have the right of self-determination. By virtue of that right they freely determine their political status and freely pursue their economic, social and cultural development.
2. All peoples may, for their own ends, freely dispose of their natural wealth and resources without prejudice to any obligations arising out of international economic co-operation, based upon the principle of mutual benefit, and international law. In no case may a people be deprived of its own means of subsistence.
3. The States Parties to the present Covenant, including those having responsibility for the administration of Non-Self-Governing and Trust Territories, shall promote the realization of the right of self-determination, and shall respect that right, in conformity with the provisions of the Charter of the United Nations.

PART II

Article 2

1. Each State Party to the present Covenant undertakes to respect and to ensure to all individuals within its territory and subject to its jurisdiction the rights recognized in the present Covenant, without distinction of any kind, such as race, colour, sex, language, religion, political or other opinion, national or social origin, property, birth or other status.
2. Where not already provided for by existing legislative or other measures, each State Party to the present Covenant undertakes to take the necessary steps, in accordance with its constitutional processes and with the provisions of the present Covenant, to adopt such laws or other measures as may be necessary to give effect to the rights recognized in the present Covenant.
3. Each State Party to the present Covenant undertakes:
    a. To ensure that any person whose rights or freedoms as herein recognized are violated shall have an effective remedy, notwithstanding that the violation has been committed by persons acting in an official capacity;
    b. To ensure that any person claiming such a remedy shall have his right thereto determined by competent judicial, administrative or

legislative authorities, or by any other competent authority provided for by the legal system of the State, and to develop the possibilities of judicial remedy;

c. To ensure that the competent authorities shall enforce such remedies when granted.

Article 3

The States Parties to the present Covenant undertake to ensure the equal right of men and women to the enjoyment of all civil and political rights set forth in the present Covenant.

Article 4

1. In time of public emergency which threatens the life of the nation and the existence of which is officially proclaimed, the States Parties to the present Covenant may take measures derogating from their obligations under the present Covenant to the extent strictly required by the exigencies of the situation, provided that such measures are not inconsistent with their other obligations under international law and do not involve discrimination solely on the ground of race, colour, sex, language, religion or social origin.
2. No derogation from articles 6, 7, 8 (paragraphs I and 2), 11, 15, 16 and 18 may be made under this provision.
3. Any State Party to the present Covenant availing itself of the right of derogation shall immediately inform the other States Parties to the present Covenant, through the intermediary of the Secretary-General of the United Nations, of the provisions from which it has derogated and of the reasons by which it was actuated. A further communication shall be made, through the same intermediary, on the date on which it terminates such derogation.

Article 5

1. Nothing in the present Covenant may be interpreted as implying for any State, group or person any right to engage in any activity or perform any act aimed at the destruction of any of the rights and freedoms recognized herein or at their limitation to a greater extent than is provided for in the present Covenant.

2. There shall be no restriction upon or derogation from any of the fundamental human rights recognized or existing in any State Party to the present Covenant pursuant to law, conventions, regulations or custom on the pretext that the present Covenant does not recognize such rights or that it recognizes them to a lesser extent.

PART III

Article 6

1. Every human being has the inherent right to life. This right shall be protected by law. No one shall be arbitrarily deprived of his life.
2. In countries which have not abolished the death penalty, sentence of death may be imposed only for the most serious crimes in accordance with the law in force at the time of the commission of the crime and not contrary to the provisions of the present Covenant and to the Convention on the Prevention and Punishment of the Crime of Genocide. This penalty can only be carried out pursuant to a final judgement rendered by a competent court.
3. When deprivation of life constitutes the crime of genocide, it is understood that nothing in this article shall authorize any State Party to the present Covenant to derogate in any way from any obligation assumed under the provisions of the Convention on the Prevention and Punishment of the Crime of Genocide.
4. Anyone sentenced to death shall have the right to seek pardon or commutation of the sentence. Amnesty, pardon or commutation of the sentence of death may be granted in all cases.
5. Sentence of death shall not be imposed for crimes committed by persons below eighteen years of age and shall not be carried out on pregnant women.
6. Nothing in this article shall be invoked to delay or to prevent the abolition of capital punishment by any State Party to the present Covenant.

Article 7

No one shall be subjected to torture or to cruel, inhuman or degrading treatment or punishment. In particular, no one shall be subjected without his free consent to medical or scientific experimentation.

Article 8

1. No one shall be held in slavery; slavery and the slave-trade in all their forms shall be prohibited.
2. No one shall be held in servitude.
3.
   a. No one shall be required to perform forced or compulsory labour;
   b. Paragraph 3 (a) shall not be held to preclude, in countries where imprisonment with hard labour may be imposed as a punishment for a crime, the performance of hard labour in pursuance of a sentence to such punishment by a competent court;
   c. For the purpose of this paragraph the term "forced or compulsory labour" shall not include:
      i. Any work or service, not referred to in subparagraph (b), normally required of a person who is under detention in consequence of a lawful order of a court, or of a person during conditional release from such detention;
      ii. Any service of a military character and, in countries where conscientious objection is recognized, any national service required by law of conscientious objectors;
      iii. Any service exacted in cases of emergency or calamity threatening the life or well-being of the community;
      iv. Any work or service which forms part of normal civil obligations.

Article 9

1. Everyone has the right to liberty and security of person. No one shall be subjected to arbitrary arrest or detention. No one shall be deprived of his liberty except on such grounds and in accordance with such procedure as are established by law.
2. Anyone who is arrested shall be informed, at the time of arrest, of the reasons for his arrest and shall be promptly informed of any charges against him.
3. Anyone arrested or detained on a criminal charge shall be brought promptly before a judge or other officer authorized by law to exercise judicial power and shall be entitled to trial within a reasonable time or to release. It shall not be the general rule that persons awaiting trial shall be detained in custody, but release may be subject to guarantees

to appear for trial, at any other stage of the judicial proceedings, and, should occasion arise, for execution of the judgement.

4. Anyone who is deprived of his liberty by arrest or detention shall be entitled to take proceedings before a court, in order that that court may decide without delay on the lawfulness of his detention and order his release if the detention is not lawful.
5. Anyone who has been the victim of unlawful arrest or detention shall have an enforceable right to compensation.

Article 10

1. All persons deprived of their liberty shall be treated with humanity and with respect for the inherent dignity of the human person.
2.
    a. Accused persons shall, save in exceptional circumstances, be segregated from convicted persons and shall be subject to separate treatment appropriate to their status as unconvicted persons;
    b. Accused juvenile persons shall be separated from adults and brought as speedily as possible for adjudication.
3. The penitentiary system shall comprise treatment of prisoners the essential aim of which shall be their reformation and social rehabilitation. Juvenile offenders shall be segregated from adults and be accorded treatment appropriate to their age and legal status.

Article 11

No one shall be imprisoned merely on the ground of inability to fulfil a contractual obligation.

Article 12

1. Everyone lawfully within the territory of a State shall, within that territory, have the right to liberty of movement and freedom to choose his residence.
2. Everyone shall be free to leave any country, including his own.
3. The above-mentioned rights shall not be subject to any restrictions except those which are provided by law, are necessary to protect national security, public order (ordre public), public health or morals or the rights

and freedoms of others, and are consistent with the other rights recognized in the present Covenant.

4. No one shall be arbitrarily deprived of the right to enter his own country.

Article 13

An alien lawfully in the territory of a State Party to the present Covenant may be expelled therefrom only in pursuance of a decision reached in accordance with law and shall, except where compelling reasons of national security otherwise require, be allowed to submit the reasons against his expulsion and to have his case reviewed by, and be represented for the purpose before, the competent authority or a person or persons especially designated by the competent authority.

Article 14

1. All persons shall be equal before the courts and tribunals. In the determination of any criminal charge against him, or of his rights and obligations in a suit at law, everyone shall be entitled to a fair and public hearing by a competent, independent and impartial tribunal established by law. The press and the public may be excluded from all or part of a trial for reasons of morals, public order (ordre public) or national security in a democratic society, or when the interest of the private lives of the parties so requires, or to the extent strictly necessary in the opinion of the court in special circumstances where publicity would prejudice the interests of justice; but any judgement rendered in a criminal case or in a suit at law shall be made public except where the interest of juvenile persons otherwise requires or the proceedings concern matrimonial disputes or the guardianship of children.
2. Everyone charged with a criminal offence shall have the right to be presumed innocent until proved guilty according to law.
3. In the determination of any criminal charge against him, everyone shall be entitled to the following minimum guarantees, in full equality:
   a. To be informed promptly and in detail in a language which he understands of the nature and cause of the charge against him;

b. To have adequate time and facilities for the preparation of his defence and to communicate with counsel of his own choosing;
c. To be tried without undue delay;
d. To be tried in his presence, and to defend himself in person or through legal assistance of his own choosing; to be informed, if he does not have legal assistance, of this right; and to have legal assistance assigned to him, in any case where the interests of justice so require, and without payment by him in any such case if he does not have sufficient means to pay for it;
e. To examine, or have examined, the witnesses against him and to obtain the attendance and examination of witnesses on his behalf under the same conditions as witnesses against him;
f. To have the free assistance of an interpreter if he cannot understand or speak the language used in court;
g. Not to be compelled to testify against himself or to confess guilt.

4. In the case of juvenile persons, the procedure shall be such as will take account of their age and the desirability of promoting their rehabilitation.
5. Everyone convicted of a crime shall have the right to his conviction and sentence being reviewed by a higher tribunal according to law.
6. When a person has by a final decision been convicted of a criminal offence and when subsequently his conviction has been reversed or he has been pardoned on the ground that a new or newly discovered fact shows conclusively that there has been a miscarriage of justice, the person who has suffered punishment as a result of such conviction shall be compensated according to law, unless it is proved that the non-disclosure of the unknown fact in time is wholly or partly attributable to him.
7. No one shall be liable to be tried or punished again for an offence for which he has already been finally convicted or acquitted in accordance with the law and penal procedure of each country.

Article 15

1. No one shall be held guilty of any criminal offence on account of any act or omission which did not constitute a criminal offence, under national or international law, at the time when it was committed. Nor shall a heavier penalty be imposed than the one that was applicable

at the time when the criminal offence was committed. If, subsequent to the commission of the offence, provision is made by law for the imposition of the lighter penalty, the offender shall benefit thereby.

2. Nothing in this article shall prejudice the trial and punishment of any person for any act or omission which, at the time when it was committed, was criminal according to the general principles of law recognized by the community of nations.

Article 16

Everyone shall have the right to recognition everywhere as a person before the law.

Article 17

1. No one shall be subjected to arbitrary or unlawful interference with his privacy, family, home or correspondence, nor to unlawful attacks on his honour and reputation.
2. Everyone has the right to the protection of the law against such interference or attacks.

Article 18

1. Everyone shall have the right to freedom of thought, conscience and religion. This right shall include freedom to have or to adopt a religion or belief of his choice, and freedom, either individually or in community with others and in public or private, to manifest his religion or belief in worship, observance, practice and teaching.
2. No one shall be subject to coercion which would impair his freedom to have or to adopt a religion or belief of his choice.
3. Freedom to manifest one's religion or beliefs may be subject only to such limitations as are prescribed by law and are necessary to protect public safety, order, health, or morals or the fundamental rights and freedoms of others.
4. The States Parties to the present Covenant undertake to have respect for the liberty of parents and, when applicable, legal guardians to ensure the religious and moral education of their children in conformity with their own convictions.

Article 19

1. Everyone shall have the right to hold opinions without interference.
2. Everyone shall have the right to freedom of expression; this right shall include freedom to seek, receive and impart information and ideas of all kinds, regardless of frontiers, either orally, in writing or in print, in the form of art, or through any other media of his choice.
3. The exercise of the rights provided for in paragraph 2 of this article carries with it special duties and responsibilities. It may therefore be subject to certain restrictions, but these shall only be such as are provided by law and are necessary:
   a. For respect of the rights or reputations of others;
   b. For the protection of national security or of public order (ordre public), or of public health or morals.

Article 20

1. Any propaganda for war shall be prohibited by law.
2. Any advocacy of national, racial or religious hatred that constitutes incitement to discrimination, hostility or violence shall be prohibited by law.

Article 21

The right of peaceful assembly shall be recognized. No restrictions may be placed on the exercise of this right other than those imposed in conformity with the law and which are necessary in a democratic society in the interests of national security or public safety, public order (ordre public), the protection of public health or morals or the protection of the rights and freedoms of others.

Article 22

1. Everyone shall have the right to freedom of association with others, including the right to form and join trade unions for the protection of his interests.
2. No restrictions may be placed on the exercise of this right other than those which are prescribed by law and which are necessary in a democratic society in the interests of national security or public safety, public

order *(ordre public)*, the protection of public health or morals or the protection of the rights and freedoms of others. This article shall not prevent the imposition of lawful restrictions on members of the armed forces and of the police in their exercise of this right.

3. Nothing in this article shall authorize States Parties to the International Labour Organisation Convention of 1948 concerning Freedom of Association and Protection of the Right to Organize to take legislative measures which would prejudice, or to apply the law in such a manner as to prejudice, the guarantees provided for in that Convention.

Article 23

1. The family is the natural and fundamental group unit of society and is entitled to protection by society and the State.
2. The right of men and women of marriageable age to marry and to found a family shall be recognized.
3. No marriage shall be entered into without the free and full consent of the intending spouses.
4. States Parties to the present Covenant shall take appropriate steps to ensure equality of rights and responsibilities of spouses as to marriage, during marriage and at its dissolution. In the case of dissolution, provision shall be made for the necessary protection of any children.

Article 24

1. Every child shall have, without any discrimination as to race, colour, sex, language, religion, national or social origin, property or birth, the right to such measures of protection as are required by his status as a minor, on the part of his family, society and the State.
2. Every child shall be registered immediately after birth and shall have a name.
3. Every child has the right to acquire a nationality.

Article 25

Every citizen shall have the right and the opportunity, without any of the distinctions mentioned in article 2 and without unreasonable restrictions:

a. To take part in the conduct of public affairs, directly or through freely chosen representatives;

b. To vote and to be elected at genuine periodic elections which shall be by universal and equal suffrage and shall be held by secret ballot, guaranteeing the free expression of the will of the electors;
c. To have access, on general terms of equality, to public service in his country.

Article 26

All persons are equal before the law and are entitled without any discrimination to the equal protection of the law. In this respect, the law shall prohibit any discrimination and guarantee to all persons equal and effective protection against discrimination on any ground such as race, colour, sex, language, religion, political or other opinion, national or social origin, property, birth or other status.

Article 27

In those States in which ethnic, religious or linguistic minorities exist, persons belonging to such minorities shall not be denied the right, in community with the other members of their group, to enjoy their own culture, to profess and practise their own religion, or to use their own language.

PART IV

Article 28

1. There shall be established a Human Rights Committee (hereafter referred to in the present Covenant as the Committee). It shall consist of eighteen members and shall carry out the functions hereinafter provided.
2. The Committee shall be composed of nationals of the States Parties to the present Covenant who shall be persons of high moral character and recognized competence in the field of human rights, consideration being given to the usefulness of the participation of some persons having legal experience.
3. The members of the Committee shall be elected and shall serve in their personal capacity.

Article 29

1. The members of the Committee shall be elected by secret ballot from a list of persons possessing the qualifications prescribed in article 28 and nominated for the purpose by the States Parties to the present Covenant.

2. Each State Party to the present Covenant may nominate not more than two persons. These persons shall be nationals of the nominating State.
3. A person shall be eligible for renomination.

Article 30

1. The initial election shall be held no later than six months after the date of the entry into force of the present Covenant.
2. At least four months before the date of each election to the Committee, other than an election to fill a vacancy declared in accordance with article 34, the Secretary-General of the United Nations shall address a written invitation to the States Parties to the present Covenant to submit their nominations for membership of the Committee within three months.
3. The Secretary-General of the United Nations shall prepare a list in alphabetical order of all the persons thus nominated, with an indication of the States Parties which have nominated them, and shall submit it to the States Parties to the present Covenant no later than one month before the date of each election.
4. Elections of the members of the Committee shall be held at a meeting of the States Parties to the present Covenant convened by the Secretary General of the United Nations at the Headquarters of the United Nations. At that meeting, for which two thirds of the States Parties to the present Covenant shall constitute a quorum, the persons elected to the Committee shall be those nominees who obtain the largest number of votes and an absolute majority of the votes of the representatives of States Parties present and voting.

Article 31

1. The Committee may not include more than one national of the same State.
2. In the election of the Committee, consideration shall be given to equitable geographical distribution of membership and to the representation of the different forms of civilization and of the principal legal systems.

Article 32

1. The members of the Committee shall be elected for a term of four years. They shall be eligible for re-election if renominated. However, the terms of nine of the members elected at the first election shall expire at the end of two years; immediately after the first election, the names of these nine members shall be chosen by lot by the Chairman of the meeting referred to in article 30, paragraph 4.
2. Elections at the expiry of office shall be held in accordance with the preceding articles of this part of the present Covenant.

Article 33

1. If, in the unanimous opinion of the other members, a member of the Committee has ceased to carry out his functions for any cause other than absence of a temporary character, the Chairman of the Committee shall notify the Secretary-General of the United Nations, who shall then declare the seat of that member to be vacant.
2. In the event of the death or the resignation of a member of the Committee, the Chairman shall immediately notify the Secretary-General of the United Nations, who shall declare the seat vacant from the date of death or the date on which the resignation takes effect.

Article 34

1. When a vacancy is declared in accordance with article 33 and if the term of office of the member to be replaced does not expire within six months of the declaration of the vacancy, the Secretary-General of the United Nations shall notify each of the States Parties to the present Covenant, which may within two months submit nominations in accordance with article 29 for the purpose of filling the vacancy.
2. The Secretary-General of the United Nations shall prepare a list in alphabetical order of the persons thus nominated and shall submit it to the States Parties to the present Covenant. The election to fill the vacancy shall then take place in accordance with the relevant provisions of this part of the present Covenant.

3. A member of the Committee elected to fill a vacancy declared in accordance with article 33 shall hold office for the remainder of the term of the member who vacated the seat on the Committee under the provisions of that article.

Article 35

The members of the Committee shall, with the approval of the General Assembly of the United Nations, receive emoluments from United Nations resources on such terms and conditions as the General Assembly may decide, having regard to the importance of the Committee's responsibilities.

Article 36

The Secretary-General of the United Nations shall provide the necessary staff and facilities for the effective performance of the functions of the Committee under the present Covenant.

Article 37

1. The Secretary-General of the United Nations shall convene the initial meeting of the Committee at the Headquarters of the United Nations.
2. After its initial meeting, the Committee shall meet at such times as shall be provided in its rules of procedure.
3. The Committee shall normally meet at the Headquarters of the United Nations or at the United Nations Office at Geneva.

Article 38

Every member of the Committee shall, before taking up his duties, make a solemn declaration in open committee that he will perform his functions impartially and conscientiously.

Article 39

1. The Committee shall elect its officers for a term of two years. They may be re-elected.
2. The Committee shall establish its own rules of procedure, but these rules shall provide, inter alia, that:
   a. Twelve members shall constitute a quorum;

b. Decisions of the Committee shall be made by a majority vote of the members present.

Article 40

1. The States Parties to the present Covenant undertake to submit reports on the measures they have adopted which give effect to the rights recognized herein and on the progress made in the enjoyment of those rights:
   a. Within one year of the entry into force of the present Covenant for the States Parties concerned;
   b. Thereafter whenever the Committee so requests.
2. All reports shall be submitted to the Secretary-General of the United Nations, who shall transmit them to the Committee for consideration. Reports shall indicate the factors and difficulties, if any, affecting the implementation of the present Covenant.
3. The Secretary-General of the United Nations may, after consultation with the Committee, transmit to the specialized agencies concerned copies of such parts of the reports as may fall within their field of competence.
4. The Committee shall study the reports submitted by the States Parties to the present Covenant. It shall transmit its reports, and such general comments as it may consider appropriate, to the States Parties. The Committee may also transmit to the Economic and Social Council these comments along with the copies of the reports it has received from States Parties to the present Covenant.
5. The States Parties to the present Covenant may submit to the Committee observations on any comments that may be made in accordance with paragraph 4 of this article.

Article 41

1. A State Party to the present Covenant may at any time declare under this article that it recognizes the competence of the Committee to receive and consider communications to the effect that a State Party claims that another State Party is not fulfilling its obligations under the present Covenant. Communications under this article may be received and considered only if submitted by a

State Party which has made a declaration recognizing in regard to itself the competence of the Committee. No communication shall be received by the Committee if it concerns a State Party which has not made such a declaration. Communications received under this article shall be dealt with in accordance with the following procedure:

a. If a State Party to the present Covenant considers that another State Party is not giving effect to the provisions of the present Covenant, it may, by written communication, bring the matter to the attention of that State Party. Within three months after the receipt of the communication the receiving State shall afford the State which sent the communication an explanation, or any other statement in writing clarifying the matter which should include, to the extent possible and pertinent, reference to domestic procedures and remedies taken, pending, or available in the matter;
b. If the matter is not adjusted to the satisfaction of both States Parties concerned within six months after the receipt by the receiving State of the initial communication, either State shall have the right to refer the matter to the Committee, by notice given to the Committee and to the other State;
c. The Committee shall deal with a matter referred to it only after it has ascertained that all available domestic remedies have been invoked and exhausted in the matter, in conformity with the generally recognized principles of international law. This shall not be the rule where the application of the remedies is unreasonably prolonged;
d. The Committee shall hold closed meetings when examining communications under this article;
e. Subject to the provisions of subparagraph (c), the Committee shall make available its good offices to the States Parties concerned with a view to a friendly solution of the matter on the basis of respect for human rights and fundamental freedoms as recognized in the present Covenant;
f. In any matter referred to it, the Committee may call upon the States Parties concerned, referred to in subparagraph (b), to supply any relevant information;

g. The States Parties concerned, referred to in subparagraph (b), shall have the right to be represented when the matter is being considered in the Committee and to make submissions orally and/or in writing;
h. The Committee shall, within twelve months after the date of receipt of notice under subparagraph (b), submit a report:
   i. If a solution within the terms of subparagraph (e) is reached, the Committee shall confine its report to a brief statement of the facts and of the solution reached;
   ii. If a solution within the terms of subparagraph (e) is not reached, the Committee shall confine its report to a brief statement of the facts; the written submissions and record of the oral submissions made by the States Parties concerned shall be attached to the report. In every matter, the report shall be communicated to the States Parties concerned.

2. The provisions of this article shall come into force when ten States Parties to the present Covenant have made declarations under paragraph I of this article. Such declarations shall be deposited by the States Parties with the Secretary-General of the United Nations, who shall transmit copies thereof to the other States Parties. A declaration may be withdrawn at any time by notification to the Secretary-General. Such a withdrawal shall not prejudice the consideration of any matter which is the subject of a communication already transmitted under this article; no further communication by any State Party shall be received after the notification of withdrawal of the declaration has been received by the Secretary-General, unless the State Party concerned has made a new declaration.

Article 42

1.
   a. If a matter referred to the Committee in accordance with article 41 is not resolved to the satisfaction of the States Parties concerned, the Committee may, with the prior consent of the States Parties concerned, appoint an ad hoc Conciliation Commission (hereinafter referred to as the Commission). The good offices of the Commission shall be made available to the States Parties concerned with a view to an amicable

solution of the matter on the basis of respect for the present Covenant;

b. The Commission shall consist of five persons acceptable to the States Parties concerned. If the States Parties concerned fail to reach agreement within three months on all or part of the composition of the Commission, the members of the Commission concerning whom no agreement has been reached shall be elected by secret ballot by a two-thirds majority vote of the Committee from among its members.

2. The members of the Commission shall serve in their personal capacity. They shall not be nationals of the States Parties concerned, or of a State not Party to the present Covenant, or of a State Party which has not made a declaration under article 41.
3. The Commission shall elect its own Chairman and adopt its own rules of procedure.
4. The meetings of the Commission shall normally be held at the Headquarters of the United Nations or at the United Nations Office at Geneva. However, they may be held at such other convenient places as the Commission may determine in consultation with the Secretary-General of the United Nations and the States Parties concerned.
5. The secretariat provided in accordance with article 36 shall also service the commissions appointed under this article.
6. The information received and collated by the Committee shall be made available to the Commission and the Commission may call upon the States Parties concerned to supply any other relevant information.
7. When the Commission has fully considered the matter, but in any event not later than twelve months after having been seized of the matter, it shall submit to the Chairman of the Committee a report for communication to the States Parties concerned:
   a. If the Commission is unable to complete its consideration of the matter within twelve months, it shall confine its report to a brief statement of the status of its consideration of the matter;
   b. If an amicable solution to the matter on tie basis of respect for human rights as recognized in the present Covenant is reached,

the Commission shall confine its report to a brief statement of the facts and of the solution reached;

c. If a solution within the terms of subparagraph (b) is not reached, the Commission's report shall embody its findings on all questions of fact relevant to the issues between the States Parties concerned, and its views on the possibilities of an amicable solution of the matter. This report shall also contain the written submissions and a record of the oral submissions made by the States Parties concerned;

d. If the Commission's report is submitted under subparagraph (c), the States Parties concerned shall, within three months of the receipt of the report, notify the Chairman of the Committee whether or not they accept the contents of the report of the Commission.

8. The provisions of this article are without prejudice to the responsibilities of the Committee under article 41.
9. The States Parties concerned shall share equally all the expenses of the members of the Commission in accordance with estimates to be provided by the Secretary-General of the United Nations.
10. The Secretary-General of the United Nations shall be empowered to pay the expenses of the members of the Commission, if necessary, before reimbursement by the States Parties concerned, in accordance with paragraph 9 of this article.

Article 43

The members of the Committee, and of the ad hoc conciliation commissions which may be appointed under article 42, shall be entitled to the facilities, privileges and immunities of experts on mission for the United Nations as laid down in the relevant sections of the Convention on the Privileges and Immunities of the United Nations.

Article 44

The provisions for the implementation of the present Covenant shall apply without prejudice to the procedures prescribed in the field of human rights by or under the constituent instruments and the conventions of the United

Nations and of the specialized agencies and shall not prevent the States Parties to the present Covenant from having recourse to other procedures for settling a dispute in accordance with general or special international agreements in force between them.

Article 45

The Committee shall submit to the General Assembly of the United Nations, through the Economic and Social Council, an annual report on its activities.

PART V

Article 46

Nothing in the present Covenant shall be interpreted as impairing the provisions of the Charter of the United Nations and of the constitutions of the specialized agencies which define the respective responsibilities of the various organs of the United Nations and of the specialized agencies in regard to the matters dealt with in the present Covenant.

Article 47

Nothing in the present Covenant shall be interpreted as impairing the inherent right of all peoples to enjoy and utilize fully and freely their natural wealth and resources.

PART VI

Article 48

1. The present Covenant is open for signature by any State Member of the United Nations or member of any of its specialized agencies, by any State Party to the Statute of the International Court of Justice, and by any other State which has been invited by the General Assembly of the United Nations to become a Party to the present Covenant.
2. The present Covenant is subject to ratification. Instruments of ratification shall be deposited with the Secretary-General of the United Nations.

3. The present Covenant shall be open to accession by any State referred to in paragraph 1 of this article.
4. Accession shall be effected by the deposit of an instrument of accession with the Secretary-General of the United Nations.
5. The Secretary-General of the United Nations shall inform all States which have signed this Covenant or acceded to it of the deposit of each instrument of ratification or accession.

Article 49

1. The present Covenant shall enter into force three months after the date of the deposit with the Secretary-General of the United Nations of the thirty-fifth instrument of ratification or instrument of accession.
2. For each State ratifying the present Covenant or acceding to it after the deposit of the thirty-fifth instrument of ratification or instrument of accession, the present Covenant shall enter into force three months after the date of the deposit of its own instrument of ratification or instrument of accession.

Article 50

The provisions of the present Covenant shall extend to all parts of federal States without any limitations or exceptions.

Article 51

1. Any State Party to the present Covenant may propose an amendment and file it with the Secretary-General of the United Nations. The Secretary-General of the United Nations shall thereupon communicate any proposed amendments to the States Parties to the present Covenant with a request that they notify him whether they favour a conference of States Parties for the purpose of considering and voting upon the proposals. In the event that at least one third of the States Parties favours such a conference, the Secretary-General shall convene the conference under the auspices of the United Nations. Any amendment adopted by a majority of the States Parties present and voting at the conference shall be submitted to the General Assembly of the United Nations for approval.

2. Amendments shall come into force when they have been approved by the General Assembly of the United Nations and accepted by a two-thirds majority of the States Parties to the present Covenant in accordance with their respective constitutional processes.
3. When amendments come into force, they shall be binding on those States Parties which have accepted them, other States Parties still being bound by the provisions of the present Covenant and any earlier amendment which they have accepted.

Article 52

1. Irrespective of the notifications made under article 48, paragraph 5, the Secretary-General of the United Nations shall inform all States referred to in paragraph I of the same article of the following particulars:
   a. Signatures, ratifications and accessions under article 48;
   b. The date of the entry into force of the present Covenant under article 49 and the date of the entry into force of any amendments under article 51.

Article 53

1. The present Covenant, of which the Chinese, English, French, Russian and Spanish texts are equally authentic, shall be deposited in the archives of the United Nations.
2. The Secretary-General of the United Nations shall transmit certified copies of the present Covenant to all States referred to in article 48.

Appendix 3

International Covenant on Economic, Social and Cultural Rights

Adopted and opened for signature, ratification and accession by General Assembly resolution 2200A (XXI) of 16 December 1966, entry into force 3 January 1976, in accordance with article 27

Preamble

The States Parties to the present Covenant

Considering that, in accordance with the principles proclaimed in the Charter of the United Nations, recognition of the inherent dignity and of the equal and inalienable rights of all members of the human family is the foundation of freedom, justice and peace in the world,

Recognizing that these rights derive from the inherent dignity of the human person,

Recognizing that, in accordance with the Universal Declaration of Human Rights, the ideal of free human beings enjoying freedom from fear and want can only be achieved if conditions are created whereby everyone may enjoy his economic, social and cultural rights, as well as his civil and political rights,

Considering the obligation of States under the Charter of the United Nations to promote universal respect for, and observance of, human rights and freedoms,

Realizing that the individual, having duties to other individuals and to the community to which he belongs, is under a responsibility to strive for the promotion and observance of the rights recognized in the present Covenant,

Agree upon the following articles:

PART I

Article 1

1. All peoples have the right of self-determination. By virtue of that right they freely determine their political status and freely pursue their economic, social and cultural development.
2. All peoples may, for their own ends, freely dispose of their natural wealth and resources without prejudice to any obligations arising out of international economic co-operation, based upon the principle of mutual benefit, and international law. In no case may a people be deprived of its own means of subsistence.
3. The States Parties to the present Covenant, including those having responsibility for the administration of Non-Self-Governing and Trust Territories, shall promote the realization of the right of self-determination, and shall respect that right, in conformity with the provisions of the Charter of the United Nations.

PART II

Article 2

1. Each State Party to the present Covenant undertakes to take steps, individually and through international assistance and co-operation, especially economic and technical, to the maximum of its available resources, with a view to achieving progressively the full realization of the rights recognized in the present Covenant by all appropriate means, including particularly the adoption of legislative measures.
2. The States Parties to the present Covenant undertake to guarantee that the rights enunciated in the present Covenant will be exercised without discrimination of any kind as to race, colour, sex, language, religion, political or other opinion, national or social origin, property, birth or other status.
3. Developing countries, with due regard to human rights and their national economy, may determine to what extent they would guarantee

the economic rights recognized in the present Covenant to nonnationals.

Article 3

The States Parties to the present Covenant undertake to ensure the equal right of men and women to the enjoyment of all economic, social and cultural rights set forth in the present Covenant.

Article 4

The States Parties to the present Covenant recognize that, in the enjoyment of those rights provided by the State in conformity with the present Covenant, the State may subject such rights only to such limitations as are determined by law only in so far as this may be compatible with the nature of these rights and solely for the purpose of promoting the general welfare in a democratic society.

Article 5

1. Nothing in the present Covenant may be interpreted as implying for any State, group or person any right to engage in any activity or to perform any act aimed at the destruction of any of the rights or freedoms recognized herein, or at their limitation to a greater extent than is provided for in the present Covenant.
2. No restriction upon or derogation from any of the fundamental human rights recognized or existing in any country in virtue of law, conventions, regulations or custom shall be admitted on the pretext that the present Covenant does not recognize such rights or that it recognizes them to a lesser extent.

PART III

Article 6

1. The States Parties to the present Covenant recognize the right to work, which includes the right of everyone to the opportunity to gain his living by work which he freely chooses or accepts, and will take appropriate steps to safeguard this right.

2. The steps to be taken by a State Party to the present Covenant to achieve the full realization of this right shall include technical and vocational guidance and training programmes, policies and techniques to achieve steady economic, social and cultural development and full and productive employment under conditions safeguarding fundamental political and economic freedoms to the individual.

Article 7

The States Parties to the present Covenant recognize the right of everyone to the enjoyment of just and favourable conditions of work which ensure, in particular:

(a) Remuneration which provides all workers, as a minimum, with:
   i. Fair wages and equal remuneration for work of equal value without distinction of any kind, in particular women being guaranteed conditions of work not inferior to those enjoyed by men, with equal pay for equal work;
   ii. A decent living for themselves and their families in accordance with the provisions of the present Covenant;
(b) Safe and healthy working conditions;
(c) Equal opportunity for everyone to be promoted in his employment to an appropriate higher level, subject to no considerations other than those of seniority and competence;
(d) Rest, leisure and reasonable limitation of working hours and periodic holidays with pay, as well as remuneration for public holidays

Article 8

1. The States Parties to the present Covenant undertake to ensure:
   a. The right of everyone to form trade unions and join the trade union of his choice, subject only to the rules of the organization concerned, for the promotion and protection of his economic and social interests. No restrictions may be placed on the exercise of this right other than those prescribed by law and which are necessary in a democratic society in the interests of national security or

public order or for the protection of the rights and freedoms of others;

b. The right of trade unions to establish national federations or confederations and the right of the latter to form or join international trade-union organizations;

c. The right of trade unions to function freely subject to no limitations other than those prescribed by law and which are necessary in a democratic society in the interests of national security or public order or for the protection of the rights and freedoms of others;

d. The right to strike, provided that it is exercised in conformity with the laws of the particular country.

2. This article shall not prevent the imposition of lawful restrictions on the exercise of these rights by members of the armed forces or of the police or of the administration of the State.
3. Nothing in this article shall authorize States Parties to the International Labour Organisation Convention of 1948 concerning Freedom of Association and Protection of the Right to Organize to take legislative measures which would prejudice, or apply the law in such a manner as would prejudice, the guarantees provided for in that Convention.

Article 9

The States Parties to the present Covenant recognize the right of everyone to social security, including social insurance.

Article 10

The States Parties to the present Covenant recognize that:

1. The widest possible protection and assistance should be accorded to the family, which is the natural and fundamental group unit of society, particularly for its establishment and while it is responsible for the care and education of dependent children. Marriage must be entered into with the free consent of the intending spouses.
2. Special protection should be accorded to mothers during a reasonable period before and after childbirth. During such period working

mothers should be accorded paid leave or leave with adequate social security benefits.

3. Special measures of protection and assistance should be taken on behalf of all children and young persons without any discrimination for reasons of parentage or other conditions. Children and young persons should be protected from economic and social exploitation. Their employment in work harmful to their morals or health or dangerous to life or likely to hamper their normal development should be punishable by law. States should also set age limits below which the paid employment of child labour should be prohibited and punishable by law.

Article 11

1. The States Parties to the present Covenant recognize the right of everyone to an adequate standard of living for himself and his family, including adequate food, clothing and housing, and to the continuous improvement of living conditions. The States Parties will take appropriate steps to ensure the realization of this right, recognizing to this effect the essential importance of international cooperation based on free consent.
2. The States Parties to the present Covenant, recognizing the fundamental right of everyone to be free from hunger, shall take, individually and through international co-operation, the measures, including specific programmes, which are needed:
   a. To improve methods of production, conservation and distribution of food by making full use of technical and scientific knowledge, by disseminating knowledge of the principles of nutrition and by developing or reforming agrarian systems in such a way as to achieve the most efficient development and utilization of natural resources;
   b. Taking into account the problems of both food-importing and food-exporting countries, to ensure an equitable distribution of world food supplies in relation to need.

Article 12

1. The States Parties to the present Covenant recognize the right of everyone to the enjoyment of the highest attainable standard of physical and mental health.
2. The steps to be taken by the States Parties to the present Covenant to achieve the full realization of this right shall include those necessary for:
   a. The provision for the reduction of the stillbirth-rate and of infant mortality and for the healthy development of the child;
   b. The improvement of all aspects of environmental and industrial hygiene;
   c. The prevention, treatment and control of epidemic, endemic, occupational and other diseases;
   d. The creation of conditions which would assure to all medical service and medical attention in the event of sickness.

Article 13

1. The States Parties to the present Covenant recognize the right of everyone to education. They agree that education shall be directed to the full development of the human personality and the sense of its dignity, and shall strengthen the respect for human rights and fundamental freedoms. They further agree that education shall enable all persons to participate effectively in a free society, promote understanding, tolerance and friendship among all nations and all racial, ethnic or religious groups, and further the activities of the United Nations for the maintenance of peace.
2. The States Parties to the present Covenant recognize that, with a view to achieving the full realization of this right:
   a. Primary education shall be compulsory and available free to all;
   b. Secondary education in its different forms, including technical and vocational secondary education, shall be made generally available and accessible to all by every appropriate means, and in particular by the progressive introduction of free education;

   c. Higher education shall be made equally accessible to all, on the basis of capacity, by every appropriate means, and in particular by the progressive introduction of free education;
   d. Fundamental education shall be encouraged or intensified as far as possible for those persons who have not received or completed the whole period of their primary education;
   e. The development of a system of schools at all levels shall be actively pursued, an adequate fellowship system shall be established, and the material conditions of teaching staff shall be continuously improved.
3. The States Parties to the present Covenant undertake to have respect for the liberty of parents and, when applicable, legal guardians to choose for their children schools, other than those established by the public authorities, which conform to such minimum educational standards as may be laid down or approved by the State and to ensure the religious and moral education of their children in conformity with their own convictions.
4. No part of this article shall be construed so as to interfere with the liberty of individuals and bodies to establish and direct educational institutions, subject always to the observance of the principles set forth in paragraph I of this article and to the requirement that the education given in such institutions shall conform to such minimum standards as may be laid down by the State.

Article 14

Each State Party to the present Covenant which, at the time of becoming a Party, has not been able to secure in its metropolitan territory or other territories under its jurisdiction compulsory primary education, free of charge, undertakes, within two years, to work out and adopt a detailed plan of action for the progressive implementation, within a reasonable number of years, to be fixed in the plan, of the principle of compulsory education free of charge for all.

Article 15

1. The States Parties to the present Covenant recognize the right of everyone:
   a. To take part in cultural life;
   b. To enjoy the benefits of scientific progress and its applications;
   c. To benefit from the protection of the moral and material interests resulting from any scientific, literary or artistic production of which he is the author.
2. The steps to be taken by the States Parties to the present Covenant to achieve the full realization of this right shall include those necessary for the conservation, the development and the diffusion of science and culture.
3. The States Parties to the present Covenant undertake to respect the freedom indispensable for scientific research and creative activity.
4. The States Parties to the present Covenant recognize the benefits to be derived from the encouragement and development of international contacts and co-operation in the scientific and cultural fields.

PART IV

Article 16

1. The States Parties to the present Covenant undertake to submit in conformity with this part of the Covenant reports on the measures which they have adopted and the progress made in achieving the observance of the rights recognized herein.
2.
   a. All reports shall be submitted to the Secretary-General of the United Nations, who shall transmit copies to the Economic and Social Council for consideration in accordance with the provisions of the present Covenant;
   b. The Secretary-General of the United Nations shall also transmit to the specialized agencies copies of the reports, or any relevant parts therefrom, from States Parties to the present Covenant which are also members of these specialized agencies in so far as these

reports, or parts therefrom, relate to any matters which fall within the responsibilities of the said agencies in accordance with their constitutional instruments.

Article 17

1. The States Parties to the present Covenant shall furnish their reports in stages, in accordance with a programme to be established by the Economic and Social Council within one year of the entry into force of the present Covenant after consultation with the States Parties and the specialized agencies concerned.
2. Reports may indicate factors and difficulties affecting the degree of fulfilment of obligations under the present Covenant.
3. Where relevant information has previously been furnished to the United Nations or to any specialized agency by any State Party to the present Covenant, it will not be necessary to reproduce that information, but a precise reference to the information so furnished will suffice.

Article 18

Pursuant to its responsibilities under the Charter of the United Nations in the field of human rights and fundamental freedoms, the Economic and Social Council may make arrangements with the specialized agencies in respect of their reporting to it on the progress made in achieving the observance of the provisions of the present Covenant falling within the scope of their activities. These reports may include particulars of decisions and recommendations on such implementation adopted by their competent organs.

Article 19

The Economic and Social Council may transmit to the Commission on Human Rights for study and general recommendation or, as appropriate, for information the reports concerning human rights submitted by States in accordance with articles 16 and 17, and those concerning human rights submitted by the specialized agencies in accordance with article 18.

Article 20

The States Parties to the present Covenant and the specialized agencies concerned may submit comments to the Economic and Social Council on any general recommendation under article 19 or reference to such general recommendation in any report of the Commission on Human Rights or any documentation referred to therein.

Article 21

The Economic and Social Council may submit from time to time to the General Assembly reports with recommendations of a general nature and a summary of the information received from the States Parties to the present Covenant and the specialized agencies on the measures taken and the progress made in achieving general observance of the rights recognized in the present Covenant.

Article 22

The Economic and Social Council may bring to the attention of other organs of the United Nations, their subsidiary organs and specialized agencies concerned with furnishing technical assistance any matters arising out of the reports referred to in this part of the present Covenant which may assist such bodies in deciding, each within its field of competence, on the advisability of international measures likely to contribute to the effective progressive implementation of the present Covenant.

Article 23

The States Parties to the present Covenant agree that international action for the achievement of the rights recognized in the present Covenant includes such methods as the conclusion of conventions, the adoption of recommendations, the furnishing of technical assistance and the holding of regional meetings and technical meetings for the purpose of consultation and study organized in conjunction with the Governments concerned.

Article 24

Nothing in the present Covenant shall be interpreted as impairing the provisions of the Charter of the United Nations and of the constitutions of the specialized agencies which define the respective responsibilities of the various organs of the United Nations and of the specialized agencies in regard to the matters dealt with in the present Covenant.

Article 25

Nothing in the present Covenant shall be interpreted as impairing the inherent right of all peoples to enjoy and utilize fully and freely their natural wealth and resources.

PART V

Article 26

1. The present Covenant is open for signature by any State Member of the United Nations or member of any of its specialized agencies, by any State Party to the Statute of the International Court of Justice, and by any other State which has been invited by the General Assembly of the United Nations to become a party to the present Covenant.
2. The present Covenant is subject to ratification. Instruments of ratification shall be deposited with the Secretary-General of the United Nations.
3. The present Covenant shall be open to accession by any State referred to in paragraph 1 of this article.
4. Accession shall be effected by the deposit of an instrument of accession with the Secretary-General of the United Nations.
5. The Secretary-General of the United Nations shall inform all States which have signed the present Covenant or acceded to it of the deposit of each instrument of ratification or accession.

Article 27

1. The present Covenant shall enter into force three months after the date of the deposit with the Secretary-General of the United Nations of the thirty-fifth instrument of ratification or instrument of accession.
2. For each State ratifying the present Covenant or acceding to it after the deposit of the thirty-fifth instrument of ratification or instrument of accession, the present Covenant shall enter into force three months

after the date of the deposit of its own instrument of ratification or instrument of accession.

Article 28

The provisions of the present Covenant shall extend to all parts of federal States without any limitations or exceptions.

Article 29

1. Any State Party to the present Covenant may propose an amendment and file it with the Secretary-General of the United Nations. The Secretary-General shall thereupon communicate any proposed amendments to the States Parties to the present Covenant with a request that they notify him whether they favour a conference of States Parties for the purpose of considering and voting upon the proposals. In the event that at least one third of the States Parties favours such a conference, the Secretary-General shall convene the conference under the auspices of the United Nations. Any amendment adopted by a majority of the States Parties present and voting at the conference shall be submitted to the General Assembly of the United Nations for approval.
2. Amendments shall come into force when they have been approved by the General Assembly of the United Nations and accepted by a two-thirds majority of the States Parties to the present Covenant in accordance with their respective constitutional processes.
3. When amendments come into force they shall be binding on those States Parties which have accepted them, other States Parties still being bound by the provisions of the present Covenant and any earlier amendment which they have accepted.

Article 30

Irrespective of the notifications made under article 26, paragraph 5, the Secretary-General of the United Nations shall inform all States referred to in paragraph I of the same article of the following particulars:

(a) Signatures, ratifications and accessions under article 26;
(b) The date of the entry into force of the present Covenant under article 27 and the date of the entry into force of any amendments under article 29.

Article 31

1. The present Covenant, of which the Chinese, English, French, Russian and Spanish texts are equally authentic, shall be deposited in the archives of the United Nations.
2. The Secretary-General of the United Nations shall transmit certified copies of the present Covenant to all States referred to in article 26.

Notes

Introduction: Resisting Rights

1 Environics Research Group, *Human Rights in Canada Today: A National Opinion Survey,* prepared for the Trudeau Foundation's 7th Annual Conference on Public Policy, Winnipeg, 18–20 November 2010.

2 UN Human Rights Council, "Universal Periodic Review Second Cycle – Canada," 26 April 2013, http://www.lan.ohchr.org/EN/HRBodies/UPR/Pages/CASession16.aspx.

3 In 2007, Canada was one of only four states to oppose the United Nations *Declaration on the Rights of Indigenous Peoples*. In 2010, Canada abstained in the vote on General Assembly Resolution 64/292, which recognized access to clean water and sanitation as a human right. In response to mounting pressure at home and at the UN, the Harper government reversed both decisions, in 2010 and 2012, respectively. In 2007, 2008, and 2010, Canada refused to co-sponsor resolutions that would call for a global moratorium on executions.

4 Amnesty International, "Matching International Commitments with National Action: A Human Rights Agenda for Canada," Amnesty International, http://www.amnesty.ca.

5 "Prime Minister Justin Trudeau's Address to the 72nd Session of the United Nations General Assembly," Office of the Prime Minister, 21 September 2017, https://pm.gc.ca/eng/news/2017/09/21/prime-minister-justin-trudeaus-address-72th-session-united-nations-general-assembly.

6 Transcripts for each of these apologies can be found on the website of the Prime Minister's Office. See "Remarks by Prime Minister Justin Trudeau," https://pm.gc.ca/eng/news/2017/11/28/remarks-prime-minister-justin-trudeau-apologize-lgbtq2-canadians; and "Prime Minister delivers apology to former students of Newfoundland and Labrador residential schools," https://pm.gc.ca/eng/news/2017/11/24/prime-minister-delivers-apology-former-students-newfoundland-and-labrador. Stephen Harper did not include the Newfoundland and Labrador

school survivors in his 2008 apology or settlement because the boarding schools they attended were not run by the Canadian federal government itself. The schools were set up before Newfoundland joined Confederation in 1949.

7 The current wording of this description of Canada's historical role in the development of international human rights, as promoted by Justin Trudeau's Liberal government, is almost identical to that promoted by Stephen Harper's Conservative government. "Canada's approach to advancing human rights," Government of Canada, Global Affairs Canada, http://international.gc.ca/wcmglobal/utilities/redirect/redirector.ashx?referrer=&errorpath=%2fworld-monde%2fworld_issues-enjeux-mondiaux%2fadvancing_rights-promouvoir_droits.aspx%3flang%3deng.

8 Amnesty International, "Matching International Commitments with National Action," 6.

9 The International Bill of Rights is also referred to as the International Bill of Human Rights. Throughout this book, I use the former title because it was most commonly used by the actors involved in developing human rights instruments at the UN in the postwar period. It was also the title used by Canadian diplomats as they discussed the UN's human rights initiatives from the 1940s to the 1970s.

10 United Nations, *Charter of the United Nations,* Chapter 1, Article 1, 24 October 1945, 1 UNTS XVI, http://www.un.org/en/documents/charter/.

11 William A. Schabas, "Canada and the Adoption of the Universal Declaration of Human Rights," *McGill Law Journal* 43, 2 (1998): 403–41; A.J. Hobbins, "Eleanor Roosevelt, John Humphrey and Canadian Opposition to the Universal Declaration of Human Rights: Looking Back on the 50th Anniversary of the UDHR," *International Journal* 53, 2 (1998): 325–42; Michael Behiels, "Canada and the Implementation of International Instruments of Human Rights: A Federalist Conundrum, 1919–1982," in *Framing Canadian Federalism: Historical Essays in Honour of John T. Saywell,* ed. Dimitry Anastakis and P.E. Bryden (Toronto: University of Toronto Press, 2009), 151–84.

12 For examples of this narrative, see Arthur Andrew, *The Rise and Fall of a Middle Power: Canadian Diplomacy from King to Mulroney* (Toronto: James Lorimer, 1993); George Ignatieff, *The Making of a Peacemonger: Memoirs of George Ignatieff* (Toronto: University of Toronto Press, 1985); Norman Hillmer and J.L. Granatstein, *Empire to Umpire: Canada and the World to the 1990s* (Toronto: Copp Clark Longman, 1994); J. King Gordon, *Canada's Role as a Middle Power* (Toronto: Canadian Institute of International Affairs, 1966); Tom Keating, *Canada and World Order: The Multilateralist Tradition in Canadian Foreign Policy* (Toronto: McClelland and Stewart, 1993).

13 Greg Donaghy, "Coming Off the Gold Standard: Re-assessing the 'Golden Age' of Canadian Diplomacy" (paper presented to "A Very Modest Ministry: Foreign Affairs and International Trade Canada," University of Saskatchewan, September 2009),

2; http://www.suezcrisis.ca/pdfs/Coming%20off%20the%20Gold%20Standard.pdf.

14 Asa McKercher, "The Centre Cannot Hold: Canada, Colonialism and the 'Afro-Asian Bloc' at the United Nations, 1960–62," *Journal of Imperial and Commonwealth History* 24, 2 (2014): 329. For other revisionist approaches to Canadian postwar diplomacy, see Adam Chapnick, "The Canadian Middle Power Myth," *International Journal* 55, 2 (2000): 188–206; Hector Mackenzie, "Golden Decades(s)? Reappraising Canada's International Relations in the 1940s and 1950s," *British Journal of Canadian Studies* 23, 2 (2010): 179–206.

15 For examples of this critique, see Laura Madokoro, Francine McKenzie, and David Meren, eds., *Dominion of Race: Rethinking Canada's International History* (Vancouver: UBC Press, 2017); David Webster, "Foreign Policy, Diplomacy, and Decolonization," in *Canada and the Third World: Overlapping Histories,* ed. Karen Dubinsky, Sean Mills, and Scott Rutherford (Toronto: University of Toronto Press, 2016), 155–82; David Webster, "Self-Fulfilling Prophesies and Human Rights in Canada's Foreign Policy: Lessons from East Timor," *International Journal* 65, 3 (Summer 2010): 739–50.

16 Madokoro, McKenzie, and Meren, ibid., 13.

17 Roger Normand and Sarah Zaidi, *Human Rights at the UN: The Political History of Universal Justice* (Bloomington and Indianapolis: Indiana University Press, 2008).

18 Dominique Clément, *Canada's Rights Revolution: Social Movements and Social Change, 1937–1982* (Vancouver: UBC Press, 2008); Dominique Clément, "The Rights Revolution in Canada and Australia," in *Taking Liberties: A History of Human Rights in Canada,* ed. David Goutor and Stephen Heathorn (Don Mills, ON: Oxford University Press, 2013), 88–113.

19 James W. St. G. Walker, *"Race," Rights and the Law in the Supreme Court of Canada: Historical Case Studies* (Toronto and Waterloo: Osgoode Society for Canadian Legal History and Wilfrid Laurier University Press, 1997); James W. St. G. Walker, "The 'Jewish Phase' in the Movement for Racial Equality in Canada," *Canadian Ethnic Studies* 34, 1 (Spring 2002): 1–29; Carmela Patrias and Ruth A. Frager, "'This Is Our Country, These Are Our Rights': Minorities and the Origins of Ontario's Human Rights Campaigns," *Canadian Historical Review* 82, 1 (2001): 1–35; Ross Lambertson, *Repression and Resistance: Canadian Human Rights Activists, 1930–1960* (Toronto: University of Toronto Press, 2005).

20 Christopher MacLennan, *Toward the Charter: Canadians and the Demand for a National Bill of Rights, 1929–1960* (Montreal and Kingston: McGill-Queen's University Press, 2003); Stephanie Bangarth, *Voices Raised in Protest: Defending North American Citizens of Japanese Ancestry, 1942–49* (Vancouver: UBC Press, 2008).

21 See, for example: David Webster, "Self-Fulfilling Prophesies and Human Rights in Canada's Foreign Policy," 739–50; David Webster, "Canada and Bilateral Human Rights Dialogues," *Canadian Foreign Policy Journal* 16, 3 (2010): 43–63; Asa McKercher, "Sound and Fury: Diefenbaker, Human Rights, and Canadian Foreign Policy," *Canadian Historical Review* 97, 2 (Summer 2016): 165–94.

22 Andrew S. Thompson, *On the Side of the Angels: Canada and the United Nations Commission on Human Rights* (Vancouver: UBC Press, 2017), 78.

23 Andrew Lui, *Why Canada Cares: Human Rights and Foreign Policy in Theory and Practice* (Montreal and Kingston: McGill-Queen's University Press, 2012). See also Chios Carmody, ed., *Is Our House in Order? Canada's Implementation of International Law* (Montreal and Kingston: McGill-Queen's University Press, 2010).

24 Ibid., 7.

25 For an overview of the field of study of Canadian foreign policy, see Brian Bow, "Paradigms and Paradoxes: Canadian Foreign Policy in Theory, Research, and Practice," *International Journal* 65, 2 (Spring 2010): 371–80.

26 For example, see Madokoro, McKenzie, and Meren, *Dominion of Race;* Dubinsky, Mills, and Rutherford, *Canada and the Third World.*

27 Walter Tarnopolsky was the Canadian scholar most associated with this classification of rights. Walter Surma Tarnopolksy, *The Canadian Bill of Rights* (Toronto: Carswell, 1966).

28 For a wider discussion of the categorization of rights, see Jack Donnelly, *Universal Human Rights in Theory and Practice,* 2nd ed. (Ithaca, NY: Cornell University Press, 2003); or Asbjorn Eide, Catarina Krause, and Allan Rosas, eds., *Economic, Social and Cultural Rights,* 2nd ed. (Dordrecht, Netherlands: Nijhoff, 2001), especially ch. 2.

29 United Nations, *Universal Declaration of Human Rights*, Preamble and Article 2, 10 December 1948, http://www.un.org/en/universal-declaration-human-rights/.

30 See, for example: Paul Gordon Lauren, *The Evolution of International Human Rights: Visions Seen* (Philadelphia: University of Pennsylvania Press, 1998); Lynne Hunt, *Inventing Human Rights: A History* (New York: W.W. Norton, 2007); Jenny S. Martinez, *The Slave Trade and the Origins of International Human Rights Law* (Oxford: Oxford University Press, 2012).

31 Samuel Moyn, *The Last Utopia: Human Rights in History* (Cambridge, MA: Belknap Press of Harvard University Press, 2010).

32 Ibid.

33 United Nations, "Definition of Key Terms Used in the UN Treaty Collection," https://treaties.un.org.

34 John Humphrey made this claim at the time of Canada's ratification of the international covenants. John Humphrey, "The International Bill of Rights: Scope and

Implementation," *William and Mary Law Review* 17, 3 (1976): 527–41. See also Hurst Hannum, "The Status of the Universal Declaration of Human Rights in National and International Law," *Georgia Journal of International and Comparative Law* 25 (1995): 287–397.

35 United Nations, UNESCO, "Glossary," http://en.unesco.org.

36 In December 2008, the UN General Assembly adopted an Optional Protocol to the ICESCR (opened for signature in June 2009), which established an individual complaints mechanism for the covenant similar to those of the Optional Protocol to the ICCPR.

37 David P. Forsythe, *Human Rights in International Relations,* 2nd ed. (Cambridge: Cambridge University Press, 2006), 12.

38 Ibid.

39 Robert Bothwell, "Foreign Affairs a Hundred Years On," in *Canada among Nations, 2008: 100 Years of Canadian Foreign Policy,* ed. Robert Bothwell and Jean Daudelin (Montreal and Kingston: McGill-Queen's University Press, 2009): 19–39; Greg Donaghy, "'A Sad, General Decline?': The Canadian Diplomat in the 20th Century," in *Canada among Nations, 2008: 100 Years of Canadian Foreign Policy,* ed. Robert Bothwell and Jean Daudelin (Montreal and Kingston: McGill-Queen's University Press, 2009): 41–59; J.L. Granatstein, *The Ottawa Men: The Civil Service Mandarins, 1935–1957* (Toronto: Oxford University Press, 1982).

40 Kevin Spooner, "'Awakening Africa': Race and Canadian Views of Decolonizing Africa," in *Dominion of Race,* ed. Laura Madokoro, Francine McKenzie, and David Meren (Vancouver: UBC Press, 2017), 211.

41 Micheline R. Ishay, *The History of Human Rights: From Ancient Times to the Globalization Era* (Berkeley: University of California Press, 2008), 4.

Chapter 1: The Roots of Resistance: Canada and the *Universal Declaration of Human Rights*

1 Memo from St. Laurent to Canadian Delegation, 8 October 1948, file 5475-DP-40, vol. 3701, RG25, Library and Archives Canada (LAC).

2 Schabas, "Canada and the Adoption of the Universal Declaration of Human Rights," 406.

3 Ibid., 441.

4 Hector Mackenzie, "Knight Errant, Cold Warrior or Cautious Ally? Canada on the United Nations Security Council, 1948–49," *Journal of Transatlantic Studies* 7, 4 (2009): 453–75.

5 For a review of the influence of the Enlightenment on ideas of rights, see Hunt, *Inventing Human Rights.*

6 For a discussion of early ideas of rights in Canadian society, see Dominique Clément, *Human Rights in Canada: A History* (Waterloo, ON: Wilfrid Laurier University Press, 2016), 32.

7 A.W. Brian Simpson, *Human Rights and the End of Empire: Britain and the Genesis of the European Convention* (Oxford: Oxford University Press, 2001), 35–37.

8 Clément, *Human Rights in Canada,* 33. For a broader discussion of the evolution of ideas of liberty in Britain, see David Goutor and Stephen Heathorn, eds., *Taking Liberties: A History of Human Rights in Canada* (Don Mills, ON: Oxford University Press, 2013), 3–4; and A.W. Brian Simpson, *Human Rights and the End of Empire,* 30–37.

9 Walter Tarnopolsky, *The Canadian Bill of Rights,* 2nd ed. (Toronto: Oxford University Press, 1964), 13.

10 *Constitution Act,* 1867, 30 & 31 Vict., c. 3, Canadian Legal Information Institute, https://www.canlii.org/t/ldsw.

11 Ibid., 93 and 133.

12 Ibid., Section 92(13). Walter Tarnopolsky, "The Historical and Constitutional Context of the Proposed Canadian Charter of Rights and Freedoms," *Law and Contemporary Problems* 44 (1981): 171; Clément, *Human Rights in Canada,* 33.

13 Walter Tarnopolsky, "Address to the Conference of Human Rights Ministers," 8 November 1974, Walter Tarnopolsky Papers, file 14, vol. 31, MG31 E55, LAC.

14 Janet Ajzenstat, *The Canadian Founding: John Locke and Parliament* (Montreal and Kingston: McGill-Queen's University Press, 2007), 48.

15 A.V. Dicey, *Introduction to the Study of the Law of the Constitution* (London: Macmillan, 1902; reprinted by Elibron Classics series, Adamant Media Corporation, 2005).

16 For a historical examination of Dicey's influence, see Richard A. Cosgrove, *The Rule of Law: Albert Venn Dicey, Victorian Jurist* (London: Macmillan, 1980); T.H. Ford, *Albert Venn Dicey: The Man and His Times* (Chichester, UK: B. Rose Publishers, 1985); and Bernard J. Hibbits, "The Politics of Principle: Albert Venn Dicey and the Rule of Law," *Anglo-American Law Review* 23, 1 (1994).

17 Ian Green, *The Charter of Rights* (Toronto: James Lorimer, 1989), 17.

18 Howard Davis, *Human Rights and Civil Liberties* (Cullompton, UK: Willan Publishing, 2003), 14.

19 Dicey, *Study of the Law,* 86.

20 Ibid., 198 and 194.

21 G.W. Jones, "The British Bill of Rights," *Parliamentary Affairs* 43, 1 (January 1990): 27–40.

22 Canada, House of Commons, *Debates,* Ian Mackenzie, 16 May 1947, 3142.

23 Ibid., Paul Martin, 7 May 1946, 1311.

24 After the British conquest of New France, the *Quebec Act* of 1774 established that "property and civil rights" in Quebec would be regulated by traditional French law. Since that point, Quebec has had a bijuridical system in which civil matters are

regulated by a civil code, and criminal law (and other areas under federal jurisdiction) are regulated by common law.

25 For an examination of Quebec society and the influence of ultramontanism, see Geneviève Zubrzycki, *Beheading the Saint: Nationalism, Religion, and Secularism in Quebec* (Chicago: University of Chicago Press, 2016), 54–57.

26 Louis St. Laurent, "Address to the Montreal Branch of the United Nations Association of Canada," 24 February 1947, file 5475-B-40, pt. 32, vol. 5111, RG25, LAC.

27 Ralph Maybank, "Statement to the Third Committee of the General Assembly," 1 October 1948, file 5475-DP-40, pt. 2.1, vol. 6425, RG25, LAC.

28 For example, in 1875 British Columbia passed legislation stating that "no Chinaman or Indian" could vote. *An Act to Make Better Provision for the Qualification and Registration of Voters,* SBC 1875, c. 2.

29 For an overview of how Indigenous rights fit into Canadian discourses of rights, see J.R. Miller, "Human Rights for Some: First Nations Rights in Twentieth-Century Canada," in *Taking Liberties: A History of Human Rights in Canada,* ed. David Goutor and Stephen Heathorn (Don Mills, ON: Oxford University Press, 2013), 233–60.

30 F.R. Scott, "Dominion Jurisdiction over Human Rights and Fundamental Freedoms," *Canadian Bar Review* 27, 5 (1949): 502–4. See also Greene, *The Charter of Rights.*

31 Walker, *"Race," Rights and the Law,* 3 and 6.

32 Ibid., 13.

33 Constance Backhouse, *Colour-Coded: A Legal History of Racism in Canada, 1900–1950* (Toronto: Osgoode Society for Canadian Legal History; University of Toronto Press, 1999), 17 and 279.

34 Ibid.

35 *Johnson v. Sparrow,* [1899] QSC 104. The plaintiff sued a Montreal theatre for denying him and a friend a seat in the orchestra section of a public theatre after they had purchased tickets. The judge held that although a theatre is a private facility, it holds a public licence and was therefore obliged to serve all members of the public.

36 See *Loew's Montreal Theatres Ltd. v. Reynolds,* [1921] 30 RJQ (Quebec KB); *Franklin v. Evans,* [1924] 55 OLR 349 (Ont HC); *Christie v. The York Corporation,* [1940] 1 DLR 81 (SCC); *Rogers v. Clarence Hotel Co. Ltd.,* [1940] 3 DLR 583 (BCCA). See also Walker, *"Race," Rights and the Law;* Backhouse, *Colour Coded;* and Henry L. Molot, "The Duty of Business to Serve the Public: Analogy to the Innkeeper's Obligation," *Canadian Bar Review* 46, 4 (December 1968): 612–42.

37 *Christie v. York Corporation,* [1940] 1 DLR 81 (SCC) at 142.

38 Walter Tarnopolsky, *Discrimination and the Law* (Toronto: Richard De Boo, 1982), 6.

39 The court decided that the federal government had exclusive authority over the rights, privileges, and disabilities of classes of persons as set out by the federal *Naturalization Act. Union Colliery Company of British Columbia v. Bryden,* [1889] AC 580 (JCPC).

40 *Cunningham and A.G. for B.C. v. Tomey Homma and A.G. for Canada,* [1903] AC 151, CCS 45 (JCPC).

41 *An Act to prevent the Employment of Female Labour in certain capacities,* SS 1912, c. 17.

42 *Quong-Wing v. The King,* [1914] 49 SCR 440 at 448.

43 Greene, *The Charter of Rights,* 15–16.

44 Ibid., 19.

45 *Reference Re Alberta Statutes* – The Bank Taxation Act; The Credit of Alberta Regulation Act; and the Accurate News and Information Act, 1938 CanLII 1 (SCC), [1938] SCR 100.

46 Ibid., 132–34.

47 Ibid., 149.

48 Lambertson, *Repression and Resistance,* ch. 1.

49 Ibid., 16–67.

50 The arrest of eight leaders of the Communist Party of Canada in 1931 led to a nationwide campaign for the repeal of Section 98. See Lorne Brown, *When Freedom Was Lost: The Unemployed, the Agitator, and the State* (Montreal and Buffalo: Black Rose Books, 1987); Lambertson, *Repression and Resistance;* and MacLennan, *Toward the Charter,* ch. 1.

51 Lambertson, ibid., 25.

52 William Kaplan, *State and Salvation: The Jehovah's Witnesses and Their Fight for Civil Rights* (Toronto: University of Toronto Press, 1989), 20.

53 Quebec politicians painted Communists and Jehovah's Witnesses as enemies of both the state and the Catholic Church. For example, see House of Commons, *Debates,* Eugène Marquis, 19 May 1947, 3223. See also Egerton, "Entering the Age of Human Rights: Religion, Politics and Canadian Liberalism, 1945–50," *Canadian Historical Review* 85, 3 (2004): 459–50.

54 For example, see Howard Palmer, "Patterns of Racism: Attitudes towards Chinese and Japanese in Alberta 1920–1950," *Histoire Sociale/Social History* 13, 25 (1980): 137–60; Patricia E. Roy, *The Oriental Question: Consolidating a White Man's Province: 1914–41* (Vancouver: UBC Press, 2003); and Peter Ward, *White Canada Forever: Popular Attitudes and Public Policy toward Orientals in British Columbia,* 2nd ed. (Montreal and Kingston: McGill-Queen's University Press, 1990).

55 David Goutor, *Guarding the Gates: The Canadian Labour Movement and Immigration, 1872–1934* (Vancouver: UBC Press, 2007).

56 Lambertson, *Repression and Resistance,* ch. 1.

57 Ibid.

58 For an examination of civil liberties violations in Canada during the Second World War, see Reginald Whitaker and Gary Marcuse, *Cold War Canada: The Making of a National Insecurity State* (Toronto: University of Toronto Press, 1994), 7–10; William

Kaplan, *State and Salvation;* Lambertson, *Repression and Resistance,* ch. 2; Clément, *Canada's Rights Revolution,* 39–40; MacLennan, *Toward the Charter,* 23–30.

59 For a study of the treatment of Canadians of Japanese ancestry during the Second World War, see Ken Adachi, *The Enemy That Never Was: A History of Japanese Canadians* (Toronto: McClelland and Stewart, 1991); Patricia E. Roy, *The Triumph of Citizenship: The Japanese and Chinese in Canada, 1941–67* (Vancouver: UBC Press, 2007); and Stephanie Bangarth, *Voices Raised in Protest.*

60 Bangarth, ibid., 2.

61 For an examination of the emergence of an egalitarian rights coalition surrounding this issue, see Bangarth, ibid.; and Lambertson, *Repression and Resistance,* ch. 3.

62 Bangarth, ibid., 2.

63 For a study of the Gouzenko Affair, see Dominique Clément, "The Royal Commission on Espionage and the Spy Trials of 1946–9: A Case Study in Parliamentary Supremacy," *Journal of the Canadian Historical Association* 11, 1 (2000): 151–72; and Amy Knight, *How the Cold War Began: The Igor Gouzenko Affair and the Hunt for Soviet Spies* (New York: Carroll and Graf Publishers, 2005).

64 The *Canadian Forum* was a left-wing literary, cultural, and political publication that began publication in 1920. Eugene Forsey, "The Padlock Act Again," *Canadian Forum* 17, 205 (February 1938): 382; "Under the Padlock," *Canadian Forum* 17, 208 (May 1938): 41–44; "The Padlock – New Style," *Canadian Forum* 18, 218 (March 1939): 362–63; "Mr. Lapointe and the Padlock," *Canadian Forum* 18, 211 (August 1938): 148–50.

65 Laski gave examples of how the DOCR in Canada had fewer restrictions than similar regulations in Britain. For example, the "classes of persons" eligible to be interned in Canada were not limited as they were in Britain. Under the Canadian regulations, the minister of justice had the right to intern any person deemed to threaten public safety. Harold Laski, "Civil Liberties in Canada and Great Britain during War," *Harvard Law Review* 55, 6 (April 1942): 1018.

66 Andrew Brewin, "Civil Liberties in Canada during Wartime," *Bill of Rights Review* 1, 2 (Winter 1941); and H. McD. Clokie, "The Preservation of Civil Liberties," *Canadian Journal of Economics and Political Science/Revue canadienne d'economique et de science politique* 13, 2 (May 1947): 208–32.

67 Bangarth, *Voices Raised in Protest,* 63–69.

68 Some examples include F.R. Scott, "Racial Discrimination and Public Policy," in *Information and Comment* (published by the Canadian Jewish Congress Committee on Social and Economic Studies) (March 1946): 2; "Duplessis versus Jehovah," *Canadian Forum* 26, 12 (1947): 222–23; "The Rights of Man," *United Nations Weekly Bulletin* 3, 25 (16 December 1947): 813; "Dominion Jurisdiction over Human Rights and Fundamental Freedoms," 497.

69 F.R. Scott, "The Trial of the Toronto Communists," *Queen's Quarterly* 39 (1932): 512.

70 Frank R. Scott, "The Privy Council and Minority Rights," *Queen's Quarterly* 37 (1930): 668–78; "Civil Liberties," *Canadian New Leader* (October 1933): 6–7; "Freedom of Speech in Canada," *Papers and Proceedings of the Canadian Political Science Association* 7 (1933): 169–89; Scott, "The Trial of the Toronto Communists," 512–13.

71 F.R. Scott, "Duplessis versus Jehovah," 223.

72 For an examination of support for and opposition to the treatment of Canadians of Japanese ancestry in the press from 1942 to 1949, see Bangarth, *Voices Raised in Protest,* 101–7.

73 Ibid., 101.

74 Clément, "The Royal Commission on Espionage," 158.

75 The Canadian legal press was highly critical of the methods of the Royal Commission on Espionage, attacking its abuse of civil liberties. Daily newspapers were split, with some supporting the actions of the Royal Commission and others criticizing perceived abuses of power. For a detailed examination of the press reaction to the espionage trials, see Clément, ibid.

76 Dominique Clément, "Spies, Lies, and a Commission: A Case Study in the Mobilization of the Canadian Civil Liberties Movement," *Left History* 7, 2 (2000), 65.

77 House of Commons, *Debates,* Alistair Stewart, 10 October 1945, 900.

78 Ibid., John Diefenbaker, 3 May 1946, 1214.

79 See, for example, Lanny Boutin, *John Diefenbaker: The Outsider Who Refused to Quit* (Toronto: Jackfruit Press, 2006); Denis Smith, *Rogue Tory: The Life and Legend of John G. Diefenbaker* (Toronto: McClelland and Stewart, 1995); and Carla Spittal, "The Diefenbaker Moment" (PhD dissertation, University of Toronto, 2011), https://tspace.library.utoronto.ca/bitstream/1807/29878/3/Spittal_Cara_201106_PhD_thesis.pdf.

80 MacLennan, *Toward the Charter,* 46.

81 House of Commons, *Debates,* 7 May 1946, 1300–3; 8 May 1946, 1339–40; 16 May 1946, 1584–85.

82 Bruce Hutchinson, ed., "Bill of Rights for Canada," *Winnipeg Free Press Pamphlet* 13 (1947). This pamphlet reprinted articles from the editorial pages of the *Winnipeg Free Press* from 30 May to 3 June 1947. "Parliament's Alarm," Bill of Rights – 1944–1953, F.R. Scott papers, vol. 3, MG30-D211, LAC.

83 *Ontario Insurance Act,* SO 1932, c. 24, s. 4; Walker, *"Race," Rights and the Law,* 193.

84 Walker, ibid., 193.

85 *Libel Act,* SM 1934, c. 23. Ira Robinson, *A History of Antisemitism in Canada* (Waterloo, ON: Wilfrid Laurier Press, 2015), 100.

86 Robinson, ibid.

87 SO 1944, c. 51. Members of the Ontario legislature had defeated a similar bill in 1933 on the grounds that it allowed government too much power to interfere with individual freedom.

88 Brian R. Howe, "The Evolution of Human Rights Policy in Ontario," *Canadian Journal of Political Science* 24, 4 (December 1991): 788.

89 James W. St. G. Walker, "Human Rights, Racial Equality, Social Justice: Can We Get There from Here?" (paper presented to "Domain Seminar on Social Justice and Multiculturalism," University of British Columbia Centre for Policy Studies in Education, Department of Canadian Heritage, 1999), 23.

90 *Saskatchewan Bill of Rights Act,* SS 1947, c. 35.

91 For an examination of why the Saskatchewan government was reluctant to test its new law in the courts, see Carmela Patrias, "Socialists, Jews, and the 1947 Saskatchewan Bill of Rights," *Canadian Historical Review* 87, 2 (June 2006): 265–92.

92 Tarnopolsky, "Address to the Conference of Human Rights Ministers."

93 Béatrice Vizkelety, *Proving Discrimination in Canada* (Toronto: Carswell, 1987), 2.

94 Patrias, "Socialists, Jews, and the 1947 Saskatchewan Bill of Rights," 292.

95 Patrias and Frager, "'This Is Our Country, These Are Our Rights,'" 2.

96 Ibid.

97 Clément, *Canada's Rights Revolution,* 12. See also Ross Lambertson, "Domination and Dissent: Equality Rights before World War II," in *A History of Human Rights in Canada: Essential Issues,* ed. Janet Miron (Toronto: Canadian Scholars' Press, 2009), 11–24.

98 For a discussion of the role of libertarian rights in Canada's early civil liberties movement, see Lambertson, *Repression and Resistance,* chs. 1–4. For a discussion of early understandings of liberty, see Ian McKay, "The Liberal Order Framework: A Prospectus for a Reconnaissance of Canadian History," *Canadian Historical Review* 81, 4 (December 2000): 624.

99 Ross Lambertson, "Suppression and Subversion: Libertarian and Egalitarian Rights up to 1960," in *A History of Human Rights in Canada: Essential Issues,* ed. Janet Miron (Toronto: Canadian Scholars' Press, 2009), 35.

100 See Ruth Frager and Carmela Patrias, "Human Rights Activists and the Question of Sex Discrimination in Postwar Ontario," *Canadian Historical Review* 93, 4 (December 2012): 583–610; and Dominique Clément, *Equality Deferred: Sex Discrimination and British Columbia's Human Rights State, 1953–84* (Vancouver: UBC Press, 2014). For a broader examination of this trend, see Alice Kessler-Harris, *In Pursuit of Equity: Men, Women, and the Quest for Economic Citizenship in 20th-Century America* (New York: Oxford University Press, 2001).

101 Frager and Patrias, ibid., 586.

102 Arès was influenced by developments within the Church and the writings of scholars such as Jacques Maritain. Richard Arès, SJ, "Les droits de l'homme devant les nations unies," *Relations* 8, 96 (December 1948): 348. He continued to write articles relating to the UDHR, including "La déclaration universelle des droits de l'homme," *Relations* 9, 97 (January 1949); "Quand les nations unies s'occupent de dieu," *Relations* 9, 99 (March 1949); and "D'où viennent les droits de l'homme?" *Relations* 9, 100 (April 1949).

103 Arès, "Les droits de l'homme devant les nations unies," 325–42.

104 Ibid., 332.

105 John Humphrey, as quoted by A.J. Hobbins, "Eleanor Roosevelt, John Humphrey and Canadian Opposition to the Universal Declaration of Human Rights," 333.

106 The role of the League of Nations in the history of human rights is debated. Some scholars, such as Dominique Marshall and Jenny Martinez, argue that debates over children's rights (1924) and the slavery convention (1926) are examples of the League's engagement with issues of human rights. See Dominique Marshall, "Reconstructing Politics, the Canadian Welfare State and the Ambiguity of Children's Rights, 1940–1950," in *Uncertain Horizons: Canadians and Their World in 1945*, ed. Greg Donaghy (Ottawa: Canadian Committee for the History of the Second World War, 1997); Martinez, *The Slave Trade and the Origins of International Human Rights*.

107 Avalon Project, "Covenant of the League of Nations," http://avalon.law.yale.edu/20th_century/leagcov.asp.

108 Mark Mazower, "The Strange Triumph of Human Rights, 1933–1950," *Historical Journal* 47, 2 (June 2004): 382–87; MacLennan, *Toward the Charter*, 61; and John P. Humphrey, "The International Law of Human Rights in the Middle Twentieth Century," in *The Present State of International Law and Other Essays: Written in Honour of the Centenary Celebration of the International Law Association, 1873–1973*, ed. Maarten Bos (Deventer, Netherlands: Kluwer, 1973), 75–105.

109 John P. Humphrey, *Human Rights and the United Nations: A Great Adventure* (New York: Transnational Publishers, 1984), 6.

110 For a more detailed examination of Canadian foreign policy prior to the Second World War, see Robert Bothwell, "The Canadian Isolationist Tradition," *International Journal* 54 (Winter 1998–99): 76–87; Adam Chapnick, "On Protocols and Fireproof Houses: The Re-emergence of Canadian Exceptionalism," *International Journal* 61, 3 (Summer 2006): 713–23.

111 Richard Veatch, *Canada and the League of Nations* (Toronto: University of Toronto Press, 1975), 181.

112 Ibid.

113 Robert Bothwell, *Alliance and Illusion: Canada and the World, 1945–1984* (Vancouver: UBC Press, 2007), 14 and 362.

114 Ibid., 11.

115 A 1945 Canadian Institute of Public Opinion poll found that 90 percent of Canadians, and 79 percent of Quebecers, supported Canada's membership in the United Nations. Cited in Adam Chapnick, *The Middle Power Project: Canada and the Founding of the United Nations* (Vancouver: UBC Press, 2005), 115.

116 Chapnick, ibid., 4.

117 Ibid., 114.

118 Bothwell, *Alliance and Illusion*, 18.

119 Mazower, "Strange Triumph of Human Rights," 388–89.

120 Samuel Moyn argues that American advocacy groups and smaller states kept human rights on the agenda for San Francisco. The addition of a Domestic Jurisdiction Clause alleviated concerns that human rights obligations would allow outside intervention in the internal affairs of a state. Samuel Moyn, *The Last Utopia*, 62. See also Mazower, "Strange Triumph of Human Rights," 391–93; and Normand and Zaidi, *Human Rights at the UN*, 127–28.

121 Article 2(7) states that the United Nations has no authority to intervene in matters that are within the domestic jurisdiction of any state. United Nations, *Charter of the United Nations*, Article 2(7), 24 October 1945, 1 UNTS 16, http://www.un.org/en/documents/charter/.

122 Kim Richard Nossal, "Cabin'd, Cribb'd, Confin'd? Canada's Interests in Human Rights," in *Human Rights in Canadian Foreign Policy*, ed. Robert O. Matthews and Cranford Pratt (Montreal and Kingston: McGill-Queen's University Press, 1988), 49–50; John W. Holmes, ed., *The Shaping of Peace: Canada and the Search for World Order*, vol. 2 (Toronto: University of Toronto Press, 1979), 44.

123 Mackenzie, "Knight Errant, Cold Warrior or Cautious Ally?," 454–55.

124 Adam Chapnick "The Department of External Affairs and the United Nations Idea, 1943–1965," in *In the National Interest: Canadian Foreign Policy and the Department of Foreign Affairs and International Trade, 1909–2009*, ed. Greg Donaghy and Michael K. Caroll (Calgary: University of Calgary Press, 2011), 86–88.

125 Lester B. Pearson, "Canada and the Post-War World," *Canadian Affairs* 1, 6 (1944): 2.

126 Ibid., 13.

127 As cited in Raymond S. Blake, "Mackenzie King and the Genesis of Family Allowances in Canada, 1939–1944," in *Social and Welfare Policy in Canada: Historical Readings*, ed. Raymond B. Blake and Jeff Keschen (Toronto: University of Toronto Press, 1995), 245.

128 The department did allow Reid to publish his draft charter anonymously. Escott Reid, *On Duty: A Canadian at the Making of the United Nations, 1945–1946* (Toronto: McClelland and Stewart, 1983), 18–23.

129 Hector Mackenzie, "Escott Reid and the Founding of the United Nations, 1945–6," in *Escott Reid: Diplomat and Scholar*, ed. Stéphane Roussel and Greg Donaghy (Montreal and Kingston: McGill-Queen's University Press, 2004), 192.

130 United Nations, *Charter of the United Nations,* Article 55, 24 October 1945. See also Normand and Zaidi, *Human Rights at the UN,* 133.

131 Original membership included Australia, Belgium, Byelorussia, Chile, China, Egypt, France, India, Iran, Lebanon, Panama, the Philippines, the Soviet Union, Ukraine, the United Kingdom, the United States, Uruguay, and Yugoslavia. Normand and Zaidi, ibid., 146.

132 Bothwell, "Foreign Affairs a Hundred Years On," 29; Donaghy, "'A Sad, General Decline?,'" 50. In the 1945 federal election, Mackenzie King's Liberals won a majority government with 125 of the 245 seats in the House of Commons. This majority grew in the summer of 1949 when St. Laurent's Liberals won 190 of the 262 seats. Government of Canada, Parliament, "Electoral Results by Party," http://www.parl.gc.ca.

133 Canada, Parliament, House of Commons and Senate, Special Joint Committee on Human Rights and Fundamental Freedoms, *Minutes of Proceedings and Evidence* (Ottawa: King's Printer, 1947), vi.

134 Hobbins, "Eleanor Roosevelt, John Humphrey and Canadian Opposition to the Universal Declaration of Human Rights," 325–26.

135 Special Joint Committee on Human Rights and Fundamental Freedoms, *Minutes of Proceedings and Evidence* (1947), 3.

136 Ibid., 64.

137 "Second and Final Report of the Special Joint Committee on Human Rights and Fundamental Freedoms" to the House of Commons of Canada, 25 June 1948, file 5475-W-2-40, pt. 1.2, vol. 6281, RG25, LAC.

138 Ibid.

139 The motion gained the support of Senator Gouin and MPs Benoît Michaud, James Turgeon, T.A. Crerar, H.W. Harridge, and Ernest Hansell. Canada, Parliament, House of Commons and Senate, Special Joint Committee on Human Rights and Fundamental Freedoms, *Minutes of Proceedings and Evidence* (Ottawa: King's Printer, 1948), 52–57.

140 Egerton, "Entering the Age of Human Rights," 451–79.

141 Ibid.

142 Memo from R.G. Riddell to Under-Secretary of State for External Affairs, 27 April 1948, file 5475-W-2-40, pt. 1.1, vol. 6281, RG25, LAC.

143 Interdepartmental Committee on Human Rights, "Draft International Declaration of Human Rights," April 1948, file 5475-W-2-40, pt. 1.1, vol. 6281, RG25, LAC.

144 Ibid.

145 "Report on the Draft International Declaration on Human Rights by the Inter-Departmental Committee on Human Rights," 1948, file 5475-W-2-40, pt. 1.1, vol. 6281, RG25, LAC.

146 House of Commons, *Debates,* Gordon Graydon, 17 June 1946, 2537.

147 Ibid., 16–19 May 1947, 2861–67.

148 Ibid., John Diefenbaker, Alistair Stewart, Stanley Knowles, J.H. Blackmore, Norman Jacques, 16–19 May 1947, 2861–67.

149 Ibid., Eugène Marquis, 19 May 1947, 3323; Roch Pinard, 16 May 1947, 3175. Pinard was opposed only to an international bill of rights if it did not contain a reference to God. Egerton, "Entering the Age of Human Rights," 457–58; MacLennan, *Toward the Charter,* 102–3.

150 House of Commons, *Debates,* John Diefenbaker, 12 February 1948, 1127; 13 February 1948, 1181.

151 Ibid., J.L. Ilsley, 9 April 1949, 2842–47.

152 Ibid., John Diefenbaker, 9 April 1948, 2857–59.

153 Ibid., 2859.

154 "Commentary for the Use of the Canadian Delegation," from the Department of External Affairs, 21 September 1948, file 5475-DG-3-40, pt. 2, vol. 3699, RG25, LAC.

155 "Report on Draft Declaration of Human Rights up to 23 November," from the Canadian Delegation in Paris to External Affairs, 25 November 1948, file 5475-DM-1-40, vol. 3700, RG25, LAC; Egerton, "Entering the Age of Human Rights," 465–66.

156 Canadian Bar Association, *1948 Yearbook of the Canadian Bar Association and the Minutes of Proceedings of the Thirtieth Annual Meeting* (Ottawa: National Printers, 1949), 142.

157 See correspondence between Mr. John T. Hackett, Canadian Bar Association, and Lester B. Pearson, Under-Secretary of State for External Affairs, October to November 1948, file 5475-DP-40, vol. 3701, RG25, LAC. For more information on Hackett's role, see A.J. Hobbins, "Humphrey and the Old Revolution: Human Rights in the Age of Mistrust," *Fontanus* 8 (1995): 122.

158 For example, see Memo from the Canadian Delegation to Lester B. Pearson, 4 October 1948, file 5475-DG-2-40, vol. 3701, RG25, LAC.

159 Ralph Maybank, "Statement to the Third Committee of the General Assembly," 1 October 1948, file 5475-DP-40, pt. 2.1, vol. 6425, RG25, LAC.

160 MacLennan, *Toward the Charter,* 61.

161 Louis St. Laurent, "Text of Address to be delivered by the Rt. Hon. L.S. St-Laurent, Secretary of State for External Affairs, Montreal Branch of the United Nations Society," 24 February 1947, file 5475-B-40, pt. 32, vol. 5111, RG25, LAC.

162 Ralph Maybank, "Statement by Ralph Maybank, M.P., Canadian Representative in the Third Committee, General Assembly, Concerning the Draft Declaration of Human Rights," 1 October 1948, file 5475-DP-40, pt. 2.1, vol. 6425, RG25, LAC.

163 Mary Ann Glendon, *A World Made New: Eleanor Roosevelt and the Universal Declaration of Human Rights* (New York: Random House, 2001).

164 Mazower, "The Strange Triumph of Human Rights."

165 See Simpson, *Human Rights and the End of Empire,* ch. 8.

166 Ibid., 336.

167 Ibid.

168 Letter from the High Commissioner for Canada to Escott Reid, Department of External Affairs, 8 September 1948, file 5475-DG-2-40, vol. 3699, RG25, LAC.

169 Memo from Canadian Delegation to Secretary of State for External Affairs, 29 September 1948, file 5475-DG-2-40, vol. 3699, RG25, LAC.

170 Memo from Canadian Delegation to the Secretary of State for External Affairs (Lester Pearson), 4 October 1948, file 5475-DG-2-40, vol. 3701, RG25, LAC.

171 Memo from Pearson to the Canadian Delegation, 7 October 1948, file 5475-DP-40, vol. 3701, RG25, LAC.

172 Memo from Canadian Delegation to Secretary of State for External Affairs, 29 September 1948, file 5475-DG-2-40, vol. 3699, RG25, LAC.

173 These drafts can be found at file 5475-DP-40, vol. 3701, RG25, LAC.

174 Memo from Canadian Delegation to the Department of External Affairs, 8 December 1948, file 5475-DP-40, vol. 3701, RG25, LAC.

175 Telegram No. 566, Canadian Delegation to the Department of External Affairs, 7 December 1948, file 5475-DP-40, vol. 3701, RG25, LAC.

176 A.J. Hobbins, ed., *On the Edge of Greatness: The Diaries of John Humphrey, First Director of the United Nations Division of Human Rights,* vol. 1, *1948–1949* (Montreal: McGill University Libraries, 1994), 89.

177 Memo from the Canadian Delegation to the Secretary of State for External Affairs, Memo 562, 7 December 1948, file 5475-DN-40, vol. 3700, RG25, LAC.

178 For membership, see United Nations, "Growth in United Nations Membership, 1945–present," http://www.un.org/en/sections/member-states/growth-united-nations-membership-1945-present/index.html; for voting results, see "Final Report: Universal Declaration of Human Rights," Canadian Delegation to the Department of External Affairs, December 1948, file 5474-DM-1-40, vol. 3700, RG25, LAC.

179 South Africa was not seen in the same negative light as the Soviet Union in this period. Canada remained supportive of South Africa at the UN in the early postwar years. Telegram from the Canadian Delegation to the Secretary of State for External Affairs, 23 November 1948, file 5475-DG-2-40, vol. 3701, RG25, LAC.

180 MacLennan, *Toward the Charter,* 65.

181 Michael Behiels, "Canada and the Implementation of International Instruments of Human Rights: A Federalist Conundrum, 1919–1982," in *Framing Canadian Federalism: Historical Essays in Honour of John T. Saywell,* ed. Dimitry Anastakis and P.E. Bryden (Toronto: University of Toronto Press, 2009), 154.

182 Canada, Parliament, House of Commons and Senate, Special Joint Committee on Human Rights and Fundamental Freedoms, *Proceedings,* 20th Parliament, 3rd and 4th Sessions, Ottawa, 1947–48, 13.

183 "Second and Final Report of the Special Joint Committee on Human Rights and Fundamental Freedoms" to the House of Commons of Canada, 25 June 1948, file 5475-W-2-40, pt. 1.2, vol. 6281, RG25, LAC.

184 House of Commons, *Debates*, J.L. Ilsley, 9 April 1948, 2844.

185 "Commentary for the Use of the Canadian Delegation," 21 September 1948, file 5475-DG-3-40, vol. 3699, RG25, LAC.

186 Memo from the Canadian Delegation to Secretary of State for External Affairs, 4 October 1948, file 5475-DG-2-40, vol. 3701, RG25, LAC.

187 Special Joint Committee on Human Rights and Fundamental Freedoms, *Proceedings*, 3.

188 Ibid., 111.

189 House of Commons, *Debates*, John Diefenbaker, 9 April 1948, 2847.

190 Ibid.

191 Ibid., J.L. Isley, 12 April 1948, 2869.

192 Lester B. Pearson, "Statement on the Universal Declaration on Human Rights," 10 December 1948, file 5475-DP-40, vol. 3701, RG25, LAC.

193 Ibid.

194 "Observations by Mr. Garson on First Draft of International Covenant on Human Rights," 27 June 1950, file 5475-W-40, pt. 2.2, vol. 6408, RG25, LAC; and Memo from Louis St. Laurent to the Canadian Delegation, October 1948, file 5475-DP-40, vol. 3701, RG25, LAC.

195 A copy of this article was sent to External Affairs. File 5475-DP-40, vol. 3701, RG25, LAC.

196 "UN General Assembly Adopts Historic Document of Rights," *Winnipeg Free Press*, 11 December 1948, 1. Similar stories ran in the *Ottawa Evening Citizen*, *Montreal Gazette*, and *Globe and Mail.*

197 "U.N. Ending Session," *Ottawa Evening Citizen*, 11 December 1948.

198 *Le Droit* reported the closing of the session on 11 December, and on 13 December included a reference to the UDHR in an article outlining the achievements of the UN session.

Chapter 2: Canada's Opposition to a Covenant on Human Rights

1 J.G.H. Halstead, "Internal Comments on Memo of August 26 on UN Activities," 6 October 1950, file 5475-W-40, pt. 3.1, vol. 6408, RG25, LAC.

2 A federal state clause would allow federal states to agree to a covenant that may include articles falling within the jurisdiction of their constituent states or provinces, without obligating those states or provinces to implement those articles. A colonial or territorial clause would permit colonial states to determine to what extent, if at all, a covenant would apply to dependent territories.

3 United Nations, General Assembly, Resolution 217 III D, 1949.
4 Department of External Affairs, Internal Memo, "Summary of Commemoration of HR Day 1953," 3 November 1952, file 5475-DP-1-40, pt. 2.1, vol. 8125, RG25, LAC.
5 See for example, "The Universal Declaration of Human Rights," *External Affairs* 1, 1, January 1949. The Ministry of Labour produced a similar article.
6 "UN Association of Canada – 2nd Anniversary Commemoration," file 5475-DP-1-40, vol. 3701, RG25, LAC.
7 "UN General Assembly Resolution to Create Human Rights Day," 5 December 1950, file 5475-DP-1-40, pt. 2.1, vol. 8125, RG25, LAC.
8 Letter from UNESCO to the Department of External Affairs, "Celebration of First Human Rights Day," 22 October 1951, file 5475-DP-1-40, pt. 2.1, vol. 8125, RG25, LAC.
9 Gordon had been the CBC's UN correspondent in the late 1940s, and became the human rights and information officer for the UN Secretariat in 1950, holding this position until 1960. Department of External Affairs, Internal Memo, "Summary of Commemoration of HR Day 1952," 25 November 1952, file 5475-DP-1-40, pt. 2.1, vol. 8125, RG25, LAC.
10 Letter from CBC to the Department of External Affairs, "Special Programming HR Day 1951," 4 December 1951, file 5475-DP-1-40, pt. 2.1, vol. 8125, RG25, LAC.
11 There is no evidence of replies from other provinces. For a sample of the replies: Memo from the Ontario Department of Education to the Department of External Affairs, December 1951, file 5475-DP-1-40, pt. 2.1, vol. 8125, RG25, LAC.
12 Speech given by Lester B. Pearson, 10 December 1953, Department of External Affairs, Internal Memo, "Summary of Commemoration of HR Day 1952," 25 November 1952, file 5475-DP-1-40, pt. 2.1, vol. 8125, RG25, LAC.
13 As discussed in the previous chapter, the 1940s witnessed the adoption of such laws as Ontario's *Racial Discrimination Act* (1944) and the *Saskatchewan Bill of Rights* (1947), as well as the repeal of the *Chinese Immigration Act* (1947) and amendments to the *Elections Act* (1948) so that race was no longer a ground for exclusion from voting in federal elections. However, anti-discrimination laws were weakly enforced in this period.
14 *Re Noble and Wolf*, [1948] OR 579 (HC). See Walker, *"Race," Rights and the Law in the Supreme Court of Canada.*
15 "Tolerance and the Law," *Globe and Mail*, 14 June 1948, 6.
16 James W. St. G. Walker, "The 'Jewish Phase' in the Movement for Racial Equality in Canada," *Canadian Ethnic Studies* 34, 1 (Spring 2002): 1–29; Patrias and Frager, "'This Is Our Country, These Are Our Rights,'" 1–35; Clément, *Canada's Rights Revolution.*
17 MacLennan, *Toward the Charter,* 83.
18 Clément, *Canada's Rights Revolution,* 50.

19 MacLennan, *Toward the Charter,* 93–94.

20 Ibid., 94; Walker, "The 'Jewish Phase' in the Movement for Racial Equality in Canada," 6.

21 Patrias and Frager, "'This Is Our Country, These Are Our Rights.'"

22 Ross Lambertson, "'The Dresden Story': Racism, Human Rights, and the Jewish Labour Committee of Canada," *Labour/Le Travail* 47 (Spring 2001): 43–82; and Walker, "The 'Jewish Phase' in the Movement for Racial Equality in Canada," 12–14.

23 Ibid.

24 MacLennan, *Toward the Charter,* 84.

25 As quoted in Lambertson, "'The Dresden Story,'" 50.

26 Scott, "Dominion Jurisdiction over Human Rights and Fundamental Freedoms."

27 Ibid., 508.

28 For an examination of the exclusion of women's rights in the human rights discourse, see Ruth Frager and Carmela Patrias, "Human Rights Activists and the Question of Sex Discrimination in Postwar Ontario"; and Clément, *Equality Deferred.* For a study of how Indigenous rights fit into the human rights discourse, see J.R. Miller, "Human Rights for Some," 233–60; and David Long, "Culture, Ideology, and Militancy: The Movement of Native Indians in Canada, 1969–91," in *Organizing Dissent: Contemporary Social Movements in Theory and Practice,* ed. W.K. Carroll (Toronto: Garamond Press, 1997).

29 For a discussion of the development of fair practices laws in the United States, see Anthony S. Chen, "The Party of Lincoln and the Politics of State Fair Employment Practices Legislation in the North, 1945–1964," *American Journal of Sociology* 112, 6 (May 2007): 1713–74; Alex Lichtenstein, "The Other Civil Rights Movement and the Problem of Southern Exceptionalism," *Journal of the Historical Society* 11, 3 (September 2011): 351–76; and Thomas J. Sugrue, *Sweet Land of Liberty: The Forgotten Struggle for Civil Rights in the North* (New York: Random House, 2008).

30 Walker, "The 'Jewish Phase' in the Movement for Racial Equality in Canada," 10–14. For an outline of the development of provincial anti-discrimination laws, see Brian Howe, *Restraining Equality: Human Rights Commissions in Canada* (Toronto: University of Toronto Press, 2000), 8.

31 Roebuck opposed the federal government's suspension of civil liberties following the Gouzenko Affair in 1945. In the 1930s, he promoted the rights of Jewish Canadians and trade unions.

32 Maurice Duplessis, the premier of Quebec, was particularly outspoken against federal interference in provincial human rights law, as was Angus Macdonald of Nova Scotia. MacLennon, *Toward the Charter,* 102; and T. Stephen Henderson, *Angus L. Macdonald: A Provincial Liberal* (Toronto: University of Toronto Press, 2007), ch. 4.

33 Canada, Parliament, Senate, *Debates,* 3 November 1949, 219; Canada, Parliament, Senate, Special Senate Committee on Human Rights and Fundamental Freedoms, *Minutes of Proceedings and Evidence* (Ottawa: King's Printer, 1950).

34 Canada, Parliament, Senate, Special Senate Committee on Human Rights and Fundamental Freedoms, *Report of the Roebuck Committee* (Ottawa: King's Printer, 1950).

35 MacLennan, *Toward the Charter,* 106.

36 As one example, in her comparative study of the incarceration of citizens of Japanese ancestry in Canada and the United States during the Second World War, Stephanie Bangarth highlights the interactions between activists resisting government action. Bangarth, *Voices Raised in Protest.*

37 Rosanne Waters, "A March from Selma to Canada: Canada and the Transnational Civil Rights Movement" (PhD dissertation, Department of History, McMaster University, 2015), https://macsphere.mcmaster.ca/bitstream/11375/17465/2/Waters_Dissertation.pdf; Patrias and Frager, "'This Is Our Country, These Are Our Rights,'" 8–9.

38 Rosanne Waters, "African Canadian Anti-Discrimination Activism and the Transnational Civil Rights Movement, 1945–1965," *Journal of the Canadian Historical Association* 24, 2 (2013): 386.

39 "A Fair Employment Practices Act and Policy," 27 May 1952, CLC Papers, vol. 230, file 17; Canadian Association for Adult Education, "Should We Have Fair Employment Practices in Canada?" (1948); and MacLennan, *Toward the Charter,* 95.

40 On 25 April, the Senate committee heard from legal expert F.R. Scott and King Gordon of the UN Division on Human Rights. On 3 May, the committee heard from Mr. L. Maynard. See Memo to Senate Committee on Human Rights and Fundamental Freedoms, 24 April 1950, file 5475-W-8-40, vol. 8118, RG25, LAC.

41 B.K. Sandwell, Statement to the Senate Committee on Human Rights and Fundamental Freedoms, 5 May 1950, 7.

42 F.R. Scott, "Brief Prepared for the Senate Committee on Human Rights and Fundamental Freedoms," 1950, file D211-28-7, MG30, LAC; and "Human Rights and Fundamental Freedoms, JCCA Submission to the Senate Committee, 1950," file 14, MG28, LAC.

43 Special Senate Committee on Human Rights and Fundamental Freedoms, *Minutes of Proceedings and Evidence* (1950).

44 Ibid., 15.

45 Lambertson, *Repression and Resistance,* 96.

46 Privy Council Office fonds, file U-41-H, vol. 206, RG2, LAC.

47 Ibid.

48 *Fair Employment Practices Act,* SO 1951, c. 24; *Fair Accommodation Practices Act,* SO 1954, c. 28.

49 Record of House of Commons Exchanges Relating to the UDHR, 18 January 1949, file 5475-DP-40, vol. 3701, RG25, LAC.

50 Ibid.

51 House of Commons, *Debates*, 28 February 1952 (submitted by David Croll), and 7 December 1953 (submitted by Alistair Stewart).

52 Robert O. Matthews and Cranford Pratt, eds., *Human Rights in Canadian Foreign Policy* (Montreal and Kingston: McGill-Queen's University Press, 1988), 29; Owen D. Carrigan, *Canadian Party Platforms, 1867–1968* (Urbana: University of Illinois Press, 1968).

53 Memo to Cabinet from Department of External Affairs, 1950, file 5475-DP-40, pt. 2.1, vol. 6425, RG25, LAC.

54 St. Laurent's Liberals won 190 of the 262 seats. Parliament of Canada, "Electoral Results by Party," Government of Canada, http://www.parl.gc.ca.

55 Mark E. Vajcner, "Stuart Garson and the Manitoba Progressive Coalition," *Manitoba History* 23 (Autumn 1993): 29–30.

56 Memo from A.J. Pick to Under-Secretary of State for External Affairs, 10 July 1950, file 5475-W-40, pt. 2.2, vol. 6408, RG25, LAC.

57 Ibid. Initially, the interest of other departments was limited to one or two articles. For example, Citizenship and Immigration was interested only in Article 8 of the draft covenant, on freedom of movement.

58 Department of External Affairs to Heads of Canadian Posts Abroad, 31 December 1953, file 5475-W-40-9, vol. 6409, RG25, LAC.

59 Stuart Garson, Minister of Justice, to Lester Pearson, Secretary of State for External Affairs, 30 June 1950, file 5475-W-40, pt. 2.2, vol. 6408, RG25, LAC.

60 A.D.P. Heeney, Under-Secretary of State for External Affairs, to N.F.H. Berlis, Secretary of the Canadian Permanent Representation to the European Office of the United Nations, 4 July 1949, file 5475-DS-1-40, vol. 3701, RG25, LAC.

61 "Minutes and Comments of the First Meeting of the Interdepartmental Committee," 26/27 July 1950, file 5475-W-40, pt. 2.2, vol. 6408, RG25, LAC.

62 "Draft Statement of Canadian Views on the International Covenant on Human Rights," A.J. Pick, Department of External Affairs, 19 April 1950, file 5475-W-40, pt. 2.1, vol. 6407, RG25, LAC; Stuart Garson, Minister of Justice, to Lester Pearson, Secretary of State for External Affairs, 30 June 1950, file 5475-W-40, pt. 2.2, vol. 6408, RG25, LAC; and Statement by L. Mayrand, Assistant Secretary of State for External Affairs, to the Special Senate Committee on Human Rights and Fundamental Freedoms, 3 May 1950, file 5475-W-8-40, vol. 8118, RG25, LAC.

63 "Minutes and Comments of the First Meeting of the Interdepartmental Committee," 26/27 July 1950, file 5475-W-40, pt. 2.2, vol. 6408, RG25, LAC.

64 Stuart Garson, Minister of Justice, to Lester Pearson, Secretary of State for External Affairs, 30 June 1950, file 5475-W-40, pt. 2.2, vol. 6408, RG25, LAC.

65 Memo to Cabinet, from the Interdepartmental Committee on Human Rights, 8 September 1950, file 5475-W-40, pt. 3.1, vol. 6408, RG25, LAC.

66 Ibid., 7.

67 Memo to the Special Senate Committee on Human Rights and Fundamental Freedoms, 24 April 1950, file 5475-W-8-40, vol. 8118, RG25, LAC.

68 Telegram from the Secretary of State for External Affairs to the Permanent Representative of Canada at the UN, "Instructions re: Covenant," 13 July 1950, file 5475-W-40, pt. 2.2, vol. 6408, RG25, LAC.

69 A.D.P. Heeney, Under-Secretary of State for External Affairs, to N.F.H. Berlis, Secretary of the Canadian Permanent Representation to the European Office of the United nations, 4 July 1949, file 5475-DS-1-40, vol. 3701, RG25, LAC.

70 For an overview of federal-provincial relations in this period, see Dimitry Anastakis and P.E. Bryden, eds., *Framing Canadian Federalism: Historical Essays in Honour of John T. Saywell* (Toronto: University of Toronto Press, 2009).

71 "Observations by Mr. Garson on First Draft of International Covenant on Human Rights," 27 June 1950, file 5475-W-40, pt. 2.2, vol. 6408, RG25, LAC.

72 Behiels, "Canada and the Implementation of International Instruments of Human Rights," 151–84.

73 Memo from A.J. Pick, Legal Division, to E. Reid, Department of External Affairs, 19 April 1950, 1, file 54-75-W-40, pt. 2.1, vol. 6407, RG25, LAC.

74 "Instructions for Canadian Delegates at the 11th Session of ECOSOC," Department of External Affairs, 17 June 1950, file 5475-DS-10-40, pt. 1, vol. 6436, RG25, LAC.

75 Speech by G. Davidson to ECOSOC, 25 July 1950, file 5475-W-40, pt. 3.1, vol. 6408, RG25, LAC.

76 Stuart Garson, Minister of Justice, to Lester Pearson, Secretary of State for External Affairs, 30 June 1950, 1, file 5475-W-40, pt. 2.2, vol. 6408, RG25, LAC.

77 "Final Report on Item No. 28: Draft International Covenants on Human Rights," 1955, file 5475-W-40, pt. 12, vol. 6923, RG25, LAC.

78 Ibid, 17.

79 A.J. Pick, Department of External Affairs, "Instructions for the Canadian Delegation to the ECOSOC Session at Geneva on Particular Articles of the Draft Covenant on Human Rights," 1950, file 5475-DS-10-40, pt. 1, vol. 6923, RG25, LAC.

80 "Memorandum to Cabinet: General Instructions to the Canadian Delegation to the Thirteenth Session of ECOSOC," 23 July 1951, file 5475-DS-18, pt. 1.1, vol. 8126, RG25, LAC.

81 Statement by L. Mayrand to the Senate Committee on Human Rights and Fundamental Freedoms, 3 May 1950, file 5475-W-8-40, vol. 8118, RG25, LAC.

82 "Memorandum to Cabinet: General Instructions to the Canadian Delegation to the Thirteenth Session of ECOSOC," 23 July 1951, file 5475-DS-18-40, pt. 1.1, vol. 8126, RG25, LAC.

83 Lester Pearson to Canadian Delegation to the Thirteenth Session of ECOSOC, 24 August 1951, ibid., pt. 1.3.

84 N.E. Curie, Department of External Affairs Memo, 22 October 1956, file 5475-W-15-40, pt. 5.1, vol. 6927, RG25, LAC.

85 "Canada and the United Nations 1951–52, Section II – Economic and Social," L.A.D. Stephens, United Nations Division, Department of External Affairs, 14 June 1952, file 5475-W-40, pt. 6, vol. 6409, RG25, LAC.

86 Howe, "The Evolution of Human Rights Policy in Ontario," 786.

87 Ibid.

88 House of Commons, *Debates,* Ernest G. Hansell, 12 April 1948, 2872.

89 Patrias, "Socialists, Jews, and the 1947 Saskatchewan Bill of Rights," 269.

90 Jules Léger to the Minister, 29 August 1957, file 5475-DP-40, pt. 2.1, vol. 6425, RG25, LAC.

91 "Report of the Interdepartmental Committee on Human Rights," April 1948, file 5475-W-2-40, pt. 1.1, vol. 6281, RG25, LAC.

92 "Observations by Mr. Garson on First Draft of International Covenant on Human Rights," 27 June 1950, file 5475-W-40, pt. 2.2, vol. 6408, RG25, LAC.

93 MacLennan, *Toward the Charter,* ch. 3.

94 "Observations by Mr. Garson on First Draft of International Covenant on Human Rights," 27 June 1950, file 5475-W-40, pt. 2.2, vol. 6408, RG25, LAC.

95 *Alberta Communal Property Act,* SA 1947, c. 16. The Interdepartmental Committee on Human Rights had noted these laws, and laws in Quebec limiting women and Jehovah's Witnesses, as conflicting with the principles of the *International Bill of Rights.*

96 Laval Fortier to Under-Secretary of State for External Affairs, 22 February 1955, file 1-24-27, pt. 1, vol. 81, RG26, LAC.

97 Letter from Laval Fortier, Citizenship and Immigration, to M.H. Wershof, External Affairs, 13 November 1956, file 5475-W-15-40, pt. 5.1, vol. 6927, RG25, LAC.

98 Letter from R.G. Robertson, Deputy Minister of Northern Affairs and Natural Resources, to Jules Léger, External Affairs, 12 March 1957, file 5475-DP-3-40, pt. 1.1, vol. 6950, RG25, LAC.

99 "Draft Statement of Canadian Views on the International Covenant on Human Rights," A.J. Pick, Department of External Affairs, 19 April 1950, file 5475-W-40, pt. 2.1, vol. 6407, RG25, LAC; Stuart Garson, Minister of Justice, to Lester Pearson, Secretary of State for External Affairs, 30 June 1950, file 5475-W-40, pt. 2.2, vol. 6408, RG25, LAC; and Statement by L. Mayrand, Assistant Secretary of State for External Affairs, to the Special Senate Committee on Human Rights and Fundamental Freedoms, 3 May 1950, file 5475-W-8-40, vol. 8118, RG25, LAC.

100 Simpson, *Human Rights and the End of Empire,* 337.

101 Australia's support for both economic and social rights and the draft covenant waned in the 1950s. Annemarie Devereux, *Australia and the Birth of the International Bill of Human Rights 1946–1966* (Annandale, NSW: Federation Press, 2005).
102 This indecisive approach to the covenants was noted in a 1956 internal memo of the Department of External Affairs. M. Cadieux, 23 October 1956, file 5475-W-15-40, pt. 5.1, vol. 6927, RG25, LAC.
103 E.G. Lee to File, 20 November 1956, ibid., pt. 5.2.
104 M. Cadieux to Legal Division, Department of External Affairs, 17 October 1956, ibid., pt. 5.1.
105 "Statement by Delegate of Canada, Mrs. R.J. Marshall, in the Third Committee of the Sixth Session of the General Assembly on the Draft International Covenant on Human Rights," 1951, file 5475-W-40, pt. 6, folder 5.2, vol. 6409, RG25, LAC.
106 Escott Reid to A.D.P. Heeney, 3 January 1952, ibid.
107 A.D.P. Heeney to David M. Johnston, Permanent Delegate of Canada to the UN, 4 January 1952, ibid.
108 "Report on work of Sixteenth Session of ECOSOC," S. Morley Scott, 1952, file 5475-W-40, vol. 6409, RG25, LAC. Canada did not sit on the Commission on Human Rights until 1963.
109 Mackenzie, "Knight Errant, Cold Warrior or Cautious Ally?," 456.
110 A.J. Pick to Escott Reid, 19 April 1950, file 5475-W-15-40, pt. 5.1, vol. 6927, RG25, LAC.
111 "Draft Statement of Canadian Views on International Covenant on Human Rights," 19 April 1950, file 5475-W-40, pt. 2.1, vol. 6407, RG25, LAC. This criticism appeared in the same report as that which called for more precise language: A.J. Pick to Escott Reid, 19 April 1950.
112 These instructions came as early as July 1950. Memo from A.D.P. Heeney to the Chairman of the Canadian Delegation to the United Nations, 13 July 1950, file 5475-W-40, pt. 2.2, vol. 6408, RG25, LAC. They were reiterated when the General Assembly began its article-by-article examination of the covenants in 1956. "Report of the Eleventh Session of the Third Committee," 1956, file 1-24-27, pt. 2, vol. 82, RG26, LAC.
113 The American member of the Commission on Human Rights (Mrs. O.B. Lord) repeated this announcement at the United Nations on 8 April 1953. Ibid., 205.
114 Glendon, *A World Made New*, ch. 11.
115 Jules Léger to John Diefenbaker, 29 August 1957, file 5475-DP-40, pt. 2.1, vol. 6425, RG25, LAC.
116 Normand and Zaidi, *Human Rights at the UN*, 241.
117 For a wider discussion of the impact of the Cold War on the United Nations, see Stanley Meisler, *United Nations: The First Fifty Years* (New York: Atlantic Monthly

Press, 1995); Norrie MacQueen, *The United Nations, Peace Operations and the Cold War*, 2nd ed. (New York: Addison-Wesley Longman, 2011).

118 These events not only influenced the tone and content of debates but were also remarked upon by Canadian delegates in their reports to External Affairs. See "Report – Survey of Political Climate and Work of 13th Session of ECOSOC," 12 November 1951, file 5475-DS-16-40, pt. 2, vol. 8126, RG25, LAC.

119 Ibid.; and "Report on the Work of the Human Rights Commission," 14 June 1952, file 5475-W-40, pt. 6, vol. 6409, RG25, LAC.

120 Ibid.

121 "Report – Survey of Political Climate and Work of 13th Session of ECOSOC," 12 November 1951, file 5475-DS-16-40, pt. 2, vol. 8126, RG25, LAC.

122 Glendon, *A World Made New*, 193.

123 Devereux, *Australia and the Birth of the International Bill of Human Rights*, 51–57.

124 Denis Stairs, "Of Medium Powers and Middling Roles," in *Statecraft and Security: The Cold War and Beyond*, ed. Ken Booth (Cambridge: Cambridge University Press, 1998): 270–86; see also Lui, *Why Canada Cares*, 51; and Robert Bothwell, *The Big Chill: Canada and the Cold War* (Ottawa: Canadian Institute of International Affairs, 1998).

125 Confidential memo from A.D.P Heeney to David M. Johnston, Permanent Delegate of Canada to the United Nations, 4 January 1952, file 5475-W-40, pt. 5.2, vol. 6409, RG25, LAC.

126 Ibid., 2.

127 Roland Burke, *Decolonization and the Evolution of International Human Rights* (Philadelphia: University of Pennsylvania Press, 2010), 1.

128 Ibid.

129 Ibid.

130 Jules Léger to John Diefenbaker, 29 August 1957, file 5475-DP-40, pt. 2.1, vol. 6425, RG25, LAC. See Normand and Zaidi, *Human Rights at the UN*.

131 The Soviets continued to use anti-colonial discourse in its attacks on the United States and other Western states into the 1960s. For example, see "Report to Under-Secretary of State for External Affairs, from UN Division," 17 October 1962, file 5475-W-15-40, pt. 10, vol. 5118, RG25, LAC.

132 Ibid.

133 Memo from the Canadian Delegation to the Department of External Affairs, 8 November 1955, file 1-24-27, pt. 1, vol. 81, RG26, LAC.

134 Meisler, *United Nations*, 208.

135 Normand and Zaidi, *Human Rights at the UN*, 200–12.

136 "Report on the work of the Human Rights Commission," from the Canadian Delegation to the Department of External Affairs, 14 June 1952, file 5475-W-40, pt. 6, vol. 6409, RG25, LAC.

137 "Report of 6th Session of HR Commission to 11th Session of ECOSOC," 21 August 1950, file 5475-W-40, pt. 3.1, vol. 6408, RG25, LAC.

138 "Instructions for the Delegation of the 13th Session of ECOSOC," Department of External Affairs, 23 July 1951, file 5475-DS-18-40, pt. 1.1, vol. 8126, RG25, LAC.

139 For a discussion of the larger political debates over economic and social rights in UN human rights debates, see Normand and Zaidi, *Human Rights at the UN,* 200–12.

140 "Report of 6th Session of HR Commission to 11th Session of ECOSOC," 21 August 1950, file 5475-W-40, pt. 3.1, vol. 6408, RG25, LAC.

141 Ibid. For a wider examination of Australia's approach to international human rights, see Devereux, *Australia and the Birth of the International Bill of Human Rights.*

142 Phillip Deery, "Communism, Security and the Cold War," *Journal of Australian Studies* 21, 54/55 (1997): 162–75.

143 "Final Report on Item 29: Draft International Covenant on Human Rights – Report of ECOSOC," 12 February 1952, file 5475-W-40, pt. 5.2, vol. 6409, RG25, LAC.

144 Internal Memo, Department of External Affairs, "Commentary for Canadian Delegation," 26 January 1951, file 5474-DS-13-40, pt. 1.1, vol. 8126, RG25, LAC.

145 Memo from the Canadian Permanent Delegation in Geneva to the Under-Secretary of State for External Affairs, 27 September 1951, file 5475-DS-16-40, pt. 1.3, vol. 8126, RG25, LAC.

146 Ibid.

147 Ibid.

148 Ibid., 7.

149 "Final Report on Item 29: Draft International Covenant on Human Rights – Report of ECOSOC," 12 February 1952, file 5475-W-40, pt. 5.2, vol. 6409, RG25, LAC.

150 The states that supported the split included India, New Zealand, Britain, the United States, Australia, Canada, France, and China. Those opposed included Pakistan, Saudi Arabia, the Soviet Bloc, and Latin America. Those that abstained included the Philippines, Thailand, the Dominican Republic, and Guatemala. "Report of the history of the Covenant," 26 February 1962, file 5475-W-40, pt. 5.2, vol. 6409, LAC.

151 This text was taken from conventions of the ILO.

152 "Report of 6th Session of HR Commission to 11th Session of ECOSOC," 21 August 1950, file 5475-W-40, pt. 3.1, vol. 6408, RG25, LAC.

153 Ibid.

154 Memo to Cabinet from the Interdepartmental Committee on Human Rights, 8 September 1950, file 5475-W-40, pt. 3.1, vol. 6408, RG25, LAC.

155 "Report of 6th Session of HR Commission to 11th Session of ECOSOC," 21 August 1950, file 5475-W-40, pt. 3.1, vol. 6408, RG25, LAC.

156 "Report – Survey of Political Climate and Work of the 13th Session of ECOSOC," 12 November 1951, file 5475-DS-16-40, pt. 2, vol. 8126, RG25, LAC.

157 Laura Madokoro, "'Belated Signing': Race-Thinking and Canada's Approach to the 1951 Convention Relating to the Status of Refugees," in *Dominion of Race: Rethinking Canada's International History*, ed. Laura Madokoro, Francine McKenzie, and David Meren (Vancouver: UBC Press, 2017), 160–82.

Chapter 3: A Reversal in Policy: The Decision to Support the Covenants

1 Stuart Garson to M. Scott, UN Division, re: Human Rights, 10 March 1952, file 5475-W-40, pt. 5.2, vol. 6409, RG25, LAC.

2 K.G. Montgomery, Speech in the Third Committee of the General Assembly, 2 November 1954, reprinted in "Final Report: Draft International Covenants on Human Rights," 252, file 5475-W-15-40, pt. 4, vol. 6412, RG25, LAC.

3 Ibid., 250.

4 The five Soviet bloc countries, Greece, Indonesia, Saudi Arabia, Iraq, Syria, Afghanistan, most Latin American states, Iran, Egypt, Philippines, China, and Yugoslavia all desired an article on self-determination, although they differed in the extent to which they wanted the current draft to be revised. For an examination of the debate over the article on self-determination, see Antonio Cassese, *Self-Determination of Peoples: A Legal Reappraisal* (Cambridge: Cambridge University Press, 1995), 47.

5 Telegram to High Commissioners in Canada, Australia, New Zealand, and South Africa, from the Commonwealth Relations Office, 15 September 1955, file 5475-W-15-40, pt. 4, vol. 6412, RG25, LAC.

6 Ibid., 3.

7 Department of External Affairs Memo, G. Grondin, UN Division, to Information Division, 24 October 1958, file 5475-DP-1-40, pt. 3, vol. 6950, RG25, LAC.

8 "Draft International Covenants on Human Rights: Background," Department of External Affairs, Twelfth Session of the General Assembly, 1957, file 5475-W-15-40, pt. 10FP, vol. 5118, RG25, LAC.

9 The following member states submitted comments: Australia, Austria, Ceylon, Hungary, Netherlands, Pakistan, Thailand, United Kingdom, USSR, and Yugoslavia. The following specialized agencies submitted comments: UNESCO and the International Labor Organization. "Report of the Third Committee re: Draft International Covenants on Human Rights," United Nations Organization, A/3077, 8 December 1955, file 5475-W-15-40, pt. 5.1, vol. 6927, RG25, LAC.

10 Department of External Affairs Memo re: Statement of the Government of Canada on United Nations Draft Covenants on Human Rights, March 1954, file 5475-W-15-40, pt. 2, vol. 6412, RG25, LAC.

11 Department of External Affairs Memo, S.F. Rae, UN Division, 5 March 1954, file 5475-W-15-40, pt. 2, vol. 6412, RG25, LAC. For a detailed explanation of Canada's position in 1954, see "Report on Civil and Political Rights" and "Report on Economic, Social and Cultural Rights" in file 1-24-27, pt. 2, vol. 82, RG26, LAC.

12 Glendon, *A World Made New,* 195. Although Eleanor Roosevelt was a champion of human rights at the UN, she drew a distinction between international human rights and the civil rights discourse within the United States. Historian Carol Anderson has referred to Roosevelt as a "master of symbolic equality," arguing she prioritized political and legal rights over economic and social rights. Carol Anderson, *Eyes Off the Prize: The United Nations and the African American Struggle for Human Rights, 1944–1955* (Cambridge: Cambridge University Press, 2003), 3–5.

13 Helle Porsdam, *Civil Religion, Human Rights and International Relations: Connecting People across Cultures and Traditions* (Cheltenham, UK, and Northampton, MA: Edward Elgar, 2012), 129–30.

14 Mary Lord represented the United States on the UN Commission on Human Rights and ECOSOC from 1953 to 1961. "Biographical Note," Mary Lord Papers, 1941–1972, Dwight D. Eisenhower Library, AC 71-6, 71-6/1, 73-22, https://eisenhower.archives.gov/Research/Finding_Aids/pdf/Lord_Mary_Papers.pdf.

15 René Cassin characterized Lord's lack of interest as "injurious to the Covenants." Normand and Zaidi, *Human Rights at the UN,* 227–29. John P. Humphrey was also extremely disappointed with the American approach (including Roosevelt's) to the covenants. Glendon, *A World Made New,* 197.

16 Lord made this announcement to the Commission on Human Rights, 8 April 1953. Department of State Bulletin, [Washington, DC]: Office of Public Communication, Bureau of Public Affairs, 1939, Bulletin 28, 579–82.

17 Simpson, *Human Rights and the End of Empire,* 817–19. Canadian delegates noted Britain's change in position. Memo from Stuart Garson, Minister of Justice, to Lester Pearson, Secretary of State for External Affairs, 14 July 1954, file 5475-W-15-40, pt. 2, vol. 6412, RG25, LAC.

18 Anthony Lester, "Fundamental Rights: The United Kingdom Isolated?" *Public Law* 10, 2 (Spring 1984): 955; Simpson, ibid., especially ch. 13.

19 Devereux, *Australia and the Birth of the International Bill of Human Rights,* 51–60.

20 Department of External Affairs Memo, S.F. Rae, UN Division, 5 March 1954, file 5475-W-15-40, pt. 2, vol. 6412, RG25, LAC.

21 Memo from Stuart Garson, Minister of Justice, to the Department of External Affairs, 31 August 1954, file 5475-W-15-40, pt. 5.1, vol. 6927, RG25, LAC.

22 See, for example, K.G. Montgomery, Speech in the Third Committee of the General Assembly, 2 November 1954, reprinted in "Final Report: Draft International Covenants on Human Rights," 252, file 5475-W-15-40, pt. 4, vol. 6412, RG25, LAC.

23 Department of External Affairs Memo, Marcel Cadieux, UN Division, to Legal Division, re: Draft Covenants on Human Rights – 11th Session of the General Assembly, 17 October 1956, file 5475-W-15-40, pt. 5.1, vol. 6927, RG25, LAC.

24 Canada voted against Article 1, on the right to self-determination. It abstained in most of the votes on economic and social rights.

25 United Nations, *Charter of the United Nations,* Article 1.2, http://www.un.org/en/documents/charter/.

26 Both Marx and Lenin argued that nations oppressed by imperialism have the right to self-determination. For a discussion of the evolution of ideas of self-determination, see Patrick Thornberry, "Self-Determination, Minorities, Human Rights: A Review of International Instruments," *International and Comparative Law Quarterly* 38, 4 (October 1989): 867–89; Frederic L. Kirgis Jr., "The Degrees of Self-Determination in the United Nations Era," *American Journal of International Law* 88, 2 (April 1994): 304–10; and Hurst Hannum, *Autonomy, Sovereignty, and Self-Determination: The Accommodation of Conflicting Rights* (Philadelphia: University of Pennsylvania Press, 1996), 33.

27 United Nations, General Assembly, Resolution 545 (VI) (5 February 1952).

28 Normand and Zaidi, *Human Rights at the UN,* 213.

29 In the final version, this article was changed to read: "All peoples have the right of self-determination. By virtue of that right they freely determine their political status and freely pursue their economic, social and cultural development." See Appendix 2 and Appendix 3, Article 1(1).

30 Ibid., Article 1(2).

31 "Final Report to the 10th Session of the General Assembly re: Human Rights," Department of External Affairs, 1955, file 5475-W-40, pt. 12, vol. 6923, RG25, LAC.

32 Burke, *Decolonization and the Evolution of International Human Rights,* 37–38.

33 Simpson, *Human Rights and the End of Empire,* 304–5.

34 Burke, *Decolonization and the Evolution of International Human Rights,* 37.

35 Moyn, *The Last Utopia,* 195–96.

36 Normand and Zaidi, *Human Rights at the UN,* 217.

37 States that routinely spoke out against the article on self-determination: Canada, Britain, Australia, New Zealand, Belgium, the Netherlands, Turkey, Brazil, Ethiopia, Israel, Norway, Sweden, and Denmark. "Final Report: Draft International Covenants on Human Rights," 1955, file 5475-W-15-40, pt. 4, vol. 6412, RG25, LAC.

38 For an overview of Canada's position, see "Final Report on Item 28: Draft International Covenant on Human Rights," 20 April 1956, file 5475-W-15-40, pt. 5.1, vol. 6927, RG25, LAC.

39 States in favour of an article on self-determination: the Soviet bloc countries (Byelorussia, Czechoslovakia, Poland, the Ukraine, and the Soviet Union), Greece,

Indonesia, Saudi Arabia, Iraq, Syria, Afghanistan, most Latin American states, Iran, Egypt, the Philippines, China, and Yugoslavia.

40 States opposed: Australia, Belgium, Canada, France, Luxembourg, the Netherlands, New Zealand, Norway, Sweden, Turkey, the United Kingdom, and the United States. Abstaining states included Brazil, Burma, China, Cuba, Denmark, the Dominican Republic, Ethiopia, Honduras, Iceland, Iran, Panama, and Paraguay.

41 N. Currie, "Statement in the Third Committee: Draft Covenant on Economic, Social and Cultural Rights," 4 January 1957, file 5475-W-15-40 pt. 5.2, vol. 6927, RG25, LAC.

42 Ann Shipley, "Speech in the Third Committee," 20 December 1956, file 5475-W-15-40, pt. 5.2, vol. 6927, RG25, LAC.

43 "Report (backgrounder) on Covenants for Other Departments," Department of External Affairs, 1956, file 1-24-27, pt. 2, vol. 82, RG26, LAC; "Comments on the Draft Covenant on Economic, Social and Cultural Rights," 17 October 1955, file 5475-W-15-40, pt. 4, vol. 6412, RG25, LAC.

44 Keating, *Canada and World Order.*

45 For an outline of the development of provincial anti-discrimination laws, see Howe, *Restraining Equality,* 8. Three provinces did not have fair practices laws by the end of the 1960s: Newfoundland, Quebec, and Alberta. All three developed anti-discrimination or human rights laws in the 1960s.

46 According to Dominque Clément, only one complaint was prosecuted under Ontario's *Fair Practices Act* in its seven years in existence. Dominique Clément, "Human Rights in Canadian Domestic and Foreign Politics: From 'Niggardly Acceptance' to Enthusiastic Embrace," *Human Rights Quarterly* 34, 3 (2012), n. 56.

47 Howe, *Restraining Equality,* 7–9.

48 For specific examples of the limitations of fair practices laws, see Clément, *Equality Deferred,* chs. 2, 3, and 4; Frager and Patrias, "Human Rights Activists and the Question of Sex Discrimination in Postwar Ontario"; and Jennifer Tunnicliffe, "'Life Together': Public Debates over Human Rights Legislation in Ontario, 1975–1981," *Histoire Sociale/Social History* 45, 92 (November 2013): 446–47.

49 For a discussion of the evolution of Canada's social policy and liberal ideology, see Rianne Mahon, "Varieties of Liberalism: Canadian Social Policy from the 'Golden Age' to the Present," *Social Policy and Administration* 42, 4 (August 2008): 342–61; and Barry Ferguson, "Remaking Liberalism: The Intellectual Legacy of Adam Shortt, OD Skelton, WC Clark & WA Mackintosh, 1890–1925," *American Review of Canadian Studies* 25, 2/3 (Summer/Fall 1995): 359.

50 Penny Bryden, *Planners and Politicians: Liberal Politics and Social Policy, 1957–1968* (Montreal and Kingston: McGill-Queen's University Press, 1997), 6.

51 These developments were all reported to the Secretary-General of the United Nations. For example, "Report on Human Rights in Canada, 1957–59 Report" Department

of External Affairs, 1959, file 5475-W-7-40, pt. 3.2, vol. 6926, RG25, LAC; "Report on the UN Yearbook on Human Rights – 1959," Department of External Affairs, 1959, file 5475-W-7-40, pt. 3.2, vol. 6926, RG25, LAC.

52 "Report on the UN Yearbook on Human Rights – 1959," 15.

53 The first province to grant voting rights to Non-Status Indians was British Columbia, in 1949. The last province was Quebec, in 1969. Although most Inuit received voting rights in 1950, there were still significant barriers to voting in the North. It is important to note that not all First Nations communities wanted voting rights, as enfranchisement brought with it other obligations that many Indigenous people did not welcome. See John Milloy, "Indian Act Colonialism: A Century of Dishonour, 1869–1969," Research paper for the National Centre for First Nations Governance, May 2008, http://fngovernance.org/ncfng_research/milloy.pdf.

54 *Noble v. Alley,* [1951] SCR 64 (SCC). In a six-to-one ruling, the Supreme Court of Canada struck down the covenant; however, the justices did not explicitly state that racial restrictions were contrary to public policy. See Walker, *"Race," Rights and the Law in the Supreme Court of Canada,* ch. 4.

55 *Hurshman, Mindlin v. Hurshman,* [1956] 6 DLR 615 (BCSC).

56 Robin Elliot, *Cases and Materials in Civil Liberties* (Vancouver: Faculty of Law, University of British Columbia, 1986); and Robin Elliot, "Civil Liberties and the Supreme Court of Canada," unpublished, University of British Columbia, Faculty of Law, 1982; and Ross Lambertson, "The BC Court and Appeal and Civil Liberties," *BC Studies* 162 (Summer 2009): 81–109.

57 *Switzman v. Elbing,* [1957] SCR 285.

58 *Roncarelli v. Duplessis,* [1959] SCR 121, 16 DLR (2d) 689.

59 Greene, *The Charter of Rights,* 33.

60 The *Yearbook on Human Rights* was published from 1946 to 1988. United Nations, Secretariat, *Yearbook on Human Rights* (New York: United Nations).

61 ECOSOC Resolution 624B (XXII), "Periodic reports on human rights," 1956.

62 Federal officials found this an onerous process, and often felt itself the "victim" of the UN's reporting system. Department of External Affairs Internal Memo, from D. Osborne to J. Holmes, re: Reports on Subjects concerning Human Rights, 21 March 1957, file 5475-DP-40, pt. 2.1, vol. 6425, RG25, LAC.

63 For a discussion of how the 1950s set the stage for these types of questions, see José E. Igartua, *The Other Quiet Revolution: National Identities in English Canada, 1945–71* (Vancouver: UBC Press, 2006); Philip Massolin, *Canadian Intellectuals, the Tory Tradition, and the Challenge of Modernity, 1939–1970* (Toronto: University of Toronto Press, 2001); Nancy Christie and Michael Gauvreau, eds., *Cultures of Citizenship in Postwar Canada, 1940–1955* (Montreal and Kingston: McGill-Queen's University Press, 2003); Leonard Kuffert, *A Great Duty: Canadian Responses to Modern Life and Mass Culture, 1939–1967* (Montreal and Kingston: McGill-Queen's University Press,

2003); and Phillip Buckner, ed., *Canada and the End of Empire* (Vancouver: UBC Press, 2005).

64 Smith, *Rogue Tory;* Garrett Wilson and Kevin Charles Wilson, *Diefenbaker for the Defence* (Toronto: James Lorimer, 1988); Boutin, *John Diefenbaker;* Arthur Slade, *John Diefenbaker: An Appointment with Destiny* (Toronto: XYZ Publishing, 2001); and Thad McIlroy, *Remembering the Chief* (Toronto: Doubleday Canada, 1984).

65 *Canadian Bill of Rights,* SC 1960, c. 44.

66 Ibid.

67 MacLennan, *Toward the Charter,* ch. 6; Lambertson, *Repression and Resistance,* 118–21; Greene, *The Charter of Rights,* 21–29; and Richard W. Pound, *Chief Justice W.R. Jacket: By the Law of the Land* (Montreal and Kingston: McGill-Queen's University Press, 1999), 115–21.

68 Senator Arthur Roebuck argued that, because the bill established no new rights and broke no new ground in protecting rights and freedoms, it did "very little for the people of Canada." MacLennan, ibid., 158; Lambertson, ibid., 362.

69 Legal scholar and rights activist Bora Laskin called the document "timid" and claimed that it was worse than had Diefenbaker done nothing. MacLennan, ibid., 158; Lambertson, ibid., 362. For legal critiques, see Bora Laskin, "Canada's Bill of Rights: A Dilemma for the Courts," *International and Comparative Law Quarterly* 11, 2 (April 1962): 519–36; and W.S. Tarnopolsky, *The Canadian Bill of Rights,* 2nd ed. (Toronto: McClelland and Stewart, 1975).

70 Lambertson, ibid., 157, 330–31, 362; MacLennan, ibid., 46, 118–21.

71 The earliest concept of human rights coming out of the UN focused on restraining state power over the individual, much as Diefenbaker's bill of rights did. By the 1960s, this had expanded to include obligations on the state to also protect the economic, social, and cultural well-being of its citizens.

72 Many of the rights found in Sections 1 and 2 of the *Canadian Bill of Rights* can be found with very similar wording in the UDHR.

73 House of Commons, *Debates,* 2 August 1960, 7446–50.

74 See, for example, "Le bill fédéral des droits de l'homme," éditoriaux, *Relations* 237 (septembre 1960), 226; "That Bill of Rights," editorial, *Saturday Night,* 27 September 1958; Pauline Jewett, "Mr. Diefenbaker's Proposed Bill of Rights," *Canadian Forum,* December 1958; M.S. Donnelly, "Why Pass a Useless Bill of Rights?" *Maclean's,* 3 January 1959; *Canadian Bar Review* 37 (March 1959); A.R.M. Lower, "The Bill of Rights," *Canadian Commentator* 3 (March 1959): 2–3.

75 Government of Canada, Special Joint Committee on Human Rights and Fundamental Freedoms, *Minutes of Proceedings and Evidence* (Ottawa: Queen's Printer, 1960).

76 Lambertson, *Repression and Resistance,* 367.

77 Ibid.

78 John Diefenbaker, 23 September 1957, quoted in Canada, *Report of the Department of External Affairs, 1957* (Ottawa: Queen's Printer, 1958), 2.

79 Chapnick, "The Department of External Affairs and the United Nations Idea, 1943–1965," 81–100.

80 Chapnick, "The Canadian Middle Power Myth," 194–95.

81 Department of External Affairs Memo to File, "Interest of Canadian Non-Governmental Organizations in U.N. Activities in the Field of the Status of Women," 19 July 1956, file 5475-W-40, pt. 14.1, vol. 6924, RG25, LAC.

82 Ibid.

83 Canada ratified the *Convention on the Political Rights of Women* in 1957.

84 External Affairs kept notes on these submissions. See file 5475-W-15-40, pt. 3, vol. 6412, RG25, LAC; and file 5475-DP-40, pt. 2.1, vol. 6425, RG25, LAC. Liberal MP David Croll introduced a private member's bill on 28 February 1953, CCF MP Alistair Stewart brought it forward again on 7 December 1953, and it was debated in January 1954.

85 House of Commons, *Debates,* Prime Minister Louis St. Laurent, 21 May 1951.

86 Collection of documents relating to House of Commons debates, collected 14 January 1954, file 5475-DP-40, pt. 2.1, vol. 6425, RG25, LAC.

87 Department of External Affairs Internal Memo, P. McDougall re: Tenth Anniversary, 7 November 1957, file 5475-DP-3-40, pt. 1.1, vol. 6950, RG25, LAC.

88 George F. Davidson, Deputy Minister of Citizenship and Immigration, to Under-Secretary of State for External Affairs, 3 August 1961, file 1-24-27-3, vol. 82, RG26, LAC.

89 Ibid., 3.

90 Davidson argues that the Canadian Labour Congress was perhaps the best example of an organization heavily involved in the dissemination of materials relating to human rights, and with a human rights committee active on all levels.

91 Patrias and Frager, "'This Is Our Country, These Are Our Rights,'" 19.

92 This resolution was endorsed by both ECOSOC and the General Assembly. ECOSOC, E/CN.4/735, 11 February 1957; and Letter from the Secretary-General of the United Nations re: Resolution on the Tenth Anniversary, 9 September 1957, file 5475-DP-1-40, pt. 3, vol. 6950, RG25, LAC.

93 Letter from the Department of External Affairs to the Department of Citizenship and Immigration, re: Government Involvement in Celebration of Tenth Anniversary, 1 March 1957, file 5475-DP-3-40, pt. 1.1, vol. 6950, RG25, LAC.

94 Department of External Affairs Internal Memo, 1 April 1957, file 5475-DP-3-40, pt. 1.1, vol. 6950, RG25, LAC.

95 Letter from Laval Fortier, Department of Citizenship and Immigration, to Jules Léger, Department of External Affairs, 6 March 1957, ibid.

96 Letter from A.H. Brown, Deputy Minister of Labour, to Jules Léger, Department of External Affairs, 11 March 1957, ibid.

97 Letter from R.G. Robertson, Deputy Minister of Northern Affairs and Natural Resources, to Jules Léger, Department of External Affairs, 12 March 1957, ibid.

98 Ibid., 2.

99 Letter from N. Currie, Department of External Affairs, to J.P. Kidd, Canadian Citizenship Council, 13 March 1957, file 5475-DP-3-40, pt. 1.1, vol. 6950, RG25, LAC.

100 Department of External Affairs Internal Memo, 27 February 1957, ibid.

101 "Report on Preparations for 1958 Conference on HR," Department of External Affairs, 7 November 1957, file 5475-DP-3-40, pt. 1.1, vol. 6950, RG25, LAC.

102 Ibid.

103 Letters and Minutes of meeting of the Human Rights Anniversary Committee for Canada, 18 September 1958, file 5475-DP-3-40, pt. 1.2, vol. 6950, RG25, LAC.

104 Documents from the Ad Hoc Committee for the Tenth Anniversary, 19 March 1958, file 5475-DP-3-40, pt. 1.1, vol. 6950, RG25, LAC.

105 "Programme – The National Human Rights Conference," 8–10 December 1958, file 1-24-27, pt. 3, Volume 82, RG26, LAC.

106 Letter from the Human Rights Anniversary Committee for Canada, to Sponsoring Organizations, 17 November 1958, folder 1631, vol. 207, MG28-I10, LAC; "Report on Preparations for 1958 Conference on HR," Department of External Affairs, 7 November 1957, 5, file 5475-DP-3-40, pt. 1.1, vol. 6950, RG25, LAC.

107 To learn about the disability rights movement in Canada, see John Lord, *Impact: Changing the Way We View Disability: The History, Perspective, and Vision of the Independent Living Movement in Canada* (Ottawa: Creative Bound International, 2010); and Michael Prince, *Absent Citizens: Disability Politics and Policy in Canada* (Toronto: University of Toronto Press, 2009).

108 Tom Warner, *Never Going Back: A History of Queer Activism in Canada* (Toronto: University of Toronto Press, 2002).

109 "Report on Preparations for 1958 Conference on HR," Department of External Affairs, 7 November 1957, 5, file 5475-DP-3-40, pt. 1.1, vol. 6950, RG25, LAC.

110 Muriel Jacobson, "Human Rights: Where Do We Stand," *Food for Thought* 19, 5 (February 1959).

111 "Report of the Eleventh Session of the Third Committee," Department of External Affairs, 1956, file 1-24-27, pt. 2, vol. 82, RG26, LAC.

112 Ibid.

113 These contradictions were pointed out by External Affairs officials. Memo from Marcel Cadieux, UN Division, to Legal Division, 23 October 1956, file 5475-W-15-40, pt. 5.1, vol. 6927, RG25, LAC.

114 Telegram from Canadian Delegation to Department of External Affairs, re: Human Rights Covenants, Constitutional Problems, 10 January 1957, file 5475-W-15-40, pt. 6.1, vol. 6927, RG25, LAC.

115 Ibid.

116 Scott, "Dominion Jurisdiction over Human Rights and Fundamental Freedoms," 497–505, 531–33; F.R. Scott, "Centralization and Decentralization," *Canadian Bar Review* 29, 10 (December 1951): 1095–1125; G.J. Szablowski, "Creation and Implementation of Treaties in Canada," *Canadian Bar Review* 34, 1 (January 1956): 28–59.

117 Szablowski, ibid., 53–54.

118 Varcoe pointed to only three articles that dealt with issues primarily under provincial jurisdiction: Articles 14 and 15 of the ICESCR, and Article 22 of the ICCPR. Letter from F.P. Varcoe to J.S. Nutt, 12 November 1956, file 5475-W-15-40, pt. 5.2, vol. 6927, RG25, LAC.

119 Letter from the Department of External Affairs to Stuart Garson, Minister of Justice, 26 May 1956, file 5475-W-15-40, pt. 5.1, vol. 6927, RG25, LAC.

120 Ibid.

121 Memo from Max Wershof to Under-Secretary of State for External Affairs, 2 November 1956, file 5475-W-15-40, pt. 5.2, vol. 6927, RG25, LAC.

122 For an example of these concerns, see Department of External Affairs Memo, M. Cadieux, UN Division, to Legal Division, re: Draft Covenants on Human Rights, 11th Session of the General Assembly, 17 October 1956, file 5475-W-15-40, pt. 5.1, vol. 6927, RG25, LAC.

123 Ibid, 1.

124 Ibid.

125 Memo from F.M. Tovell, UN Divison, to M. Scott, re: Human Rights – Mr. Garson's Views, 10 March 1952, file 5475-W-40, pt. 5.2, vol. 6409, RG25, LAC.

126 "Final Report on the Thirteenth Session, Third Committee of the General Assembly," 8 January 1959, file 5475-W-15-40, pt. 7.2, vol. 6928, RG25, LAC.

127 "Draft International Covenants on Human Rights – Correspondence," 1957, file 5475-W-15-40, pt. 6.1, vol. 6927, RG25, LAC.

128 Letter from Laval Fortier, Department of Citizenship and Immigration, to M.H. Wershof, Department of External Affairs, 13 November 1956, file 5475-W-15-40, pt. 5.2, vol. 6927, RG25, LAC.

129 Memo from Laval Fortier to Minister, Department of External Affairs, February 1955, file 1-24-27, pt. 1, vol. 81, RG26, LAC.

130 Letter from A.H. Brown, Deputy Minister of Labour, to M.H. Wershof, Department of External Affairs, 14 November 1956, file 5475-W-15-40, pt. 5.2, vol. 6927, RG25, LAC. Brown argued that the article providing for the right to work was vague and open to multiple interpretations, potentially causing problems for Canada.

131 Letter from R.G. Robertson, Deputy Minister of Northern Affairs and Natural Resources, to Jules Léger, Under-Secretary of State for External Affairs, 22 November 1956, file 5475-W-15-4, pt. 5.2, vol. 6927, RG25, LAC.

132 Ibid.

133 UN General Assembly, *Convention on the Political Rights of Women*, 20 December 1952, A/RES/640(VII); UN General Assembly, *Convention on the Nationality of Married Women*, 29 January 1957, A/RES/1040(XI); UN General Assembly, *Declaration of the Rights of the Child*, 20 November 1959, A/RES/1386(XIV); UN General Assembly, *International Convention on the Elimination of All Forms of Racial Discrimination*, 21 December 1965, A/RES/2106(XX).

134 The League of Nations first passed a *Declaration of the Rights of the Child* in 1924, and this was revised by the UN after the Second World War. Dominique Marshall, "Children's Rights from Below," in *Taking Liberties: A History of Human Rights in Canada*, ed. David Goutor and Stephen Heathorn (Don Mills, ON: Oxford University Press, 2013), 195.

135 There is a remarkable continuity in reports from January 1957 (when the Liberals were in power) to the Twelfth and Thirteenth Sessions of the General Assembly (in 1958 and 1959, under the Diefenbaker government). See vols. 6425, 6927, 6928, and 6535 of RG25, LAC.

136 Kevin A. Spooner, *Canada, the Congo Crisis, and UN Peacekeeping, 1960–64* (Vancouver: UBC Press, 2009), 2.

137 For example, see Telegram from the Canadian Delegation to the Department of External Affairs re: Human Rights Covenant, 10 January 1957, file 5475-W-15-40, pt. 6.1, vol. 6927, RG25, LAC; and "Final Report on the Thirteenth Session of the Third Committee of the General Assembly," 8 January 1959, file 5475-W-15-40, pt. 7.2, vol. 6928, RG25, LAC.

138 "Growth in United Nations Membership, 1945–present," United Nations Organization, http://www.un.org/en/sections/member-states/growth-united-nations-membership-1945-present/index.html.

139 Ibid.

140 Asian membership increased by fourteen between 1946 and 1957, and African membership by thirty between 1956 and 1962. The proportion of European and American nations dropped from over 70 percent to 50 percent in just over fifteen years. Ibid.

141 McKercher, "The Centre Cannot Hold," 329–49.

142 Bothwell, *Alliance and Illusion*, 8.

143 Burke, *Decolonization and the Evolution of International Human Rights*, especially 35–58 (ch. 3). Other vocal states included Indonesia, the Philippines, and Syria.

144 The Soviet bloc tried to use anti-colonial arguments to win support from non-aligned states, but Western nations increasingly argued that the Soviet Union was a colonial power in its own right.

145 The delegation described the anti-colonial majority in detail to External Affairs in 1956. "Final Report on Item 28: Draft International Covenant on Human Rights," Report from the Canadian Delegation to the Department of External Affairs, 20 April 1956, file 5475-W-15-40, pt. 5.1, vol. 6927, RG25, LAC.

146 Memo to Minister, 2 September 1959, file 5475-W-15-40, pt. 8, vol. 6928, RG25, LAC.

147 Ibid.

148 "Canadian Position on Draft International Covenants on Human Rights," Department of External Affairs, 25 January 1962, file 5475-W-15-40, pt. 9, vol. 5118, RG25, LAC.

149 "Report on the Seventeenth Regular Session of the General Assembly of the United Nations," New Zealand Government Report, file 5475-W-15-40, pt. 10, vol. 5118, RG25, LAC. This folder contains other reports from the New Zealand government. For samples of reports from Australia, see vol. 5116 (W-40, pt. 17) and vol. 4215 (W-40, pt. 11).

150 Walter Tarnopolsky, "Address to the Conference of Human Rights Ministers," 7–8 November 1974, 82-001, box 5, folder 6, Thomas Symons Papers, Trent University Archives (TUA).

151 The dates are as follows: Ontario (1962), Nova Scotia (1963), Alberta (1966), New Brunswick (1967), Prince Edward Island (1968), British Columbia (1969), and Manitoba (1970).

152 "Report on Human Rights in Canada (Report/DEA) [1957–59]," file 5475-W-7-40, pt. 3.2, vol. 6926, RG25, LAC.

153 For example, F.R. Scott, *Civil Liberties and Canadian Federalism* (Toronto: University of Toronto Press, 1959); Douglas Schmeiser, *Civil Liberties in Canada* (London: Oxford University Press, 1964); Edward McWhinney, "Mr. Justice Rand's Rights of the Canadian Citizen-The Padlock Case," *Wayne Law Review* 4 (1957): 115; Laskin, "Canada's Bill of Rights"; and S.J. Godfrey, "Freedom of Religion and the Canadian Bill of Rights," *Faculty Law Review* 22 (1964): 60.

154 For example, M.L. Ross, "Freedom with Strings Attached," *Saturday Night* 76 (June 1961): 2; "Maintient le droit," *Canadian Forum* 43 (July 1963):76–77; and G. Labrosse, "'Pacem in Terris' et notre déclaration des droits de l'homme," *Relations* (23 June 1963): 177–78.

155 "Teaching about the United Nations – Progress Made since 1959," Department of External Affairs, 25 June 1963, file 5139-CZ-40, pt. 6, vol. 6950, RG25, LAC.

156 Ibid.

157 "Educational Role of the United Nations Association in Canada," ECOSOC Report, 1963, file 5139-CZ-40, pt. 6, vol. 6950, RG25, LAC.

158 Memo from N.A. Robertson to the Minister of External Affairs re: Fifteenth Anniversary Celebrations, 27 May 1963, file 5475-DP-3-40, pt. 1.2, vol. 6950, RG25, LAC.

159 United Nations, General Assembly, Resolution 1775(XVII). The special committee was to consider suggestions for the format of celebrations, and to provide information about resources that might be useful for member states in their national preparations. For communications regarding Canada's participation, see file 5475-DP-3-40, pt. 1.2, RG25, LAC.

160 Minutes and Documentation for founding meeting of Canadian Anniversary Conference of Canada, June – August 1963, file 5475-DP-3-40, pt. 1.2, vol. 6950, RG25, LAC.

161 For example, the committee consulted with the French and English networks of the CBC, a number of national presses, the Canadian Film Institute, and the National Film Board in order to encourage a variety of media resources for local communities.

162 "Canadian Anniversary Conference on Human Rights – Executive Committee Meeting," 13 August 1963, file 5475-DP-3-40, pt. 2, vol. 6950, LAC.

163 For a full listing of voluntary organizations that attended the meeting, see file 5475-DP-3-40, pt. 2, vol. 6950, RG25, LAC.

164 "Report to the United Nations' Secretary-General on Canada's Celebrations, 1962," 27 February 1963, file 5475-DP-3-40, pt. 2, vol. 6950, LAC.

165 Letters from the Provinces re: 15th Anniversary, June 1963, file 5475-DP-3-40, pt. 2, vol. 6950, LAC.

166 Attorney General of New Brunswick to N.A. Robertson, Under-Secretary of State for External Affairs, 24 June 1963, file 5475-DP-3-40, pt. 2, vol. 6950, RG25, LAC.

167 This term is taken from the title of Peter Regenstreif's 1965 monograph. Peter Regenstreif, *The Diefenbaker Interlude* (Toronto: Longmans Canada, 1965).

168 Many authors have shown the forces at work in the postwar world that influenced the Quiet Revolution. See Michael Behiels, *Prelude to Quebec's Quiet Revolution: Liberalism Versus Neo-nationalism, 1945–1960* (Montreal and Kingston: McGill-Queen's University Press, 1985); B.L. Vigod, "Some Reflections on the State and Social Welfare in Quebec before the Quiet Revolution," in *The Benevolent State: The Growth of Welfare in Canada*, ed. Allan Moscovitch and Jim Albert (Toronto: Garamond Press, 1987), 175–86; and Michael Gauvreau, *The Catholic Origins of Quebec's Quiet Revolution, 1931–1970* (Montreal and Kingston: McGill-Queen's University Press, 2005).

169 Dominique Clément, "Quebec," Canada's Human Rights History, https://historyofrights.ca/encyclopaedia/social-movements/rights-associations-second-generation/quebec/.

170 José Igartua, "The Sixties in Quebec," in *Debating Dissent: Canada in the 1960s*, ed. Lara Campbell, Dominique Clément, and Gregory S. Keeley (Toronto: University of Toronto Press, 2012), 249–51; and Matthew Hayday, "Reconciling the Two Solitudes?

Language Rights and the Constitutional Question from the Quiet Revolution to the Victoria Charter," in *Debating Dissent,* 233.

171 Hayday, ibid., 235; and Canada, Royal Commission on Bilingualism and Biculturalism, *Report of the Royal Commission on Bilingualism and Biculturalism* (Ottawa: Queen's Printer, 1967).

172 Canada, Royal Commission on Bilingualism and Biculturalism, ibid.; Hayday, ibid., 236.

173 Lara Campbell and Dominique Clément, "Time, Age, Myth: Towards a History of the Sixties," in Campbell, Clément, and Keeley, *Debating Dissent,* 6.

174 Department of External Affairs Internal Memo re: Draft Report on Human Rights in Canada, 1960–62, June 1963, file 1-24-27, pt. 4, vol. 82, RG26, LAC.

175 Ibid.

176 "Report of the Fourteenth Session of the Third Committee of the General Assembly," Department of External Affairs, 1959, file 5475-W-15-40, pt. 8, vol. 6928, RG25, LAC.

177 Department of External Affairs Memo to the Minister re: Canada's candidature for the Human Rights Commission, file 5475-W-40, pts. 16.1 and 16.2, vol. 6924, RG25, LAC.

178 Department of External Affairs Memo to the Minister re: United Nations Commission on Human Rights: Nomination of Canadian Representative to the Commission, 5 October 1962, file 5475-DP-40, pt. 2.2, vol. 6425, RG25, LAC.

179 S. Morley Scott, "Report on work of Sixteenth Session of ECOSOC," 1952, file 5475-W-40, vol. 6409, RG25, LAC.

180 Department of External Affairs Memo to the Minister, N.A. Robertson, re: Canadian Focus while on the Human Rights Commission, 18 February 1963, file 5457-W-40, pt. 18, vol. 5116, RG25, LAC.

181 Memo from the UN Division to the Legal Division, Department of External Affairs, re: Canadian Position on Draft International Covenants on Human Rights (Civil and Political Rights), 25 January 1962, file 5475-W-15-40, pt. 9, vol. 5118, RG25, LAC.

182 "Human Rights Policy and Plans – United Nations Human Rights Commission (1966–67)," file 45-13-1-1, pt. 4, vol. 14949, RG25, LAC.

183 Memo from M.H. Wershof, Department of External Affairs, to UN Division re: Canada's Position on the Human Rights Covenants, 17 December 1963, file 45-13-2-3, pt. 1, vol. 13112, RG25, LAC.

184 Ibid., 1.

185 This was reminiscent of an earlier argument, put forth by J.G.H. Halstead and John Holmes when the draft First Covenant was released in 1949. J.G.H Halstead, Department of External Affairs Internal Memo, 6 October 1950, file 5475-W-40, pt. 3.2, vol. 6408, RG25, LAC.

186 The report pointed to Articles 2, 3, 9, 11, 22, 23, 24, and 25 of the *Covenant on Civil and Political Rights,* and Articles 3, 8, 13, and 14 of the *Covenant on Economic, Social and Cultural Rights*. Memo from E.G. Lee to G.S. Murray re: Procedure for Study of Canadian Constitutional Position on the Human Rights Covenants, 20 January 1964, file 45-13-2-3, pt. 1, vol. 13112, RG25, LAC.

187 Memo from the UN Division to the Legal Division, Department of External Affairs, re: Canadian Position on Draft International Covenants on Human Rights, 25 January 1962, file 5475-W-15-40, pt. 4, vol. 5118, RG25, LAC.

188 Ibid.

189 Memo from A.J. Pick, Legal Division, External Affairs, to E. Reid, 19 April 1950, file 5475-W-40, pt. 2.1, vol. 6407, RG25, LAC.

190 Ibid., 5.

191 The Optional Protocol to the *International Covenant on Civil and Political Rights* is a separate instrument from the covenant itself. It sets up the Human Rights Committee, and outlines the process for dealing with communications from individuals claiming to be victims of violations of any of the rights set out in the covenant.

192 For a copy of the *International Covenant on Civil and Political Rights,* see Appendix 2. For a copy of the *International Covenant on Economic, Social and Cultural Rights,* see Appendix 3.

193 Letter from the Department of External Affairs to the Prime Minister re: Statement for Human Rights Day, 7 December 1962, file 5475-DP-3-40, pt. 1.2, vol. 6950, RG25, LAC.

194 In October 1965, Jean H. Lagassé, the director of the Citizenship Branch of the Department of Citizenship and Immigration, inquired as to the level of provincial consultation that had taken place. W.H. Barton, the head of the UN Division of External Affairs, replied that not only had the federal government not consulted with the provinces but the department had no intention to invite the provinces to any meetings in the near future regarding possible ratification of the documents. Letter from W.H. Barton, Head of UN Division of External Affairs, to Jean H. Lagassé, Department of Citizenship and Immigration, re: Provincial Consultations, file 17-2-4, pt. 1, vol. 146, RG6, LAC.

195 Draft letter from UN Division of Department of External Affairs to the Deputy Attorneys-General of the Provinces, and to Mr. Claude Morin, Deputy Minister of Federal-Provincial Affairs in Quebec, 21 September 1966, file 45-13-2-3, pt. 1, vol. 13112, RG25, LAC.

Chapter 4: The Road to Ratification, 1966–76

1 House of Commons, *Debates,* John G. Diefenbaker, 19 January 1967, 11983.

2 Ibid., Lester B. Pearson.

3 Ibid., 23 January 1967, 12102.

4 The arguments for and against obtaining provincial support are best laid out in a confidential memo written to Cabinet in 1976. Memo to Cabinet from the Department of External Affairs, re: Accession to the UN Covenant on Civil and Political Rights, April 1976, file 45-13-2-3, pt. 10, vol. 13650, RG25, LAC. See also Behiels, "Canada and the Implementation of International Instruments of Human Rights," 151–84.

5 R.J. Buchan of the Legal Operations Division of the Department of External Affairs. "Canada in the International Field of Human Rights," 10 May 1974, file 45-13-2-3, pt. 9, vol. 13650, RG25, LAC.

6 Memo from W.H. Barton, Chair, to the Interdepartmental Committee on Human Rights, 26 January 1967; and from G.S. Shortliffe, Department of External Affairs, to W.H. Barton, 8 February 1967, file 45-CDA-13-1-1, vol. 14947, RG25, LAC.

7 Minutes, Interdepartmental Committee on Human Rights Meeting, 9 February 1967, file 45-CDA-13-1-1, vol. 14947, RG25, LAC.

8 Memo from G.S. Shortliffe, Department of External Affairs, to W.H. Barton, 8 February 1967, file 45-CDA-13-1-1, vol. 14947, RG25, LAC.

9 "Report for the United Nations Yearbook on Human Rights for 1967," file 566-11, pt. 5, vol. 887, RG76, LAC.

10 "Canadian Position on Draft International Covenants on Human Rights," Department of External Affairs, 25 January 1962, file 5475-W-15-40, pt. 9, vol. 5118, RG25, LAC.

11 On 29 May 1967, the Alberta government wrote to the federal government recommending that Canada ratify the covenants. Confidential Internal Memo, Department of External Affairs, 28 June 1967, file 45-CDA-13-1-1, vol. 14947, RG25, LAC.

12 The Pearson Government outlined these priorities in five throne speeches. Government of Canada, "Speeches from the Throne," 17 May 1963 – 9 May 1967, Parliament of Canada, https://lop.parl.ca/sites/ParlInfo/default/en_CA/Parliament/procedure/throneSpeech.

13 For an analysis of the Pearson government's policies and priorities, see John English, *The Worldly Years: The Life of Lester Pearson, 1949–1972*, vol. 2 (Toronto: Vintage Books Canada, 1992); Norman Hillmer, ed., *Pearson: The Unlikely Gladiator* (Montreal and Kingston: McGill-Queen's University Press, 1999); and Lester B. Pearson, *Mike: The Memoirs of the Right Honourable Lester B. Pearson* (Toronto: University of Toronto Press, 1972).

14 Mme Roquet, Speech to the Third Committee of the General Assembly, 29 November 1968, file 45-13-1-6, pt. 6, vol. 14952, RG20, LAC.

15 Canada, Royal Commission on Bilingualism and Biculturalism, *Preliminary Report* (Ottawa: Queen's Printer, 1966), 13.

16 Hayday, "Reconciling the Two Solitudes?," 233.

17 Scholars have identified a number of variables to explain why the 1960s are seen as a particularly crucial decade, including changes in attitudes among youth to sexuality and morality, the women's liberation movement, the impact of radical politics, the wider criticism of authority structures across society, the waning of group and ethno-political identities, and postwar affluence, with its emphasis upon consumer choice and personal satisfaction.

18 Eva Mackey, *House of Difference: Cultural Politics and National Identity in Canada* (London: Routledge, 1999), 72.

19 Bryan D. Palmer, *Canada's 1960s: The Ironies of Identity in a Rebellious Era* (Toronto: University of Toronto Press, 2009). See also Campbell, Clément, and Keeley, *Debating Dissent*.

20 For a study of how dominant understandings of identity in Canada were challenged in this period, see Igartua, *The Other Quiet Revolution;* and Eve Haque, *Multiculturalism within a Bilingual Framework: Language, Race, and Belonging in Canada* (Toronto: University of Toronto Press, 2012).

21 Doug Owram, *Born at the Right Time: A History of the Baby Boom Generation* (Toronto: University of Toronto Press, 1996).

22 Dominique Clément, "Generations and the Transformation of Social Movements in Postwar Canada," *Histoire sociale/Social History* 42, 84 (2009): 361.

23 According to Marjorie Griffin Cohen, the commission was "the most significant single event in establishing a sense of a women's movement in Canada." Marjorie Griffin Cohen, "The Canadian Women's Movement," in *Canadian Women's Issues, Volume 1: Strong Voices, Twenty-Five Years of Women's Activism in English Canada*, ed. Ruth Roach Pierson and Marjorie Griffin Cohen (Toronto: James Lorimer, 1993), 4.

24 Interview with Pierre Elliott Trudeau, 21 December 1967, CBC Digital Archives, http://www.cbc.ca/player/play/1811727781.

25 Cornelia Navari, *Internationalism and the State in the Twentieth Century* (London and New York: Routledge, 2000), 172.

26 See Nataša Miškovic, Harald Fischer-Tiné, and Nada Boškovska, *The Non-Aligned Movement and the Cold War: Delhi – Bandung – Belgrade* (Abingdon, UK: Routledge, 2014); Lorenz M. Lüthi, "The Non-Aligned Movement and the Cold War, 1961–1973," *Journal of Cold War Studies* 18, 4 (Fall 2016): 98–147.

27 David F. Schmitz, *The Tet Offensive: Politics, War, and Public Opinion* (Lanham, MD: Rowman and Littlefield, 2005).

28 Kieran Williams, *The Prague Spring and Its Aftermath: Czechoslovak Politics 1968–1970* (Cambridge and New York: Cambridge University Press, 1998).

29 Carole Fink, Phillip Gassert, and Detleff Junker, eds., *1968: The World Transformed* (Cambridge and New York: Cambridge University Press, 1998), 3.

30 Jeremi Suri, *Power and Protest: Global Revolution and the Rise of Détente* (Cambridge, MA: Harvard University Press, 2003).

31 Peter B. Levy, "The Dream Deferred: The Assassination of Martin Luther King, Jr., and the Holy Week Uprisings of 1968," in *Baltimore '68: Riots and Rebirth in an American City*, ed. Elizabeth Nix (Philadelphia: Temple University Press, 2011), 6.

32 Most scholars identity the protests of 1968 as an American and Western European phenomenon. There is work, however, showing that similar protests took place around the world. See Nora Farik, ed., *1968 Revisited: 40 Years of Protest Movements* (Brussels: Heinrich Böll Foundation, 2008).

33 UN General Assembly Resolution A/RES/21/2217, 19 December 1966.

34 Report of the 20th Session of the General Assembly, 1965, file 17-2-4-1, vol. 146, RG6, LAC.

35 Myer Belkin, Head of the Human Rights Division, Citizenship Branch, "Report on International Conference on Human Rights Held in Tehran, April 22 – May 13, 1968," *Resource: A Publication of the Canadian Commission, International Year for Human Rights*, July/August 1968, 9.

36 The Canadian delegation was led by Under-Secretary of State for External Affairs G.G.E. Steele, and included Canadian Ambassador to France Paul Beaulieu, director of the Ontario Human Rights Commission Daniel G. Hill, the Honourable James M. Harding, the Honourable Harry Batshaw, and Ronald St. John Macdonald, dean of law at the University of Toronto.

37 Report on UK-Canada talks on ECOSOC questions from 1967, 23 June 1967, file 45-CDA-13-1-1, vol. 14947, RG25, LAC.

38 Belkin, "Report on International Conference on Human Rights Held in Tehran."

39 Andrew Thompson, "Teheran 1968 and the Origins of the Human Rights Council?" (Paper presented at the 2011 annual meeting of the Academic Council on the United Nations System), 2, https://acuns.org.

40 Roland Burke, "From Individual Rights to National Development: The First UN Conference on Human Rights, Tehran, 1968," *Journal of World History* 19, 3 (September 2008): 276.

41 Ibid., 278.

42 United Nations, *Final Act of the International Conference on Human Rights, Teheran, 22 April to 13 May 1968* (New York: United Nations Publications, 1968), 4, http://legal.un.org/avl/pdf/ha/fatchr/Final_Act_of_TehranConf.pdf. See also Daniel J. Whelan, *Indivisible Human Rights: A History* (Philadelphia: University of Pennsylvania Press, 2010), 149.

43 "International Year for Human Rights – OHRC 1968," Records of the Ontario Human Rights Commission, barcode B270372, 76-3-0-1353, RG76-3, Archives of Ontario (AO).

44 Series 84, box 3, file 3, "Montreal Assembly for Human Rights, December 1967 – April 1968," United Nations Archives, New York (UNA).

45 For general information relating to the Montreal assembly and its connection to the Tehran conference, see ibid.; for the goals of the assembly, see Letter from Leslie

Paffrath to Mr. C.V. Narasimhan, Chef de Cabinet, UN, 3 March 1967, 801.4 series 0198, box 3, file 8, "Human Rights – International Year for Human Rights," UNA.

46 Daniel Barstow Magraw, "Louis B. Sohn: Architect of the Modern International Legal System," *Harvard International Law Journal* 48, 1 (Winter 2007): 1–11.

47 There were participants from various states, including Canada, the United States, Uganda, Belgium, United Arab Republic, Tanzania, France, Israel, Mexico, Turkey, Costa Rica, Iran, Ceylon, Uruguay, Switzerland, Brazil, Sweden, New Zealand, Finland, Indonesia, Britain, Senegal, Kenya, and Trinidad and Tobago.

48 "Montreal Statement of the Assembly for Human Rights," brochure, series 84, box 3, file 3, "Montreal Assembly for Human Rights, December 1967 – April 1968," UNA.

49 In addition to these representatives, forty-five Canadian observers attended the event. List of Participants, Montreal World Assembly for Human Rights, brochure, series 84, box 3, file 3, "Montreal Assembly for Human Rights, December 1967 – April 1968," UNA.

50 "Montreal Statement of the Assembly for Human Rights," *Journal of the International Commission of Jurists* 9, 1 (June 1968): 94–212; also brochure, "Montreal Assembly for Human Rights, December 1967 – April 1968," UNA.

51 "Final Report of the International NGO Conference, Paris 16–20 September 1968," file 45-13-1-6, pt. 5, vol. 14952, RG25, LAC.

52 Information on a number of international conferences in 1968 can be found in file 45-13-1-6, pt. 5, vol. 14952, RG25, LAC.

53 "Proposal for Canadian Observance of International Year for Human Rights," Canadian Citizenship Branch, Citizenship and Immigration, 14 May 1965, file 17-2-4-1, vol. 146, RG6, LAC.

54 Ibid.

55 For an outline of the initial plans for the year, see ibid.

56 Minutes of the Meeting of the Interdepartmental Committee on Human Rights, 4 April 1966, file 45-CDA-13-1-1, pt. 1, vol. 14947, RG25, LAC.

57 Minutes, Meeting of the Executive Committee, Canadian Commission, IYHR, 15 September 1967, file 161-3-4/4, pt. 2, vol. 12, RG6, LAC. Additional funds were later granted by the Department of the Secretary of State and the Canadian National Association for UNESCO.

58 For a list of the representatives involved in planning the IYHR and attending the national consultations and conferences, see "Minutes of Executive Committee, IYHR 1967 and 1968," file 12-161-3, pt. 4, RG4, LAC; Report on the National Consultation on International Year for Human Rights, 12–14 September 1966, file 17-2-4, pt. 1, vol. 146, RG6, LAC; and International Year for Human Rights, Walter Tarnopolsky fonds, file 8, vol. 8, MG31-E55, LAC.

59 Report on the Genesis and Role of the Canadian Commission, IYHR, December 1968, file 17-2-4, pt. 4, vol. 146, RG6, LAC.

60 Memo to Cabinet from the Department of External Affairs re: Human Rights Program, October 1968, file 45-13-1, pt. 6, vol. 14952, RG25, LAC.

61 Montreal Planning Conference, 31 March to 2 April 1967, file 161-3-4/4, pt. 2, vol. 12, RG6, LAC.

62 "Proposal for Canadian Observance of International Year for Human Rights," Canadian Citizenship Branch, Citizenship and Immigration, 14 May 1965, file 17-2-4-1, vol. 146, RG6, LAC.

63 J.G.H. Halstead, internal memo, Department of External Affairs, 6 October 1950, filc 5475-W-40, pt. 3.2, vol. 6408, RG25, LAC.

64 Cabinet approved the letter on 4 January 1967. Letter from Prime Minister Lester Pearson to the Provincial Governments, re: Federal Role in International Year for Human Rights, 1 February 1967, file 45-CDA-13-11, vol. 14947, RG25, LAC.

65 Ibid.

66 A summary of Ontario's participation can be found in International Year for Human Rights, Ontario Committee (1967–68), barcode B270204, RG76-3, AO. See also Letter from W.A. Jones, Chair of the Planning Committee, Ontario Committee for Human Rights, 1 February 1968, barcode B270392, Ontario Human Rights Commission fonds, RG 76-3-0-1351, AO.

67 Letter from the Ontario Committee, IYHR to provincial governments, barcode B270392, Ontario Human Rights Commission fonds, RG 76-3-0-1351, AO.

68 Report to the Canadian Committee, IYHR, reprinted in the May 1968 edition of *Resource,* file 45-13-1-6, pt. 5, vol. 14952, RG25, LAC.

69 A summary of New Brunswick's participation in the IYHR can be found in the announcement, New Brunswick Department of Labour, March 1968, Provincial Archives of New Brunswick (PANB).

70 Lesage actually gave a speech before the Third Committee of the General Assembly in 1950 justifying Canada's resistance to the draft covenant. "Speech to Third Committee on First 18 Articles of Draft Covenant," 19 October 1050, file 5475-W-40, pt. 3.2, vol. 6408, RG25, LAC.

71 A summary of Quebec's participation in the IYHR can be found in "International Year for Human Rights" (Quebec Commission), file 1, pt. 1, vol. 475, Canadian Labour Congress fonds, MG28-I103, LAC.

72 Ibid.

73 Ibid.

74 Quebec's participation generated considerable media coverage. For example, "All-out War on Discrimination Promised by Quebec," *Montreal Star,* 4 November 1968, 3; and "Le gouvernement encourage la discrimination en ne faisant rien pout combaitre la propaganda haineuse," *Le Soleil,* 4 November 1968, 11. Other examples can be found in the following papers: *Montreal Star* (8 October 1968, 4 November 1968), *L'Action* (29 October 1968, 4 November 1968), *Journal de*

Québec et Montreal (18 September 1968), *La Presse* (31 October 1968); *Le Devoir* (18 October 1968).

75 For a summary of various provincial governments' participation in the year, see "List of Events and Plans Undertaken by Various Organizations for International Year for Human Rights," 15 December 1967, file 17-2-4, pt. 3, vol. 146, RG6, LAC.

76 Program, IYHR, box 12, pt. 2, vol. 161, RG6, LAC.

77 Prince Edward Island's activities were printed in the *Resource* newsletter, file 45-13-1-6, pt. 6, vol. 14952, RG25, LAC.

78 Letters discussing Newfoundland's participation in the International Year for Human Rights, 17 July 1967, file 17-2-4, pt. 3, vol. 146, RG6, LAC; see also Dominque Clément, "Searching for Rights in the Age of Activism: The Newfoundland-Labrador Human Rights Association, 1968–1982," *Newfoundland Studies* 19, 2 (2003): 347–72.

79 The CAALL was the predecessor of the Canadian Association of Statutory Human Rights Legislators, which formed in 1970. "History of CASHRA," Canadian Association of Statutory Human Rights Legislators, http://www.cashra.ca/history.html.

80 Letter from Daniel Hill, Director of the Ontario Human Rights Commission, 31 March 1966, file 17-2-4, pt. 2, vol. 146, RG6, LAC.

81 Two reports on the achievements of the IYHR were generated in December 1968: Report on the Genesis and Role of the Canadian Commission IYHR, December 1968; and Report by the Department of Citizenship and Immigration re: Origins of Canadian Involvement in International Year for Human Rights, 20 December 1968. Both can be found in file 17-2-4-4, vol. 146, RG6, LAC.

82 These reports were organized into a final report. "International Year for Human Rights National Conference – Report of Seminars," 1, file 8, vol. 8, Canadian Council for Human Rights, Walter Surma Tarnopolsky fonds, LAC.

83 Ibid., 11.

84 Report on the Montreal Planning Conference, 1967, file 161-3-4/4, pt. 2, vol. 12, RG6, LAC.

85 Judy LaMarsh, Secretary of State, Speech to the National Consultation on Human Rights, 12 September 1966, file 161-3-4/4, pt. 2, vol. 12, RG6, LAC.

86 Ibid. Cohen's speech was reprinted by Canada's Anti-Defamation League of B'nai Brith in its newsletter. Maxwell Cohen, "Human Rights: A Cause or Catch-All," *Intercom* (September-November 1971), B'nai Brith Canada.

87 This did not extend to its policies towards other nations, as it was not until the 1970s that Ottawa was prepared to assign resources to promote international respect for human rights. Matthews and Pratt, *Human Rights in Canadian Foreign Policy*, 285–311.

88 Maxwell Cohen, "Human Rights: Programme or Catchall? A Canadian Rationale," *Canadian Bar Review* 46, 4 (December 1968): 554–64.

89 Ibid., 554.
90 Ibid., 555.
91 Ibid., 557.
92 There are many archival sources outlining the events that took place in Canada throughout 1968. See Report by the Government of Canada to the Secretary-General of the United Nations re: Canadian Involvement in International Year for Human Rights, 1969, file 17-2-4, pt. 4, vol. 146 RG6, LAC; and Donald MacDonald, President of the Canadian Labour Congress, to All Principal Officers, 10 July 1968, IYHR, List of Events, Canadian Labour Congress fonds, on microfiche, H-553, LAC.
93 Copies of this publication can be found in file 45-13-1-6, pts. 5 and 6, vol. 14952, RG25, LAC.
94 Canadian Commission, IYHR, Minutes of Meetings, 16 February 1968, file 161-3-4/4, pt. 2, vol. 12, RG6, LAC.
95 Report by the Department of Citizenship and Immigration re: Origins of Canadian Involvement in IYHR, 20 December 1968, file 17-2-4/4, vol. 146, RG6, LAC.
96 Program, Canadian National Conference IYHR, 1–3 December 1968, Ottawa, file 17-2-4-4, vol. 146, RG6, LAC.
97 Canadian Commission, IYHR, "Canada & Human Rights: 21 Questions and Answers," pamphlet, 1968, file 161-3-4/4, vol. 12.2, RG6-F-4, LAC.
98 Ibid.
99 Ibid.
100 Palmer, *Canada's 1960s,* 221, 261, 382.
101 Canadian Human Rights Foundation, "Research into Economic, Social and Cultural Rights: Critical Survey of Human Rights Legislation in Canada," August 1974, file 45-13-2-3, pt. 10, vol. 13650, RG25, LAC.
102 The Canadian Labour Congress also reprinted excerpts from Borovoy's speech in its monthly publication. "The Divine Right to be Human," *Labour Gazette,* February 1969, 68.
103 The Canadian Department of Labour reprinted excerpts from Humphrey's speech in its monthly publication. Ibid., 66–71.
104 Krista Maecots, "Ex-UN Official Raps Canada on Its Human Rights Record," *Ottawa Citizen,* 14 November 1968, 29.
105 For the evolution of provincial human rights acts and commissions, see Howe, *Restraining Equality,* especially ch. 1.
106 Ibid.; Clément, "Searching for Rights in the Age of Activism"; and Dominique Clément, "Alberta's Rights Revolution," *British Journal of Canadian Studies* 26, 1 (2013): 59–77.
107 One suggestion was for the council to campaign for the ratification of various UN covenants, but most members opposed the focus on international instruments, feeling

that it was more prudent to focus on domestic endeavours. Members Arthur Stinson, Louis Sabourin, Ranjit Hall, Kalmen Kaplansky, and Neil Morrison all argued that a conference on the ratification of international covenants was not the best use of the council's resources. Minutes of Meeting of Provisional Executive Committee, Canadian Council for Human Rights, 3 July 1969, file 8, vol. 8, Walter Tarnopolsky fonds, MG31-E55, LAC.

108 Letter from Kalmen Kaplansky to Members of the Provisional Executive Commission, Canadian Council for Human Rights, 5 August 1970, file 8, vol. 8, Walter Tarnopolsky fonds, MG31-E55, LAC.

109 Canadian Commission, IYHR, Minutes of Meetings, 8 April 1968, box 12, pt. 2, vol. 161, RG6, LAC. Also Clément, "Human Rights in Canadian Domestic and Foreign Politics," 774.

110 For example, "The Divine Right to Be Human," 71.

111 House of Commons, *Debates,* R.N. Thompson, 10 December 1968, 3743.

112 Ibid., Mr. Haidasz, 17 November 1969, 915; David Lewis, 17 November, 1969, 889; and Ian Wahn, 9 April 1970, 5700.

113 Ibid., John Gilbert, 8 May 1970, 6737; and Andrew Brewin, 26 June 1970, 8645.

114 Walker, "The 'Jewish Phase' in the Movement for Racial Equality in Canada."

115 Interview with Roland de Corneille, February 2013.

116 Ibid.

117 For files relating to the League for Human Rights' Petition Campaign, see containers 105 and 106, vol. 133, MG28, LAC.

118 Pamphlet, League for Human Rights of B'nai Brith Canada, "Canada – Speak Up for Human Rights!," file 3, F16, vol. 19, League for Human Rights, Roland de Corneille fonds, MG31, LAC.

119 Minutes of Meeting of Committee on Human Rights Covenants ("Petition Committee"), 22 July 1971, file 12, F16, vol. 19, League for Human Rights, Roland de Corneille fonds, MG31, LAC.

120 News Release, League for Human Rights of B'nai Brith, 28 May 1971, file 3, F16, vol. 19, League for Human Rights, Roland de Corneille fonds, MG31, LAC.

121 All three were printed in the 24 November 1971 edition of the paper. "Mayor Proclaims Human Rights Petition Week," *Oshawa Times,* 24 November 1971. Similar articles and photos appeared in other newspapers. For clippings, see file 12, F16, vol. 19, League for Human Rights of B'nai Brith, Roland de Corneille fonds, MG31, LAC.

122 Letter from Roland de Corneille, League for Human Rights, to Lou Copeland, Chair of the Petition Campaign, 20 October 1971, file 12, F16, vol. 19, League for Human Rights of B'nai Brith, Roland de Corneille fonds, MG31, LAC.

123 "Human Rights Petition Presentation Statement," 10 December 1971, file 12, F16, vol. 19, League for Human Rights of B'nai Brith, Roland de Corneille fonds, MG31, LAC.

124 Anti-Defamation League, *Intercom,* published by the Anti-Defamation League of Canada/League for Human Rights of B'nai Brith (March 1972), file 6, vol. 19, Roland de Corneille fonds, MG31-F16, LAC.

125 Pierre Trudeau, as quoted in "Reception from Trudeau," ibid.

126 House of Commons, *Debates,* David MacDonald and Pierre Trudeau, 13 December 1971, 10396.

127 Roland de Corneille, Speech given to Jaycees National Convention in Kingston, Ontario, July 1973, file 7, F16, vol. 19, Roland de Corneille fonds, MG31, LAC.

128 Memo to Cabinet from the Department of External Affairs, "Human Rights Program," October 1968, file 45-13-1, pt. 6, vol. 14952, RG25, LAC.

129 "Secretariat Report on Proceedings – Constitutional Conference, Committee of Ministers on Fundamental Rights," Minister of Labour's General Correspondence, barcode B355540, RG7-1, AO.

130 Pierre Elliott Trudeau, "Economic Rights," *McGill Law Journal* 8 (1961–62): 125.

131 Hon. Pierre Elliott Trudeau, Minister of Justice, *A Canadian Charter of Human Rights* (Ottawa: Queen's Printer, 1968), 27.

132 Matthew Hayday, "From Repression to Renaissance: French-Language Rights in Canada before the Charter," in *A History of Human Rights in Canada,* ed. Janet Miron (Toronto: Canadian Scholars' Press, 2009), 191–95; and Maxwell Yalden, *Transforming Rights: Reflections from the Front Lines* (Toronto: University of Toronto Press, 2009), 46–47.

133 Hugh Donald Forbes, "Trudeau as the First Theorist of Canadian Multiculturalism," in *Multiculturalism and the Canadian Constitution,* ed. Stephen Tierney (Vancouver: UBC Press, 2007), 27–42.

134 Constitutional conferences were held in February, June, and December 1969, September 1970, and June 1971. Behiels, "Canada and the Implementation of International Instruments of Human Rights," 151–84.

135 This sentiment was expressed in several interviews conducted with human rights activists from the period, and in documents outlining the planning for the Canadian Council for Human Rights. Interviews with Thomas Symons, Roy Romanow, Harish Jain, and Roland de Corneille. Minutes of Meeting of Provisional Executive Committee, Canadian Council for Human Rights, 3 July 1969, file 8, vol. 8, Walter Tarnopolsky fonds, MG31-E55, LAC.

136 House of Commons, *Debates,* Andrew Brewin, 8 March 1974, 33.

137 For a more thorough examination of Trudeau's policies and his balance of foreign and domestic issues, see J.L. Granatstein and Robert Bothwell, *Pirouette: Pierre Trudeau and Canadian Foreign Policy* (Toronto: University of Toronto Press, 1990); John English, *Citizen of the World: The Life of Pierre Elliott Trudeau,* vol. 1, *1919–1968* (Toronto: Knopf Canada, 2006); John English, *Just Watch Me: The Life of Pierre Elliott*

Trudeau, vol. 2, *1968–2000* (Toronto: Knopf Canada, 2009); and Pierre Elliott Trudeau, *Memoirs* (Toronto: McClelland and Stewart, 1993).

138 Letters from Mitchell Sharp, Secretary of State for External Affairs, to Quebec Premier Robert Bourassa, November 1971 and 24 January 1973, file 45-13-2-3, pt. 3, vol. 13649, RG25, LAC.

139 Bourassa wrote: "Plusiers droits defines aux articles 2 à 15 du Pacte international relative aux droits économiques, sociaux et culturels ou aux articles 6 à 27 du Pacte international relative aux droits civils et politiques font déjà l'objet de plusiers legislations provincials, en particulier au Québec, et l'Assemblée nationale peut être appellee dans l'avenir à se prononcer sur des projets de lois susceptibles de les affecter." Robert Bourassa to Mitchell Sharp, 16 March 1973, file 45-13-2-3, pt. 3, vol. 13649, RG25, LAC.

140 Ibid.

141 Hayday, "Reconciling the Two Solitudes?," 234.

142 Granatstein and Bothwell, *Pirouette,* 201.

143 Letter from Barbara Arnott on behalf of the Canadian Unitarian Council, to the Department of External Affairs, 6 May 1974, file 45-13-2-3, vol. 9, RG25, LAC.

144 Letter from Betty M. Stillwell to the Department of External Affairs, 30 April 1974, file 45-13-2-3, vol. 9, RG25, LAC.

145 Samples of letters written to the Saskatchewan government in 1973 and 1974 can be found in file 70, pts. 1–8, vol. 8, R-900, 82–127, Roy Romanow fonds, Saskatchewan Archives (SA). Several of these letters were forward to Prime Minister Trudeau.

146 Walter Tarnopolsky, "The Development of Human Rights Legislation and Activity in Canada" (paper delivered at the Conference of Human Rights Administrators, Victoria, BC, 8 November 1974). A copy of this paper can be found in the Walter Tarnopolsky fonds, file 11, vol. 33, MG31-E 55, LAC. Subsequent media reports included Derek Sidenius, "Rights Issue 'A Time Bomb,'" *Victoria Times,* 9 November 1974; "Osgoode Hall Dean Fears Race Clashes," *Toronto Star,* 8 November 1974, A5.

147 Memo from W.H. Barton, UN Division, to A. Gotlieb, Legal Division, Department of External Affairs, 18 January 1968, file 45-13-1, pt. 6, vol. 14952, RG25, LAC.

148 A.W. Robertson, Director of Legal Advisory Division of Department of External Affairs, 22 July 1974, file 45-CDA-13-1-1, vol. 14947, RG25, LAC.

149 Internal Memo, from R.G.H. Mitchell, Acting Director of the Federal-Provincial Coordination Division of External Affairs, 24 July 1974, file 45-CDA-13-1-1, vol. 14947, RG25, LAC.

150 House of Commons, *Debates,* Gordon Fairweather, 10 December 1973, 8548.

151 Ibid., Andrew Brewin, 10 December 1973, 8548. A statement was also made by René Matte, who argued that Canada needed to set a better example at the international level.

152 Noël Kinsella, "Involvement of Provinces in United Nations Human Rights Activities," Report prepared for the Department of External Affairs, 1 November 1972, file 45-13-2-3, pt. 3, vol. 13649, RG25, LAC.

153 Ibid., 6.

154 Ibid., 5–6.

155 Ibid.

156 CASHRA was established in 1972. Its predecessor was the Canadian Association of Administrators of Labour Legislation (CAALL).

157 The course was sponsored by the Department of the Secretary of State. Memo from J.E. Thibault, External Affairs, to File, 21 February 1973, file 45-13-2-3, pt. 3, vol. 13649, RG25, LAC.

158 Memo to File, Department of Justice, re: "Canadian Accession to the Human Rights Covenants and Protocol," file 45-13-2-3, pt. 9, vol. 13650, RG25, LAC.

159 Internal Memo, A.W. Robertson, Director of Legal Advisory Services, External Affairs, re: Government Positions on Ratification, 23 January 1975, file 45-13-2-3, pt. 9, vol. 13650, RG25, LAC.

160 Ibid.

161 Letter from J.E. Harlick to Mr. Stanford re: "Briefing Book Entry: Canada's Proposed Accession to the International Human Rights Instruments," 21 May 1975, file 45-13-2-3, pt. 10, vol. 13650, RG25, LAC.

162 Internal Memo, A.W. Robertson, Director of Legal Advisory Services, External Affairs, re: Government Positions on Ratification, 23 January 1975, file 45-13-2-3, pt. 9, vol. 13650, RG25, LAC.

163 Memo to the Minister re: Canada's Accession to the Human Rights Covenants, 19 September 1975, file 45-13-2-3, pt. 10, vol. 13650, RG25, LAC.

164 Internal Memo, A.W. Robertson, Director of Legal Advisory Services, Department of External Affairs, re: Government Positions on Ratification, 23 January 1975, file 45-13-2-3, pt. 9, vol. 13650, RG25, LAC.

165 Federal Provincial Meeting on HR – Talking Points, 28 October 1975, file 45-13-2-3, pt. 10, vol. 13650, RG25, LAC.

166 The representatives in the working group were Mr. Symons (Ontario), Mr. McKay (Nova Scotia), Mr. Smith (Saskatchewan), Mr. Dufour (Quebec), and Mr. Copithorne (federal Department of External Affairs). Interview with Thomas Symons, 15 January 2013.

167 Federal-Provincial Conference on Human Rights, Ottawa, 27 and 28 October 1975, file 9, box 32; Letter from Philippe LeBlanc, Coordinator, Federal-Provincial Conference on Human Rights, accession #01-003, Additions, Thomas Symons Papers, TUA.

168 Memo from the Saskatchewan Department of the Attorney General to Mr. K. Lysyk, 10 November 1975, file 153, vol. V, R-900, R-82-127, Roy Romanow fonds, SA.

169 Memo from Cabinet to the Department of External Affairs, 4 December 1975, file 45-13-2-3, pt. 10, vol. 13650, RG25, LAC.

170 François Cloutier, "Preliminary Declaration of the Minister of Intergovernmental Affairs," 12 December 1975, box 16, accession #82-001, Human Rights, Thomas Symons Papers, TUA.

171 Ibid.

172 Confidential Memo to Cabinet, from External Affairs, re: Accession to the UN Covenant on Civil and Political Rights, April 1976, file 45-13-2-3, pt. 10, vol. 13650, RG25, LAC.

173 Ibid.

174 Communique, Federal-Provincial Conference on Human Rights, 12 December 1975, file 1, box 16, accession #82-001, Human Rights, Thomas Symons Papers, TUA.

175 Memo from J.S. Stanford, Director of the Legal Advisory Division, 12 April 1976, file 45-13-2-3, pt. 10, vol. 13650, RG25, LAC.

176 Ibid.

177 Confidential Memo to Cabinet, from External Affairs, re: Accession to the UN Covenant on Civil and Political Rights, April 1976, file 45-13-2-3, pt. 10, vol. 13650, RG25, LAC.

178 Ibid.

179 Ibid.

180 Ibid.

181 Memo from J.S. Stanford, Director of the Legal Advisory Division, 27 April 1976, file 45-13-2-3, pt. 10, vol. 13650, RG25, LAC.

182 The examples provided were the *International Road Traffic Convention,* for which the province of Newfoundland made the federal government wait, and the *Vienna Convention on Consular Relations,* for which British Columbia and Manitoba were the last provinces to agree.

183 Memo from J.S. Stanford, Director of the Legal Advisory Division, 27 April 1976, file 45-13-2-3, pt. 10, vol. 13650, RG25, LAC.

184 Memo for Minister, 13 May 1976, file 45-13-2-3, pt. 10, vol. 13650, RG25, LAC.

185 House of Commons, *Debates,* Allan MacEachern, 18 May 1976, 13609.

186 English, *Just Watch Me,* 139.

Conclusion: The Making of the Myth

1 Thompson, *On the Side of the Angels,* 11. For general documents on the activities of the UN Commission on Human Rights in this period, see file 45-13-1-1, folders 10–15, vol. 13645, RG25, LAC.

2 Matthews and Pratt, *Human Rights in Canadian Foreign Policy,* 91.

3 Thompson, *On the Side of the Angels,* 64–72.

4 Matthews and Pratt, *Human Rights in Canadian Foreign Policy,* 91.
5 Letter from Elizabeth Smith, Toronto Branch of the UN Association of Canada, to the Department of Secretary of State, 1 October 1971, file 17, CB 10-2-2, vol. 319, RG 6, LAC.
6 Historian Andrew Thompson details how Canada became increasingly vocal in this period, calling out nation states such as South Africa or Chile for their failure to protect the rights of their citizens. Thompson, *On the Side of the Angels,* 64.
7 Ibid., 5.
8 For a thorough examination of how Canada dealt with this issue at the UNCHR, see Thompson, *On the Side of the Angels,* ch. 5. For a broader discussion of the movement for Indigenous rights, see Sheryl Lightfoot, *Global Indigenous Politics: A Subtle Revolution* (New York: Routledge, 2016).
9 Thompson, ibid., 78.
10 The other opposing states were Australia, the United States, and New Zealand.
11 The Centre for International Governance Innovation, "The Internationalization of Indigenous Rights: UNDRIP in the Canadian Context," 2014, https://www.cigionline.org/publications/internationalization-indigenous-rights-undrip-canadian-context.
12 T.A. Keenleyside, "Aiding Rights: Canada and the Advancement of Human Dignity," in *Canadian International Development Assistance Policies,* ed. Cranford Pratt (Montreal and Kingston: McGill-Queen's University Press, 1994), 244; and Paul Gecelovsky and T.A. Keenleyside, "Canada's International Human Rights Policy in Practice: Tiananmen Square," *International Journal* 50, 3 (1995): 564–93.
13 Cranford Pratt, "Conclusion," in Pratt, *Canadian International Development Assistance Policies.*
14 David R. Morrison, *Aid and Ebb Tide: A History of CIDA and Canadian Development Assistance* (Waterloo, ON: Wilfrid Laurier University Press, 1998).
15 Keenleyside, "Aiding Rights," 244.
16 For example: Mark MacGuigan and P. Whitney Lackenbauer, *An Inside Look at External Affairs during the Trudeau Years: The Memoirs of Mark MacGuigan* (Calgary: University of Calgary Press, 2002); Nossal, "Cabin'd, Cribb'd, Confin'd?," 46–58; Webster, "Self-Fulfilling Prophesies and Human Rights in Canada's Foreign Policy."
17 Webster, "Canada and Bilateral Human Rights Dialogues," 56.
18 Amnesty International, "Matching International Commitments with National Action: A Human Rights Agenda for Canada," Amnesty International, http://www.amnesty.ca.
19 News Release, First Federal-Provincial Conference on Human Rights, Ottawa, 10 December 1975, file 1, box 16, "Human Rights," accession #82-001, Thomas Symons Papers, TUA.

20 Background Paper on the International Human Rights Covenants, September 1975, container 47282, Human Rights Commission fonds, RS972, PANB.

21 House of Commons, *Debates,* Lester Pearson, 23 January 1967, 12102.

22 Memo for the Minister, Department of External Affairs, from J.D. Livermore, UN Division, re: "Canadian Representation on Human Rights" and "Tone of Letter to the Public," 1976, file 45-13-1-1, folder 15, vol. 13645, RG25, LAC.

23 Ibid., 2.

24 V.M. Edelstein, "The Impact of Human Rights on Canadian Foreign Policy," United Nations Division, Department of External Affairs, 18 May 1979, file 45-CDA-13-1-1, pt. 2, vol. 15901, RG25, LAC.

25 Ibid., 7.

26 P.E. Trudeau, "Canadian Charter of Rights and Freedoms," 1982, http://charter.ofrightsandfreedoms.ca.

27 Desmond Morton, 1997, as quoted in Sheila Petty, Gary Sherbert, and Annie Gérin, eds., *Canadian Cultural Poesis: Essays on Canadian Culture* (Waterloo, ON: Wilfrid Laurier University Press, 2006), 72.

28 Erin Peters, "The 'Heritage Minutes' and Canadian Collective Memory: An Analysis of the Use of Nostalgia and Nationalism to Build a Unifying Cultural Memory (PhD dissertation, Institute of Germanic and Romance Studies, 2009), 67, http://sas-space.sas.ac.uk/2289/1/Peters%20-%20Heritage%20Minutes%20-%20Text.pdf.

29 Historica Canada, "John Humphrey," 1997, https://www.historicacanada.ca/content/heritage-minutes/john-humphrey. The full transcript of the Heritage Minute can be found at https://heritageminutes.wordpress.com/2015/07/10/john-humphrey-heritage-minute/.

30 Emily West, "Selling Canada to Canadians: Collective Memory, National Identity, and Popular Culture," *Critical Studies in Media Communication* 19, 2 (2002): 212–29.

31 The stamp was designed by Jim Hudson, based on a photograph by Rod Stears found in the McGill University Archives. Canadian Postage Stamps, https://www.canadianpostagestamps.ca/stamps/17092/john-peters-humphrey-universal-declaration-of-human-rights-canada-postage-stamp.

32 Dubinsky, Mills, and Rutherford, *Canada and the Third World,* 11.

33 James W. St. G. Walker, "Decoding the Rights Revolution: Lessons from the Canadian Experience," in *Taking Liberties: A History of Human Rights in Canada,* ed. David Goutor and Stephen Heathorn (Don Mills, ON: Oxford University Press, 2013), 48–49.

34 Ibid.

Bibliography

Archival Sources

Library and Archives Canada

B'nai Brith Canada fonds
Bora Laskin fonds
Canadian Bar Association fonds
Canadian Council on Social Development fonds
Canadian Labour Congress fonds
CBC fonds
Department of Citizenship and Immigration fonds
Department of External Affairs fonds
Department of the Secretary of State of Canada fonds
F.R. Scott fonds
Japanese Canadian Citizens Association fonds
Jewish Labour Committee fonds
John Diefenbaker fonds
John King Gordon fonds
Lester B. Pearson fonds
Louis St. Laurent fonds
National Council of YMCAs of Canada fonds
Privy Council Office fonds
Roland de Corneille fonds
United Nations Association of Canada fonds
Walter Tarnopolksy fonds
William Lyon Mackenzie King fonds

Archives of Ontario

Correspondence of the Deputy Minister of Labour fonds
John P. Robarts fonds
Leslie M. Frost fonds
Minister of Labour's General Correspondence fonds
Ontario Human Rights Commission fonds

Provincial Archives of New Brunswick

Human Rights Commission fonds

Saskatchewan Archives

Alan Blakeney fonds
Roy Romanow fonds
Tommy Douglas fonds
Woodrow Lloyd fonds

United Nations Archives

Bill of Rights, UN ESCOR series
Human Rights, International Year for Human Rights (1968) series
Relations with Human Rights Commissions, Economic/Social Commissions series
Social Affairs – Human Rights Division series

Trent University Archives

Thomas Symons Papers

Government Documents

Canada. Parliament. House of Commons. *Debates.*

Canada. Parliament. House of Commons and Senate. Special Joint Committee on Human Rights and Fundamental Freedoms. *Minutes of Proceedings and Evidence.* Ottawa: King's Printer, 1947.

Canada. Parliament. Senate. *Debates.*

Canada. Parliament. Senate. Special Senate Committee on Human Rights and Fundamental Freedoms. *Report of the Roebuck Committee.* Ottawa: King's Printer, 1950.

–. Special Joint Committee on Human Rights and Fundamental Freedoms. *Minutes of Proceedings and Evidence.* Ottawa: King's Printer, 1948.

–. Special Joint Committee on Human Rights and Fundamental Freedoms. *Minutes of Proceedings and Evidence.* Ottawa: Queen's Printer, 1960.

–. Special Senate Committee on Human Rights and Fundamental Freedoms. *Minutes of Proceedings and Evidence*. Ottawa: King's Printer, 1950.

Canada. Royal Commission on Bilingualism and Biculturalism. *Preliminary Report*. Ottawa: Queen's Printer, 1966.

–. *Report of the Royal Commission on Bilingualism and Biculturalism*. Ottawa: Queen's Printer, 1967.

Canadian Bar Association. *1948 Yearbook of the Canadian Bar Association and the Minutes of Proceedings of the Thirtieth Annual Meeting*. Ottawa: National Printers, 1949.

Trudeau, Hon. Pierre Elliott, Minister of Justice. *A Canadian Charter of Human Rights*. Ottawa: Queen's Printer, 1968.

United Nations. General Assembly. *Convention on the Nationality of Married Women*. 29 January 1957. A/RES/1040(XI).

United Nations. General Assembly. *Convention on the Political Rights of Women*. 20 December 1952. A/RES/640(VII).

United Nations. General Assembly. *Declaration of the Rights of the Child*. 20 November 1959. A/RES/1386(XIV).

United Nations. General Assembly. *International Convention on the Elimination of All Forms of Racial Discrimination*. 21 December 1965. A/RES/2106(XX).

United Nations. Secretariat. *Yearbook on Human Rights*. New York: United Nations, 1946–88.

Legislation

Accurate News and Information Act, SA 1937, c. 5.

Alberta Communal Property Act, SA 1947, c. 16.

An Act to Make Better Provision for the Qualification and Registration of Voters, SBC 1875, c. 2.

An Act to Prevent the Employment of Female Labour in Certain Capacities, SS 1912, c. 17.

Bank Taxation Act, SA 1937, c. 1.

Canadian Bill of Rights, SC 1960, c. 44.

The Constitution Act, 1867, 30 & 31 Vict., c 3. http://canlii.ca/t/ldsw.

Credit of Alberta Regulation Act, SA 1937, c. 2.

Libel Act, SM 1934, c. 23.

Ontario Insurance Act, SO 1932, c. 24, s. 4.

Racial Discrimination Act, SO 1944, c. 51.

Saskatchewan Bill of Rights Act, SS 1947, c. 35.

Cases Cited

Christie v. The York Corporation, [1940] 1 DLR 81 (SCC).

Cunningham and A.G. for B.C. v. Tomey Homma and A.G. for Canada, [1903] AC 151.

Franklin v. Evans, [1924] 55 OLR 349 (Ont HC).

Hurshman, Mindlin v. Hurshman, [1956] 6 DLR. 615 (BCSC).

Johnson v. Sparrow, [1899] QSC 104.

Loew's Montreal Theatres Ltd. v. Reynolds, [1921] 30 RJQ (Quebec KB).

Noble v. Alley, [1951] SCR 64 (SCC).

Quong-Wing v. The King, [1914] 49 SCR 440.

Reference Re Alberta Statutes – The Bank Taxation Act; The Credit of Alberta Regulation Act; and the Accurate News and Information Act, [1938] SCR 100, 1938 CanLII 1 (SCC).

Rogers v. Clarence Hotel Co. Ltd., [1940] 3 DLR 583 (BCCA).

Roncarelli v. Duplessis, [1959] SCR 121, 16 DLR (2d) 689.

Switzman v. Elbing, [1957] SCR 285.

Union Colliery Co. of British Columbia v. Bryden, [1899] AC 580 (JCPC).

Other Sources

Adachi, Ken. *The Enemy That Never Was: A History of Japanese Canadians.* Toronto: McClelland and Stewart, 1991.

Ajzenstat, Janet. *The Canadian Founding: John Locke and Parliament.* Montreal and Kingston: McGill-Queen's University Press, 2007.

Amnesty International. "Matching International Commitments with National Action: A Human Rights Agenda for Canada." Amnesty International, http://www.amnesty.ca.

Anastakis, Dimitry, and P.E. Bryden, eds. *Framing Canadian Federalism: Historical Essays in Honour of John T. Saywell.* Toronto: University of Toronto Press, 2009. https://doi.org/10.3138/9781442688131.

Anderson, Carol. *Eyes Off the Prize: The United Nations and the African American Struggle for Human Rights, 1944–1955.* Cambridge: Cambridge University Press, 2003.

Andrew, Arthur. *The Rise and Fall of a Middle Power: Canadian Diplomacy from King to Mulroney.* Toronto: James Lorimer, 1993.

Arès, Richard. "D'où viennent les droits de l'homme?" *Relations* 9, 100 (April 1949): 96–99.

–. "La déclaration universelle des droits de l'homme." *Relations* 9, 97 (January 1949) : 9–13.

–. "Les droits de l'homme devant les nations unies." *Relations* 8, 96 (December 1948): 348.

–. "Quand les nations unies s'occupent de dieu." *Relations* 9, 99 (March 1949): 63–67.

Avalon Project. "Covenant of the League of Nations." http://avalon.law.yale.edu/20th_century/leagcov.asp.

Backhouse, Constance. *Colour-Coded: A Legal History of Racism in Canada, 1900–1950*. Toronto: Osgoode Society for Canadian Legal History; University of Toronto Press, 1999.

Bangarth, Stephanie. *Voices Raised in Protest: Defending North American Citizens of Japanese Ancestry, 1942–49*. Vancouver: UBC Press, 2008.

Behiels, Michael. "Canada and the Implementation of International Instruments of Human Rights: A Federalist Conundrum, 1919–1982." In *Framing Canadian Federalism: Historical Essays in Honour of John T. Saywell*, ed. Dimitry Anastakis and P.E. Bryden, 151–84. Toronto: University of Toronto Press, 2009. https://doi.org/10.3138/9781442688131-008.

–. *Prelude to Quebec's Quiet Revolution: Liberalism Versus Neo-nationalism, 1945–1960*. Montreal and Kingston: McGill-Queen's University Press, 1985.

Belkin, Myer (Head of the Human Rights Division, Citizenship Branch). "Report on International Conference on Human Rights Held in Tehran, April 22 – May 13, 1968." *Resource: A Publication of the Canadian Commission, International Year for Human Rights*, July/August 1968.

Blake, Raymond S. "Mackenzie King and the Genesis of Family Allowances in Canada, 1939–1944." In *Social and Welfare Policy in Canada: Historical Readings*, ed. Raymond B. Blake and Jeff Keschen, 244–54. Toronto: University of Toronto Press, 1995.

Bothwell, Robert. *Alliance and Illusion: Canada and the World, 1945–1984*. Vancouver: UBC Press, 2007.

–. *The Big Chill: Canada and the Cold War*. Ottawa: Canadian Institute of International Affairs, 1998.

–. "The Canadian Isolationist Tradition." *International Journal (Toronto)* 54, 1 (Winter 1998–99): 76–87. https://doi.org/10.2307/40203356.

–. "Foreign Affairs a Hundred Years On." In *Canada among Nations, 2008: 100 Years of Canadian Foreign Policy*, ed. Robert Bothwell and Jean Daudelin, 19–39. Montreal and Kingston: McGill-Queen's University Press, 2009.

Boutin, Lanny. *John Diefenbaker: The Outsider Who Refused to Quit*. Toronto: Jackfruit Press, 2006.

Bow, Brian. "Paradigms and Paradoxes: Canadian Foreign Policy in Theory, Research, and Practice." *International Journal* 65, 2 (Spring 2010): 371–80.

Brewin, Andrew. "Civil Liberties in Canada during Wartime." *Bill of Rights Review* 1, 2 (Winter 1941): 112–22.

Brown, Lorne. *When Freedom Was Lost: The Unemployed, the Agitator, and the State.* Montreal and Buffalo: Black Rose Books, 1987.

Bryden, Penny. *Planners and Politicians: Liberal Politics and Social Policy, 1957–1968.* Montreal and Kingston: McGill-Queen's University Press, 1997.

Buckner, Phillip, ed. *Canada and the End of Empire.* Vancouver: UBC Press, 2005.

Burke, Roland. *Decolonization and the Evolution of International Human Rights.* Philadelphia: University of Pennsylvania Press, 2010. https://doi.org/10.9783/9780812205329.

–. "From Individual Rights to National Development: The First UN International Conference on Human Rights, Tehran, 1968." *Journal of World History* 19, 3 (2008): 275–96. https://doi.org/10.1353/jwh.0.0020.

Campbell, Lara, Dominique Clément, and Gregory S. Keeley, eds. *Debating Dissent: Canada and the Sixties.* Toronto: University of Toronto Press, 2012.

Carmody, Chios, ed. *Is Our House in Order? Canada's Implementation of International Law.* Montreal and Kingston: McGill-Queen's University Press, 2010.

Carrigan, Owen D. *Canadian Party Platforms, 1867–1968.* Urbana: University of Illinois Press, 1968.

Cassese, Antonio. *Self-Determination of Peoples: A Legal Reappraisal.* Cambridge: Cambridge University Press, 1995.

Centre for International Governance Innovation. "The Internationalization of Indigenous Rights: UNDRIP in the Canadian Context" (2014). https://www.cigionline.org/publications/internationalization-indigenous-rights-undrip-canadian-context.

Chapnick, Adam. "The Canadian Middle Power Myth." *International Journal (Toronto)* 55, 2 (2000): 188–206. https://doi.org/10.1177/002070200005500202.

–. "The Department of External Affairs and the United Nations Idea, 1943–1965." In *In the National Interest: Canadian Foreign Policy and the Department of Foreign Affairs and International Trade, 1909–2009*, ed. Greg Donaghy and Michael K. Caroll, 81–100. Calgary: University of Calgary Press, 2011.

–. *The Middle Power Project: Canada and the Founding of the United Nations.* Vancouver: UBC Press, 2005.

–. "On Protocols and Fireproof Houses: The Re-emergence of Canadian Exceptionalism." *International Journal (Toronto)* 61, 3 (Summer 2006): 713–23.

Chen, Anthony S. "The Party of Lincoln and the Politics of State Fair Employment Practices Legislation in the North, 1945–1964." *American Journal of Sociology* 112, 6 (May 2007): 1713–74. https://doi.org/10.1086/512709.

Christie, Nancy, and Michael Gauvreau, eds. *Cultures of Citizenship in Postwar Canada, 1940–1955.* Montreal and Kingston: McGill-Queen's University Press, 2003.

Clément, Dominique. "Alberta's Rights Revolution." *British Journal of Canadian Studies* 26, 1 (2013): 59–77. https://doi.org/10.3828/bjcs.2013.4.

–. *Canada's Rights Revolution: Social Movements and Social Change, 1937–1982.* Vancouver: UBC Press, 2008.

–. *Equality Deferred: Sex Discrimination and British Columbia's Human Rights State, 1953–84.* Vancouver: UBC Press, 2014.

–. "Generations and the Transformation of Social Movements in Postwar Canada." *Histoire Sociale/Social History* 42, 84 (2009): 361–87. https://doi.org/10.1353/his.0.0077.

–. *Human Rights in Canada: A History.* Waterloo, ON: Wilfrid Laurier University Press, 2016.

–. "Human Rights in Canadian Domestic and Foreign Politics: From 'Niggardly Acceptance' to Enthusiastic Embrace." *Human Rights Quarterly* 34, 3 (2012): 751–78. https://doi.org/10.1353/hrq.2012.0044.

–. "The Rights Revolution in Canada and Australia." In *Taking Liberties: A History of Human Rights in Canada*, ed. David Goutor and Stephen Heathorn, 88–113. Don Mills, ON: Oxford University Press, 2013.

–. "The Royal Commission on Espionage and the Spy Trials of 1946–9: A Case Study in Parliamentary Supremacy." *Journal of the Canadian Historical Association* 11, 1 (2000): 151–72. https://doi.org/10.7202/031135ar.

–. "Searching for Rights in the Age of Activism: The Newfoundland-Labrador Human Rights Association, 1968–1982." *Newfoundland Studies* 19, 2 (2003): 347–72.

–. "Spies, Lies, and a Commission: A Case Study in the Mobilization of the Canadian Civil Liberties Movement." *Left History* 7, 2 (2000): 53–79.

Clokie, H. McD."The Preservation of Civil Liberties." *Canadian Journal of Economics and Political Science/Revue canadienne d'economique et de science politique* 13, 2 (May 1947): 208–32.

Cohen, Marjorie Griffin. "The Canadian Women's Movement." In *Canadian Women's Issues, Volume 1: Strong Voices, Twenty-Five Years of Women's Activism in English Canada*, ed. Ruth Roach Pierson and Marjorie Griffin Cohen, 1–32. Toronto: James Lorimer, 1993.

Cohen, Maxwell. "Human Rights: Programme or Catchall? A Canadian Rationale." *Canadian Bar Review* 46, 4 (December 1968): 554–64.

Cosgrove, Richard A. *The Rule of Law: Albert Venn Dicey, Victorian Jurist.* London: Macmillan, 1980. https://doi.org/10.1007/978-1-349-05814-3.

Davis, Howard. *Human Rights and Civil Liberties.* Cullompton, UK: Willan Publishing, 2003.

Deery, Phillip. "Communism, Security and the Cold War." *Journal of Australian Studies* 21, 54/55 (1997): 162–75. https://doi.org/10.1080/14443059709387347.

Devereux, Annemarie. *Australia and the Birth of the International Bill of Human Rights 1946–1966*. Annandale, NSW: Federation Press, 2005.

Dicey, A.V. *Introduction to the Study of the Law of the Constitution*. London: Macmillan, 1902. Reprinted by Elibron Classics series, Adamant Media Corporation, 2005.

Donaghy, Greg. "'A Sad, General Decline?' The Canadian Diplomat in the 20th Century." In *Canada among Nations, 2008: 100 Years of Canadian Foreign Policy*, ed. Robert Bothwell and Jean Daudelin, 41–59. Montreal and Kingston: McGill-Queen's University Press, 2009.

–. "Coming Off the Gold Standard: Re-assessing the 'Golden Age' of Canadian Diplomacy." Paper presented to "A Very Modest Ministry: Foreign Affairs and International Trade Canada," University of Saskatchewan, September 2009. http://www.suezcrisis.ca/pdfs/Coming%20off%20the%20Gold%20Standard.pdf.

Donaghy, Greg, and Michael Carroll, eds. *In the National Interest: Canadian Foreign Policy and the Department of Foreign Affairs and International Trade, 1909–2009*. Calgary: University of Calgary Press, 2011.

Donnelly, Jack. *Universal Human Rights in Theory and Practice*. 2nd ed. Ithaca, NY: Cornell University Press, 2003.

Dubinsky, Karen, Sean Mills, and Scott Rutherford, eds. *Canada and the Third World: Overlapping Histories*. Toronto: University of Toronto Press, 2016.

Egerton, George. "Entering the Age of Human Rights: Religion, Politics and Canadian Liberalism, 1945–50." *Canadian Historical Review* 85, 3 (2004): 451–79.

Eide, Asbjorn, Catarina Krause, and Allan Rosas, eds. *Economic, Social and Cultural Rights*. 2nd ed. Dordrecht, Netherlands: Nijhoff, 2001.

Elliot, Robin. *Cases and Materials in Civil Liberties*. Vancouver: Faculty of Law, University of British Columbia, 1986.

English, John. *Citizen of the World: The Life of Pierre Elliott Trudeau*. Vol. 1, *1919–1968*. Toronto: Knopf Canada, 2006.

–. *Just Watch Me: The Life of Pierre Elliott Trudeau*. Vol. 2, *1968–2000*. Toronto: Knopf Canada, 2009.

–. *The Worldly Years: The Life of Lester Pearson*. Vol. 2, 1949–72. Toronto: Vintage Books Canada, 1992.

Farik, Nora, ed. *1968 Revisited: 40 Years of Protest Movements*. Brussels: Heinrich Böll Foundation, 2008.

Ferguson, Barry. "Remaking Liberalism: The Intellectual Legacy of Adam Shortt, OD Skelton, WC Clark & WA Mackintosh, 1890–1925." *American Review of Canadian Studies* 25, 2/3 (Summer/Fall 1995): 359.

Fink, Carole, Phillip Gassert, and Detleff Junker, eds. *1968: The World Transformed*. Cambridge and New York: Cambridge University Press, 1998. https://doi.org/10.1017/CBO9781139052658.

Forbes, Hugh Donald. "Trudeau as the First Theorist of Canadian Multiculturalism." In *Multiculturalism and the Canadian Constitution*, ed. Stephen Tierney, 27–42. Vancouver: UBC Press, 2007.

Ford, T.H. *Albert Venn Dicey: The Man and His Times*. Chichester, UK: B. Rose Publishers, 1985.

Forsey, Eugene. "Mr. Lapointe and the Padlock." *Canadian Forum* 18, 211 (August 1938): 148–50.

–. "The Padlock Act Again." *Canadian Forum* 17, 205 (February 1938): 382.

–. "The Padlock – New Style." *Canadian Forum* 18, 218 (March 1939): 362–63.

–. "Under the Padlock." *Canadian Forum* 17, 208 (May 1938): 41–44.

Forsythe, David. *Human Rights in International Relations*. 2nd ed. Cambridge: Cambridge University Press, 2006. https://doi.org/10.1017/CBO9780511808357.

Frager, Ruth, and Carmela Patrias. "Human Rights Activists and the Question of Sex Discrimination in Postwar Ontario." *Canadian Historical Review* 93, 4 (December 2012): 583–610. https://doi.org/10.3138/chr.732.

Gauvreau, Michael. *The Catholic Origins of Quebec's Quiet Revolution, 1931–1970*. Montreal and Kingston: McGill-Queen's University Press, 2005.

Gecelovsky, Paul, and T.A. Keenleyside. "Canada's International Human Rights Policy in Practice: Tiananmen Square." *International Journal* 50, 3 (1995): 564–93.

Glendon, Mary Ann. *A World Made New: Eleanor Roosevelt and the Universal Declaration of Human Rights*. New York: Random House, 2001.

Godfrey, S.J. "Freedom of Religion and the Canadian Bill of Rights." *Faculty Law Review* 22 (1964): 60.

Gordon, J. King. *Canada's Role as a Middle Power*. Toronto: Canadian Institute of International Affairs, 1966.

Goutor, David. *Guarding the Gates: The Canadian Labour Movement and Immigration, 1872–1934*. Vancouver: UBC Press, 2007.

Goutor, David, and Stephen Heathorn, eds. *Taking Liberties: A History of Human Rights in Canada*. Don Mills, ON: Oxford University Press, 2013.

Granatstein, J.L. *The Ottawa Men: The Civil Service Mandarins, 1935–1957*. Toronto: Oxford University Press, 1982.

Granatstein, J.L., and Robert Bothwell. *Pirouette: Pierre Trudeau and Canadian Foreign Policy*. Toronto: University of Toronto Press, 1990.

Greene, Ian. *The Charter of Rights*. Toronto: J. Lorimer, 1989.

Hannum, Hurst. *Autonomy, Sovereignty, and Self-Determination: The Accommodation of Conflicting Rights*. Philadelphia: University of Pennsylvania Press, 1996. https://doi.org/10.9783/9780812202182.

–. "The Status of the Universal Declaration of Human Rights in National and International Law." *Georgia Journal of International and Comparative Law* 25 (1995): 287–397.

Haque, Eve. *Multiculturalism within a Bilingual Framework: Language, Race, and Belonging in Canada*. Toronto: University of Toronto Press, 2012.

Hayday, Matthew. "From Repression to Renaissance: French-Language Rights in Canada before the Charter." In *A History of Human Rights in Canada*, ed. Janet Miron, 182–200. Toronto: Canadian Scholars' Press, 2009.

–. "Reconciling the Two Solitudes? Language Rights and the Constitutional Question from the Quiet Revolution to the Victoria Charter." In *Debating Dissent: Canada in the 1960s*, ed. Lara Campbell, Dominique Clément, and Greg Kealey, 231–48. Toronto: University of Toronto Press, 2012.

Henderson, T. Stephen. *Angus L. Macdonald: A Provincial Liberal*. Toronto: University of Toronto Press, 2007. https://doi.org/10.3138/9781442684034.

Heron, Craig. *The Canadian Labour Movement: A Brief History*. 2nd ed. Toronto: James Lorimer, 1996.

Hibbits, Bernard J. "The Politics of Principle: Albert Venn Dicey and the Rule of Law." *Anglo-American Law Review* 23, 1 (1994): 1–31.

Hillmer, Norman, ed. *Pearson: The Unlikely Gladiator*. Montreal and Kingston: McGill-Queen's University Press, 1999.

Hillmer, Norman, and J.L. Granatstein. *Empire to Umpire: Canada and the World to the 1990s*. Toronto: Copp Clark Longman, 1994.

Hobbins, A.J. "Eleanor Roosevelt, John Humphrey and Canadian Opposition to the Universal Declaration of Human Rights: Looking Back on the 50th Anniversary of the UDHR." *International Journal (Toronto)* 53, 2 (1998): 325–42.

–. "Humphrey and the Old Revolution: Human Rights in the Age of Mistrust." *Fontanus* 8 (1995): 121–36.

–, ed. *On the Edge of Greatness: The Diaries of John Humphrey, First Director of the United Nations Division of Human Rights, 1948–99*. Vol 1. Montreal: McGill University Libraries, 1994.

Holmes, John W., ed. *The Shaping of Peace: Canada and the Search for World Order*. Vol. 2. Toronto: University of Toronto Press, 1979.

Howe, R. Brian. "The Evolution of Human Rights Policy in Ontario." *Canadian Journal of Political Science* 24, 4 (December 1991): 783–802. https://doi.org/10.1017/S0008423900005667.

–. *Restraining Equality: Human Rights Commissions in Canada*. Toronto: University of Toronto Press, 2000. https://doi.org/10.3138/9781442679276.

Hucker, Daniel. *Public Opinion and the End of Appeasement in Britain and France*. London: Routledge, 2011.

Humphrey, John P. *Human Rights and the United Nations: A Great Adventure*. New York: Transnational Publishers, 1984.

–. "The International Bill of Rights: Scope and Implementation." *William and Mary Law Review* 17, 3 (1976): 527–41.

–. "The International Law of Human Rights in the Middle Twentieth Century." In *The Present State of International Law and Other Essays: Written in Honour of the Centenary Celebration of the International Law Association, 1873–1973,* ed. Maarten Bos, 75–105. Deventer, Netherlands: Kluwer, 1973. https://doi.org/10.1007/978-94-017-4497-3_6.

Hunt, Lynne. *Inventing Human Rights: A History*. New York: W.W. Norton, 2007.

Igartua, José E. *The Other Quiet Revolution: National Identities in English Canada, 1945–71*. Vancouver: UBC Press, 2006.

–. "The Sixties in Quebec." In *Debating Dissent: Canada in the 1960s,* ed. Lara Campbell, Dominique Clément, and Greg Kealey, 249–68. Toronto: University of Toronto Press, 2012.

Ignatieff, George. *The Making of a Peacemonger: Memoirs of George Ignatieff*. Toronto: University of Toronto Press, 1985. https://doi.org/10.3138/9781442654105.

Ishay, Micheline R. *The History of Human Rights: From Ancient Times to the Globalization Era*. Berkeley: University of California Press, 2008.

Jones, G.W. "The British Bill of Rights." *Parliamentary Affairs* 43, 1 (January 1990): 27–40.

Kaplan, William. *State and Salvation: The Jehovah's Witnesses and Their Fight for Civil Rights*. Toronto: University of Toronto Press, 1989.

Keenleyside, T.A. "Aiding Rights: Canada and the Advancement of Human Dignity." In *Canadian International Development Assistance Policies,* ed. Cranford Pratt, 240–67. Montreal and Kingston: McGill-Queen's University Press, 1994.

Kessler-Harris, Alice. *In Pursuit of Equity: Men, Women, and the Quest for Economic Citizenship in 20th-Century America*. New York: Oxford University Press, 2001.

Kirgis, Frederic L., Jr. "The Degrees of Self-Determination in the United Nations Era." *American Journal of International Law* 88, 2 (April 1994): 304–10. https://doi.org/10.2307/2204101.

Knight, Amy. *How the Cold War Began: The Igor Gouzenko Affair and the Hunt for Soviet Spies*. New York: Carroll and Graf Publishers, 2005.

Kuffert, Leonard. *A Great Duty: Canadian Responses to Modern Life and Mass Culture, 1939–1967*. Montreal and Kingston: McGill-Queen's University Press, 2003.

Lambertson, Ross. "The BC Court and Appeal and Civil Liberties." *BC Studies* 162 (Summer 2009): 81–109.

–. "Domination and Dissent: Equality Rights before World War II." In *A History of Human Rights in Canada: Essential Issues,* ed. Janet Miron, 11–24. Toronto: Canadian Scholars' Press, 2009.

–. "'The Dresden Story': Racism, Human Rights, and the Jewish Labour Committee of Canada." *Labour/Le Travail* 47 (Spring 2001): 43–82.

–. *Repression and Resistance: Canadian Human Rights Activists, 1930–1960*. Toronto: University of Toronto Press, 2005.

–. "Suppression and Subversion: Libertarian and Egalitarian Rights up to 1960." In *A History of Human Rights in Canada: Essential Issues,* ed. Janet Miron, 27–42. Toronto: Canadian Scholars' Press, 2009.

Laski, Harold. "Civil Liberties in Canada and Great Britain during War." *Harvard Law Review* 55, 6 (April 1942): 1006–18. https://doi.org/10.2307/1334632.

Laskin, Bora. "Canada's Bill of Rights: A Dilemma for the Courts." *International and Comparative Law Quarterly* 11, 2 (April 1962): 519–36. https://doi.org/10.1093/iclqaj/11.2.519.

Lauren, Paul Gordon. *The Evolution of International Human Rights: Visions Seen.* Philadelphia: University of Pennsylvania Press, 1998.

Lester, Anthony. "Fundamental Rights: The United Kingdom Isolated?" *Public Law* 10, 2 (Spring 1984): 955–71.

Levy, Peter B. "The Dream Deferred: The Assassination of Martin Luther King, Jr., and the Holy Week Uprisings of 1968." In *Baltimore '68: Riots and Rebirth in an American City,* ed. Elizabeth Nix, 3–25. Philadelphia: Temple University Press, 2011.

Lichtenstein, Alex. "The Other Civil Rights Movement and the Problem of Southern Exceptionalism." *Journal of the Historical Society* 11, 3 (September 2011): 351–76. https://doi.org/10.1111/j.1540-5923.2011.00342.x.

Lightfoot, Sheryl. *Global Indigenous Politics: A Subtle Revolution.* New York: Routledge, 2016.

Long, David. "Culture, Ideology, and Militancy: The Movement of Native Indians in Canada, 1969–91." In *Organizing Dissent: Contemporary Social Movements in Theory and Practice,* ed. W.K. Carroll, 151–70. Toronto: Garamond Press, 1997.

Lord, John. *Impact: Changing the Way We View Disability: The History, Perspective, and Vision of the Independent Living Movement in Canada.* Ottawa: Creative Bound International, 2010.

Lui, Andrew. *Why Canada Cares: Human Rights and Foreign Policy in Theory and Practice.* Montreal and Kingston: McGill-Queen's University Press, 2012.

Lüthi, Lorenz M. "The Non-Aligned Movement and the Cold War, 1961–1973." *Journal of Cold War Studies* 18, 4 (Fall 2016): 98–147. https://doi.org/10.1162/JCWS_a_00682.

MacGuigan, Mark, and P. Whitney Lackenbauer. *An Inside Look at External Affairs during the Trudeau Years: The Memoirs of Mark MacGuigan.* Calgary: University of Calgary Press, 2002.

Mackenzie, Hector. "Escott Reid and the Founding of the United Nations, 1945–6." In *Escott Reid: Diplomat and Scholar,* ed. Stéphane Roussel and Greg Donaghy. Montreal, Kingston: McGill-Queen's University Press, 2004.

–. "Golden Decades(s)? Reappraising Canada's International Relations in the 1940s and 1950s." *British Journal of Canadian Studies* 23, 2 (2010): 179–206. https://doi.org/10.3828/bjcs.2010.10.

–. "Knight Errant, Cold Warrior or Cautious Ally? Canada on the United Nations Security Council, 1948–49." *Journal of Transatlantic Studies* 7, 4 (2009): 453–75. https://doi.org/10.1080/14794010903286300.

Mackey, Eva. *House of Difference: Cultural Politics and National Identity in Canada.* London: Routledge, 1999.

MacLennan, Christopher. *Toward the Charter: Canadians and the Demand for a National Bill of Rights, 1929–1960.* Montreal and Kingston: McGill-Queen's University Press, 2003.

MacQueen, Norrie. *The United Nations, Peace Operations and the Cold War.* 2nd ed. New York: Addison-Wesley Longman, 2011.

Madokoro, Laura. "'Belated Signing': Race-Thinking and Canada's Approach to the 1951 Convention Relating to the Status of Refugees." In *Dominion of Race: Rethinking Canada's International History,* ed. Laura Madokoro, Francine McKenzie, and David Meren, 160–82. Vancouver: UBC Press, 2017.

Madokoro, Laura, Francine McKenzie, and David Meren, eds. *Dominion of Race: Rethinking Canada's International History.* Vancouver: UBC Press, 2017.

Magraw, Daniel Barstow. "Louis B. Sohn: Architect of the Modern International Legal System." *Harvard International Law Journal* 48, 1 (Winter 2007): 1–11.

Mahon, Rianne. "Varieties of Liberalism: Canadian Social Policy from the 'Golden Age' to the Present." *Social Policy and Administration* 42, 4 (August 2008): 342–61. https://doi.org/10.1111/j.1467-9515.2008.00608.x.

Marshall, Dominique. "Children's Rights from Below." In *Taking Liberties: A History of Human Rights in Canada,* ed. David Goutor and Stephen Heathorn, 189–212. Don Mills, ON: Oxford University Press, 2013.

–. "Reconstructing Politics, the Canadian Welfare State and the Ambiguity of Children's Rights, 1940–1950." In *Uncertain Horizons: Canadians and Their World in 1945,* ed. Greg Donaghy. Ottawa: Canadian Committee for the History of the Second World War, 1997.

Martinez, Jenny. *The Slave Trade and the Origins of International Human Rights Law.* Oxford: Oxford University Press, 2012. https://doi.org/10.1093/acprof:osobl/9780195391626.001.0001.

Massolin, Philip. *Canadian Intellectuals, the Tory Tradition, and the Challenge of Modernity, 1939–1970.* Toronto: University of Toronto Press, 2001. https://doi.org/10.3138/9781442672246.

Matthews, Robert O., and Cranford Pratt, eds. *Human Rights in Canadian Foreign Policy.* Montreal and Kingston: McGill-Queen's University Press, 1988.

Mazower, Mark. "The Strange Triumph of Human Rights, 1933–1950." *Historical Journal* 47, 2 (June 2004): 379–98. https://doi.org/10.1017/S0018246X04003723.

McIlroy, Thad. *Remembering the Chief.* Toronto: Doubleday Canada, 1984.

McKay, Ian. "The Liberal Order Framework: A Prospectus for a Reconnaissance of Canadian History." *Canadian Historical Review* 81, 4 (December 2000): 616–45.

McKercher, Asa. "The Centre Cannot Hold: Canada, Colonialism and the 'Afro-Asian Bloc' at the United Nations, 1960–62." *Journal of Imperial and Commonwealth History* 42, 2 (2014): 329–49. https://doi.org/10.1080/03086534.2013.851870.

–. "Sound and Fury: Diefenbaker, Human Rights, and Canadian Foreign Policy." *Canadian Historical Review* 97, 2 (Summer 2016): 165–94. https://doi.org/10.3138/chr.3241.

McWhinney, Edward. "Mr. Justice Rand's Rights of the Canadian Citizen – the Padlock Case." *Wayne Law Review* 4 (1957): 115.

Meisler, Stanley. *United Nations: The First Fifty Years*. New York: Atlantic Monthly Press, 1995.

Miedema, Gary R. *For Canada's Sake: Public Religion, Centennial Celebrations, and the Re-making of Canada in the 1960s*. Montreal and Kingston: McGill-Queen's University Press, 2005.

Miller, J.R. "Human Rights for Some: First Nations Rights in Twentieth-Century Canada." In *Taking Liberties: A History of Human Rights in Canada*, ed. David Goutor and Stephen Heathorn, 233–60. Don Mills, ON: Oxford University Press, 2013.

Milloy, John. "Indian Act Colonialism: A Century of Dishonour, 1869–1969." Paper for the National Centre for First Nations Governance (May 2008). http://fngovernance.org/ncfng_research/milloy.pdf.

Miron, Janet, ed. *A History of Human Rights in Canada: Essential Issues*. Toronto: Canadian Scholars' Press, 2009.

Miškovic, Nataša, Harald Fischer-Tiné, and Nada Boškovska. *The Non-Aligned Movement and the Cold War: Delhi – Bandung – Belgrade*. Abingdon, UK: Routledge, 2014.

Molot, Henry L. "The Duty of Business to Serve the Public: Analogy to the Innkeeper's Obligation." *Canadian Bar Review* 46, 4 (December 1968): 612–42.

Morrison, David R. *Aid and Ebb Tide: A History of CIDA and Canadian Development Assistance*. Waterloo, ON: Wilfrid Laurier University Press, 1998.

Moyn, Samuel. *The Last Utopia: Human Rights in History*. Cambridge, MA: Belknap Press of Harvard University Press, 2010.

Navari, Cornelia. *Internationalism and the State in the Twentieth Century*. London and New York: Routledge, 2000.

Normand, Roger, and Sarah Zaidi. *Human Rights at the UN: The Political History of Universal Justice*. Bloomington and Indianapolis: Indiana University Press, 2008.

Nossal, Kim Richard. "Cabin'd, Cribb'd, Confin'd? Canada's Interests in Human Rights." In *Human Rights in Canadian Foreign Policy*, ed. Robert O. Matthews and Cranford Pratt, 46–58. Montreal and Kingston: McGill-Queen's University Press, 1988.

Owram, Doug. *Born at the Right Time: A History of the Baby Boom Generation*. Toronto: University of Toronto Press, 1996.

Palmer, Bryan D. *Canada's 1960s: The Ironies of Identity in a Rebellious Era*. Toronto: University of Toronto Press, 2009.

Palmer, Howard. "Patterns of Racism: Attitudes towards Chinese and Japanese in Alberta 1920–1950." *Histoire Sociale/Social History* 13, 25 (1980): 137–60.

Patrias, Carmela. "Socialists, Jews, and the 1947 Saskatchewan Bill of Rights." *Canadian Historical Review* 87, 2 (June 2006): 265–92. https://doi.org/10.3138/CHR/87.2.265.

Patrias, Carmela, and Ruth Frager. "'This Is Our Country, These Are Our Rights': Minorities and the Origins of Ontario's Human Rights Campaigns." *Canadian Historical Review* 82, 1 (2001): 1–35. https://doi.org/10.3138/CHR.82.1.1.

Pearson, Lester B. "Canada and the Post-War World." *Canadian Affairs* 1, 6 (1944): 2.

–. *Mike: The Memoirs of the Right Honourable Lester B. Pearson*. Toronto: University of Toronto Press, 1972.

Peters, Erin. "The 'Heritage Minutes' and Canadian Collective Memory: An Analysis of the Use of Nostalgia and Nationalism to Build a Unifying Cultural Memory." PhD dissertation, Institute of Germanic and Romance Studies, 2009. http://sas-space.sas.ac.uk/2289/1/Peters%20-%20Heritage%20Minutes%20-%20Text.pdf.

Pierson, Ruth Roach, and Marjorie Griffin Cohen, eds. *Canadian Women's Issues, Volume 1: Strong Voices, Twenty-Five Years of Women's Activism in English Canada*. Toronto: James Lorimer, 1993.

Porsdam, Helle. *Civil Religion, Human Rights and International Relations: Connecting People across Cultures and Traditions*. Cheltenham, UK, and Northampton, MA: Edward Elgar, 2012.

Pound, Richard W. *Chief Justice W.R. Jacket: By the Law of the Land*. Montreal and Kingston: McGill-Queen's University Press, 1999.

Prince, Michael. *Absent Citizens: Disability Politics and Policy in Canada*. Toronto: University of Toronto Press, 2009.

Regenstreif, Peter. *The Diefenbaker Interlude*. Toronto: Longmans Canada, 1965.

Reid, Escott. *On Duty: A Canadian at the Making of the United Nations, 1945–1946*. Toronto: McClelland and Stewart, 1983.

Robinson, Ira. *A History of Antisemitism in Canada*. Waterloo, ON: Wilfrid Laurier Press, 2015.

Roy, Patricia E. *The Oriental Question: Consolidating a White Man's Province: 1914–41*. Vancouver: UBC Press, 2003.

–. *The Triumph of Citizenship: The Japanese and Chinese in Canada, 1941–67*. Vancouver: UBC Press, 2007.

Schabas, William A. "Canada and the Adoption of the Universal Declaration of Human Rights." *McGill Law Journal/Revue de Droit de McGill* 43, 2 (1998): 403–41.

Schmeiser, Douglas. *Civil Liberties in Canada*. London: Oxford University Press, 1964.

Schmitz, David F. *The Tet Offensive: Politics, War, and Public Opinion*. Lanham, MD: Rowman and Littlefield, 2005.

Scott, F.R. "Centralization and Decentralization." *Canadian Bar Review* 29, 10 (December 1951): 1095–1125.

–. "Civil Liberties." *Canadian New Leader* (October 1933): 6–7.

–. *Civil Liberties and Canadian Federalism*. Toronto: University of Toronto Press, 1959.

–. "Dominion Jurisdiction over Human Rights and Fundamental Freedoms." *Canadian Bar Review* 27, 5 (1949): 497–536.

–. "Duplessis versus Jehovah." *Canadian Forum* 22 (1947): 222–23.

–. "Freedom of Speech in Canada." *Papers and Proceedings of the Canadian Political Science Association* 22 (1933): 169–89.

–. "The Privy Council and Minority Rights." *Queen's Quarterly* 37 (1930): 668–78.

–. "Racial Discrimination and Public Policy." *Information and Comment* (published by the Canadian Jewish Congress Committee on Social and Economic Studies) (March 1946): 2.

–. "The Rights of Man." *United Nations Weekly Bulletin* 3, 25 (16 December 1947): 813.

–. "The Trial of the Toronto Communists." *Queen's Quarterly* 39 (1932): 512.

Simpson, A.W. Brian. *Human Rights and the End of Empire: Britain and the Genesis of the European Convention*. Oxford: Oxford University Press, 2001.

Slade, Arthur. *John Diefenbaker: An Appointment with Destiny*. Toronto: XYZ Publishing, 2001.

Smith, Denis. *Rogue Tory: The Life and Legend of John G. Diefenbaker*. Toronto: Macfarlane Walter and Ross, 1995.

Spittal, Carla. "The Diefenbaker Moment." PhD dissertation, University of Toronto, 2011. https://tspace.library.utoronto.ca/bitstream/1807/29878/3/Spittal_Cara_201106_PhD_thesis.pdf.

Spooner, Kevin A. "'Awakening Africa': Race and Canadian Views of Decolonizing Africa." In *Dominion of Race: Rethinking Canada's International History*, ed. Laura Madokoro, Francine McKenzie, and David Meren, 206–27. Vancouver: UBC Press, 2017.

–. *Canada, the Congo Crisis, and UN Peacekeeping, 1960–64*. Vancouver: UBC Press, 2009.

Stairs, Denis. "Of Medium Powers and Middling Roles." In *Statecraft and Security: The Cold War and Beyond,* ed. Ken Booth, 270–86. Cambridge: Cambridge University Press, 1998. https://doi.org/10.1017/CBO9780511558962.015.

Sugrue, Thomas J. *Sweet Land of Liberty: The Forgotten Struggle for Civil Rights in the North*. New York: Random House, 2008.

Suri, Jeremi. *Power and Protest: Global Revolution and the Rise of Détente*. Cambridge, MA: Harvard University Press, 2003.

Szablowski, G.J. "Creation and Implementation of Treaties in Canada." *Canadian Bar Review* 34, 1 (January 1956): 28–59.

Tarnopolksy, Walter Surma. *The Canadian Bill of Rights*. 2nd ed. Toronto: McClelland and Stewart, 1975.

–. *Discrimination and the Law*. Toronto: Richard De Boo, 1982.

–. "The Historical and Constitutional Context of the Proposed Canadian Charter of Rights and Freedoms." *Law and Contemporary Problems* 44 (1981): 169–93.

Thompson, Andrew S. *On the Side of the Angels: Canada and the United Nations Commission on Human Rights*. Vancouver: UBC Press, 2017.

–. "Teheran 1968 and the Origins of the Human Rights Council?" Paper presented at the 2011 annual meeting of the Academic Council on the United Nations System. Academic Council on the United Nations System (ACUNS), https://acuns.org.

Thornberry, Patrick. "Self-Determination, Minorities, Human Rights: A Review of International Instruments." *International and Comparative Law Quarterly* 38, 4 (October 1989): 867–89. https://doi.org/10.1093/iclqaj/38.4.867.

Trudeau, Pierre Elliott. "Economic Rights." *McGill Law Journal/Revue de droit de McGill* 8 (1961–62): 125.

–. *Memoirs*. Toronto: McClelland and Stewart, 1993.

Tunnicliffe, Jennifer. "'Life Together': Public Debates over Human Rights Legislation in Ontario, 1975–1981." *Histoire Sociale/Social History* 45, 92 (November 2013): 443–70.

United Nations. "Charter of the United Nations." http://www.un.org/en/documents/charter/.

–. "Definition of Key Terms Used in the UN Treaty Collection." https://treaties.un.org.

–. "Growth in United Nations Membership, 1945-present." http://www.un.org/en/sections/member-states/growth-united-nations-membership-1945-present/index.html.

–. UNESCO. "Glossary." http://en.unesco.org.

Vajcner, Mark E. "Stuart Garson and the Manitoba Progressive Coalition." *Manitoba History* 23 (Autumn 1993): 29–35.

Valverde, Mariana. *The Age of Light, Soap and Water: Moral Reform in English Canada, 1885–1925*. Toronto: McClelland and Stewart, 1991.

Veatch, Richard. *Canada and the League of Nations*. Toronto: University of Toronto Press, 1975.

Vigod, B.L. "Some Reflections on the State and Social Welfare in Quebec before the Quiet Revolution." In *The Benevolent State: The Growth of Welfare in Canada*, ed. Allan Moscovitch and Jim Albert, 175–86. Toronto: Garamond Press, 1987.

Vizkelety, Béatrice. *Proving Discrimination in Canada*. Toronto: Carswell, 1987.

Walker, James W. St. G. "Decoding the Rights Revolution: Lessons from the Canadian Experience." In *Taking Liberties: A History of Human Rights in Canada*, ed. David Goutor and Stephen Heathorn, 29–58. Don Mills, ON: Oxford University Press, 2013.

–. "Human Rights, Racial Equality, Social Justice: Can We Get There from Here?" Paper presented to "Domain Seminar on Social Justice and Multiculturalism," University of British Columbia Centre for Policy Studies in Education, Department of Canadian Heritage, 1999.

–. "The 'Jewish Phase' in the Movement for Racial Equality in Canada." *Canadian Ethnic Studies* 34, 1 (Spring 2002): 1–29.

–. *"Race," Rights and the Law in the Supreme Court of Canada: Historical Case Studies*. Toronto and Waterloo: Osgoode Society for Canadian Legal History and Wilfrid Laurier University Press, 1997.

Ward, Peter. *White Canada Forever: Popular Attitudes and Public Policy toward Orientals in British Columbia*. 2nd ed. Montreal and Kingston: McGill-Queen's University Press, 1990.

Warner, Tom. *Never Going Back: A History of Queer Activism in Canada*. Toronto: University of Toronto Press, 2002.

Waters, Rosanne. "A March from Selma to Canada: Canada and the Transnational Civil Rights Movement." PhD dissertation, Department of History, McMaster University, 2015. https://macsphere.mcmaster.ca/bitstream/11375/17465/2/Waters_Dissertation.pdf.

–. "African Canadian Anti-Discrimination Activism and the Transnational Civil Rights Movement, 1945–1965." *Journal of the Canadian Historical Association* 24, 2 (2013): 386–424. https://doi.org/10.7202/1025083ar.

Webster, David. "Canada and Bilateral Human Rights Dialogues." *Canadian Foreign Policy Journal* 16, 3 (2010): 43–63. https://doi.org/10.1080/11926422.2010.9687319.

–. "Foreign Policy, Diplomacy, and Decolonization." In *Canada and the Third World: Overlapping Histories*, ed. Karen Dubinsky, Sean Mills, and Scott Rutherford, 155–82. Toronto: University of Toronto Press, 2016.

–. "Self-Fulfilling Prophesies and Human Rights in Canada's Foreign Policy: Lessons from East Timor." *International Journal (Toronto)* 65, 3 (Summer 2010): 739–50. https://doi.org/10.1177/002070201006500313.

West, Emily. "Selling Canada to Canadians: Collective Memory, National Identity, and Popular Culture." *Critical Studies in Media Communication* 19, 2 (2002): 212–29.

Whelan, Daniel J. *Indivisible Human Rights: A History*. Philadelphia: University of Pennsylvania Press, 2010. https://doi.org/10.9783/9780812205404.

Whitaker, Reginald, and Gary Marcuse. *Cold War Canada: The Making of a National Insecurity State*. Toronto: University of Toronto Press, 1994.

Williams, Kieran. *The Prague Spring and Its Aftermath: Czechoslovak Politics 1968–1970*. Cambridge and New York: Cambridge University Press, 1998.

Wilson, Garrett, and Kevin Charles Wilson. *Diefenbaker for the Defence*. Toronto: J. Lorimer, 1988.

Yalden, Maxwell. *Transforming Rights: Reflections from the Front Lines*. Toronto: University of Toronto Press, 2009. https://doi.org/10.3138/9781442670167.

Zubrzycki, Geneviève. *Beheading the Saint: Nationalism, Religion, and Secularism in Quebec*. Chicago: University of Chicago Press, 2016.

Index